Principles of Accounting

based on

International Standards, 3e

(English Version)

Dai-Sun Lee, Kee-Shin Song, Kyung-Man Jung, Ho-Gap Lee, Sung-Whan Park

Yulgok Publishing Company

As we release the 3rd edition a Korean·English translation

It has been 7 years since Accounting Principles based on International Standards was published. Because the several revisions made over this period were not considered in-depth enough, this time we've done a major overhaul of the whole book. We consider the following points in this revision.

1. Highlight international standards that are different from the old standards

Up to now, this book was written and revised as an introduction to overall international standards, so it was somewhat short on explaining the specific, detailed requirements of the international standards. This revision highlights in detail the following items, which the international standards require be carried out differently than under the old standards.

	Old standards	International standards	Text
Estimating bad debts	Select one amongst the individual method, percentage method, and aging method.	If information obtained by the individual method is not enough, the aging method should be applied.	p.276
Presenting trade receivables	Indirect method, showing gross amount of trade receivables less allowance for uncollectible accounts.	Both direct method, showing net amount of trade receivables, and indirect method are allowed. If direct method is used, allowance for uncollectible accounts balance should be disclosed in a footnote.	p.274
Inventory valuation	Select one amongst specific identification method, FIFO, LIFO, or weighted average method.	LIFO is not allowed. Must apply specific identification method first. If inventories are exchangeable, FIFO or weighted average can be applied.	p.326
Checking whether depreciation expense reflects economic reality	No standard.	Must check every year whether depreciation expense reflects economic reality and, if it does not reflect, must change depreciation method, useful life, and residual value.	p.371
Presenting accumulated depreciation	Indirect method showing accumulated depreciation as a deduction.	Both direct method, showing net amount, and indirect method are allowed. If direct method is used, balance of accumulated depreciation should be disclosed in a footnote.	p.376
Presenting bonds payable	Indirect method showing discount on bonds payable as a reduction.	Direct method showing amortized cost.	p.428
Classification of interest received, dividend received, and interest paid in statement of cash flows	Classified as operating activities applying an exception to the theory.	Allows both the exceptional old standards and the theory, classifying interest received and dividend received as investing activities and interest paid as a financing activity. (This book applies classification by the theory).	p.511
Classification of financial assets	Trading, Available-for-sale, Held-to-maturity financial assets	Amortized cost, Fair value through profit or loss, Fair value through other comprehensive income financial assets	p.582

2. Use of revised terminology

We revise and use the titles of the income statement account (Korean) that can be understood as cash flows rather than expense or revenue as below.

Before revision	After revision
Rent (paid)	Rent expense
Insurance premium	Insurance expense
Salaries	Salaries expense
Rent(received)	Rent revenue
Service fees	Service fees revenue

3. Inclusion of IFRS (International Financial Reporting Standards) footnotes

Each time IFRS is quoted or referenced, a footnote is created, and the related standards are listed in the 'IFRS References (http://www.kasb.or.kr)' section included at the end of each Chapter. Therefore, it becomes clear that the definitions of key terms and important accounting methods are determined by IFRS. If a student wishes to conduct in-depth research on a related topic, he or she can easily identify the relevant standards and so conduct the research more effectively by using the information provided. In addition, when the student publishes his or her research outputs, he or she can easily quote or reference the related standards.

4. A Korean-English translation

We have created a Korean · English translation, in response to the internationalization of the accounting environment. When translating, we attempt to consider both the Korean and English version as independent texts. We first translate each sentence from Korean version into English and then re-translate this English version back into Korean, to ensure we arrive at a consistent result. Accounting can be difficult to both understand and effectively communicate. We expect that this Korean-English translation will help minimize these problems.

As we hurry to revise, we know that there will be some errors and typos. We politely ask for your understanding and for kindly notifying us of any errors. We also promise to revise continuously from now on. We express our profound thanks to all staff of Yulgok publishing company for their invaluable work.

February 21, 2019
Authors

As we write this book

As of 2011, all listed companies in Korea should apply K-IFRS (Korean-International Financial Reporting Standards) when preparing and reporting financial statements, to internationalize their accounting information. To cope with this change, this book introduces the principles of accounting based on the international standards. To help readers easily understand the international standards and principles of accounting, we incorporate the following thoughts in the book.

1. We explain the formats and elements of financial statements based on international standards through cases that we often face in real life.

In Chapters 1 and 2, we introduce the case of a start-up retail business, to explain the formats and elements of financial statements that are required by the international standards: the statement of financial position, the comprehensive income statement, the statement of changes in equity, and the statement of cash flows. In this way, readers can reach a practical understanding of what accounting information is reported in these financial statements.

2. We explain the double-entry bookkeeping, an accounting information generating system in three steps : 1) recording and closing cash transactions, 2) adjustments required by the accrual basis of accounting, and 3) comprehensive cases. With these three steps in mind, readers can systematically and easily understand how to prepare financial statements (including the income statement, statement of financial position, statement of changes in equity, and statement of cash flows), using the double-entry bookkeeping system.

In Chapter 3, we introduce only cash transactions, so that readers can easily learn the ways to prepare financial statements and the ways to close accounting books. In Chapter 4, we mainly review adjustments, which are needed when financial statements are prepared on the accrual basis. In Chapter 5, we introduce comprehensive cases, to explain the process of recording transactions and preparing financial statements for both the first year of operation and the following year. We also introduce key financial ratios, based on accounting information reported in the financial statements, to show how we can use accounting information in real life.

3. We introduce the real-life financial statements, footnotes, and financial ratios as case studies, to help readers understand accounting practices and study accounting in a practical setting.

In between Chapters 5 and 6, we introduce the real financial statements, footnotes, and financial ratios, allowing readers to see financial statements prepared by companies in the real world. We clearly mark the case study financial statements and footnotes to show what part of them are related with the subjects covered in Chapters 6～11 and in the Appendix. In this way, readers can associate their learning with real accounting case studies.

4. We classify and examine the elements of the statement of financial position, the income statement, and statement of cash flows into operating activities, investing activities, and financing activities. This allows readers to understand how the various activities of a company are reflected in their financial statements. And we select and explain the international standards that are appropriate to the Principles of Accounting course.

In Chapters 6 and 7, we review the elements related to operating activities. More specifically, in Chapter 6 we explain sales and trade receivables and accounting methods for bad debts per the international standards. In Chapter 7, we review the cost of goods sold, inventory, and trade payables. And we introduce inventory recording and valuation methods, per the international standards.

In Chapter 8, we study non-current assets that are related to investing activities. More specifically, we review depreciation methods and impairment loss, per the international standards.

In Chapters 9 and 10, we study elements related to financing activities. In Chapter 9, we review liabilities, or capital derived from non-owners. More specifically, we introduce borrowing and bonds payable, examples of financial liabilities. We also explain accounting methods for bonds payable, per international standards. Next, we introduce provisions—non-financial liabilities. In Chapter 10, we review equity, or so-called 'owner's capital,' More specifically, we review share capital, share premium, and retained earnings. We also introduce the statement of changes in equity.

5. Understanding the statement of cash flows can be challenging. To help the reader to easily understand, both conceptually and practically, the preparation of this statement, in each chapter, we introduce the parts related with the statement of cash flows. A separate chapter is also devoted to explaining comprehensively how to prepare a statement of cash flows.

In Chapters 3~5, which deal with the accounting information production process, the direct method for preparing the statement of cash flows is generally introduced. In Chapters 6~10, which deal with the reporting of accounting information for each of the company's activities, we also explain how items in the statement of financial position and the income statement are related to cash flows. Last, in Chapter 11, the direct and indirect methods for preparing the statement of cash flows are thoroughly reexamined, along with an explanation of how to utilize information in the statement of cash flows.

6. Although their difficulty level is too high to introduce them in Principles of Accounting course, consolidated financial statements (which are those basically required by the international standards) and other comprehensive income (which is included in a comprehensive income statement) deserve the minimum explanation. They are therefore introduced in the Appendix.

In the Appendix, we briefly explain the equity method of carrying investments in associates and introduce the method for preparing consolidated financial statements, with simple cases, so that the concepts and components of consolidated financial statements can be understood. We examine the gain on valuation of available-for-sale financial assets and the gain on revaluation of tangible assets, as examples of other comprehensive income. We introduce also accounting procedures for the valuation and disposition of these financial assets and of the tangible assets producing these gains, with simple cases.

7. Because most students taking the Principles of Accounting course will be working in a department other than the accounting department after graduation, this book concentrates more on understanding and using accounting information than on preparing it.

While we deal with accounting technique at the minimum level, to assist in understanding accounting information, in general we write the main text of the book in a style that introduces easy-to-understand cases and fully explain difficult concepts so that readers can understand accounting information easily. Items that are needed to understand accounting information, but that are difficult or lack direct relevance to the key accounting topics, are explained in textboxes. So that readers can understand each subject effectively without losing the book's overall flow of thought. At the end of each chapter, definitions of key accounting terminology are summarized, with Korean terminology in parentheses, so they can be used as a reference. Each chapter's exercises are kept at the minimum level needed for students to comprehend the textbook materials. It is arranged that the answers can be checked through the solutions manual available for sale.

The international standards and the American standards convergence project is ongoing, and there are a lot of issues to be discussed for the international standards. Therefore, the international standards will be changed quite a bit in the near future. The authors will keep revising this book to reflect the newly changed international standards. We're very sorry if any errors and typos emerge in the printing, even though we've done our best to avoid them. We politely ask for your understanding and request that you kindly notify us of any errors. Last, we express our sincere gratitude to the President and staff members of Yulgok Publishing Company.

August 25, 2011
Authors

Contents

Accrual Basis and Preparation of Financial Statements

Comprehensive Illustration of Preparing and Using Financial Statements

Case Financial Statements of Daehan Department Store

Operating Activities—Sales and Trade Receivables

Operating Activities—Cost of Goods Sold, Inventory, and Trade Payables

Investing Activities—Non-current Assets

Financing Activities—Liabilities

Financing Activities—Equity

Statement of Cash Flows

Special Issues

Key Financial Ratios

Business Activities and Financial Statements

Section 1 Business enterprises and business activities

Section 2 Business activities and accounting system

Section 3 Preparing and disclosing financial statements

Chapter 1 Overview

In this chapter, we review the types of information that are needed by investors who put money into business enterprises, by creditors who lend money to business enterprises, and by managers who operate business enterprises, as well as how these pieces of information are provided. First, we explain the basic activities of business enterprises—investing, financing, and operating activities—and review how these activities are interrelated. Next, we explain that the accounting information is a systematic summary of the contents and results of each of these activities, and the financial statements are tools for providing this information. We also review why this accounting information is needed and what we can learn from it.

Business enterprises and business activities

1.1 What is a business enterprise?

Accounting is a system for preparing and providing information about a business enterprise to those who invest in the enterprise, to those who lend to this enterprise, and to those who operate this business enterprise. Therefore, to understand accounting properly, one has to understand what a business enterprise is and what kind of activities are conducted by a business enterprise. If I ask students who are taking a principles of accounting course whether they understand what a business enterprise is, the majority of them will usually say "Yes." But if I carry the conversation a little further, I find that there are very few students who know, especially systematically know, what a business enterprise is. To help us better understand a business enterprise and its activities, let us review the case of Mr. Kim, a student who is taking the principles of accounting course.

(1) Oh-so-seo Mart

Mr. Kim's uncle (Uncle, hereafter) worked for a department store as a very able employee for long time until he honorably retired from the store following a company restructuring. Uncle tried to get a job with other companies, but it was not easy. So, he tried to come up with the best option that would allow him to make the most out of his experience and know-how, and he concluded that the best choice was to open a small discount store. Uncle decided that he would start out on a small scale and then expand it into a big discount store using ₩10 billion from his severance benefit payment and proceeds from selling some real estate.

Uncle decided to open a discount store in a shopping mall located in a newly built apartment complex that was very close to his residence. Before opening, he conducted research to determine the income level of his neighbors and to find items that would sell well. He analyzed the general commerce around the store site and researched the operations of nearby discount stores. He made a detailed plan for the store, including the size of the store, the type of interior, the total funds needed, and the number of employees that he would need to hire. As a result, he was confident that he would be successful if he could attract customers who usually went to department stores or super-size discount marts, by being very kind to the customers and providing merchanise at a lower price. He named the store Oh-so-seo Mart (OSS Mart, hereafter), which means "Please come to our discount store."

Uncle prepared a basic plan to open OSS Mart, and he invited two co-investors, who promised to invest ₩60 billion. He purchased a store and registered the company at the courthouse. He issued 70 million shares of common stock with a par value of ₩1,000. Of these, he distributed 60 million shares to the co-investors, who invested ₩60 billion, and gave himself 10 million shares for his investment of ₩10 billion. He also received a loan of ₩30 billion from a bank. Uncle had interior work done to install the display shelves and other necessary fixtures. He then purchased an automobile to deliver merchandise to customers and a separate warehouse to store merchandise. He also purchased office equipment, such as computers and supplies. He hired administrative and sales personnel and provided them with training on operating policies, sales methods, proper attitude toward customers, bookkeeping methods, etc.

Last, he had a large sign made for OSS Mart and hung it neatly on the wall. Next, he purchased and displayed merchandise and started to sell it, while running advertising and promotional programs. After opening the store, he developed a good reputation with customers because he identified items they needed and provided them at a low price. Uncle's family members, including Mr. Kim, were very happy because the store was running smoothly.

(2) Types of business enterprise

Some companies are similar to OSS Mart, which purchases and sells merchandise that is produced by other companies, while other companies directly manufacture and sell goods. Companies that purchase and sell merchandise produced by other companies are called merchandising companies. A typical example in this category is a department store. Companies that directly produce and sell goods are called manufacturing companies, and the Samsung Electronics Corporation and the Hyundai Motors Corporation belong in this category. Companies that provide services rather than selling products are called service companies.

Examples in this category are accounting firms, law firms, medical service organizations, and consulting firms.

This textbook mainly examines the business activities of merchandising companies and explains the process of producing accounting information for them. The accounting process for manufacturing companies will be reviewed in advanced accounting courses.

〈Box 1-1〉 Classification of business enterprises by ownership

Sole proprietorship

The subject of a **sole proprietorship (개인기업)** is the owner of the company, an actual person. Therefore, the owner and the company are not recognized as separate and independent subjects. In addition, sometimes two or more people contribute capital and operate the company together, and they call this type of company a **partnership (조합기업)**. The characteristics of a partnership are similar to those of a sole proprietorship.

Law created company

The type of company that directly contrasts to a sole proprietorship is a law-created company. A law-created company is a company whose subject is a legal person rather than an actual person. In other words, a law-created company is considered a person under the law (called a 'legal person') and carries out its own activities. In Korea, there are four different kinds of law-created companies based on the limits of the participants' responsibility, namely a general partnership, a joint venture, a limited company, and a **corporation (주식회사)**. A corporation can generate the funds needed for operation by issuing stock to numerous people, and it is the most common form of company.

1.2 Concerns of corporate interest groups

Those who would typically be interested in the operation of OSS Mart are the investors who contributed capital (Uncle and his co-investors), the creditors who lent money (bank), and the managers who are responsible for running the company (Uncle is an investor but also a manager). Because the investors, creditors, and managers have an economic interest on the company, they are called interest groups. What kind of concerns do the interest groups at OSS Mart have?

Uncle and his co-investors, as the investors, want to maximize the return on their investment. For example, the co-investors expect that OSS Mart will succeed as a business so the value of their initial investment of ₩60 billion will grow. The bank, as a creditor, wants to receive back the money it lent, and the interest on it, without any problem. That is, the bank that lent money to OSS Mart expects to receive the interest and the principal of ₩30 billion on schedule. Uncle, as a manager of OSS Mart, wants to know whether the mart is operating well and according to plan, so that it continues to grow.

As seen in this review, each interest group has a different concern. We can summarize these interest groups' concerns as follow :

First, they want to know whether the company is doing well as a business and making a profit so that the investment value increases.

Second, they want to know whether the company is capable of paying back both the principal amount borrowed and the interest on time.

Third, they want to know whether the company is running well, as planned, so that it continues to grow.

1.3 Three activities of a business enterprise

Business activities can be classified in many different ways based on nature of activity. The concerns of a company's interest groups, as explained above, are mainly related to the following three activities. The first are investing activities (투자활동), which are the activities of acquiring resources needed for business operation, such as store space, vehicles and fixtures. The second are operating activities (영업활동), which are the activities of purchasing and selling merchandise by utilizing acquired resources. The third are financing activities (재무활동), which are the activities of providing the funds needed for the above-mentioned activities. In the case of OSS Mart, the activities of acquiring resources like the store space, automobiles and equipment needed to operate the store are investing activities, and the operating activities are activities of purchasing merchandise and selling it to customers. Obtaining funds from Uncle and his co-investors and obtaining loans from the bank are financing activities.

⟨Diagram 1-1⟩ Relationship among investing activities, operating activities, and financing activities

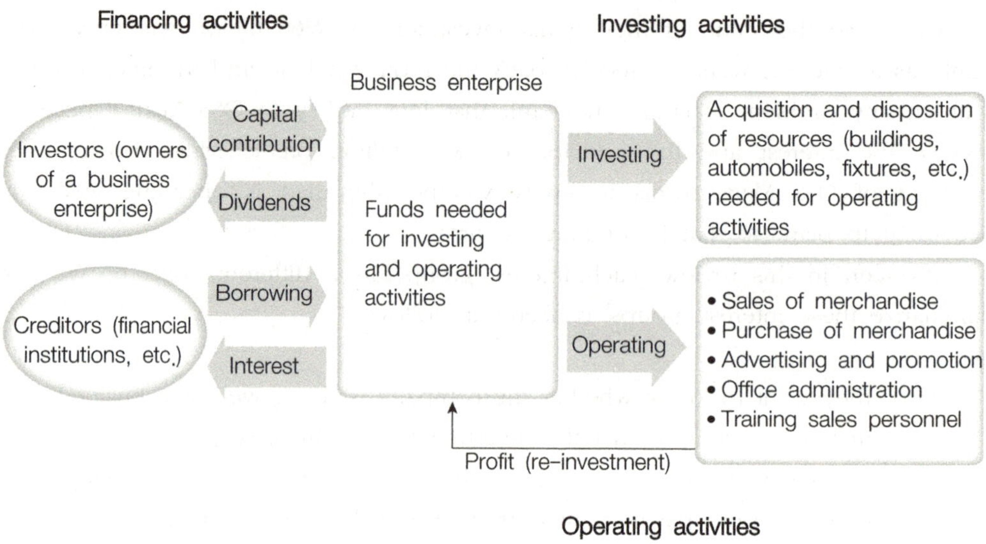

Business enterprises grow and progress through investing activities, operating activities and financing activities. Those three activities do not occur independently; instead, they are linked together closely as they are carried out, as we can see in ⟨Diagram 1-1⟩. Let us review more closely these three basic activities of a business enterprise.

1.3.1 Definition of business activities

(1) Investing activities

Investing activities are, as we can see in ⟨Diagram 1-1⟩, activities by which a company acquires the resources needed to carry out business activities, such as buildings, automobiles and office appliance and equipment. If a company acquires resources through investing activities, the quantity and composition of resources possessed by the company will change.

(2) Operating activities

As we can see in ⟨Diagram 1-1⟩, operating activities include all selling and administrating activities that are associated with purchasing merchandise and selling that merchandise to customers. Therefore, operating activities include such activities as purchasing and selling merchandise, advertising to promote a product, and office administration. If a company does these operating activities well, it makes a profit. If it does not, it will take a loss. Companies making a lot of profit can reinvest it and grow continuously ; on the contrary, those companies that cannot make a profit will run short of money and go bankrupt. Since the success or failure of a company depends on operating activities, they are considered the core activities of a company.

(3) Financing activities

Financing activities are, as we can see in ⟨Diagram 1-1⟩, activities by which a company can generate the funds needed for investing and operating activities. Companies need funds to buy buildings and automobiles, and to purchase and promote merchandise. All activities aimed at generating the funds needed by a company are financing activities.

The methods by which companies can generate funds can be divided into two categories. The first method is generating funds through the business owners' investment. The second method is borrowing from financing institutions, such as banks. In the case of OSS Mart, the funds of ₩10 billion from Uncle and of ₩60 billion from two co-investors generated by issuing common stock are by the former method. The ₩30 billion borrowed from the bank are funds generated by the latter method. On the other hand, as companies pay interest on the loans, these paying interest activities are also financing activities. (An exception is allowed when a statement of cash flow is prepared, so that paying interest can be classified as an operating activity. A detailed explanation will be made in Chapter 11, 'Statement of Cash Flows.')

1.3.2 Examples of classifying business activities

The following ⟨Table 1-1⟩ is a summary of business activities of OSS Mart, classified by the three activity types defined above.

⟨Table 1-1⟩ Classification of activities of OSS Mart

Classification	No.	Description
Investing Activities	①	Purchasing the store
	②	Purchasing an automobile
	③	Paying interior decoration fees
	④	Purchasing office furniture and equipment such as desks, computers and copy machines
Operating Activities	⑤	Purchasing merchandise
	⑥	Selling merchandise
	⑦	Paying advertising expense
	⑧	Paying employee salaries
	⑨	Paying electric and telephone bills
	⑩	Purchasing office supplies such as copying paper and stationary.
	⑪	Paying store repair expense
Financing Activities	⑫	Generating funds by issuing stock
	⑬	Obtaining a loan from the bank
	⑭	Paying interest on the bank loan

Business activities and accounting system

2.1 Information needed by interest groups of a business enterprise

If we summarize the information that typical interest groups of a business enterprise—investors, creditors, and managers, need in common, it is as follows:

First, information concerning the value of the resources the company possesses, and the amount of debt to be paid off.

Second, information concerning how much profit has been generated by conducting the operating activities.

Third, information concerning how funds needed for business activities have been generated and used.

2.2 What is the accounting system?

The accounting system provides information that is needed by interest groups like those reviewed above. More specifically, as shown in 〈Diagram 1-2〉, the accounting system classifies business activities into three activities: investing activities, operating activities and financing activities. It records these activities, and then prepares financial statements by summarizing and aggregating the outcomes of the information recorded. It then provides the interest groups with the information they need, through these financial statements.

⟨Diagram 1-2⟩ Function of accounting system

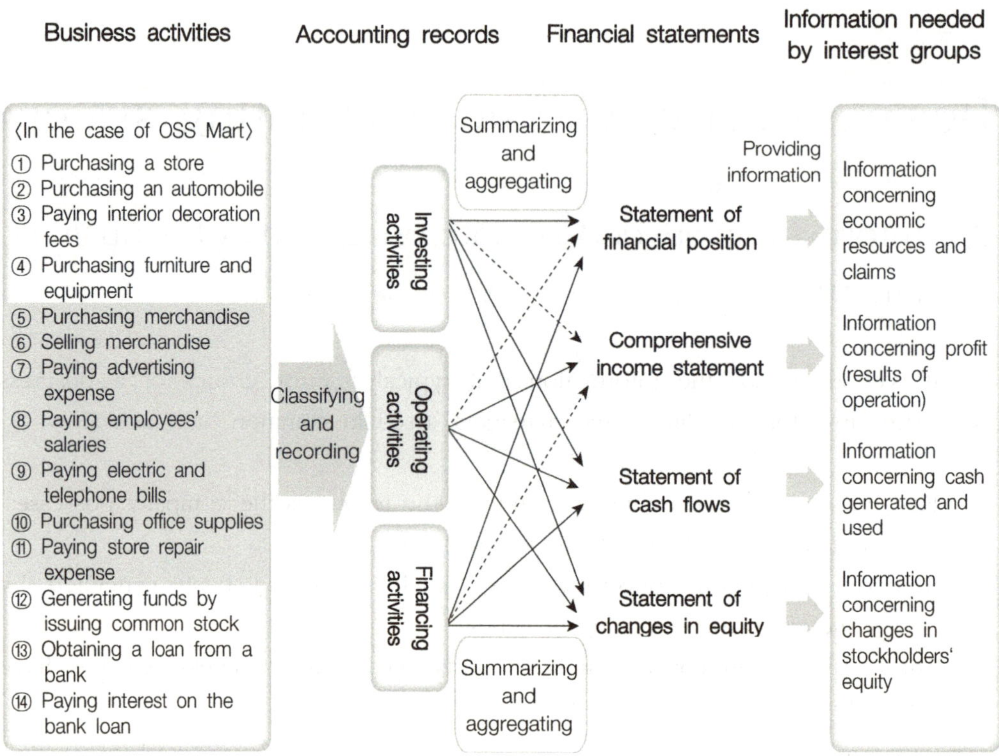

Financial statements are comprised of a statement of financial position, a comprehensive income statement, a statement of cash flows, and a statement of changes in equity. The statement of financial position provides information concerning the resources a company possesses and the debts it has to pay off. The comprehensive income statement supplies information on how much profit has been generated. The statement of cash flows shows information concerning how cash has been generated and used. The statement of changes in equity furnishes information on the increase and decrease in capital that forms stockholders' claim (stockholders' equity.)

⟨Box 1-2⟩ What is accounting?

Accounting is an information system **identifying (식별)**, **measuring (측정)** and **communicating (전달)** financial information concerning a business enterprise so that stockholders (investors) and creditors, managers and other accounting information users can make rational decisions.

2.3 Financial statements

As can be seen in 〈Diagram 1-2〉, the key financial statements (재무제표) include : the statement of financial position (which summarizes investing and financing activities), the comprehensive income statement (which summarizes operating activities), the statement of cash flows (which summarizes cash flows from the three activities), and the statement of changes in equity (which summarizes changes in equity). Strictly speaking, some of the operating activities are reported in the statement of financial position, and some of the investing and financing activities are reported in the comprehensive income statement. In 〈Diagram 1-2〉 these linkages have been marked with dotted lines to highlight the basic relationships between business activities and financial statements. Here we briefly review what each financial statement reports. A detailed explanation of each financial statement will be made in Chapter 2.

(1) Statement of financial position

The statement of financial position (재무상태표) is an accounting report that shows the financial position of a company at a specific point in time, summarizing mainly the results of the company's investing and financing activities. As explained above, investing activities are activities by which companies acquire resources such as buildings, automobiles and office equipment that are needed to conduct business activities. These acquired resources are called assets. Financing activities are activities by which companies generate the funds needed for investing and operating activities. In the case of OSS Mart, money borrowed from the bank—that is, from a creditor—is called a liability. The funds provided by Uncle, as an owner-investor, and by the other co-investors, are called equity.

The statement of financial position reports the outcomes of investing activities as assets and the outcomes of financing activities as liabilities and equity at the year's end. Therefore, if we read a statement of financial position we can understand the value of assets that can be used for the operation of the company, as well as the debts to be repaid by the company and the amount of investment by stockholders as of the end of the year. The current status of a company's assets, liabilities and equity is called its financial position (재무상태), and the statement of financial position summarizes these. In the past, the statement of financial position used to be called a balance sheet (B/S : 대차대조표). Its name was changed to 'statement of financial position' when IFRS (See 3.2 of this chapter for details) was adopted.

(2) Comprehensive income statement

A company usually conducts a series of operating activities to purchase and sell merchandise. Companies make their profit out of these operating activities. The comprehensive income statement (포괄손익계산서) reports on whether a company has earned income or incurred loss over a specific period of time, by subtracting the money used for operating activities from the money earned from operating activities. If the amount earned is greater than the amount used, the difference is called a profit. If, instead, the amount used is greater than the amount earned, the difference is called a loss. Money earned from the operation of a business is called 'revenue' and money spent to earn profit is called 'expense.' Revenues mainly come from selling merchandise. Expenses include the purchase price of merchandise, as well as the cost of human resources, advertising, electricity, telephone, etc.

The comprehensive income statement is prepared for a one-year period. It reports comprehensive income or comprehensive loss by subtracting total expenses from total revenues for that year. Because we can consider the comprehensive income as the performance of the company's management, the comprehensive income statement is also called the 'management performance report.'

(3) Statement of cash flows

Cash is important for a business enterprise, as well as for a family, and in both instances it's especially important to understand how cash is generated and used. In general, each investing activity, operating activity and financing activity constitutes either cash inflow or cash outflow. The statement of cash flows (현금흐름표) classifies cash flows for a specific period (one year) into these three business activities, and reports cash inflow and outflows for each activity.

(4) Statement of changes in equity

Because various and complex equity transactions are made in these days, it has become very important for stockholders to know how—and how much—each component of their equity has increased or decreased. The statement of changes in equity (자본변동표) reports on why and how much each component of stockholders' equity has increased or decreased over a one-year period. Examples of these components include capital contributed by stockholders, as well as earnings retained by the company.

〈Box 1-3〉 Objective of financial reporting[1]

The objective of financial reporting is to provide information—concerning financial position, results of operation and changes in financial position—that is useful to the various users of accounting information in making economic decisions. To achieve this objective, the following information is provided :

- Information about economic resources, liabilities, and stockholders' equity
- Information about operating performance, especially about profitability
- Information about cash flows
- Information about changes in stockholders' equity

2.4 Other users of accounting information

Various individuals or groups need accounting information. So far, we have reviewed the key users of accounting information : investors (stockholders), creditors, and managers. We've taken a look at what these groups are interested in, and the role of accounting information. Here we will review other users of accounting information, apart from those key users. Other users include government, customers, suppliers, employees, and labor unions, etc. These people also use accounting information to readjust their relationships with the company, and to make their own decisions to achieve their objectives. 〈Diagram 1-3〉 provides an overall summary of the various interest groups, including key users and other users of accounting information, as well as their specific interests.

〈Diagram 1-3〉 Interest groups and their objectives for the use of accounting information

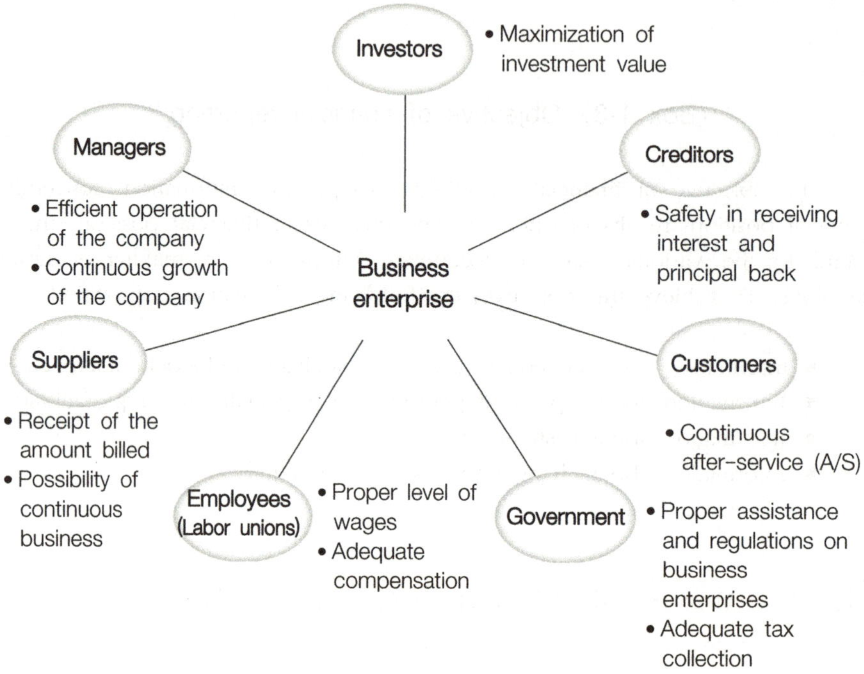

〈Box 1-4〉 Accounting is a business language

These days, accounting is recognized as the most systematic means to provide comprehensive information about a company. It is used extensively as a communication tool by which various interest groups can make rational decisions concerning a business enterprise. As such, accounting information is called a **business language (기업경영의 언어)**.

(1) Government

The government assists and sometimes regulates business enterprises. Therefore, the government is an important interest group of a business enterprise. One of the problems the government contends with is that of determining what kinds of assistance programs and regulations should be provided and applied to business enterprises. Another important task for the government is to collect an adequate amount of taxes. The government needs accounting information to regulate business operations, as well as to set up tax policies, policies to allocate resources efficiently, and other economic policies. For example, the accounting information reported in a business enterprise's financial statements is a crucial judgment factor in determining the amount of tax a business company has to pay, as well as in determining the price of goods supplied to the government. Accounting information is also used when the government is setting up policies to encourage small-and medium-sized companies and venture companies, and to regulate monopolistic businesses.

(2) Employees and labor unions

Employees and labor unions must decide what level of wage increase they should demand when they negotiate with managers. The level of wage increase that can effectively be agreed upon is one that's based on the actual operational results of the company. Therefore, accounting information can be an excellent barometer in deciding whether the requested level of wage increase is realistic and achievable. Accounting information can also help employees and labor unions to understand whether the company is growing continuously and, therefore, whether it may be capable of paying severance benefits in the future. In addition, accounting information can help job applicants to understand not only the operational performance but also future prospects of the company they are interested in.

(3) Suppliers

Suppliers are concerned, most of all, with ensuring that they will receive the amount billed, and with the continuation of business. They use accounting information to make their own decisions on such matters. Therefore, suppliers pay great attention to the soundness of a company's financial position and to its profitability.

(4) Customers

Customers that purchase merchandise sold by a company hope that A/S (after-service) on the merchandise they've bought will be provided continuously. Using accounting information, customers can assess whether A/S is likely to be provided continuously. They can also gauge with accounting information whether the price of merchandise is irrationally high in comparison with cost.

〈Box 1-5〉 Classification of accounting

- **Financial accounting**: Deals with information needed by external users, such as investors and creditors.
- **Managerial accounting**: Deals with information needed by internal users, including managers.
- **Tax accounting**: Accounting that aims to help compute and pay taxes.
- **Accounting for non-profit organizations**: Accounting for organizations run as nonprofits, such as government, schools, scholarship foundations.

〈Box 1-6〉 Capital market and accounting information

A capital market is a market where transactions are made between fund providers, such as investors and creditors, and fund users such as the managers of companies. The fund providers make their business decisions based on all sorts of information about the companies that are potential users of their funds. If information is not available to the fund providers in the proper quantity and quality, they cannot make proper decisions. Furthermore, if the fund providers experience losses because of misleading information, they will no longer provide funds to the market. If these things happen, the market will be short of money. As a result, companies (the fund users) will lose business opportunities and their business activities will be suppressed. This can impact the entire economy and even lead to its collapse. Therefore, adequate information must be provided to the fund suppliers to keep the capital market functioning properly. Accounting information is at the core of this.

Preparing and disclosing financial statements

It is the responsibility of managers to prepare financial statements. As seen in ⟨Diagram 1-4⟩, managers record, classify, and summarize the outcomes of investing, operating and financing activities; prepare financial statements through the accounting system. The standards that are applied by managers when they prepare financial statements are called financial accounting standards. The financial statements prepared by managers are audited by certified public accountants (CPA : 공인회계사), and are disclosed to the users of accounting information.

⟨Diagram 1-4⟩ Preparing and disclosing financial statements

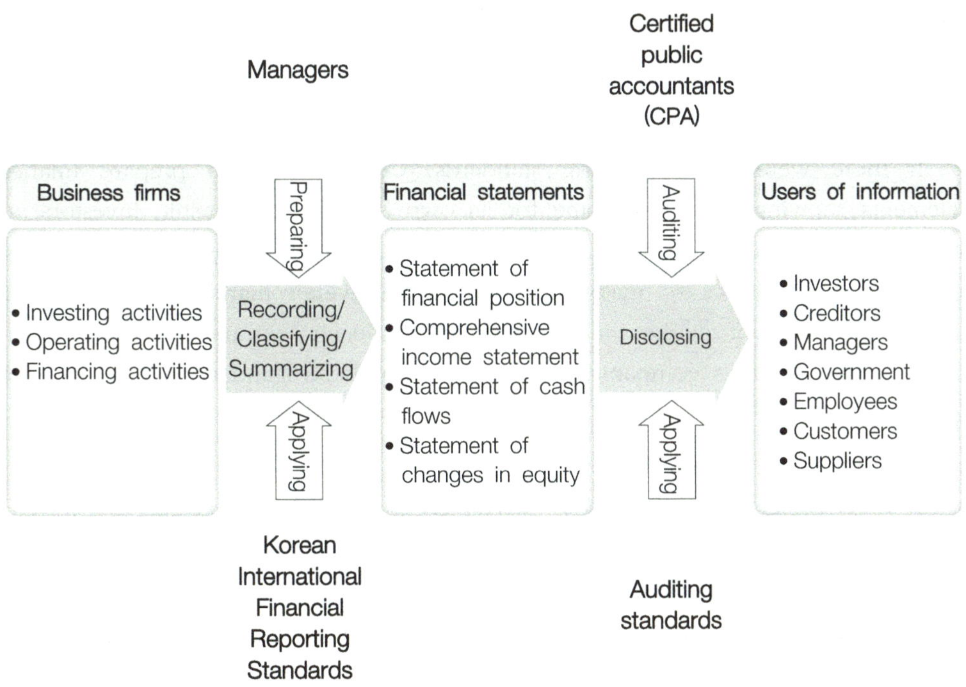

3.1 The need of accounting standards

Accounting standards—the set of standards to be followed when preparing financial statements—are crucial. As explained above, there is a high demand for accounting information by the interested parties. If business firms were allowed to prepare financial statements and disclose accounting information freely, each firm would likely prepare financial statements in the way that it deemed most beneficial to itself, and would then provide the information to users. If they were free to do so, the contents of financial statements would be distorted and it would be very difficult to make an informed comparison between firms. Accounting information users would find the financial statements untrustworthy and far less useful. Therefore, financial statements must be prepared in accordance with a set of certain standards.

Let's take a look at how OSS Mart generates the funds it needs to expand. Business at OSS Mart has grown well, ever since the store opened, by maintaining efficient operations and building good relationships with its customers. Uncle plans to expand the store space, as a new apartment complex is being constructed in a nearby neighborhood. If OSS Mart wants to generate the funds it needs for the expansion from outsiders, it must first provide financial statements reporting its current financial position and operational results. Banks and investors—potential providers of the funds—will then review those financial statements and decide whether to lend or invest money or not.

If there were no accounting standards, OSS Mart could prepare financial statements showing inflating income for its own benefit. As a result, investors and creditors could suffer economic losses and, if this happened with enough companies, it could cause major disorder in the overall market and society. To prevent this kind of market and societal chaos, each country issues accounting standards and requires companies to comply with those standards when preparing their financial statements.

3.2. Korean accounting standards and issuing body

As noted, accounting standards aim to give consistency and objectivity to the accounting information that is provided by firms. Until 1999, the Korean government led the way in defining these standards. Generally speaking, if a government is in charge of determining the standards, it tends to be inflexible when making and amending them. This makes it difficult for the standards to reflect changes in both business itself and in the business environment, especially in the international environment in a timely manner.

In 1997, when we had a foreign currency crisis, IMF (International Monetary Fund) provided us with a bail out fund subject to a condition that we should adopt an accounting system based on international standards. As a result, the Korean government decided to delegate its standards-making function to the private sector and established the Korean Accounting Institute (KAI : 한국회계기준원, up to March 2006 회계연구원) in 1999, with the Korean Accounting Standards Board (KASB : 회계기준위원회) as an umbrella unit making and amending accounting standards. KAI issued the Korean International Financial Reporting Standards (한국채택국제회계기준 : K-IFRS hereafter) in December 2007, adopting International Accounting Standards (refer to the ⟨Box 1-7⟩ below) altogether. K-IFRS consists of International Accounting Standards and International Financial Reporting Standards that were translated by the KAI. Starting from 2011, all listed companies must prepare their financial statements applying K-IFRS. You can find a great deal of information concerning Korean Accounting Standards on the home page of the Korean Accounting Standards Board (http://www.kasb.co.kr).

⟨Box 1-7⟩ International Accounting Standards

Each country has different sets of accounting standards, due to their different economic environments. As a result, it becomes difficult to compare accounting information across different countries. This means that companies can experience difficulty in generating funds through the international capital market. To solve the problems caused by differences in accounting standards among countries, nine nations, including the United States and the United Kingdom, formed IASC (International Accounting Standards Committee) in 1973, and issued **International Accounting Standards (IAS : 국제회계기준)**. In 2001, they changed the IASC into the IASB (International Accounting Standards Board), and the Board began to issue **International Financial Reporting Standards (IFRS : 국제재무보고기준)**. Korea became a member of this organization in 1975.

⟨Box 1-8⟩ Constitution of Korean accounting standards

Korean accounting standards are comprised of 'K-IFRS,' 'Korean Financial Accounting Standards in General,' 'Accounting Standards for Small and Medium Size Companies,' and 'Accounting Standards for Special Topics.' The Accounting Standards for Small and Medium Size Companies are issued by the Ministry of Law ; all the remaining standards are issued by KAI. K-IFRS is applicable to the listed companies. Korea Financial Accounting Standards in General are applicable to non-listed companies that are subject to external auditing. Non-listed companies that are not subject to external auditing must apply Accounting Standards for Small and Medium Size Companies. Accounting Standards for Special Topics are standards set up to reflect legal requirements and typical Korean transactions and environments. Except for the Accounting Standards for Small and Medium Size Companies, each set of standards is composed of statements of the standards and interpretations of the standards. The statements provide not only comprehensive guidelines concerning accounting methods, presentation and disclosure, but also detail practical application methods. The interpretations provide guidelines for newly emerging financial reporting issues not covered by the standards. They also provide interpretation and guidelines for the practical application of the standards.

⟨Box 1-9⟩ GAAP

The standards that are more comprehensive than the accounting standards issued are generally accepted accounting principles (GAAP : 일반적으로 인정된 회계처리기준) (In the past the English was directly translated, so it used to be called '일반적으로 인정된 회계원칙'). Because business activities vary a great deal and business environments are different from one company to another, there is a limit to fulfilling all the needs in practice by issuing accounting standards. Therefore, accounting rules that are generally accepted, and that are both universally valid and rational within a specific society, have emerged and are used in preparing financial statements. The term "generally accepted" means that certain methods of preparing financial statements have been well accepted and used for a long time in practice. Therefore, generally accepted accounting principles can be considered as principles that possess 'majority supports and real authority.'

3.3 Auditing

After OSS Mart prepared its financial statements and gave them to its bank, hoping to borrow the money it needed to expand, the bank's loan officer said he could not trust those financial statements and demanded that they be audited before resubmission. Auditing (회계감사), which is sometimes called financial statements auditing, is an examination of financial statements to check whether those financial statements are prepared fairly in accordance with financial accounting standards.

Financial statements significantly affect both a company's interest groups and society at large, so they should be prepared in such a way that users can rely on them. Therefore, financial statements are audited by professional accountants called CPAs. CPAs examine financial statements to determine whether they are prepared in accordance with accounting standards; they then express an audit opinion. If a material distortion is noted during the audit, then the company cannot receive an unqualified opinion and may receive disadvantageous treatment. Audit scopes, field auditing methods and audit reporting methods that are to be followed by CPAs when they audit financial statements are incorporated in the auditing standards.

〈Box 1-10〉 Types of audit opinions

Audit opinions, as expressed by CPAs on financial statements, are of the following four types:

Unqualified opinion: Opinion expressed when the financial statements prepared by the company are in accordance with accounting standards.

Qualified opinion: Opinion expressed when a part of the financial statements is in violation of the accounting standards, or when audit materials are insufficient.

Adverse opinion: Opinion expressed when the financial statements, as a whole, severely violate the accounting standards.

Disclaimer: No audit opinion is expressed because the auditor lacks independence or it is impossible to conduct an audit.

3.4 Disclosing financial statements

Financial statements should be provided to users of accounting information on a timely basis. IFRS[2] recommends that the company prepare and disclose the financial statements every half year (6 months), and require the company to report financial statements at least once a year.

(1) Interim financial statements

Interim financial statements are financial statements that we prepare during the accounting period. Financial statements that we prepare for an accounting period of 3 months are called quarterly financial statements ; those that we prepare at the end of the second quarter, covering an accounting period of 6 months, are called semi-annual financial statements. Interim financial statements are prepared to provide the operational results and financial position of a company to outside interest groups on a timely basis. Interim financial statements should be prepared in the same format as the annual financial statements which will be reviewed below. The company can, however, prepare them in a summary format. The listed companies disclose quarterly financial statements and semi-annual financial statements, due to their requirement by 'the Capital Market and Financial Investment Service Act.'

(2) Annual financial statements

Annual financial statements are statements prepared at the end of a fiscal year to report a company's financial position, its operational results and changes in financial position for the period of one year, to the company's external interest groups. In general, they are simply called financial statements. Annual financial statements include the statement of financial position, the comprehensive income statement, the statement of cash flows, the statement of changes in equity, and footnotes. Korean 'Law on External Audit of Corporations' requires that companies larger than a certain size should have these statements audited by CPAs before they are disclosed.

〈Box 1-11〉 Separate financial statements and consolidated financial statements

There is no problem deciding whether **consolidated financial statements (연결재무제표)** should be prepared or not, when the company has no subsidiary (an investee company that is controlled by the investor company). But when the company becomes a parent because it has a subsidiary, the preparation of the consolidated financial statement itself becomes an issue. A parent can either prepare **separate financial statements (별도재무제표)** for an accounting entity that includes the parent only ; or it can prepare consolidated financial statements for an accounting entity including both the parent and subsidiary. K-IFRS (KAI issued)[3] requires to apply applicable K-IFRS when the separate financial statements and the consolidated financial statements, both of which are required for parents by Korean 'Law on External Audit of Corporations' are prepared.

Because preparing consolidated financial statements is a difficult task, one that is a level more difficult than the level this book introduces, it is explored later in Advanced Accounting, a course taken after Intermediate Accounting. This book mainly focuses on financial statements for companies without subsidiaries, and only introduces a simple case of consolidated financial statements in its Appendix.

(3) Electronic disclosing system

In the past, companies had to print financial statements in a booklet format and submitted to the Financial Supervisory Service, Korean Stock Exchange, and Korean Institute of Certified Public Accountants. Starting in 2001, companies disclose financial statements through the electronic disclosing system of the Financial Supervisory Service.

If you visit DART (Data Analysis, Retrieval and Transfer System), which is an electronic disclosing system of the Financial Supervisory Service (http://dart.fss.or.kr), you can find all the electronically disclosed financial statements (both interim and annual), business reports, and certified public auditors' reports, etc. We can download these reports and use them if we need.

〈Box 1-12〉 Qualitative characteristics of accounting information[4]

The qualitative characteristics of accounting information are the key attributes that accounting information should have to be useful to information users in making decisions. There are two fundamental qualitative characteristics, four enhancing qualitative characteristics, and one constraint.

Fundamental qualitative characteristics :

- **Relevance** : If accounting information is to be useful, it must be relevant by making a difference in the decisions made by users. To be relevant, it should have the value of predicting the entity's future and the value of confirming that prediction.
- **Faithful representation** : If accounting information is to be useful it must faithfully represent the phenomena that it purports to represent. To do so, the accounting information should be complete to include all necessary information, it should be neutral among various users, and it should be free from errors.

Enhancing qualitative characteristics :

These are qualitative characteristics that enhance the fundamental characteristics explained above.

- **Comparability** : Qualitative characteristic that enables users to identify and understand similarities and differences between items. Accounting information is more useful if it can be compared with similar information from other entities, or of the same entity during another period of time.
- **Verifiability** : Qualitative characteristic by which knowledgeable and independent observers could reach a consensus as to whether a faithful representation of economic phenomena is made.
- **Timeliness** : Accounting information should be provided to information users in useful time periods.
- **Understandability** : Accounting information should be clearly and concisely classified, characterized and presented ; thus, it should be understandable for the users.

Information cost constraint :

Information cost is a pervasive constraint on accounting reporting. If the cost of the information exceeds the benefits expected from the accounting information provided, that piece of information cannot be reported.

IFRS references (http://www.kasb.or.kr)

[1] *The Conceptual Framework for Financial Reporting*, par. 1.2, 1.4.
[2] IAS 34 *Interim Financial Reporting*, par. 35.
IAS 1 *Presentation of Financial Statements*, par. 2.
[3] IAS 27 *Separate Financial Statements*, par. Korean 1.1.
IFRS 10 *Consolidated Financial Statements*, par. Korean 3.1.
[4] *The Conceptual Framework for Financial Reporting*, par. 2.1～2.39.

Key terms

Annual financial statements (연차재무제표) : Financial statements prepared for one fiscal year, at the end of that fiscal year. (p.22)

Auditing (회계감사) : An examination of financial statements to check whether those financial statements are prepared fairly in accordance with accounting standards. (p.21)

Creditors (채권자) : Persons that lend money to a company. (p.4)

Financial statements (재무제표) : Statements that summarize the outcomes of a company's business activities and are composed of a statement of financial position, a comprehensive income statement, a statement of cash flows, and a statement of changes in equity. (p.11)

Financing activities (재무활동) : Activities by which a company generates the funds needed for investing and operating activities. (p.5)

Interim financial statements (중간재무제표) : Financial statements prepared during an accounting year for a quarter (3 months), or for a half of a year (6 months). (p.22)

Investing activities (투자활동) : Activities by which a company acquires resources such as buildings, automobiles, and office equipment. (p.5)

Investors (투자자) : Persons that invest money in a company. (p.4)

Korean International Financial Reporting Standards (K-IFRS : 한국채택국제회계기준) : Accounting standards issued by the Korean Accounting Institute (KAI), mostly based on a translation of International Accounting Standards (IAS) and International Financial Reporting Standards (IFRS). (p.19)

Manufacturing company (제조기업) : A company that produces goods and sells those goods to customers. (p.3)

Merchandising company (상품매매기업) : A company that sells goods produced by other companies. (p.3)

Operating activities (영업활동): Selling and administration activities that are associated with purchasing merchandise and selling that merchandise to customers to make a profit. (p.5)

Service company (서비스기업): A company that renders services to clients. (p.3)

Exercises

1. Activities of a company—a merchandising company

The following are the activities of Daeshin Trading Co., a merchandising business :

① Issued 30 million shares of common stock with par value of ₩1,000, receiving ₩30 billion.
② Borrowed ₩20 billion from a bank.
③ Paid rent of ₩10 billion for a building used for an office and a store.
④ Paid ₩6 billion for interior decoration of the store and installation of sales facilities.
⑤ Purchased office furniture and equipment, such as desks and computers, and paid ₩5 billion.
⑥ Hired two administrative staff and three salespersons.
⑦ Purchased office supplies such as copying paper and stationary, and paid ₩1 billion in cash.
⑧ Purchased merchandise at ₩100 billion in cash.
⑨ Sold merchandise at ₩150 billion in cash.
⑩ Paid employee salaries of ₩50 billion.
⑪ Paid electricity bill of ₩5 billion.
⑫ Paid telephone bill of ₩2 billion.
⑬ Purchased merchandise at ₩30 billion and paid cash of ₩20 billion, leaving a remaining balance of ₩10 billion in its account.
⑭ Paid employee travel expense of ₩3 billion.
⑮ Paid sales promotion and advertising fees of ₩7 billion
⑯ Paid ₩1 billion of the amount of merchandise purchased on credit.
⑰ Paid educational fees of ₩1 billion to teach employees how to be kind to customers.
⑱ Paid interest of ₩25 billion to the bank.
⑲ Purchased K-Mart stock worth ₩5 billion on the stock market with idle cash.

《Question》

Fill in the activity numbers of those to be reported under each of the following activities.

(1) Operating activities : ________ (2) Investing activities : ____________________
(3) Financing activities : ________ (4) Not reported in financial statements : ________

2. **Activities of a company—a service company**

The following are activities of AC Consulting, a service company.

① Issued 50 million shares of common stock with par value of ₩1,000 and received cash of ₩50 billion.
② Borrowed ₩100 billion from a bank.
③ Paid office rent of ₩10 billion.
④ Purchased office equipment and paid ₩20 billion.
⑤ Purchased office supplies and paid ₩1 billion.
⑥ Provided consulting services to a client and received ₩300 billion.
⑦ Paid employee salaries of ₩150 billion.
⑧ Paid employee travel expense of ₩2 billion.
⑨ Purchased an automobile to be used for business and paid ₩4 billion.
⑩ Paid customer entertainment expense of ₩1 billion.
⑪ Paid interest of ₩10 billion to the bank.
⑫ Paid utility expense of ₩3 billion, such as the water and sewage bills, the electricity bill and the gas bill.
⑬ Paid telephone bill of ₩2 billion.
⑭ Purchased S-Electronics stock of ₩5 billion on the stock market with idle cash.

《Question》

Write down activity numbers of those to be reported under each of the following activities.

(1) Operating activities : __________ (2) Investing activities : ____________
(3) Financing activities : __________

3. **Activities of a company—a manufacturing company**

The following are the activities of TS Electronics, which manufactures and sells electronic equipment.

① Issued ₩10 million shares of common stock with par value of ₩1,000 and received ₩100 billion.
② Borrowed ₩200 billion form a bank.
③ Paid main office building rent of ₩3 billion.
④ Purchased land and a factory and paid ₩170 billion.
⑤ Purchased an electronic equipment manufacturing machine and paid ₩20 billion.
⑥ Purchased raw materials for ₩50 billion in cash.
⑦ Paid factory laborer wages of ₩10 billion
⑧ Purchased factory supplies and paid ₩1 billion.
⑨ Paid factory utility expense of ₩5 billion, such as the water and sewage bills, the electricity bill and the gas bill.

⑩ Paid sales and administrative employee salaries of ₩15 billion.
⑪ Sold finished goods at ₩330 billion in cash.
⑫ Purchased an automobile to be used for business and paid ₩2 billion.
⑬ Paid casualty insurance premium of ₩8 billion.
⑭ Paid employee welfare expense of ₩3 billion.
⑮ Paid interest of ₩40 billion to the bank.
⑯ Purchased H-Trading stock at ₩5 billion on the stock market with idle cash.

《Question》
Write down activity numbers of those to be reported under each of the following activities.

(1) Operating activities : ____________ (2) Investing activities : ____________
(3) Financing activities : ____________

Nature of Financial Statements

Chapter 2 Overview

In this chapter, we study financial statements, which an accounting system prepares to provide accounting information to the various interested parties of a company. First of all, the structures of key financial statements, the statement of financial position, the comprehensive income statement, the statement of cash flows, and the statement of changes in equity, as well as the concepts applied to each of these statements, are examined. Next, the information that each of these statements provides is explained. It will be very helpful to have the set of financial statements of a specific company downloaded from the electronic disclosing system of the Financial Supervisory Service (http://dart.fss.or.kr) and to review the contents of those financial statements while studying this chapter.

Statement of financial position

1.1 What is a statement of financial position?

The statement of financial position (재무상태표) is a statement showing the compositions of assets, liabilities, and equity, which constitute the financial position of a company at the end of an accounting year. In other words, it is an accounting report showing how much assets a company owns for its operation, how much liabilities (debts) the company has to pay off, and how much equity (stockholders' equity) of the company is.

To understand financial position better, let's examine the following simple example. Assume that the total properties of C Company, which President Choi operates, are worth ₩100 billion and that the debts (amount owed) of that company to be paid off total ₩40 billion. If anyone asks how much C Company's properties are worth, one can answer "₩100 billion"; however, one can describe the properties and debts of C Company better by answering that net properties are worth ₩60 billion after excluding the debts of ₩40 billion from the total properties worth ₩100 billion. Here in this case, the ₩100 billion in gross properties of C Company are called assets, the ₩40 billion outstanding debts are called liabilities, and the ₩60 billion worth of net properties are called equity. In accounting, detailed contents of assets, liabilities, and equity are called its financial position, and a statement showing that financial position as in the following ⟨Table 2-1⟩ is called the statement of financial position.

⟨Table 2-1⟩ An example of reporting financial position

Statement of financial position

C Company (Numbers in billions of ₩)

Gross properties (Assets)	100	Debts (Liabilities)	40
		Net properties (Equity)	60
Total	100	Total	100

Because a statement of financial position is a statement showing the financial position of a company, if anyone wants to know the size of the assets a company has, he or she has to examine its statement of financial position. Also, if outstanding loans from banks or any individual person are in question, we should examine the statement of financial position. It can be also understood through the statement of financial position how much in assets remained as stockholders' equity after paying off all liabilities.

1.2 Structure of statement of financial position

The statement of financial position is composed of a heading and a body. The heading includes the title of the statement (the statement of financial position), the name of the company for whom the statement has been prepared, and the preparation date of the statement. In the body, below the heading, the details and amount of assets (자산) that the company owns are stated, and the sources of the funds used to acquire those assets are classified into liabilities (부채) and equity (자본) and are stated.

A statement of financial position is a sheet of paper, divided into two parts, that reports the details and amounts of the acquired properties as assets on the left side and then the sources and amounts of funds as liabilities and equity on the right side so that the two sides contrast with each other. In accounting, traditionally, the left side is called the debit (Dr.: 차변), and the right side is called the credit (Cr.: 대변). In the past, the statement of financial position used to be called '대차대조표,' which means this statement (표) symmetrically contrasts (대조) the credit and the debit. [In the past, the statement of financial position used to be called 'B/S'(balance sheet) which means this sheet (표) reports balances (잔액) of assets, liabilities, and equity items so that the credit and the debit are in balancing (균형).]

To help with understanding a statement of financial position, let's reexamine in detail the example of OSS Mart, which was introduced in Chapter 1. The funds generated and the assets acquired when OSS Mart was organized on January 1, 20×1 are as follows in 〈Illustration 2-1〉.

According to 〈Illustration 2-1〉, Uncle issued 70 million shares of common stock with a par value of ₩1,000, distributed them to himself and to his co-investors, generated ₩70 billion, and founded a corporation called OSS Mart. Then, he borrowed ₩30 billion from a bank so that a total fund of ₩100 billion was generated. With this fund, he purchased a piece of land at ₩20 billion and facilities, such as a store building, and equipment at ₩37 billion. And then he purchased K-Mart stock at ₩13 billion as a long-term investment and decided to classify it as a fair value through other comprehensive income (FVOCI) financial asset, and made a short-term loan of ₩27 billion to a supplier. A remaining cash balance of ₩3 billion was kept in hand for operation.

〈Illustration 2-1〉 Financial position of OSS Mart (January 1, 20×1)

(Numbers in billions of ₩)

Fund generated

① Fund generated by issuing 70 million shares of common stock with par value of ₩1,000 to stockholders, Uncle and co-investors : 70

② Borrowing from a bank : 30

Assets acquired

① Land : 20

② Facilities, such as building and equipment : 37

③ FVOCI (fair value through other comprehensive income) financial asset : 13

④ Short-term loan : 27

⑤ Cash in hand : 3

The following 〈Table 2-2〉 is statement of financial position of OSS Mart as of January 1, 20×1 using information in 〈Illustration 2-1〉.

〈Table 2-2〉 Statement of financial position (account format)

OSS Mart　　As of January 1, 20×1　　(Numbers in billions of ₩)

Account titles	Amount	Account titles	Amount
Assets		**Liability**	
Current assets		**Current liability**	
Cash	3	Short-term borrowing	30
Short-term loan	27		
Non-current assets			
FVOCI financial asset	13		
Land	20	**Equity**	
Plant assets	37	Share capital-common stock	70
Total assets	100	**Total liability and equity**	100

The heading of OSS Mart's statement of financial position shows the title of the statement, name of the company (OSS Mart) for which the statement was prepared, preparation date (January 1, 20×1), and monetary units. Below the heading, the body of the statement is divided into the left side and the right side. On the left side, the composition and amount of assets are listed, and the total amount of assets is reported on the bottom. On the right side, the compositions and amounts of liabilities and equity are listed, and the total liabilities and total equity are reported on the bottom. In this illustration, because the compositions of liability and equity are one item, the total liability and total equity are not reported. However, if each composition is more than two items, the total amount of liabilities and the total amount of equity should be reported separately.

The statement of financial position in 〈Table 2-2〉 shows that OSS Mart as of January 1, 20×1, owns five kinds of assets : cash, shot-term loan, FVOCI financial asset, land, and plant assets, and the total amount of assets is ₩100 billion. Also, it shows that ₩30 billion out of the ₩100 billion used to purchase those assets came from a creditor, and the remaining ₩70 billion came from stockholders.

If we examine the statement of financial position of OSS Mart, we can find that the total amount on the left side (debit) equals the total amount on the right side (credit). The reason why the debit total equals the credit total is that the total amount of assets the company purchased—the debit total, ought to be the same as the total amount of funds used to purchase those assets-the credit total. If we put this relationship in a formula, it looks as follows.

Assets	=	**Liabilities**	+	**Equity**
₩100 billion		₩30 billion		₩70 billion

The above formula is called the statement of financial position equation or the accounting equation, and it means that the total amount of assets equals the addition of total liabilities and total equity.

In the statement of financial position, there ought to be a preparation date, which is a date of statement of financial position. In the case of OSS Mart, a business opening date of January 1, 20×1, was set up as the date of statement of financial position to explain the structure of the statement of financial position. However, in general, the statement of financial position is prepared as of the last day of the fiscal year (usually December 31). The reason for preparing it at the end of the fiscal year is to report the financial position at the end of a period (one year) during which the company conducts various activities.

A statement of financial position can be prepared in two different formats. The statement of financial position of OSS Mart of ⟨Table 2-2⟩ was prepared in the traditional style by dividing reports into two parts, left and right, and reported assets on the left side and liabilities and equity on the right side. This style is called the account format because the format separating the left side and the right side resembles the format of account where transactions are recorded (account will be explained in detail in Chapter 3). A statement of financial position can be prepared in another way by laying out the compositions and amounts of assets, liabilities, and equity from top to bottom as can be seen in ⟨Table 2-3⟩. This kind of style is called the report format. In these days, the report format has become a general one because the items to be reported in the statement of financial position have been increased greatly and have become more complex. The statements of financial position stored in the electronic disclosing system of the Financial Supervisory Service are in this report format.

⟨Table 2-3⟩ Statement of financial position (report format)

OSS Mart As of January 1, 20×1 (Numbers in billions of ₩)

Account titles	Amount
Assets	
Current assets	
Cash	3
Short-term loan	27
Non-current assets	
FVOCI financial asset	13
Land	20
Plant assets	37
Total assets	100
Liability	
Current liability	
Short-term borrowing	30
Equity	
Share capital-common stock	70
Total liability and equity	100

1.3 Classification of components of statement of financial position

The components of the statement of financial position are called account titles, are listed according to the characteristics of those components as shown in 〈Table 2-4〉. Assets are classified and reported into current assets and non-current assets; liabilities into current liabilities and non-current liabilities; and equity into share capital, share premium, retained earnings, accumulated other comprehensive income, and other components of equity. Next, detailed account titles and the amount belonging to each component are reported.

〈Table 2-4〉 Classification of statement of financial position items

Classification		Detailed account titles
A	Current assets	Cash and cash equivalents Trade receivables Accrued revenue Cost financial assets : Short-term loans Prepaid expense Inventory : Merchandise
	Non-current assets	Cost financial assets : Long-term loans FVOCI financial assets Tangible assets : Land Plant assets Construction in progress Intangible assets : Industrial property rights

Classification		Detailed account titles
L	Current liabilities	Trade payables Accrued expense Unearned revenue Cost financial liabilities : Short-term borrowings
	Non-current liabilities	Cost financial liabilities : Long-term borrowings Amortized cost financial liabilities : Bonds payable Provisions
E	Share capital	Share capital-common stock Share capital-preferred stock
	Share premium	Share premium-common stock
	Retained earnings	Retained earnings
	Accumulated other comprehensive income	Accumulated gain on valuation of FVOCI financial assets
	Other components of equity	Treasury stock

A : Assets L : Liabilities E : Equity

Most Korean companies (including companies in the United States and Japan) present current items first and non-current items next in the statement of financial position. However, most European companies present non-current items first. ⟨Table 2-5⟩ is the statement of financial position of OSS Mart prepared in this European presentation style.

⟨Table 2-5⟩ Statement of financial position (European style)

OSS Mart As of January 1, 20×1 (Numbers in billions of ₩)

Account titles	Amount
Assets	
Non-current assets	
FVOCI financial asset	13
Land	20
Plant assets	37
Current assets	
Cash	3
Short-term loan	27
Total assets	100
Equity	
Share capital-common stock	70
Liability	
Current liability	
Short-term borrowing	30
Total liability and equity	100

⟨Box 2-1⟩ Criterion for current and non-current classification

When a statement of financial position is prepared, the **one-year rule (1년 기준)** is used to classify assets and liabilities into current assets and non-current assets as well as current liabilities and non-current liabilities. According to this rule, assets that can be converted into cash or that can be used up for operation within one year from the date of the statement of financial position are classified as current assets, and those that are converted into cash or used for operation for a period beyond one year are classified as non-current assets. In the case of liabilities, liabilities with a maturity date falling within one year from the date of the statement of financial position are classified as current liabilities, and liabilities with a maturity date falling beyond one year are classified as non-current liabilities.

⟨Box 2-2⟩ Order of presenting components of statement of financial position

IFRS[1] requires to classify assets and liabilities current/non-current. Only if it is more reliable and more relevant not to classify current/non-current and to report all items in order of liquidity, current/non-current classification can be waived. Also in this case, we can present highest liquid items first or the lowest liquid item first. **Liquidity (유동성)** means, for assets, the degree of easiness of converting assets into cash, and for liabilities, it is the degree of urgency to pay them back in cash.

1.4 Components of statement of financial position

1.4.1 Concept and key components of assets

Assets are economic resources that a company can use in carrying out its operations. An asset is defined as "a present economic resource controlled by the entity as a result of past events." And an economic resource is defined as "a right that has the potential to produce economic benefits," per IFRS[2]. Through this definition, we can identify what to include in assets and what not to include. However, it is okay for students who are studying accounting for the first time to understand assets as properties that a company owns.

(1) Current assets

Current assets are assets that can be converted into cash or can be sold or used for operations within one year from the date of the statement of financial position and are assets that are held for short-term trading or to be sold within one year.

① Cash and cash equivalents : include cash such as currency (money), checks that banks draw, checks that other companies draw, deposits in checking and saving accounts, and financial instruments that are highly liquid and thus are easily converted into cash and come with an insignificant amount of risk in changes in value. (Although cash and cash equivalents are financial assets, they are separated from other financial assets and are reported in the statement of financial position as a separate item.)

② Trade receivables : represent the right to receive proceeds in the future from the credit sales of merchandise and includes accounts receivable and notes receivable. If merchandise is sold on account, it is recorded in accounts receivable, but if merchandise is sold on credit and a note is received from a customer, it is recorded in notes receivable. (Although trade receivables are financial assets, they are separated from other financial assets and are reported on the statement of financial position as a separate item.)

③ Accrued revenue : represents revenue earned by rendering service to a client but not received in cash yet, so it is expected to be collected in cash in the future.

④ Short-term financial assets : A financial asset means a contractual right to receive cash or a financial asset from another entity. Per IFRS[3], financial assets are classified into amortized cost financial assets, fair value through profit or loss (FVPL) financial assets, and fair value through other comprehensive income (FVOCI) financial assets. This book has separated cost financial assets from the amortized cost financial assets for educational purposes. Financial assets that are expected to receive cash within 12 months are classified as current assets. Here, short-term loans, a form of cost financial asset, are used as an example to explain a short-term financial asset. Amortized cost financial assets, FVPL financial assets, and FVOCI financial assets will be reviewed in the Appendix of this book. (FVOCI financial assets held for long-term are introduced as an example of long-term financial assets under non-current assets below.)

- Short-term loans : A loan means money lent to other companies or other persons and represents the right to collect that money in the future. Loans with maturity dates falling within one year are classified as short-term loans. As short-term loans are reported at cost, they are classified as cost financial assets.

⑤ Prepaid expense : represents future economic benefits expected as a result of the prepayment of expenses that will occur in the future. For example, if one year rent is paid in advance when a building is rented, the rent is reported as a prepaid rent, one of the prepaid expenses.

⑥ Merchandise inventory : means merchandise (goods) which are purchased from other companies for the purpose of selling. In the case of a department store, an air conditioner displayed in the store to sell is merchandise. However, an air conditioner installed in an office is kept to use, not to sell. Therefore, it is classified as a plant asset called an appliance.

〈Box 2-3〉 Inventories of manufacturing companies

- **Finished goods** : mean products manufactured by a company for the purpose of selling. They are called finished goods to distinguish them from merchandise of merchandising companies.
- **Raw material** : means material to use for production of finished goods.
- **Work in process** : means unfinished goods that are in process of manufacturing.

(2) Non-current Assets

Non-current assets are assets which are other than current assets and to be possessed by the company for a period longer than 1 year from the date of statement of financial position, and are composed following items.

① Long-term financial assets : mean financial assets that are expected to be converted into cash after one year is elapsed. Here, FVOCI financial assets and long-term loans, one kind of cost financial assets, are used as examples to explain long-term financial assets.

- FVOCI financial assets : include long-term investments in stock the company decided to measure at fair value and recognize gain or loss on valuation as an other comprehensive income and long-term investments in bonds held not only for 'holding to maturity' but also for 'selling.' (Refer to the Appendix of this book for the composition and classification of financial assets.)
- Long-term loans : mean money lent to other companies or other persons with a loan period longer than one year. As long-term loans are reported at cost, they are classified as cost financial assets.

② Tangible assets : mean assets with physical substance.

- Land : represents a plot of ground and forests that are used for operations.
- Plant assets : include buildings, machinery, ships, airplanes, automobiles and vehicles, appliances, and office equipment.
- Construction in progress : means assets in a stage of incompletion among plant assets that the company has constructed itself.

③ Intangible assets : mean assets without physical substance.

- Industrial property rights : include patents, trademarks, the rights of a practical new device, design rights, etc., that a company owns.

1.4.2 Concept and key components of liabilities

Liabilities are debts that the company has to pay back to other companies or other persons. A liability is defined as "a present obligations of the entity as a result of past events," per IFRS[4]. Liabilities are classified into current liabilities and non-current liabilities.

(1) Current liabilities

Short-term obligations with a maturity date falling within one year from the date of the statement of financial position are called current liabilities, and the key components are as follows :

① Trade payables : Accounts payable and notes payable not yet paid are called trade payables. If we purchase merchandise on credit, we record the purchased amount in accounts payable. If we purchase merchandise on credit and issued notes, we record the purchased amount in notes payable. However, if we purchase plant assets, such as machinery and vehicles that are not for sale, on credit, we record the purchased amount in non-trade payables. (Although a trade payable is a financial liability, it is separate from other financial liabilities and is reported on the statement of financial position as a separate item.)

② Accrued expense : means an expense that has occurred already but has not been paid yet. For example, in the case of interest expense that occurs on borrowings from a bank but are not paid yet because the interest payment date has not arrived, the interest amount is reported as interest payable, an accrued expense.

③ Unearned revenue : means obligation to provide services in the future because the revenue that will be earned in the future has been received in cash. For example, if rent is received in advance when a building is rented, the rent is reported as an unearned rent, one of the unearned revenues.

④ Short-term financial liabilities : Financial liabilities are contractual obligations to pay cash or financial assets to another entity. Per IFRS[5], financial liabilities are classified into amortized cost financial liabilities and fair value through profit or loss (FVPL) financial liabilities. This book has separated cost financial liabilities from amortized cost financial liabilities for educational purposes. Financial liabilities that are expected to be paid off in cash within one year are classified as current liabilities. Here, short-term borrowings, one type of cost financial liability, is used as an example to explain short-term financial liability. Amortized cost financial liabilities, FVPL financial liabilities will be reviewed in Chapter 9. (Bonds payable reported as amortized cost financial liabilities are introduced as an example of long-term financial liabilities under non-current liabilities below.)

- Short-term borrowings : mean money borrowed from financial institutions, etc. that should be paid back within one year. As short-term borrowings are reported at cost, they are classified as cost financial liabilities.

⑤ Other current liabilities : include liabilities that should be paid within one year, such as a bank overdraft, dividends payable, and income tax payable.

(2) Non-current liabilities

A long-term obligation with a maturity date later than one year from the date of the statement of financial position is classified as a non-current liability. Key components are long-term financial liabilities and provisions.

① Long-term financial liabilities : mean financial liabilities that should be paid after one year. Here, long-term borrowings, one kind of cost financial liabilities, and bonds payable, one kind of amortized cost financial liabilities are used as examples to explain long-term financial liabilities.

- Long-term borrowings : mean borrowings from financial institutions, etc. with maturity dates falling after one year. As long-term borrowings are reported at cost, they are classified as cost financial liabilities.
- Bonds payable : mean funds generated by issuing bonds. Bonds are documents that a company issues to borrow money for a long time from a number of people through the security market. Bonds may be issued at a premium (discount). In that case, bonds payable are reported cost after amortizing premium (discount). Therefore, bonds payable are classified as amortized cost financial liabilities. (Refer to Chapter 9 for detail explanation for amortization method, etc.)

② Provisions : Provisions are present obligations caused by past transactions, such as a product warrant, and are reported when it is provable that they can be paid off and the amount to be paid can be reliably estimated. If a provision is expected to be paid within one year, it should be classified as a current liability.

1.4.3 Concept and key components of equity

Equity (자본) means a residual after taking liabilities from the total assets of a firm. Therefore, equity represents the owner's (stockholders') claim (equity) among assets of a firm. Equity is defined as "the residual interest in the assets of the entity after deducting all its liabilities," per IFRS[6]. If we define equity as a residual claim, the statement of financial position equation (Assets = Liabilities + Equity) changes as follows.

Equity = Assets − Liabilities

The outcome of this computation is called net assets (순자산) because this amount is the net amount after taking liabilities off from gross assets.

Equity includes the funds that owners have contributed and the portion of earnings retained within the company. In the case of a corporation, the equity is classified and reported by sources in the statement of financial position. The par value of stocks issued to stockholders is reported as share capital, and contributed capital in excess of par is reported as share premium. Earnings not paid as dividends but retained within the company are reported as retained earnings. However, in the case of a single-ownership company, investment by owners and retained earnings together without making any distinction between them are reported as a capital. Because a form of business that we come across often is the corporate form, the equity of a corporation is reviewed in this book.

(1) Share capital

Share capital is the total par value of stock issued by a company. Par value is a legal denominator determined by the company. Most of them are ₩5,000 ; however, some of them are ₩1,000, ₩500, and ₩100.

① Share capital-common stock : means total amount of par value of common stock issued.

② Share capital-preferred stock : means total amount of par value of preferred stock issued. (Refer to 〈Box 2-4〉 for differences between common stock and preferred stock.)

(2) Share premium

Share premium is capital contributed by stockholders in excess of par value. A typical example is share premium-common stock.

① Share premium-common stock : means capital contributed by common stockholders in excess of par value of common stock issued.

(3) Retained earnings

With earnings generated through operating activities, a company can either pay dividends or, instead of paying dividends, retain the earnings in the company for re-investment purposes. Earnings retained in the company are called retained earnings.

(4) Accumulated other comprehensive income

As the accumulated amount of income not paid as dividends is reported as retained earnings, the accumulated amount of other comprehensive income is reported as accumulated other comprehensive income. (Net income and other comprehensive income are reviewed in detail on the comprehensive income statement below.) Typical examples of accumulated other comprehensive income are accumulated gain on valuation of FVOCI financial assets and revaluation surplus.

① Accumulated gain (or loss) on valuation of FVOCI financial assets : means accumulated differences between the market value of FVOCI financial assets owned at the beginning of the year and that at the end of the year.
② Revaluation surplus : means accumulated differences between the fair value of tangible assets when that value at the end of the year is increased from that value at the beginning of the year

(5) Other components of equity

Other components of equity include items that are an addition to or a deduction from equity other than share capital, share premium, retained earnings, and accumulated other comprehensive income. A typical example is treasury stock.

① Treasury stock : means stock repurchased back and kept by a company that is issued by that company itself.

⟨Box 2-4⟩ Common stock and preferred stock

■ **Common stock**

Common stock is the most general form of stock that corporations issue. Common stock holders can exercise voting rights in stockholder meetings.

■ **Preferred stock**

In general, preferred stock is a stock with the preferential right to receive dividends over common stock. Preferred stock holders cannot exercise voting rights in a stockholder meeting. (Various classes of preferred stock : Refer to Chapter 10 2.1 : 'Classes of stock')

Comprehensive income statement

2.1 What is a comprehensive income statement?

The comprehensive income statement (포괄손익계산서) is a statement reporting the results of operation for a specific length of time, usually one year. In other words, it shows how much income has been generated though operating activities by a company for one year. More specifically, the comprehensive income statement shows the amount of income of a company by subtracting the cost of the merchandise sold, salespersons' salaries, and all expenses incurred for administrating activities from sales revenues generated by selling merchandise for one year. Therefore, if you closely examine the comprehensive income statement, you can find whether or not a company generated income by doing good business and made more income than other companies did.

Revenues are returns received or will be received by providing goods or services to customers, and expenses are the acquisition costs of goods or services that are used up to generate revenues. (Detailed definitions will be reviewed in 2.3 'Components of comprehensive income statement.') When revenues are greater than expenses, income is reported, and in the reversal, when revenue is less than expenses, loss is reported.

In practice, sometimes the income statement is called P/L (p and l). It means that the income statement reports (P : profit) or (L : loss). The income statement used to be called the statement of profit or loss. Income statement in Korean (손익계산서) is identical with the statement of profit or loss.

2.2 Structure of comprehensive income statement

Comprehensive income (포괄이익) is all income earned by a company through business activities. Some incomes are included in comprehensive income but are not included in net income. These items are called other comprehensive income (OCI :

기타포괄이익). Therefore, comprehensive income is the addition of net income and other comprehensive income. (For the sake of convenience, only income is reviewed here. If there is a loss, loss should be recorded instead of income.)

As can be seen in ⟨Table 2-6⟩, the comprehensive income statement reports the revenues generated by a company and the expenses that occurred for an accounting period, and it computes the difference of these two and reports it as net income. Total comprehensive income is reported by adding other comprehensive income to the net income. The comprehensive income statement can be prepared in a single statement reporting net income and other comprehensive income together as shown in ⟨Table 2-6⟩ (1), or as two statements separately reporting net income and other comprehensive income as shown in ⟨Table 2-6⟩ (2).

⟨Table 2-6⟩ Structure of comprehensive income statement

(1) Single report format

Comprehensive income statement

×× Co. From January 1, 20×1 to December 31, 20×1 (Numbers in billions of ₩)

Revenues	×××
(−) Expenses	(−) ×××
Net income	×××
(+) Other comprehensive income	(+) ×××
Total comprehensive income	×××

(2) Two reports format

Income statement

×× Co. From January 1, 20×1 to December 31, 20×1 (Numbers in billions of ₩)

Revenues	×××
(−) Expenses	(−) ×××
Net income	×××

Comprehensive income statement

×× Co. From January 1, 20×1 to December 31, 20×1 (Numbers in billions of ₩)

Net income	×××
(+) Other comprehensive income	(+) ×××
Total comprehensive income	×××

2.2.1 Classification of expenses

We can classify expenses by two different methods when we prepare an income statement. The first one involves classifying by function, such as the cost of goods sold, operating expenses (selling expense and administrative expense), and other expenses. The second one involves classifying by nature, such as the purchase of merchandise, delivery expense, employee salaries expense, advertising expense, and depreciation expense.

IFRS[7] does not rigidly require the format of comprehensive income statements and just asks to prepare the comprehensive income statement in a format that is helpful to users for understanding the performance of the company. Therefore, a company can classify expenses by function or by nature. The functional classification is the method that old Korean accounting standards required and currently most manufacturing companies and merchandising companies are using. Hence, we mainly review the method of classifying expenses by function below. The method for 'classifying by nature' will be reviewed briefly with an illustration in 2.4.2 below. From Chapter 3 onward we will exclusively discuss the method of 'classifying by function.'

2.3 Components of comprehensive income statement

As briefly reviewed above, the comprehensive income statement reports revenues, expenses and other comprehensive income. Here, we review concepts and detailed components of these items.

2.3.1 Concepts and key components of revenue

Revenue (수익) is a return a company has received or will receive by providing goods or services to customers for a certain period. Revenue is defined as "income arising in the course of an entity's ordinary activities." And income is defined as "increases in assets or decreases in liabilities, that result in an increase in equity, other than those relating to contributions from holders of equity claims," per IFRS[8]. To help with understanding revenue, we take simple ⟨Illustration 2-2⟩ below.

> ⟨Illustration 2-2⟩ Revenue vs. Income
>
> How much is the revenue if Company A bought product Q at ₩8,000 and sold it at ₩10,000?

Because the return obtained by providing merchandise to a customer is ₩10,000, the revenue is ₩10,000. The amount of ₩2,000 computed by subtracting the purchase cost of ₩8,000 (Cost of goods sold, is examined in 2.3.2 (1) below.) from the revenue of ₩10,000 is called income. However, some people in the real world use the terminology of revenue to indicate income so that they bring quite a bit of confusion. (Refer to ⟨Box 2-5⟩ 'Revenue vs. Income vs. Receipt' below.) Revenues are classified into (1) operating revenues and (2) other revenues.

(1) Operating revenues

Operating revenues are revenues obtained from the main operating activities, and sales revenues generated by selling merchandise belong to this category. Sales revenues are the biggest among various revenues and constitute a primary source of income. The operating revenues of service firms, such as accounting firms, a lawyer's office, and consulting firms generated by rendering service are called service fee revenues. (Some service companies label service fee revenues as service revenues, and they label service revenues as sales revenues.) Revenue earned from incidental operating activities, such as rent revenue from leasing assets, is classified as other operating revenue.

(2) Other revenues

Other revenues are revenues generated from investing or financing activities. Interest revenues received by making loans and dividend revenues received by holding the stocks of other companies are examples of other revenues.

〈Box 2-5〉 Revenue vs. Income vs. Receipt

Revenue, **income**, and receipt (수입) are used a lot without making any distinction among them ; however, in accounting, they are used with strict differentiation. Revenue means the sales amount of merchandise sold, and income means net amount after deducting expenses from revenues. In other words, revenue is the **gross amount (총액)**, and income is the **net amount (순액)**. **Receipt** means the same as a cash receipt and is a term referring to cash inflow. If merchandise is sold in cash, 'revenue' and 'receipt' are same ; however, if merchandise is sold, some in cash and some on credit, there would be a difference of credit sales amount between the 'revenue' and 'receipt.'

2.3.2 Concepts and key components of expenses

Expense (비용) means goods or services consumed to generate revenue. Expenses are defined as "decreases in assets, or increases in liabilities, that result in decrease in equity, other than those relating to distributions to holders of equity claims," per IFRS[9]. Expenses are classified into (1) cost of goods sold, (2) operating expenses, (3) other expenses and (4) income tax expense.

(1) Cost of goods sold

If a company sells merchandise to earn sales revenue, an asset called merchandise is consumed (flow-out to outside of the company). The purchase amount—that is, the cost of the merchandise consumed—is called the cost of goods sold or cost of sales (매출원가). '매출원가' in Korean is identical with the 'cost of sales' in English. In 〈Illustration 2-2〉 above, the purchase cost of Product Q sold of ₩8,000 is the cost of goods sold. Cost of goods sold is a typical example of expense of merchandising companies, and in many cases, this amount is the biggest among expense items.

(2) Operating expenses

Operating expenses are composed of selling expenses, including logistics expenses and administrative expenses that occur to repair and maintain facilities. Selling expenses, such as salespersons' salaries expense, advertising expense, sales promotion expense, entertainment expense, and administrative expenses, such as administrative staff salaries expense, building rent expense, utility expense, and repair and maintenance expense belong to this category.

(3) Other expenses

Other expenses are expenses occurred not from operating activities but from investing or financing activities. Interest expense, which is a finance expense, is a typical example of other expenses. IFRS[10] requires to report finance expenses separately. (In this book, we present the caption of 'finance expense' to highlight that finance expense should be reported separately. You can omit the caption as long as you present finance expense separately.)

(4) Income tax expense

Income tax expense is an expense levied on earnings that are the income of a company. If a person earns money, he or she has to pay personal income tax to the government. Corporate income tax is income tax paid by a corporation to the government as a law-created entity. This corporate income tax is an expense of using various infrastructure provided by the government.

〈Box 2-6〉 Rent received vs. Rent revenue
Rent paid vs. Rent expense

If we rent a building as a landlord, we receive rent. If we rent a building as a tenant, we pay rent. All rent received is not always rent revenue. Only rent earned in the current year is reported as rent revenue. All rent paid is not always rent expense. Only rent expired in the current year is reported as rent expense. Rent is a term used to mean cash received or cash paid and is not a proper term to mean revenue or expense on an income statement. The same confusion is made when we use insurance premium and salaries as account titles on an income statement. Therefore, this book uses terms shown in the following 〈Table 2-7〉 on an income statement to minimize confusion.

〈Table 2-7〉 Revising terms in income statement

Current terms (Korea)	Terms used in this book
Rent (received)	Rent revenue
Rent (paid)	Rent expense
Insurance premium	Insurance expense
Salaries	Salaries expense

2.3.3 Concept and key components of other comprehensive income

Comprehensive income is the total income combining net income and other comprehensive income. Other comprehensive income means income not included in net income because if it is included in net income, net income might be biased or fluctuate a great deal from one period to another. Mainly gain from valuing assets at fair value belongs to this income, and examples are gain on valuation of FVOCI financial assets and gain on revaluation of tangible assets.

Because other comprehensive income is a rather difficult issue, no further explanation is made here, but basic concepts and simple examples will be reviewed in the Appendix of this book.

2.3.4 Income on each step on comprehensive income statement

We reviewed various formats of comprehensive income statements above. Here, we review information provided by income on each step on a comprehensive income statement. (Note : The comprehensive income statement classifying expenses by function above is a multiple-step comprehensive income statement presenting incomes step by step. On the contrary, the comprehensive income statement classifying expenses by nature is a single-step comprehensive income statement presenting only one net income.)

⟨Table 2-8⟩ shows that income on each step on the comprehensive income statement is a result of various activities of a company.

⟨Table 2-8⟩ Income on each step on comprehensive income statement and activities of a company

Comprehensive income statement

××Company From January 1, 20×1 to December 31, 20×1 (Numbers in billions of ₩)

<table>
<tr><th>Account titles</th><th>Amount</th><th colspan="2">Activities of a company</th></tr>
<tr><td>Sales</td><td>×××</td><td rowspan="3">Sales of merchandise</td><td rowspan="5">Operating activities</td></tr>
<tr><td>Cost of goods sold</td><td>(−)××</td></tr>
<tr><td>Gross profit</td><td>××</td></tr>
<tr><td>Operating expenses</td><td>(−)××</td><td rowspan="2">Selling and administrative activities</td></tr>
<tr><td>Income from operations</td><td>××</td></tr>
<tr><td>Other revenues</td><td>×</td><td colspan="2" rowspan="3">Investing and financing activities</td></tr>
<tr><td>Other expenses</td><td>(−)×</td></tr>
<tr><td>Income before income tax expense</td><td>××</td></tr>
<tr><td>Income tax expense</td><td>(−)×</td><td colspan="2">Corporate income tax</td></tr>
<tr><td>Net income</td><td>××</td><td colspan="2" rowspan="4">Results of operation</td></tr>
<tr><td>Other comprehensive income</td><td>×</td></tr>
<tr><td>Comprehensive income</td><td>××</td></tr>
<tr><td>Earnings per share</td><td>₩×××</td></tr>
</table>

Let's review in detail the concepts and meanings of income on each step of the comprehensive income statement.

(1) Gross profit

Gross profit is computed by subtracting cost of goods sold, which is the acquisition cost of merchandise sold from sales, which is merchandise sales revenue. It is called gross profit because expenses should be subtracted additionally from this figure to compute net income.

(Numbers in billions of ₩)

Sales	xxx
Cost of goods sold	(−)xx
Gross profit	xx

Gross profit is called the sales margin (판매마진) and is the most fundamental data by which one can evaluate the profitability of a firm.

(2) Income from operations

Income from operations is computed by subtracting operating expenses from the gross profit. The reason it is called income from operations is that it shows the results of operating activities. Operating expenses are data by which one can evaluate the efficiency of the selling and administrative activities of a company.

(Numbers in billions of ₩)

Gross profit	xx
Operating expenses	(−)xx
Income from operations	xx

If the result of operating activities that are the main activities of a company is presented, combined together with those of non-operating activities (investing activities and financing activities), the comparability of the results of operation between companies is jeopardized. Therefore, K-IFRS(KAI issued)[11] requires to present income from operations separately on a comprehensive income statement. (IFRS[12] dose not require disclosing income from operations, but allows a company to elect to disclose this income if the operating activities are well defined.)

(3) Net income before income tax expense

Net income before income tax expense is income after adding other revenues and subtracting other expenses from income from operations. Other revenues and other expenses are reported separately from income from operations because they are generated from the investing and financing activities of a firm.

(Numbers in billions of ₩)

Income from operations	××
Other revenues	×
Other expenses	(−)×
Net income before income tax expense	××

(4) Net income and earnings per share

1) Net Income

Net income is income computed by subtracting income tax expenses from net income before income tax expense. Income tax expense includes corporate income tax levied on the income of a corporation and the resident tax levied on that income tax. The computation of income tax will be examined in the tax accounting course.

(Numbers in billions of ₩)

Net income before income tax expense	××
Income tax expense	(−)×
Net income	××
Earnings per share	₩×××

Because net income is an outcome of subtracting the total amount of all kinds of expenses from the total revenues generated during an accounting period, it shows the final results of the operation of a company. With net income, a company can pay dividends to stockholders or retain earnings in the company and reinvest them.

2) Earnings per share

Earnings per share (EPS : 주당이익) is computed by dividing number of common shares outstanding into the net income. The number of common shares outstanding means number of common shares issued by the company that are being held by external common stockholders, thus outstanding. Detailed method of computation will be reviewed in Chapter 5.

Stock price and dividends are stated per share basis. Therefore, earnings per share can be very useful in valuing a company because it can be directly compared with stock price and dividends one to one. For example, the most frequently used method of valuing a company is the price earnings multiple showing how many times of earnings the stock price represents. Earnings used in that price earnings multiple is earnings per share. [Various price multiples including PER (price earnings ratio : 주가이익비율) will be reviewed in Chapter 5.] For these reasons, IFRS[13] requires to present earnings per share on a comprehensive income statement.

〈Box 2-7〉 Net income vs. Earnings per share

Net income is a gross amount considering neither the size of the company nor the number of stocks. Let us assume that the net income of Company A, a company competing with OSS Mart, for 20×1 is ₩21 billion, the same as that of OSS Mart. In this case, does an information user evaluate that the operational performance of OSS Mart and that of Company A are the same? No, he or she does not. Let us assume that the number of outstanding common stock of OSS Mart is 70 million shares, and that of Company A is 35 million shares. In the case of OSS Mart, earnings of ₩300 is applicable to one share of common stock. However, in the case of Company A, earnings of ₩600 is applicable to one share. Therefore, a stockholder of Company A enjoys twice the earnings per share in comparison with a stockholder of OSS Mart.

Let us assume that the net income of OSS Mart for 20×2 increases to ₩25 billion. If 30 million shares of common stocks were issued in 20×2 and the number of outstanding common stocks became 100 million shares, the earnings per share for 20×2 decreases to ₩250. Although the absolute amount of net income was increased, the earnings applicable to a stockholder who owns one share of common stock is decreased. In this way, the **earnings per share** can be used very usefully in comparing performance between different companies and different periods of one company.

(5) Total comprehensive income

Total comprehensive income is computed by adding other comprehensive income to net income.

(Numbers in billions of ₩)

Net income	××
Other comprehensive income	×
Total comprehensive income	××

Total comprehensive income is income that includes not only net income but also other comprehensive income from valuing assets at fair value. Therefore, this income is an index showing the comprehensive performance of a company by including all income from all transactions except for transactions with stockholders of the company.

2.4 Preparing a comprehensive income statement

To understand the format of a comprehensive income statement, we will use the example of OSS Mart. The following is a summary of detailed revenues earned by conducting operating activities and detailed expenses to generate those revenues for one year starting when OSS Mart opened at the beginning January of 20×1.

〈Illustration 2-3〉 Detailed revenues and expenses of OSS Mart (20×1)

(Numbers in billions of ₩)

Detailed revenues

① Merchandise sales amount (sales amount) : 118
② Interest revenue on a short-term loan : 2

Detailed expenses

① Acquisition cost of merchandise sold (Cost of goods sold) : 65
② Salespersons' salaries expense : 15
③ Vehicle rent expense : 7
④ Interest expense on borrowing from a bank : 3
⑤ Income tax expense : 9

Detailed other comprehensive income

① Gain on valuation of FVOCI financial assets : 2

According to the above data, the revenues of OSS Mart for 20×1 are ₩118 billion in sales revenues generated by selling merchandise and the interest revenue of ₩2 billion on a short-term loan. Expenses are ₩65 billion for the cost of merchandise sold, ₩15 billion for salespersons' salaries, ₩7 billion for rent expense, ₩3 billion for interest expense on borrowing from a bank, and ₩9 billion for income tax expense. The gain on the valuation of FVOCI financial assets, which is one of the other comprehensive incomes, is ₩2 billion.

2.4.1 When expenses are classified by function

(1) Single comprehensive income statement

The following 〈Table 2-9〉 is a single comprehensive income statement of OSS Mart for 20×1 classifying expenses by their function.

〈Table 2-9〉 Single comprehensive income statement of OSS Mart (classifying expenses by function)

Comprehensive income statement

OSS Mart From January 1 20×1 to December 31 20×1 (Numbers in billions of ₩)

Account titles	Amount	
Sales		118
Cost of goods sold		(−)65
Gross profit		53
Operating expenses		(−)22
Salaries expense	(−)15	
Rent expense	(−)7	
Income from operations		31
Other revenue		2
Interest revenue	2	
Other expense		(−)3
Finance expense :		
Interest expense	(−)3	
Income before income tax expense		30
Income tax expense		(−)9
Net Income		21
Other comprehensive income		2
Gain on valuation of FVOCI financial assets	2	
Total comprehensive income		23
Earnings per share		₩300

As we examine the above single comprehensive income statement, it can be found that a comprehensive income statement is composed of a heading and a body, just as the statement of financial position is. The heading is the same as that of the statement of financial position, but we should present the period prepared for (from January 1, 20×1 to December 31, 20×1) instead of the preparation date. Also, in the body, revenues and expenses are classified and presented by function.

In the case of OSS Mart, the gross profit generated by the main operating activities of selling merchandise is ₩53 billion, and from this gross profit, if we subtract the operating expenses of ₩220 billion, which are composed of salaries expense and rent expense, we can get income from the operations totaling ₩31 billion. From this income from operations, if we add interest revenue of ₩2 billion on a short-term loan, which is a part of other revenues, and deduct the interest expense of ₩3 billion on borrowing from a bank, which is a financing expense and a part of other expenses, we can get net income before the income tax expense of ₩30 billion. From this amount, if we deduct the income tax expense, which is tax paid by a corporation as a law-created entity of ₩9 billion, we can get a net income of ₩21 billion. The total comprehensive income that is computed by adding other comprehensive income of ₩2 billion to net income is ₩23 billion. Earnings per share are ₩300, that are computed by dividing 70 million common shares outstanding into net income of ₩21 billion. When a single comprehensive income statement is prepared, the earnings per share are presented on the bottom line of the statement after total comprehensive income.

(2) Preparing two statements : income statement and comprehensive income statement

The following 〈Table 2-10〉 features two statements : the income statement and the comprehensive income statement prepared by separating the single comprehensive income statement of OSS Mart shown above. In this case, the earning per share is presented on the bottom line of the income statement.

〈Table 2-10〉 Comprehensive income statement of OSS Mart (classifying expenses by function–two statements)

Income statement

OSS Mart From January 1 20×1 to December 31 20×1 (Numbers in billions of ₩)

Account titles	Amount	
Sales		118
Cost of goods sold		(−)65
Gross profit		53
Operating expenses		(−)22
Salaries expense	(−)15	
Rent expense	(−)7	
Income from operations		31
Other revenue		2
Interest revenue	2	
Other expense		(−)3
Finance expense :		
Interest expense	(−)3	
Net income before income tax expense		30
Income tax expense		(−)9
Net income		21
Earnings per share		₩300

Comprehensive income statement

OSS Mart From January 1 20×1 to December 31 20×1 (Numbers in billions of ₩)

Account titles	Amount	
Net income		21
Other comprehensive income		2
Gain on valuation of FVOCI financial assets	2	
Total comprehensive income		23

2.4.2 When expenses are classified by nature

(1) Single comprehensive income statement

The following ⟨Table 2-11⟩ is a single comprehensive income statement of OSS Mart for 20×1 classifying expenses by their nature.

⟨Table 2-11⟩ Single comprehensive income statement of OSS Mart (classifying expense by nature)

Comprehensive income statement

OSS Mart From January 1 20×1 to December 31 20×1 (Numbers in billions of ₩)

Account titles	Amount	
Revenues		120
Sales revenue	118	
Other revenue	2	
Expenses		(−)90
Merchandise purchased	(−)65	
Salaries expense	(−)15	
Rent expense	(−)7	
Finance expense :		
Interest expense	(−)3	
Net income before income tax expense		30
Income tax expense		(−)9
Net income		21
Other comprehensive income		2
Gain on valuation of FVOCI financial assets	2	
Total comprehensive income		23
Earning per share		₩300

As can be seen in ⟨Table 2-11⟩ if expenses are classified by their nature, net income before income tax expense is computed by subtracting total expenses from total revenue. Therefore, gross profit and income from operations are not reported.

(2) Prepairing two statements : income statement and comprehensive income statement

We can also prepare a comprehensive income statement classifying expense by nature separating two statements, income statement and comprehensive income statement. In that case, we can prepare an income statement same as in ⟨Table 2-11⟩ and a comprehensive income statement same as in ⟨Table 2-10⟩. Thus, we omit an illustration of preparing two statements here.

As explained above, companies can prepare a single comprehensive income statement or can prepare a comprehensive income statement separating into two statements. This book examines only income statements in chapters 3, 4 and 5, where bookkeeping methods are introduced and examines other comprehensive income in the Appendix. A case comprehensive income statement introduced between Chapter 5 and Chapter 6 is a single comprehensive income statement.

Statement of cash flows

3.1 What is a statement of cash flows?

A statement of cash flows (현금흐름표) is a financial report showing cash flows for a specific period, usually one year. To be more specific, the statement of cash flows classifies the cash flows of a company into operating activities, investing activities, and financing activities and then reports the detailed contents of cash inflows and cash outflows in each activity and reports how much cash balance is increased or decreased during an accounting period.

Although the statement of financial position and the comprehensive income statement reviewed above report the financial position and results of operation, which are outcomes of three activities of a company, they do not report detailed cash flows of each activity. A statement of cash flows reports the cash flows of each activities of a company so that it enables users of information to understand how and how much cash is generated, and for what purpose the cash is used.

If a company's cash flow is not good, even though it reports income, it may experience financial distress and fall into bankruptcy. (We call this kind of bankruptcy as a bankruptcy in black. Black refers to profit and red refers to loss). If one uses cash flow information provided by a statement of cash flows along with information provided by a comprehensive income statement, he or she can more effectively identify such companies on the brink of bankruptcy in advance. In Chapter 11 'Statement of Cash Flows', we will study how to prepare a statement of cash flows in detail, and here, we review the structure and contents of the statement of cash flows.

3.2 Issues in preparing statement of cash flows

(1) Individually reporting items

Interest received and dividends received are investing activities, and interest paid and dividends paid are financing activities. As an exception is allowed by IFRS[14], these items can be classified as operating activities. No matter what activities these items are classified as, these items should be reported as individually reporting items. As an individually reporting item beside these items, there is an item of income tax paid that is reported as an operating activity. Throughout this textbook, it is assumed no exception is allowed in classifying these individually reporting items. (In this book, we present the caption of 'individually reporting item' to highlight that these items should be reported individually. You can omit the caption as long as you report these items individually.) The classification and reporting method of these items will be explained in Chapter 11.

(2) Direct method and indirect method

Cash flows from operating activities are computed by subtracting income tax paid, an individually reporting item, from cash generated from operations. Cash generated from operation can be computed by either the direct method or indirect method. Under the direct method cash generated from operations is directly computed by subtracting cash paid to suppliers for merchandise purchased and cash paid for operating expenses such as employees' salaries, etc., from cash received from customers as a result of selling merchandise. The indirect method indirectly computes cash generated from operations by adjusting an income figure on a comprehensive income statement.

Because the direct method shows detailed sources of the cash flows, it is easy to understand. However, because the indirect method is easy to apply, most companies (in Korea, 100% of listed companies) use this method. This Chapter and Chapter 3, 4 and 5, where the basic method of preparing financial statements is introduced, will exclusively review the direct method. The indirect method will be reviewed in Chapter 11.

3.3 Preparing a statement of cash flows

To understand the statement of cash flows, here we prepare the statement of cash flow of OSS Mart for 20×1. Let's assume that OSS Mart paid dividends of ₩7 billion to stockholders, ₩100 per share. Let the illustration used in preparing the statement of cash flows be the following ⟨Illustration 2-4⟩, which is a combination of ⟨Illustration 2-1⟩ (used to prepare the statement of financial position above) and ⟨Illustration 2-3⟩ (used to prepare the comprehensive income statement above). Here, we assume that all revenues and expenses in ⟨Illustration 2-3⟩ were transacted in cash.

⟨Illustration 2-4⟩ Detailed cash flows of OSS Mart (20×1)

(Numbers in billions of ₩)

- Detailed cash flows from operating activities
  ① Sales of merchandise : 118
  ② Purchase of merchandise : (−)65
  ③ Payment of employees' salaries : (−)15
  ④ Payment of rent : (−)7
  ⑤ Payment of income tax : (−)9

- Detailed cash flows from investing activities
  ① Receipt of interest on a loan : 2
  ② Making a loan to a supplier : (−)27
  ③ Purchase of FVOCI financial assets : (−)13
  ④ Purchase of land : (−)20
  ⑤ Purchase of plant assets : (−)37

- Detailed cash flows from financing activities
  ① Borrowing from a bank : 30
  ② Issuance of common stock : 70
  ③ Payment of interest on borrowing : (−)3
  ④ Payment of dividends : (−)7

⟨Table 2-12⟩ is a statement of cash flows of OSS Mart for 20×1. As we examine ⟨Table 2-12⟩, we can find that the statement of cash flows is composed of a heading and a body same as other financial statements. The heading is the same as that of the comprehensive income statement reviewed above. In the body, cash flows during a period for which the statements are prepared are classified into operation activities, investing activities, and financing activities. In the case of OSS Mart, we can understand that there was a net cash inflow of ₩22 billion from operating activities, a net cash outflow of ₩95 billion from investing activities, and a net cash inflow of ₩90 billion from financing activities, resulting in a net increase of ₩17 billion in cash balance during 20×1.

In the case of OSS Mart, because it started in 20×1, the beginning balance of cash was '0'; therefore, a ₩14 billion increase of cash itself became the ending balance of cash. Because the statement of financial position in ⟨Table 2-2⟩ was prepared for learning purposes on January 1, 20×1, which was not the end of the accounting year, the cash balance (₩3 billion) in the statement of financial position was not same as the ending balance of cash (₩17 billion) on the statement of cash flows. Also, because it was assumed that all revenue and expense transactions were made in cash, the cash generated from operations on the statement of cash flows and the income from operations on the comprehensive income statement were the same amount. In reality, some of the revenue and expense transactions are made on credit or through prepayment, so those two amounts are not the same. More details will be reviewed in Chapter 5.

〈Table 2-12〉 Statement of cash flows (direct method)

From January 1, 20×1 to December 31, 20×1

OSS Mart (Numbers in billions of ₩)

Description	Amount	
Cash flows from operating activities		
Cash receipts from customers	118	
Cash paid to suppliers and employees	(−)87	
Cash generated from operations	31	
Individually reporting item :		
Income tax paid	(−)9	
Net cash from operating activities		**22**
Cash flows from investing activities		
Individually reporting item :		
Interest received	2	
Short-term loan (made)	(−)27	
Purchase of FVOCI financial assets	(−)13	
Purchase of land	(−)20	
Purchase of plant assets	(−)37	
Net cash used in investing activities		**(−)95**
Cash flows from financing activities		
Proceeds from short-term borrowing	30	
Proceeds from issuing common stock	70	
Individually reporting items :		
Interest paid	(−)3	
Dividends paid	(−)7	
Net cash from financing activities		**90**
Net increase in cash		**17**
Cash at beginning of period		**0**
Cash at end of period		**17**

Statement of changes in equity

4.1 What is a statement of changes in equity?

Statement of changes in equity (자본변동표) is a financial report showing changes in equity (stockholders' equity) by each component for a certain period, generally one year. More specifically, statement of changes in equity reports changes in share capital, share premium, retained earnings, and accumulated other comprehensive income, and other components of equity.

Although the statement of financial position and comprehensive income statement explained above report the financial position and results of operation, they do not report detailed changes in equity—that is, the equity of stockholders. The statement of changes in equity shows how each component of equity changed from the beginning balance till the ending balance. Therefore, information users can find information concerning additional contribution made by stockholders, dividends, earnings and other comprehensive income reflected in equity, and other transactions with stockholders.

4.2 Structure of statement of changes in equity

The statement of changes in equity is prepared in a format presenting beginning balance, explanation and amount of changes, and ending balance for each component of equity. To help with understanding the statement of changes in equity, we will prepare a statement of changes in equity of OSS Mart for 20×1. The following 〈Illustration 2-5〉 is a summary of changes in equity of OSS Mart during 20×1, which are extracted from the statement of financial position, comprehensive income statement, and statement of cash flows reviewed above.

〈Illustration 2-5〉 Detailed changes in equity of OSS Mart during 20×1

(Numbers in billions of ₩)

- Changes in share capital-common stock
  Cash received by issuing 7 million shares of common stock with par value of ₩1,000 : 70

- Changes in retained earnings and accumulated other comprehensive income by total comprehensive income

  ▲ Changes in retained earnings
  Net income : 21

  ▲ Changes in accumulated other comprehensive income (accumulated gain on valuation of FVOCI financial assets).
  Gain on valuation of FVOCI financial assets : 2

- Changes in retained earnings because of dividend payment
  Cash dividends paid : (−)7

〈Table 2-13〉 is a statement of changes in equity of OSS Mart for 20×1 prepared by using data in 〈Illustration 2-5〉. As can be seen in 〈Table 2-13〉, a statement of changes in equity is composed of a heading and a body same as other financial statements. The heading is the same as those of the comprehensive income statement and the statement of cash flows reviewed above. In the body, changes in equity for the period are presented by each component.

In the case of OSS Mart, share capital-common stock was increased by ₩70 billion by issuing common stocks. Total comprehensive income of ₩23 billion affected retained earnings and accumulated other comprehensive income. Retained earnings was increased by ₩21 billion due to net income, and accumulated gain on valuation of FVOCI financial assets was increased by ₩2 billion due to gain on valuation of FVOCI financial assets. Also, retained earnings was decreased by ₩7 billion due to cash dividends. Because 20×1 was the founding year, there was no balance in all equity accounts at the beginning of the year. Therefore, the ending balances were results of an increase or decrease that occurred in each component of equity during the year. The ending balances of share capital-common stock, retained earnings, and accumulated gain on valuation of FVOCI financial assets were ₩70 billion, ₩14 billion, and ₩2 billion, respectively, and the ending balance of the total equity was ₩86 billion.

〈Table 2-13〉 Statement of changes in equity

From January 1, 20×1 to December 31, 20×1

OSS Mart (Numbers in billions of ₩)

Description	Share capital	Retained earnings	Accumulated OCI	Total
	Common stock		Accumulated gain on valuation of FVOCI financial assets	
Balance at January 1, 20×1	–	–	–	–
Changes in equity for 20×1 :				
Issuance of common stock	70			70
Total comprehensive income		21	2	23
Cash dividends		(−)7		(−)7
Balance at December 31, 20×1	70	14	2	86

OCI : other comprehensive income

The total equity of ₩86 billion in the statement of changes in equity above is not identical with total equity of ₩70 billion in 〈Table 2-2〉 statement of financial position because 〈Table 2-2〉 statement of financial position was prepared intentionally as of January 1, 20×1, not the end of the year for learning purposes. Details about the statement of changes in equity will be reviewed in Chapter 10.

〈Box 2-8〉 Disclosing statement of retained earnings

The **statement of retained earnings (이익잉여금처분계산서)** is a statement reporting the anticipated balance of unappropriated retained earnings after reflecting a plan to appropriate retained earnings that include the net income reported in the comprehensive income statement. As explained above, the statement of changes in equity reports changes in all components of equity, including retained earnings. Therefore, the statement of retained earnings—which used to be prepared as one of the basic financial statements—is currently disclosed in the footnotes. [see K-IFRS(KAI issued)[15]] Details of the statement of retained earning will be reviewed in 〈Box 10-3〉 in Chapter 10.

Basic assumption and limitations of financial statements

5.1 Basic assumption of financial statements : going concern

Basic assumption in preparing financial statements is certain fact or observation taken for granted in preparing financial statements without any process of proving it. The reason is that it can be a foundation for another principle or standard. IFRS[16] takes a going concern assumption as a basic assumption in preparing financial statements. The going concern assumption is an assumption that a company will stay in business and not go out of business for the foreseeable future. That is an assumption that makes fair value accounting and historical cost accounting possible.

In most cases, financial statements are prepared with a going concern assumption. Therefore, assets and liabilities can be measured at fair value or historical cost. Fair value means that 1) market value when there is active market (reviewed in the Appendix), 2) net realizable value : value that can be obtained by selling (reviewed in Chapter 7), 3) net present value : discounted future cash flows (reviewed in Chapter 9), and 4) professional appraiser's appraisal value (reviewed in the Appendix). Historical cost means the acquisition cost : purchase price paid (applied in all the Chapters). If the going concern assumption cannot be kept, one must use accounting standard which is different from the ones justified by the going concern assumption. For example, if there is an intention or a need to liquidate the business entity itself or to stop a major part of the operation, assets should be valued at the forced disposal value—that is, the liquidation value.

5.2 Limitations of financial statements

As reviewed up to this point, it is understood that the statement of financial position, comprehensive income statement, statement of cash flows, and statement of changes in equity provide useful information to various users, such as investors and creditors, in making decisions. However, financial statements have a few limitations. They are summarized below.

(1) Omission of qualitative information

Financial statements provide mainly information stated in amount of monetary unit, and they do not provide qualitative information that is difficult to measure in monetary amount. For example, although information concerning human resources, such as the quality of employees and capability of management, is a very important factor in evaluating the growth and profitability of a company, it is not reported in the statement of financial position. In addition, although the development of new products, achievement of competitive advantage within an industry, and improvement of corporate image are important barometers measuring operating performance, they are not reported in financial statements, either.

(2) Impairment of comparability

Titles and amounts of account reported on financial statements are results of accounting treatment in accordance with accounting standards. Accounting standards sometimes allow more than two accounting methods for a certain transaction because circumstances and contents of business each company conducts are quite different from one another. As a result, sometimes comparability of accounting information can be impaired. It is because if two different companies chose different accounting methods although their businesses are identical, numbers reported in financial statements are different.

(3) Limit on reflection of price level change

If a statement of financial position is prepared at acquisition cost, it is more reliable but has a problem of not reporting a price level change. For example, even though the fair value of land, which was acquired at ₩5 billion several years ago, is ₩7 billion due to a price level change, it is continuously reported at ₩5 billion on the acquisition cost based statement of financial position. IFRS[17] allows for property, plant and equipment to be evaluated at fair value or acquisition cost.

Hence, there is a limit of not reflecting a price level change because some assets are reported at acquisition cost.

The above mentioned limitations are minor when we compare them with usefulness of financial statements. However, we should continuously work to overcome these limitations and improve the usefulness of financial statements.

IFRS references (http://www.kasb.or.kr)

[1] IAS 1 *Presentation of Financial Statements*, par. 60.
[2] *The Conceptual Framework for Financial Reporting*, par. 4.3, 4.4.
[3] IFRS 9 *Financial Instruments.*, par. 4.1.2, 4.1.2A, 4.1.4.
[4] *The Conceptual Framework for Financial Reporting*, par. 4.26.
[5] IFRS 9 *op. cit.*, par. 4.2.1, 4.2.2.
[6] *The Conceptual Framework for Financial Reporting*, par. 4.63.
[7] IAS 1 *op. cit.*, par. 99.
[8] IFRS 15 *Revenue from Contracts with Customers*, Appendix A Defined terms : Revenue.
The Conceptual Framework for Financial Reporting, par. 4.68.
[9] *The Conceptual Framework for Financial Reporting*, par. 4.69
[10] IAS 1 *op. cit.*, par. 82.
[11] IAS 1 *op. cit.*, par. Korean 138.2 138.3.
[12] IAS 1 *op. cit.*, par. BC55, 56.
[13] IAS 33 *Earnings per Share*, par. 9.
[14] IAS 7 *Statement of Cash Flows*, par. 31.
[15] IAS 1 *op. cit.*, par. Korean 138.1.
[16] *The Conceptual Framework for Financial Reporting*, par. 3.9.
[17] IAS 18 *Property, Plant and Equipment*, par. 29.

Key terms

Accounting equation (회계등식) : A formula showing that the total amount of assets equals the addition of total liabilities and total equity (Assets = Liabilities + Equity). (p.35)

Assets (자산) : Economic resources that can be used by a company in carrying out operation. (p.39)

Comprehensive income statement (포괄손익계산서) : A statement reporting total comprehensive income that is an addition of net income and other comprehensive income for an accounting period. (p.47)

Current assets (유동자산) : Assets that can be converted into cash or used for operation within one year. (p.39)

Current liabilities (유동부채) : Short-term obligation with maturity date falling within one year. (p.42)

Equity (자본) : Stockholders' equity, residual claim or net assets computed by subtracting liabilities from total assets of a company. (p.44)

Expense (비용) : Acquisition cost of goods or services which are used up to generate revenues. (p.51)

Intangible assets (무형자산) : Non-current assets without physical substance that provide economic benefits to company. (p.42)

Inventories (재고자산) : Assets that are held by a company for the purpose of sales (example : merchandise). (p.41)

Liabilities (부채) : Obligation (debts) that the company has to pay back to other companies or other persons. (p.42)

Net assets (순자산) : Gross assets less liabilities, that is equity. (p.44)

Non-current assets (비유동자산) : Assets that are other than current assets and to be possessed longer period than one year. (p.41)

Non-current liabilities (비유동부채) : Long-term obligation with maturity date arriving later than one year. (p.43)

Other comprehensive income (기타포괄이익) : Fair value valuation gain that is not included in net income but included in comprehensive income because if it is included in net income, it might distort net income or make net income fluctuate a lot. (p.53)

Plant assets (설비자산) : Assets, such as buildings, machinery, automobiles, office equipment, that are used for operation. (p.42)

Retained earnings (이익잉여금) : Earnings not paid to stockholders by dividends but retained within the company. (p.45)

Revenue (수익) : A return received or will be received by providing goods or services to customers. (p.50)

Share capital (자본금) : Total par value of stock issued by a company. (p.45)

Share premium (자본잉여금) : Capital contributed by stockholders in excess of par value. (p.45)

Statement of cash flows (현금흐름표) : A statement reporting cash inflows and outflows of each of operating activities, investing activities, and financing activities for an accounting period. (p.64)

Statement of changes in equity (자본변동표) : A statement reporting changes in equity components, such as share capital, share premium, and retained earnings, accumulated other comprehensive income, and other components of equity for an accounting period. (p.69)

Statement of financial position (재무상태표) : A statement showing the contents of assets, liabilities, and equity that constitute the financial position of a company at the end of an accounting period. (p.32)

Tangible assets (유형자산) : Non-current assets with physical substances. (p.42)

Exercises

1. Classification of components of statement of financial position

The following are account titles reported in a statement of financial position of Daeil Trading Co. at the end of 20×1.

① Cash ② Merchandise ③ Short-term loans ④ Long-term loans
⑤ Trade receivables ⑥ Trade Payables ⑦ Short-term borrowings
⑧ Accrued expense ⑨ Land ⑩ Plant assets
⑪ Long-term borrowings ⑫ Bonds payable
⑬ Share capital-common stock ⑭ Retained earnings
⑮ Share premium-common stock
⑯ Accumulated gain on valuation of FVOCI financial assets
⑰ FVOCI financial assets (long-term investment)

《Question》

Write down account numbers that should be reported under each of following item.

(1) Current assets : ________ (2) Non-current assets : ________
(3) Current liabilities : ________ (4) Non-current liabilities : ________
(5) Equity : ________

2. Classification of components of comprehensive income statement

The following are account titles reported in a comprehensive income statement of Usung Trading Co. for 20x1.

① Sales ② Cost of goods sold ③ Salaries expense ④ Rent expense
⑤ Interest revenue ⑥ Interest expense
⑦ Advertising expense ⑧ Employees welfare expense
⑨ Dividends revenue ⑩ Rent revenue
⑪ Entertainment expense ⑫ Gain on disposal of tangible assets
⑬ Tax and dues expense ⑭ Insurance expense
⑮ Gain on valuation of FVOCI financial assets
⑯ Gain on revaluation of land

《Question》

Write down account numbers that are reported under each of following item.

(1) Operating revenue : ________ (2) Other revenues : ________
(3) Cost of goods sold : ________ (4) Operating expenses : ________
(5) Other expense : ________ (6) Other comprehensive income : ________

3. Preparation of statement of financial position ①

The following is data for a statement of financial position of Jinju Trading Co. as of December 31, 20×1.

(Numbers in billions of ₩)

Account titles	Amount	Account titles	Amount
Cash	18	Trade receivables	445
Merchandise	250	Short-term loans	23
Prepaid expense	5	Land	318
Plant assets	660	Industrial property rights	76
Trade payables	260	Short-term borrowings	140
Interest payable	4	Unearned rent	70
Long-term borrowings	232	Bonds payable	400
Share capital-common stock	700	Retained earnings	171
Accumulated gain on valuation of FVOCI financial assets	3	FVOCI financial assets (long-term investment)	185

《Question》 Prepare a statement of financial position in account format.

4. Preparation of a statement of financial position ②

The following is data for a statement of financial position of Buil Inc. as of December 31, 20×1.

(Numbers in billions of ₩)

Account titles	Amount	Account titles	Amount
Cash	8	Trade receivables	48
Short-term loans	21	Interest receivable	8
Prepaid insurance	6	Merchandise	35
Long-term loans	30	Land	84
Plant assets	98	Industrial property rights	12
Trade payables	45	Short-term borrowings	28
Interest payable	8	Unearned rent	7
Bonds payable	60	Long-term borrowings	31
Share capital-common stock	75	Share premium-common stock	35
Retained earnings	46	Land revaluation surplus	15

《Question》 Prepare a statement of financial position in report format.

5. Preparation of a comprehensive income statement ①

The following is for a comprehensive income statement of Yonam Inc. for 20×1.

(Numbers in billions of ₩)

Account titles	Amount	Account titles	Amount
Cost of goods sold	390	Salaries expense	92
Advertising expense	30	Rent expense	15
Insurance expense	20	Utility expense	10
Interest expense	48	Interest revenue	35
Sales	630	Gain on valuation of FVOCI financial assets	4
Gain on revaluation of land	3	Income tax expense	20

※ Yonam Inc.'s outstanding number of common stock is 20 million share.

《Questions》

(1) Prepare a single comprehensive income statement.
(2) Prepare a comprehensive income statement in two statements.

6. Preparation of a comprehensive income statement ②

The following is data for a comprehensive income statement of Korea Trading Co. for 20×1.

(Numbers in billions of ₩)

Account titles	Amount	Account titles	Amount
Sales	230	Cost of goods sold	150
Salaries expense	56	Advertising expense	5
Insurance expense	4	Entertainment expense	1
Interest expense	9	Interest revenue	8
Income tax expense	2	Gain on valuation of FVOCI financial assets	1
Gain on revaluation of land	3		

※ Korea Trading Co.'s outstanding number of common stocks is 4 million shares.

《Questions》

(1) Prepare a single comprehensive income statement.
(2) Prepare a comprehensive income statement in two statements.

7. Preparation of statement of cash flows ①

The following is detailed cash inflow and outflow of Onchun Trading Co. for 20×1.

Cash inflows and cash outflows

Onchun Trading Co. From Jan. 1, 20×1 to Dec. 31, 20×1 (Numbers in billions of ₩)

Description	Amount	
Cash inflows		383
Sales of merchandise	260	
Sales of plant assets	70	
Interest received	3	
Short-term borrowings	50	
Cash outflows		(−)378
Cash paid to suppliers and employees	(−)240	
Income tax paid	(−)2	
Short-term loans made	(−)35	
Purchase of plant assets	(−)90	
Interest paid	(−)6	
Dividends paid	(−)5	
Net increase in cash		5
Cash at beginning of period		6
Cash at end of period		11

《Question》

Prepare a statement of cash flows (direct method). (It is assumed that no exception is allowed in classifying interest received, interest paid and dividends paid.)

8. Preparation of a statement of cash flows ②

The following is detailed cash flow data of Daehan Trading Co. for 20×1.

(Numbers in billions of ₩)

Description	Amount	Description	Amount
Cash receipts from customers	250	Cash paid to suppliers and employees	190
Interest received	20	Interest paid	30
Dividends received	15	Short-term borrowings	24
Proceeds from sales of plant assets	35	Purchase of land	110
Proceeds from issuing bonds	20	Proceeds from issuing common stock	30
Retirement of short-term borrowings	30	Cash at beginning of period	5
Income tax paid	25	Dividends paid	2

《Question》

Prepare a statement of cash flows (direct method). (It is assumed that no exception is allowed in classifying interest received, dividends received, interest paid and dividends paid.)

9. Preparation of a statement of changes in equity

The following are equity account balances of Daegu Trading Co. at beginning of 20×1 and details of increase and decrease in equity during 20×1.

Equity account balances at beginning of 20×1

(Numbers in billions of ₩)

Account titles	Amount	Account titles	Amount
Share capital-common stock	50	Share premium-common stock	30
Retained earnings	8	Accumulated gain on valuation of FVOCI financial assets	1
Land revaluation surplus	2		

Increase and decrease in equity

(Numbers in billions of ₩)

Description	Amount	
Issuance of stock (10 million shares of common stock with par value of 1,000)		12
Comprehensive income		9
Net income	6	
Gain on valuation of FVOCI financial assets	2	
Gain on revaluation of land	1	
Dividends paid		(-)5

《Question》 Prepare a statement of changes in equity.

Recording Transactions and Preparation of Financial Statements —Cash Transactions

Section 1 Transactions and bookkeeping

Section 2 Recording transactions under the double-entry bookkeeping system

Section 3 Accounting cycle (cash)

Chapter 3 Overview

In this chapter, first we review what is meant by 'transaction' in accounting. We likewise review the single-entry and double-entry bookkeeping systems as transaction recording methods. Next, the accounting recording procedures in the double-entry bookkeeping system that is used by corporations is explained in detail. Since the purpose of recoding transactions is to prepare financial statements, an accounting cycle (cash) that is an accounting system by which financial statements are prepared when all transactions are made in cash, is reviewed in the last section of this chapter.

Transactions and bookkeeping

1.1 Transactions

A transaction (거래) in accounting means a measurable economic event that affects the financial position of a company. Many economic events occur in a company every single day. For example, every business activity, from purchasing merchandise from suppliers, to selling merchandise to customers and hiring prominent managers, can be considered an economic event. But among those events, transactions are events that affect the financial position of a company, the position of its assets, and its liabilities, and equity, all of which can be measured in monetary units. Therefore, hiring a prominent manager is not considered as a transaction because managers are not owned by the company ; hence, they cannot be assets of the company. And because their value is difficult to measure in monetary units even if they were considered as assets.

1.2 Bookkeeping

Bookkeeping (부기) means recording transactions in accounting books. We can observe bookkeeping quite often in our daily life. For example, the cash book used in our family is an accounting book, and recording cash in and cash out, in that book, is bookkeeping. Using the following illustration, let's examine what kind of outcomes we can get if we record transactions in a cash book.

〈Illustration 3-1〉 Transactions

The following are Daehan Consulting's transactions for 20×1, its founding year.

① Issued 100 million shares of common stock with par value of ₩1,000 at the beginning of the year and received ₩100 billion in cash.
② Borrowed ₩200 billion from a bank for 5 years.
③ Purchased a piece of land and paid ₩290 billion in cash.
④ Provided consulting services and received ₩110 billion in cash.
⑤ Paid employees' salaries of ₩50 billion for 20×1.
⑥ Paid office rent of ₩20 billion for 20×1.
⑦ Paid interest of ₩10 billion for 20×1 on the bank loan.
⑧ Paid income tax of ₩12 billion for 20×1 in cash.

Although the format of a cash book is not uniform, usually it is composed of a column recording cash receipts, a column recording cash payments, and a column recording balance. 〈Table 3-1〉 shows a cash book with transactions in 〈Illustration 3-1〉 recorded.

〈Table 3-1〉 Cash book

(Numbers in billions of ₩)

T. no.	Description of transaction	Receipt	Payment	Balance
①	Issuance of common stock	100		100
②	Long-term borrowing	200		300
③	Purchase of land		290	10
④	Receipt of service fees	110		120
⑤	Payment of salaries		50	70
⑥	Payment of rent		20	50
⑦	Payment of interest		10	40
⑧	Payment of income tax		12	28

Transaction ①, issued common stocks ; transaction ②, borrowed money from a bank ; and Transaction ④, provided consulting service are the ones with cash receipts. The cash amount received from each of these transactions should be recorded in the cash receipt column. Transaction ③, purchased a piece of land ; Transaction ⑤, paid employees' salaries ; Transaction ⑥, paid office rent ; Transaction ⑦, paid interest on loan ; Transaction ⑧, paid income tax involve cash payments. The cash amount paid from these transactions should therefore be recorded in the cash payment column. The balance obtained by adding each of cash receipt amounts and subtracting each of the cash payment amounts should be recorded in the balance column. The balance computed after recording all the transactions from ① to ⑧ is ₩28 billion.

Under the method of recording in a cash book, as reviewed above, we record each transaction only once, either in the receipt column or in the payment column when a transaction occurs. This kind of recording system, requiring only one entry when a transaction occurs, is called the single-entry bookkeeping system (단식부기). A report of cash receipts and payments prepared for a nonprofit organization—such as a government, a school, a religious organization, or a social gathering—is an example of a typical accounting report based on the single-entry bookkeeping system. Because cash receipts and payments are not classified by their causes in the single-entry bookkeeping system, it is rather difficult to understand the financial position and operational results of the organization using the report of cash receipt and payment.

Several hundred years ago people engaged in the merchandising business used the double-entry bookkeeping system to record transactions. The double-entry bookkeeping system (복식부기) is a system of recording a cash receipt or payment and then, after that, additionally recording the cause of each cash receipt or payment. For example, in Transaction ① of 〈Illustration 3-1〉, 'cash' was increased by ₩100 billion, and the reason was an increase in 'share capital-common stock' from the issuance of common stock. Under the double-entry bookkeeping system, when this transaction occurs, first, the increase in 'cash' is recorded, and next, the increase in 'share capital-common stock' is additionally recorded. Again, it is called double-entry bookkeeping because each transaction is recorded twice, as per this example.

Recording transactions under the double-entry bookkeeping system

The double-entry bookkeeping system was originally developed to prepare a statement of financial position and an income statement. Therefore, explanation of the double-entry bookkeeping system will be limited to these two statements. The statement of cash flows and the statement of changes in equity are statements that have only begun to be required recently. These two more recent statements are also prepared using outcomes of the double-entry system, but they are not directly related to the basic principles of the double-entry system. The methods for preparing the statement of cash flows and statement of changes in equity are explained in Section 3, after reviewing the double-entry system in Section 2.

2.1 Accounting equation

The method of recording and summarizing transactions under the double-entry book-keeping system is based on the following accounting equation studied in Chapter 2.

Assets = Liabilities + Equity

Equity can be classified into contributed capital and retained earnings, based on their generating sources. Contributed capital is generated through capital transactions, such as issuing stock to stockholders, and retained earnings are generated from income-creating activities. Therefore, the above equation can be expressed as follows.

Assets = Liabilities + Contributed capital + Retained earnings

The components of the statement of financial position are continually changing as transactions are recorded. Therefore, the financial position at the end of an accounting period is different from that at the beginning of the accounting period.

The following is a formula classifying changes in contributed capital.

Beginning contributed capital + Increase in contributed capital − Decrease in contributed capital = Ending contributed capital

Increases in contributed capital are achieved by issuing additional stock. Decreases in contributed capital are made by retiring stock that has already been issued.

The following is a formula classifying changes in retained earnings by resources.

Beginning retained earnings + Net income − Dividends = Ending retained earnings

As can be seen in above equation, retained earnings are increased by net income and decreased by dividends.

Net income is computed by subtracting expenses from revenues. The following is a formula expressing the relationship among these items.

Net income = Revenues − Expenses

〈Diagram 3-1〉 is a comprehensive illustration of the above equations.

〈Diagram 3-1〉 Comprehensive illustration of accounting equation

Beginning assets	=	Beginning liabilities	+	Beginning equity	
				Beginning contributed capital	Beginning retained earnings
+ Increase in assets − Decrease in assets	=	+ Increase in liabilities − Decrease in liabilities	+	+ Increase in contributed capital − Decrease in contributed capital	+ Revenues − Expenses − Dividends
‖		‖		‖	‖
Ending assets	=	Ending liabilities	+	Ending contributed capital	Ending retained earnings
				Ending equity	

〈Diagram 3-1〉 shows what is reported in a statement of financial position and in an income statement. As shown on the bottom part of the diagram, a statement of financial position reports assets, liabilities and equity at end of a period. As shown on the right side of the diagram an income statement reports revenues and expenses that form part of changes in retained earnings.

〈Box 3-1〉 Application of accounting equation

Using 〈Illustration 3-2〉 below, let's review the relationship between components of the accounting equation in detail.

〈Illustration 3-2〉 Accounting equation

〈Table 3-2〉 below shows data obtained by an accountant, Mr. Kim, who is auditing K Co. (Case ⓐ) and Y Co. (Case ⓑ). Let's compute the amounts applicable to ①, ②, and ③.

〈Table 3-2〉 Accounting equation

(Numbers in billions of ₩)

Case		Beginning			Increase in CC	Decrease in CC	Revenues	Expenses	Dividends	Ending		
		A	L	E						A	L	E
ⓐ	K Co.	30	20	10	2	1	①	40	3	400	250	150
ⓑ	Y Co.	50	30	20	4	2	70	60	5	600	③	②

A : Assets L : Liabilities E : Equity CC : Contributed capital

Case ⓐ is a case of verifying revenue using the accounting equation. In this case, the revenues depicted as ① can be verified as follows. The equation of 〈Beginning equity + Increase in contributed capital − Decrease in contributed capital + Revenues − Expenses − Dividends = Ending equity〉 in 〈Diagram 3-1〉 can be rearranged as an equation of 〈Revenues = Ending equity − Beginning equity − Increase in contributed capital + Decrease in contributed capital + Expenses + Dividends〉. Using this rearranged equation, revenues ① is computed to be ₩47 billion (15 − 10 − 2 + 10 + 40 + 3).

Case ⓑ is a case of using the equation to verify the ending equity and ending liabilities of Y Co. In this case, ending equity is depicted as ② and can be verified as follows. Using the equation of 〈Ending equity = Beginning equity + Increase in contributed capital − Decrease in contributed capital + Revenues − Expenses − Dividends〉 in 〈Diagram 3-1〉, the ending equity is computed to be

₩27 billion (20 + 4 − 2 + 70 − 60 − 5). Using the equation of 〈Ending liabilities = Ending assets − Ending equity〉, ending liabilities ③ is computed to be ₩33 billion (60 − 27).

2.2 Recording transactions using the accounting equation

Let's review here the method for preparing financial statements using the outcomes of recording accounting transactions in 〈Illustration 3-1〉 in the accounting equation. The following 〈Table 3-3〉 is an analysis of the effects of the transactions in 〈Illustration 3-1〉 on financial statements.

〈Table 3-3〉 Analysis of transactions

T No.	Description	Effect of transaction	
		Increase or decrease in cash	Cause for increase or decrease in cash
①	Issuance of common stock	Increased by ₩100 billion	Share capital-common stock (equity) increased by ₩100 billion.
②	Long-term borrowings	Increased by ₩200 billion	Long-term borrowings (liability) increased by ₩200 billion.
③	Purchase of land	Decreased by ₩290 billion	Land (asset) increased by ₩290 billion.
④	Receipt of service fees	Increased by ₩110 billion	Service fees revenue of ₩110 billion incurred.
⑤	Payment of salaries	Decreased by ₩50 billion.	Salaries expense of ₩50 billion incurred
⑥	Payment of rent	Decreased by ₩20 billion	Rent expense of ₩20 billion incurred.
⑦	Payment of interest	Decreased by ₩10 billion	Interest expense of ₩10 billion incurred.
⑧	Payment of income tax	Decreased by ₩12 billion	Income tax expense of ₩12 billion incurred.

Cash was increased due to transaction ①; the cause was that share capital-common stock (equity) was increased.

Cash was increased due to Transaction ②; the cause was that long-term borrowing (liability) was increased.

Cash was decreased due to Transaction ③; the cause was that land (asset) was increased. (If land is not used for operating activities, it should be classified as an investment in real estate. But we classify it as land here based on an assumption that the land is used for operating activities).

Cash was increased due to Transaction ④; the cause was that service fees revenue was incurred.

Cash was decreased due to each Transaction ⑤, ⑥, ⑦ and ⑧; the causes were salaries expense, rent expense, interest expense and income tax expense were incurred, respectively.

The following ⟨Diagram 3-2⟩ records the transactions in ⟨Illustration 3-1⟩ using the accounting equation.

⟨Diagram 3-2⟩ Recording accounting transactions using accounting equation

(Numbers in billions of ₩)

	Assets			=	Liability	+	Equity										
									Retained earnings								
	Cash	+	Land	=	Long-term borrowings	+	Share capital – common stock	+	Service fees revenue	–	Salaries expense	–	Rent expense	–	Interest expense	–	Income tax expense
Beginning balance	0		0		0		0		0		0		0		0		0
①	+100			=			+100										
②	+200			=	+200												
③	−290		+290	=													
④	+110			=					+110								
⑤	−50			=							+50						
⑥	−20			=									+20				
⑦	−10			=											+10		
⑧	−12			=													+12
Ending balance	28	+	290	=	200	+	100	+	110	–	50	–	20	–	10	–	12

There was no beginning balance on any of the items in ⟨Diagram 3-2⟩, because 20×1 was the first year of operation. Cash increases and decreases from all transactions from ① to ⑧ are recorded in the cash column, in assets, as '+' and '−'. The reason for each increase and decrease in cash was additionally recorded, as in the following. For Transaction ① + ₩100 billion was recorded in share capital-common stock, in the column of equity. For Transaction ② + ₩200 billion was recorded in the long-term borrowings column of liability. For Transaction ③ + ₩290 billion was recorded in the land column of assets. For Transaction ④, + ₩110 billion was recorded in the service fees revenue column of retained earnings. For each of Transactions ⑤, ⑥, ⑦ and ⑧: + ₩50 billion was listed in the salaries expense column; + ₩20 billion in the rent expense column ; + ₩10 billion in the interest expense column ; and + ₩12 billion in the income tax expense column of retained earnings, respectively. After recording all transactions, the ending balance of each column was computed.

Now we can prepare financial statements using the information in 〈Diagram 3-2〉. First, we prepare the income statement, as shown in 〈Table 3-4〉, by listing the ending balances of the revenue and expense columns of retained earnings.

〈Table 3-4〉 Income statement

Daehan Consulting From Jan. 1 to Dec. 31, 20×1 (Numbers in billions of ₩)

Account titles	Amount	
Service fees revenue		110
Operating expenses		(−)70
Salaries expense	(−)50	
Rent expense	(−)20	
Income from operations		40
Other expense		(−)10
Finance expense :		
Interest expense	(−)10	
Net income before income tax expense		30
Income tax expense		(−)12
Net income		18
Earnings per share		₩180

Service fees revenue, in the income statement shown in 〈Table 3-4〉, is ₩110 billion from Transaction ④. Operating expenses are ₩70 billion, composed of salary expense of ₩50 billion from Transaction ⑤ and rent expense of ₩20 billion from Transaction ⑥. Income from operations of ₩40 billion is computed by subtracting operating expenses of ₩70 billion from service fees revenue of ₩110 billion. Interest expense of ₩10 billion from Transaction ⑦ are classified as a finance expense, in 'other expense,' because it is from financing activities. Net income before income tax expense of ₩30 billion is computed by subtracting other expense of ₩10 billion from income from operations of ₩40 billion. Net income of ₩18 billion is computed by subtracting Transaction ⑧ income tax expense of ₩12 billion from net income before income tax expense of ₩30 billion. Earnings per share are computed by dividing the number of outstanding common stock of 100 million shares into the net income of ₩18 billion.

The following 〈Table 3-5〉 is a statement of the financial position of Daehan Consulting. It was prepared by classifying the ending balances of items in assets, liability and equity in 〈Diagram 3-2〉.

Cash of ₩28 billion is classified as a current asset, and land of ₩290 billion is classified as a tangible asset under non-current asset. The company's total assets of ₩318 billion are derived by adding these two assets. Long-term borrowings of ₩200 billion, which is a cost financial liability because it is reported at cost, is classified as a non-current liability. This is the only liability, so total liability is ₩200 billion. Share capital-common stock of ₩100 billion is classified as share capital. Retained earnings are ₩18 billion of net income ; this is computed by adding and subtracting the detailed items in the retained earnings columns as shown in the income statement. Total equity is ₩118 billion ; this figure is derived through the addition of share capital-common stock of ₩100 billion and retained earnings of ₩18 billion. Total equity and liability is ₩318 billion ; this is an addition of the total liability of ₩200 billion plus the total equity of ₩118 billion.

〈Table 3-5〉 Statement of financial position

Daehan Consulting　　As of December 31, 20×1　　(Numbers in billions of ₩)

Account titles	Amount		Account titles	Amount	
Assets			Liability		
Current asset		28	Non-current liability		200
Cash	28		Cost financial liability :		
Non-current asset		290	Long-term borrowings	200	
Tangible asset :			Total liability		200
Land	290		Equity		
			Share capital		100
			Common stock	100	
			Retained earings		18
			Total equity		118
Total assets		318	Total liability and equity		318

〈Box 3-2〉 Valuation of assets

In 〈Table 3-5〉, Daehan Consulting's statement of financial position, the land was valued at ₩290 billion, which was the amount of money paid at the time of acquisition. The principle of valuing an asset at the amount paid at the time of acquisition, that is at its acquisition cost is called the **acquisition cost principle (취득원가원칙)**. It is also called the **historical cost principle (역사적 원가원칙)** because the acquisition cost is the amount paid at the acquisition time, which is now in the past (history). It is called the cost model in IFRS[1].

If **fair value (공정가치)** of an asset changes after its acquisition and the fair value can be measured reliably, that asset can be valued at fair value. For example, if an appraisal value made by a professional appraising organization for the land owned by Daehan Consulting is ₩300 billion, we can present in the statement of financial position at ₩300 billion. IFRS[2] calls this valuation method as the **fair value model**. (See Appendix of this book for further details.)

2.3 Accounts

There is a limit to the method of recording transactions in the accounting equation shown in 〈Diagram 3-2〉. If few transactions are made and the types of transactions are simple, as in 〈Illustration 3-1〉 above, there may be no problem. But if the number of transactions is high and the types of transaction vary greatly—thus making the number of reported items very high—it may be physically nearly impossible to record transactions in this accounting equation. Due to this problem, a method has been developed to set up accounting books for each item to be reported in the financial statements. And then we record transactions in the accounting books rather than in the accounting equation. The accounting books that are set up for each item to be reported in financial statements are called accounts (계정).

If we look at 〈Table 3-2〉, we record an increase as '+' and a decrease as '−'. But if we use accounts, instead of '+' and '−', we use a concept of left and right side. That is, we devide an account into two parts, the left side and the right side, and record an increase and decrease in any item. An example of an account is shown in 〈Diagram 3-3〉 below.

〈Diagram 3-3〉 Example of T account

Account title

The account in 〈Diagram 3-3〉 is called a T account, because it looks like the letter 'T.' Accounts are set up for each item : assets, liabilities, equity, revenues and expenses. For example, an account with the title of 'cash' is set up to record cash, which is one of a company's assets. An accounting book where all the accounts are gathered is called the general ledger (총계정원장). The left side of a T account is called debit (Dr.: 차변) and the right side is called credit (Cr.: 대변).

〈Diagram 3-1〉 reviewed above is a comprehensive illustration of the accounting equation. The equation showing that total assets equal total liabilities and equity can be seen at both the beginning and the end of an accounting period. If we put this equation into the account format, assets are reported on the debit (left) side of the equation and liabilities and equity are reported on the credit (right) side of the equation. We know that changes made due to any transactions during an accounting period in 〈Diagram 3-1〉 are can be also put into the equation as shown below.

+ Increase in assets − Decrease in assets = + Increase in Liabilities − Decrease in Liabilities + Increase in contributed capital − Decrease in contributed capital + Revenues − Expenses − Dividends

The following equation emerges, if we : 1) separate revenues and expenses ; 2) treat any increase in equity apart from revenues (shown as an increase in contributed capital, in the above equation) as an increase in equity ; and 3) treat any decrease in equity besides expenses (shown as a decrease in contributed capital and dividends in the above equation) as a decrease in equity in the above equation.

+ Increase in assets − Decrease in assets = Increase in Liabilities − Decrease in Liabilities + Increase in equity − Decrease in equity + Revenues − Expenses

To use an account to record an increase or decrease in financial statement items, we should first decide which side of the account should be used to record an increase. It has been our convention to use the debit side of the account to record an increase in any item that would have appeared on the debit side of the equation. This way, account balances can be formed on the debit side of the account. (Remember that an account balance is formed when the increase is more than the decrease.) Assets are on the debit side of the equation, so we record an increase on the debit side of an account and record a decrease on the credit side of an account. Based on same logic, we record an increase in liabilities and equity on the credit side of the account, and record a decrease in liabilities and equity on the debit side of the account. Expenses decrease retained earnings, which are a form of equity, so we record them on the debit side of the account. Revenues increase retained earnings, so record them on the credit side of the account. The following equation shows how each item on the equation is recorded, and on which side of the account.

+	Increase in assets (Debit)	−	Decrease in assets (Credit)	=	Increase in Liabilities (Credit)	−	Decrease in Liabilities (Debit)
+	Increase in equity (Credit)	−	Decrease in equity (Debit)	+	Revenues (Credit)	−	Expenses (Debit)

If we want to have all items recorded on the debit side of the account on the debit side of the equation, and all items recorded on the credit side of the account on the credit side of the equation, we should transfer all items with a '−' to the opposite side of the equation. The equation, after these items are transferred, is as follows.

+	Increase in assets (Debit)	+	Decrease in liabilities (Debit)	+	Decrease in equity (Debit)	+	Expenses (Debit)
=	Decrease in assets (Credit)	+	Increase in liabilities (Credit)	+	Increase in equity (Credit)	+	Revenues (Credit)

⟨Diagram 3-4⟩, to follow, shows a T account summarizing items to be recorded on the debit side of the account and items to be recorded on the credit side of an account. As the above equation, after transfer, should be intact at any time, the total of the items to be recorded on the debit side of the account in ⟨Diagram 3-4⟩, which are on the debit side of the above equation, should equal the total items to be recorded on the credit side of the account in ⟨Diagram 3-4⟩, which are on the credit side of the above equation.

So when each transaction occurs, we should pick and record one item from the debit side of ⟨Diagram 3-4⟩ and we should pick and record one item from the credit side of ⟨Diagram 3-4⟩. (An event that combines the occurrence of an expense on the debit side and an occurrence of revenue on the credit side is an exception.) For example, if we record an increase in asset on the debit side of an account due to a transaction, we must record, one of a decrease in asset, an increase in liability, an increase in equity, or an occurrence of revenue, on the credit side of another account. Recording twice, once on the debit side and another on the credit side as shown in this example, is the core of the double-entry bookkeeping system.

⟨Diagram 3-4⟩ Principles of recoding in accounts

Increase in assets Decrease in liabilities Decrease in equity Occurrence of expenses	Decrease in assets Increase in liabilities Increase in equity Occurrence of revenues

2.4 Journal entries

If we record transactions on accounts directly, it is difficult to know when and how each transaction has occurred and to check recording accuracy. Therefore, companies go through an additional step of preparing journal entries prior to recording transactions in accounts. A journal entry (분개) is an order as to what amount should be recorded, to what account, and on which side, in accordance with the principles of recording in accounts. An accounting book where we record these journal entries is called a journal (분개장). The word 'journalize' (분개하다) is used as a verb to describe the action of preparing journal entries. The following ⟨Table 3-6⟩ is a journal that lists all journal entries for the transactions in ⟨Illustration 3-1⟩.

⟨Table 3-6⟩ Journal

(Numbers in billions of ₩)

①	(Dr.) Cash	100	(Cr.) Share capital-common stock	100
②	(Dr.) Cash	200	(Cr.) Long-term borrowings	200
③	(Dr.) Land	290	(Cr.) Cash	290
④	(Dr.) Cash	110	(Cr.) Service fees revenue	110
⑤	(Dr.) Salaries expense	50	(Cr.) Cash	50
⑥	(Dr.) Rent expense	20	(Cr.) Cash	20
⑦	(Dr.) Interest expense	10	(Cr.) Cash	10
⑧	(Dr.) Income tax expense	12	(Cr.) Cash	12

Journal entries are prepared by applying the double-entry bookkeeping principles, as follows. Because cash is an asset, an increase in asset should be recorded on the debit side and a decrease in asset should be recorded on the credit side. So the increase in cash and decrease in cash from Transaction ① to Transaction ⑧ are journalized on the debit side of the cash account and on the credit side of the cash account, respectively. Transaction ① is a transaction that creates an increase in equity : share capital-common stock. An increase in equity should be recorded on the credit side, so ₩100 billion is journalized on the credit side of the share capital-common stock account. Transaction ② is a transaction with an increase in liability : long-term borrowings. An increase in liability should be recorded on the credit side, so ₩200 billion is journalized on the credit side of the long-term borrowings account. Transaction ③ is a transaction involving an increase in an asset : land. Any increase in asset should be recorded on the debit side, so ₩290 billion is journalized on the debit side of the land account. Transaction ④ is a revenue transaction : revenue from service fees is incurred. Incurrence of revenue should be recorded on the credit side, so ₩110 billion is journalized on the credit side of the service fees revenue account. Transactions ⑤, ⑥, ⑦ and ⑧ are transactions having expenses incurred. Incurrence of expense should be recorded on the debit side, so ₩50 billion, ₩20 billion, ₩10 billion and ₩12 billion are journalized on the debit side of the salaries expense account, rent expense account, interest expense account and income tax expense account, respectively.

2.5 Posting

If a transaction occurs, it is first journalized in a journal. Then the journal entry is recorded in the accounts. The process of recording a journal entry in accounts is called posting (전기).

Here we review how a journal entry for Transaction ① in 〈Illustration 3-1〉 is posted. In Transaction ①, cash is increased by ₩100 billion and share capital-common stock is increased by ₩100 billion. The journal entry for this transaction is posted as shown in 〈Diagram 3-5〉.

〈Diagram 3-5〉 Posting a journal entry

(Numbers in billions of ₩)

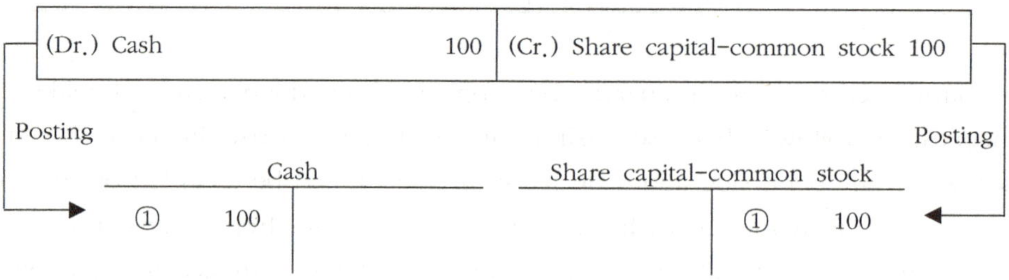

If we prepare journal entries in a journal and post those journal entries to accounts, instead of recording transactions directly to accounts, then we can easily trace items recorded on accounts back through the journal and identify the detail transactions. To make more effective tracking possible, a transaction number or transaction date may also be recorded when a journal entry is posted.

2.6 Computation of account balance

After posting is done we should compute account balances. When we use T accounts, we determine the account balance by calculating the difference between the debit side total and the credit side total of each account. For example, the cash account balance of Daehan Consulting is computed as follows. (Numbers in ⟨Diagram 3-6⟩ through ⟨Diagram 3-8⟩ are in billions of ₩.)

⟨Diagram 3-6⟩ Computation of T account balance — general approach

Cash

	Debit	Credit
	① 100	③ 290
	② 200	⑤ 50
	④ 110	⑥ 20
		⑦ 10
		⑧ 12
Total	410	382
		28
	410	410
Balance	28	

As can be seen in ⟨Diagram 3-6⟩, the debit total of the cash account is ₩410 billion and the credit total is ₩382 billion. The difference between the two totals is ₩28 billion. Based on our conventions, we insert the difference of ₩28 billion on the credit side, the side with a lower total, to make the totals of each side equal, and double underline underneath. We then show the balance on a separate line, as can be seen in ⟨Diagram 3-6⟩.

However, for the sake of convenience, some people omit this computation process and just single underline at the bottom of the account and show only the balance as shown in ⟨Diagram 3-7⟩.

〈Diagram 3-7〉 Computation of T account balance—shortcut approach

Cash

	Debit	Credit
	① 100	③ 290
	② 200	⑤ 50
	④ 110	⑥ 20
		⑦ 10
		⑧ 12
Balance	28	

T accounts are used when we need to explain the basic concepts of the double-entry bookkeeping system, or to briefly summarize debit and credit entries on each account. However, balance column accounts are used more extensively in practice. Balance column accounts are simply T accounts with an additional column for the account balance, as can be seen in 〈Diagram 3-8〉. From now on, this book uses balance column accounts to show what we will see in real-life practice.

〈Diagram 3-8〉 Balance column account

Cash

Debit	Credit	Balance
① 100		100(Dr.)
② 200		300(Dr.)
	③ 290	10(Dr.)
④ 110		120(Dr.)
	⑤ 50	70(Dr.)
	⑥ 20	50(Dr.)
	⑦ 10	40(Dr.)
	⑧ 12	28(Dr.)

If we use balance column accounts, we should compute a new account balance every time when we post a journal entry on an account. The accounting system is computerized, in practice, so this calculation is made by the computer. For example, in the case of Daehan Consulting, when ₩100 billion from Transaction ① is posted on the debit side of the cash account, the debit balance of ₩100 billion should be recorded in the balance column. [Because it is a debit balance, it was recorded as 100(Dr.). If it was a credit balance, it should be recorded as 100(Cr.)]. And when ₩200 billion from Transaction ② is posted on the debit side of the cash account, the new debit balance of ₩300 billion should be recorded.

⟨Diagram 3-9⟩ is the general ledger of Daehan Consulting, showing balances of each account after posting all the journal entries in ⟨Table 3-6⟩.

⟨Diagram 3-9⟩ General ledger after posting journal entries

(Numbers in billions of ₩)

Land

③ 290		290(Dr.)

Long-term borrowings

	② 200	200(Cr.)

Share capital-common stock

	① 100	100(Cr.)

Service fees revenue

	④ 110	110(Cr.)

Salaries expense

⑤ 50		50(Dr.)

Rent expense

⑥ 20		20(Dr.)

Interest expense

⑦ 10		10(Dr.)

Income tax expense

⑧ 12		12(Dr.)

Now we can prepare an income statement and a statement of financial position, using the balances of the accounts in the general ledger in the same way as we did when the accounting equation was used. It is more efficient to set up accounts and record transactions, as above, than to record transactions in the accounting equation. Thus, this method is used in practice.

Accounting cycle (cash)

Up to now, we have reviewed the principles and concepts of the double-entry bookkeeping system. In this section, using a simple illustration, we will study a process of preparing financial statements that is referred to as an accounting cycle (회계순환과정). An accounting cycle (cash), when all transactions are made in cash, is composed as in ⟨Diagram 3-10⟩. An accounting cycle (accrual) when revenues and expenses are prereceived and prepaid, respectively and revenue and expense transaction's are made on credit, will later be reviewed in detail in Chapter 4.

⟨Diagram 3-10⟩ Accounting cycle (cash)

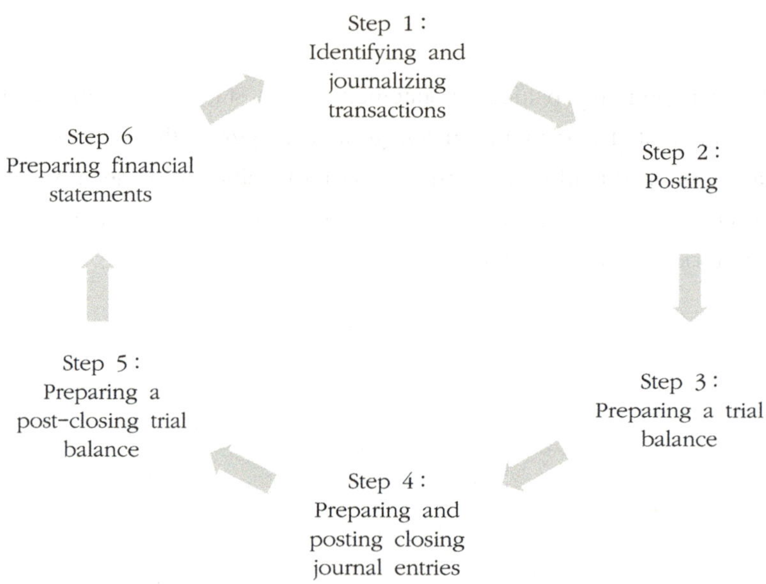

Step 1 is the task of identifying and journalizing transactions. Step 2 requires posting the journal entries to accounts. Step 3 is a task of preparing a trial balance. Step 4 is the task of preparing and posting closing journal entries. In Step 5, a post-closing trial balance is prepared. Last in Step 6, financial statements are prepared.

Step 1 and Step 2 are performed every time a transaction occurs during an accounting period. From Steps 3 to the last step, Step 6 are performed when financial statements are prepared at the end of a period. Since these steps are repeated every period, the process is called a cycle.

In the first year of operation of a company, because there is no beginning balance in each account, all accounts start with a '0' balance. But, from the second year of operation onward, accounting record keeping is done based on a beginning balance. Using simple illustrations, we will now explain the recording process, step by step, for each of these two situations. Here we will focus only on the recording process to prepare an income statement, as a part of the comprehensive income statement studied in Chapter 2. We will cover the recording process to report other comprehensive income in the Appendix.

3.1 When there is no beginning balance (the founding year)

〈Illustration 3-3〉 Accounting cycle(cash)—a merchandising company: When there is no beginning balance

The transactions of Saehan Department Store (hereafter, SH Department Store), for its founding year of 20×1, are as follow.

① Issued 100 million shares of common stock with par value of ₩1,000 at the beginning of 20×1 and received ₩100 billion.
② Borrowed ₩200 billion from a bank for 3 years.
③ Rented a building and paid rent of ₩30 billion for 20×1 in cash.
④ Purchased merchandise of ₩120 billion in cash.
⑤ Sold merchandise costing ₩100 billion at ₩250 in cash.
⑥ Purchased a piece of land and paid ₩220 billion in cash.
⑦ Made a loan of ₩80 billion to a supplier for 3 years.
⑧ Paid employees' salaries of ₩40 billion for 20×1 in cash.
⑨ Paid interest of ₩20 billion on the borrowing for 20×1 in cash.
⑩ Received interest of ₩4 billion on the loan for 20×1 in cash.
⑪ Paid dividends of ₩10 billion in cash.
⑫ Paid income tax of ₩15 billion for 20×1 in cash.

1 Journal entries

The first step is the task of identifying and journalizing transactions. 〈Table 3-7〉 shows a list of the journal entries prepared for transactions in 〈Illustration 3-3〉.

〈Table 3-7〉 Journal entries

(Numbers in billions of ₩)

No.		Debit		Credit	
①		(Dr.) Cash	100	(Cr.) Share capital-common stock	100
②		(Dr.) Cash	200	(Cr.) Long-term borrowings	200
③		(Dr.) Rent expense	30	(Cr.) Cash	30
④		(Dr.) Merchandise	120	(Cr.) Cash	120
⑤	⑤a	(Dr.) Cash	250	(Cr.) Sales	250
	⑤b	(Dr.) Cost of goods sold	100	(Cr.) Merchandise	100
⑥		(Dr.) Land	220	(Cr.) Cash	220
⑦		(Dr.) Long-term loans	80	(Cr.) Cash	80
⑧		(Dr.) Salaries expense	40	(Cr.) Cash	40
⑨		(Dr.) Interest expense	20	(Cr.) Cash	20
⑩		(Dr.) Cash	4	(Cr.) Interest revenue	4
⑪		(Dr.) Dividends	10	(Cr.) Cash	10
⑫		(Dr.) Income tax expense	15	(Cr.) Cash	15

The journal entries in 〈Table 3-7〉 for which the types of entries are not explained in 〈Illustration 3-1〉 are for transactions ④, ⑤, ⑦, ⑩, and ⑪. Since the journal entries for increases and decreases in cash has been explained above, here we will explain only the remaining part of journal entries.

Transaction ④ is a transaction that incurs an increase in an asset : merchandise. An increase in an asset should be recorded on the debit side, so here ₩120 billion is journalized on the debit side of the merchandise account.

In transaction ⑤, merchandise costing ₩100 billion was sold at ₩250 billion in cash. This transaction is analyzed by dividing it into two sub-transactions : in transaction ⑤a, sales revenue of ₩250 billion is generated, while in transaction ⑤b, merchandise is decreased by ₩100 billion.

Transaction ⑤a incurs revenue through sales. An incurrence of revenue should be recorded on the credit side, so ₩250 billion is journalized on the credit side of the sales account.

The cost of merchandise provided to generate sales revenue is called the cost of goods sold (an expense). Transaction ⑤b is a transaction that carries an expense, the cost of goods sold; as well as an asset, merchandise, that is decreased. An incurrence of expense should be recorded on the debit side, so ₩100 billion is journalized on the debit side of the cost of goods sold account. A decrease in an asset should be recorded on the credit side, so ₩100 billion is journalized on the credit side of the merchandise account.

Transaction ⑦ shows an increase in an asset: a long-term loan. An increase in an asset should be recorded on the debit side, so ₩80 billion is journalized on the debit side of the long-term loans account.

Transaction ⑩ shows incurred revenue: interest revenue. An incurrence of revenue should be recorded on the credit side, so ₩4 billion is journalized on the credit side of the interest revenue account.

Transaction ⑪ shows a dividend payment. A dividend payment should be recorded on the debit side, so ₩10 billion is journalized on the debit side of the dividends account.

2 Posting

The second step is posting the journal entries to accounts. 〈Diagram 3-11〉 shows the general ledger after posting the journal entries in 〈Table 3-7〉 to balance column accounts.

〈Diagram 3-11〉 General ledger after posting

(Numbers in billions of ₩)

Cash

Debit	Credit	Balance
① 100		100(Dr.)
② 200		300(Dr.)
	③ 30	270(Dr.)
	④ 120	150(Dr.)
⑤a 250		400(Dr.)
	⑥ 220	180(Dr.)
	⑦ 80	100(Dr.)
	⑧ 40	60(Dr.)
	⑨ 20	40(Dr.)
⑩ 4		44(Dr.)
	⑪ 10	34(Dr.)
	⑫ 15	19(Dr.)

Merchandise

Debit	Credit	Balance
④ 120		120(Dr.)
	⑤b 100	20(Dr.)

Long-term loans

Debit	Credit	Balance
⑦ 80		80(Dr.)

Land

Debit	Credit	Balance
⑥ 220		220(Dr.)

Long-term borrowings

Debit	Credit	Balance
	② 200	200(Cr.)

Share capital-common stock

Debit	Credit	Balance
	① 100	100(Cr.)

Dividends

Debit	Credit	Balance
⑪ 10		10(Dr.)

Sales

Debit	Credit	Balance
	⑤a 250	250(Cr.)

Interest revenue

Debit	Credit	Balance
	⑩ 4	4(Cr.)

Cost of goods sold

Debit	Credit	Balance
⑤b 100		100(Dr.)

Salaries expense

Debit	Credit	Balance
⑧ 40		40(Dr.)

Rent expense

Debit	Credit	Balance
③ 30		30(Dr.)

Interest expense

Debit	Credit	Balance
⑨ 20		20(Dr.)

Income tax expense

Debit	Credit	Balance
⑫ 15		15(Dr.)

3 Preparing a trial balance

The third step is preparing a trial balance. A trial balance aims to check whether transactions are recorded correctly, without any errors, before financial statements are prepared. (If T accounts are used, the balance of each account should be computed using the methods shown in 〈Diagram 3-6〉 or 〈Diagram 3-7〉, before the trial balance is prepared).

In a trial balance, the accounts and account balances are listed following the order of the accounts in the general ledger : assets, liabilities, equity, revenues and expenses. In general, assets and expenses have debit balances while liabilities, equity and revenues have credit balances. If all transactions are correctly journalized and posted, the debit total and the credit total in a trial balance should be equal. Of course, just because debit total equals credit total in a trial balance does not mean we can be sure that there was no error in the recording process. For example, the debit total and credit total would still be equal if we overlooked an entire transaction, failing to prepare a journal entry for it at all ; or if we made the mistake of recording the same wrong amount on both the debit side and the credit side of a journal entry.

The following ⟨Table 3-8⟩ is the trial balance of SH Department Store at the end of 20×1.

⟨Table 3-8⟩ Trial Balance

SH Department Store　　December 31, 20×1　　(Numbers in billions of ₩)

Debit	Account titles	Credit
19	Cash	
20	Merchandise	
80	Long-term loans	
220	Land	
	Long-term borrowings	200
	Share capital-common stock	100
10	Dividends	
	Sales	250
	Interest revenue	4
100	Cost of goods sold	
40	Salaries expense	
30	Rent expense	
20	Interest expense	
15	Income tax expense	
554	Total	554

As a result of preparing the trial balance, we know that the debit total and credit total are equal at ₩554 billion. While we still need to investigate further, this is a first positive sign showing that we made no recording errors.

4 Preparing and posting closing journal entries

The forth step is the task of preparing and posting closing journal entries to clear the ledger accounts so the next year's transactions can be recorded.

⟨Diagram 3-12⟩ shows the process of closing the revenue, expense and dividends accounts into the retained earnings account. Conventionally, the closing of revenue and expense accounts are done via an income summary (집합손익) account. This aims to simplify the retained earnings account by reflecting only the summary of revenues and expenses therein.

⟨Diagram 3-12⟩ Revenues, expenses, dividends, and retained earnings

(Numbers in billions of ₩)

			Beg. Retained Earnings	(0)
Revenue	(254)	→	Net Income	(49)
− Expenses	(205)	(Income summary)	− Dividends	(10)
Net Income	(49)		End. Retained Earnings	(39)

(1) Closing revenue and expense accounts : closing journal entries and posting

The first step in closing is to close revenue accounts and expense accounts and to transfer their balances into the income summary account.

Closing journal entry Ⓐ : ⟨Table 3-9⟩, below, shows an entry to close sales and interest revenue accounts, and to transfer their balances into the income summary account. (It is a compound entry. You can prepare two single entries although it is not recommended. See : ⟨Box 3-3⟩ 'Multiple single entries vs. A compound entry') Account closure is done by recording each revenue account's credit balance on the debit side of said account. The transfer of the balance is achieved by recording the total balances of these revenue accounts on the credit side of the income summary account.

〈Table 3-9〉 Journal entry closing revenue accounts

(Numbers in billions of ₩)

Ⓐ	(Dr.) Sales	250	(Cr.) Income summary	254
	Interest revenue	4		

〈Box 3-3〉 Multiple single entries vs. A compound entry

A **single entry** is an entry debiting one account and crediting another account. A **compound entry** is an entry combining two or more single entires sharing same debit or credit entry ; hence, it makes that task of preparing and posting entries simple. For example, the entry in 〈Table 3-9〉 is a compound entry combining two single entries shown below.

(Dr.) Sales	250	(Cr.) Income summary	250

(Dr.) Interest revenue	4	(Cr.) Income summary	4

Closing journal entry Ⓑ : 〈Table 3-10〉, below, shows an entry to close the accounts pertaining to the cost of goods sold, salaries expense, rent expense, interest expense, and income tax expense, and to transfer their balances into the income summary account. The closing of accounts is done by recording the debit balance of each expense account on the credit side of said expense account. The transfer of the balance is done by recording the total balances of these expense accounts on the debit side of the income summary account.

〈Table 3-10〉 Journal entry closing expense accounts

(Numbers in billions of ₩)

Ⓑ	(Dr.) Income summary	205	(Cr.) Cost of goods sold	100
			Salaries expense	40
			Rent expense	30
			Interest expense	20
			Income tax expense	15

〈Diagram 3-13〉 shows the income summary account, as well as the revenue and expense accounts, after posting the closing journal entries in ⟨Table 3-9⟩ and ⟨Table 3-10⟩.

⟨Diagram 3-13⟩ Posting journal entries closing revenue accounts and expense accounts

(Numbers in billions of ₩)

Cost of goods sold

Debit	Credit	Balance
⑤b 100		100(Dr.)
	Ⓑ 100	0

Income summary

Debit	Credit	Balance
	Ⓐ 254	254(Cr.)
Ⓑ 205		49(Cr.)

Sales

Debit	Credit	Balance
	⑤a 250	250(Cr.)
Ⓐ 250		0

Salaries expense

Debit	Credit	Balance
⑧ 40		40(Dr.)
	Ⓑ 40	0

Interest revenue

Debit	Credit	Balance
	⑩ 4	4(Cr.)
Ⓐ 4		0

Rent expense

Debit	Credit	Balance
③ 30		30(Dr.)
	Ⓑ 30	0

Interest expense

Debit	Credit	Balance
⑨ 20		20(Dr.)
	Ⓑ 20	0

Income tax expense

Debit	Credit	Balance
⑫ 15		15(Dr.)
	Ⓑ 15	0

As can be seen in ⟨Diagram 3-13⟩, when revenue accounts and expense accounts are closed, these account balances are transferred to the income summary account and become '0'. Because revenue accounts and expense accounts are nominal accounts that are temporarily used to summarize revenues and expenses for an accounting period, these accounts are called temporary accounts (임시계정) or nominal accounts (명목계정). In ⟨Diagram 3-13⟩, double rulings can be seen after closing temporary accounts. This is the convention in practice, and it signifies that these temporary accounts are closed.

If we look at the income summary account, we can tell whether income was incurred or loss was incurred. If the income summary account balance shows a credit balance, net income has been incurred, and if it is a debit balance, net loss has been incurred. Since the income summary account in ⟨Diagram 3-13⟩ shows a credit balance of ₩49 billion, we know that there was a net income of ₩49 billion.

(2) Closing income summary account and dividends account : closing journal entries and posting

The second step in closing is transferring the income summary account balance and dividends account balance to the retained earnings account. Net income, shown as an income summary account credit balance, should be transferred to the credit side of the retained earnings account ; dividends should be transferred to the debit side of the retained earnings account. The closing journal entries Ⓒ and Ⓓ demonstrating these transfers can be seen in ⟨Table 3-11⟩. As a reference, net loss, shown as an income summary account debit balance, is to be transferred to the debit side of the retained earnings accounts. If the retained earnings account balance shows a debit balance after closing, it is called accumulated loss.

⟨Table 3-11⟩ Journal entries closing income summary account and dividends account

(Numbers in billions of ₩)

Ⓒ	(Dr.) Income summary	49	(Cr.) Retained earnings	49
Ⓓ	(Dr.) Retained earnings	10	(Cr.) Dividends	10

When the income summary account balance and dividends account balance are transferred to the retained earnings account by closing journal entries, as in ⟨Table 3-11⟩, these two account balances become '0,' as seen in ⟨Diagram 3-14⟩ below.

⟨Diagram 3-14⟩ Posing journal entries closing income summary account and dividends account

(Numbers in billions of ₩)

Dividends		
⑪ 10		10(Dr.)
	Ⓓ 10	0

Retained earnings		
	Ⓒ 49	49(Cr.)
Ⓓ 10		39(Cr.)

Income summary		
	Ⓐ 254	254(Cr.)
Ⓑ 205		49(Cr.)
Ⓒ 49		0

Through closing journal entries, not only revenue and expense account but also income summary and dividends account balances become '0.' With these balances at

'0,' recording for the next accounting period is now possible.

The statement of financial position accounts, such as assets, liabilities and equity accounts, have balances even after closing journal entries are posted. Because the statement of financial position accounts, unlike the income statement accounts, continuously have balances even after closing journal entries are posted, they are called permanent accounts (영구계정) or real account (실질계정). There is no need to close these accounts. (Refer to 〈Box 3-4〉 'Closing permanent accounts?')

〈Box 3-4〉 Closing permanent accounts?

Temporary accounts are accounts set up to use for just one accounting period, like income statement accounts, income summary account and dividends account. If we compare it to a watch, a temporary account is like a stopwatch. After it is used for one 100m race, its needle should be returned to '0' for the next race. The mechanism that sets the needle of the temporary account back to '0' is the closing journal entry.

Permanent accounts, in contrast, are accounts that have balances permanently, regardless of accounting periods, such as the statement of financial position accounts. In the watch analogy, a permanent account is like a normal watch that we use every day. Just as we do not return the needle of a normal watch back to '0' when one race is over, there is no need to set permanent account balances back to '0'. Therefore, there is no need to close permanent accounts.

T accounts are not formal accounting books, but are set up temporally. So if T accounts are used, new T accounts should be set up for the next year not just for temporary accounts but also for permanent accounts. If permanent accounts have beginning balances, the beginning balances should be recorded in new T accounts before journal entries are posted. (Methods to record beginning balance in T accounts and balance column T accounts are explained in 3.2 'When there is a beginning balance,' and in 2, 'Posting,' in this chapter). In practice, nearly all companies continuously use not T accounts but balance column ledger accounts year after year, so there is no need to set up new accounts for next year. The current year's ending balances automatically become the following year's beginning balances.

5 Preparing a post-closing trial balance

The fifth step is the task of preparing a post-closing trial balance. A post-closing trial balance is prepared to check whether the closing is done accurately, without any errors.

The following ⟨Table 3-12⟩ shows the post-closing trial balance of SH Department Store at the end of 20×1.

⟨Table 3-12⟩ Post-closing trial balance

SH Department Store　　December 31, 20×1　　(Numbers in billions of ₩)

Debit	Account titles	Credit
19	Cash	
20	Merchandise	
80	Long-term loans	
220	Land	
	Long-term borrowings	200
	Share capital-common stock	100
	Retained earnings	39
339	Total	339

As the debit balance total and the credit total balance are equal in the post-closing trial balance in ⟨Table 3-12⟩, this is a first sign that there may have been no errors made in the preparing and posting of closing journal entries.

6 Preparing financial statements

The sixth and final step is the task of preparing the financial statements, including the income statement, statement of financial position, statement of cash flows and statement of changes in equity. Using account balances in the trial balance, we prepare an income statement and using account balances in the post-closing trial balance we prepare a statement of financial position. The next step is to prepare the statement of cash flows, by analyzing the cash account ; as well as the statement of changes in equity, by analyzing the equity accounts.

(1) Income statement

〈Table 3-13〉 shows the income statement of SH Department Store for 20×1. The store's earnings per share of ₩490 are computed by dividing the net income of ₩49 billion by 100 million common shares outstanding.

〈Table 3-13〉 Income statement

SH Department Store From Jan. 1, 20×2 to Dec. 31 20×2 (Numbers in billions of ₩)

Account titles	Amount	
Sales		250
Cost of goods sold		(−)100
Gross profit		150
Operating expenses		(−)70
Salaries expense	(−)40	
Rent expense	(−)30	
Income from operations		80
Other revenue		4
Interest revenue	4	
Other expense		(−)20
Finance expense :		
Interest expense	(−)20	
Net income before income tax expense		64
Income tax expense		(−)15
Net income		49
Earnings per share		₩490

(2) Statement of financial position

〈Table 3-14〉 shows a statement of the financial position of SH Department Store, as of December 31, 20×1.

〈Table 3-14〉 Statement of financial position

SH Department Store As of Dec. 31, 20×1 (Numbers in billions of ₩)

Account titles	Amount		Account titles	Amount	
Assets			Liability		
Current assets		39	Non-current liability		200
Cash	19		Cost financial liability :		
Inventory :			Long-term borrowings	200	
Merchandise	20		Total liability		200
Non-current assets		300	Equity		
Cost financial asset :			Share capital		100
Long-term loans	80		Common stock	100	
Tangible asset :			Retained earnings		39
Land	220				
			Total equity		139
Total assets		339	Total liability and equity		339

(3) Statement of cash flows

A statement of cash flows is prepared by analyzing the cash account, as in 〈Table 3-15〉.

〈Table 3-15〉 Cash account analysis

Cash

(Numbers in billions of ₩)

T No.	Activities	Opposite account	Amount	T No.	Activities	Opposite account	Amount
①	Financing	Share capital-common stock	100	③	Operating	Rent expense	30
②	Financing	Long-term borrowings	200	④	Operating	Merchandise	120
⑤a	Operating	Sales	250	⑥	Investing	Land	220
⑩	Investing	Interest revenue	4	⑦	Investing	Long-term loans	80
				⑧	Operating	Salaries expense	40
				⑨	Financing	Interest expense	20
				⑪	Financing	Dividends	10
				⑫	Operating	Income tax expense	15

The activities column in 〈Table 3-15〉 shows which of the company's activities each transaction represents. The opposite account, shown as a reference, is the account title that is opposite the cash account in the journal entry.

〈Box 3-5〉 How a direct method statement of cash flows is prepared in practice?

Transactions in 〈Illustration 3-3〉 are the minimum number of cash transactions needed to explain the accounting cycle. Thus, it is possible to prepare a **direct method statement of cash flows** by conducting a cash account analysis as shown in 〈Table 3-15〉.

But in practice, number of cash transactions occurred in a year is so big, it is impossible to conduct a cash account analysis. Therefore, first, we prepare an **indirect method statement of cash flows** using the income statement and the statement of financial position as explained in Chapter 11 'Statement of Cash Flows' and then convert it into a direct method statement of cash flows. (Refer to chapter 11 5.6 'Preparing a direct method statement of cash flows by the indirect method.')

Transaction ① and Transaction ② are typical financing activities, generating funds from stockholders and creditors respectively. Because interest paid by Transaction ⑧ is rewarded to the borrowing from Transaction ②, and dividends paid by Transaction ⑨ are rewarded to the capital contributed by stockholders from Transaction ①, these two transactions are also financing activities.

Transaction ④ and Transaction ⑥ refer to purchasing assets. Because merchandise purchased in Transaction ④ will be sold to customers as an operating activity, Transaction ④ is classified as an operating activity. Since land purchased by Transaction ⑥ will be used by the company for a long time, Transaction ⑥ is classified as an investing activity. Purchasing supply—that is an asset—is classified as an operating activity. This is because the supply will be consumed in a short period of time, and therefore becomes an operating expense.

Transaction ⑦, which is a long-term loan, and Transaction ⑩, which is the interest received from that long-term loan, are investing activities.

Transaction ⑤, which is a cash receipt of sales revenue, is a typical operating activity. Transactions ③ and ⑧ are also typical operating activities of paying operating expenses.

Transaction ⑩, of paying income tax, is also classified as an operating activity. The reason is that an assumption was made that income tax cannot be classified by the company's activities to simplify the case. If classification by activities is possible, then income tax can be reported for each activity.

As K-IFRS[3] allows exceptions in classifying interest receipts, interest payments and dividend payments, they can be classified as operating activities. It is required, however, that these items and the income tax payment should be reported individually. (More details of exceptional classifications and of individually reporting items will be reviewed in Chapter 11).

The following ⟨Table 3-16⟩ is a statement of cash flows of SH Department Store for 20×1.

⟨Table 3-16⟩ Statement of cash flows

SH Department Store From Jan. 1, 20×1 to Dec. 31 20×1 (Numbers in billions of ₩)

Description	Amount	
Cash flows from operating activities		
Cash receipts from customers	250	
Cash paid to suppliers and employees	(−)190	
Cash generated from operations	60	
Individually reporting item :		
Income tax paid	(−)15	
Net cash from operating activities		45
Cash flows from investing activities		
Individually reporting item :		
Interest received	4	
Long-term loans (made)	(−)80	
Purchase of land	(−)220	
Net cash used in investing activities		(−)296
Cash flows from financing activities		
Proceed from issuing common stock	100	
Proceeds from long-term borrowings	200	
Individually reporting items :		
Interest paid	(−)20	
Dividends paid	(−)10	
Net cash from financing activities		270
Net increase in cash		19
Cash at beginning of period		0
Cash at end of period		19

The cash flows from operating activities are computed by deducting the income tax paid from the cash generated through operations, which in turn refers to the difference between cash receipts from customers and cash paid to suppliers and employees. Cash receipts from customers correspond to the sales amount of ₩250 billion that is seen in Transaction ⑤a. Cash paid to suppliers and employees is ₩190 billion. It is a total of ₩30 billion in rent paid in Transaction ③; a ₩120 billion purchase of merchandise in Transaction ④; and ₩40 billion in salaries paid in Transaction ⑧. Therefore, the cash generated from operations is ₩60 billion. Next, by subtracting the income tax paid of ₩15 billion, which is an individually reporting item, net cash from operating activities is computed at ₩45 billion.

The cash flows from investing activities are computed by deducting cash outflows for investing activities from cash inflows from investing activities. Cash inflows from investing activities, here, are ₩4 billion from Transaction ⑩ of interest received. Cash outflows for investing activities include ₩220 billion from Transaction ⑥ of purchasing land, and ₩80 billion from Transaction ⑦ of making a long-term loan. Therefore, net cash used for investing activities is (-) ₩296 billion. The interest received in Transaction ⑩ is an individually reporting item.

The cash flows incurred through financing activities are computed by deducting the cash outflows for financing activities, from the cash inflows due to financing activities. Here, the cash inflows from financing activities are ₩100 billion due to the issuance of stock in Transaction ①, and ₩200 billion in long-term borrowing from Transaction ②. The cash inflows from financing activities are the addition of these two inflow amounts, which total ₩300 billion. The cash outflows for financing activities are ₩30 billion, an addition of interest payment of ₩20 billion from Transaction ⑧ and dividend payment of ₩10 billion from Transaction ⑨. The net cash from financing activities is ₩270 billion. The interest payment from Transaction ⑧ and the dividend payment from Transaction ⑨ are individually reporting items.

A net increase in cash of ₩19 billion is computed by subtracting the net cash used in investing activities of ₩296 billion from the net cash from operating activities of ₩45 billion, and adding the net cash from financing activities of ₩270 billion. Because there was no cash at the beginning of the period, the cash account at the end of the period is same as the net cash increase of ₩19 billion.

(4) Statement of changes in equity

The statement of changes in equity is prepared by conducting T account analysis for each of equity accounts as in ⟨Diagram 3-15⟩ below. The T account analysis is a task of tracking debit entries and credit entries in the applicable account and identifying their causes.

〈Diagram 3-15〉 T account analysis for equity accounts

(Numbers in billions of ₩)

Share capital-common stock

Debit	Credit	Balance
	① Issuance of common stock 100	100(Cr.)

Retained earning

Debit	Credit	Balance
	Ⓒ Net income 49	49(Cr.)
Ⓓ Cash dividends 10		39(Cr.)

The following 〈Table 3-17〉 is SH Department Store's statement of changes in equity for 20×1.

〈Table 3-17〉 Statement of changes in equity

SH Department Store From Jan. 1, 20×1 to Dec. 31 20×1 (Numbers in billions of ₩)

Description	Share capital	Retained earnings	Total
	Common stock		
Balance as of January 1, 20×1	–	–	–
Changes in equity during 20×1 :			
Issuance of common stock	100		100
Net income		45	45
Cash dividends		(−)10	(−)10
Balance as of December 31, 20×1	100	35	135

In the case of the share capital-common stock of SH Department Store, although there was no beginning balance, it was increased by ₩100 billion due to the issuance of common stock during the year, so the ending balance became ₩100 billion. In the case of retained earnings, although there was no beginning balance, it was increased by a net income of ₩45 billion and decreased by cash dividends of ₩10 billion during the year, so the ending balance became ₩35 billion. Hence, the ending balance for the total equity of SH Department Store became ₩135 billion.

3.2 When there are beginning balances (after the founding year)

In 〈Illustration 3-3〉, we explain an accounting cycle(cash) to prepare financial statements in the founding year. In the founding year, there are no beginning balances in all accounts. But, starting from the second year after foundation, there are beginning balances in the statement of financial position accounts : the asset, liability, and equity accounts. 〈Illustration 3-4〉 is a continuation of 〈Illustration 3-3〉, and shows the transactions of SH Department Store in the second year from its foundation.

〈Illustration 3-4〉 Accounting cycle(cash)—a merchandising company : When there are beginning balances

The transactions of SH Department Store for 20×2, the second year from its foundation, are as follow.

① Issued 100 million shares of common stock with par value ₩1,000 and at the beginning of 20×2 received cash of ₩100 billion.
② Borrowed ₩90 billion from a bank for 3 years.
③ Purchased merchandise at ₩160 billion in cash.
④ Sold merchandise costing ₩150 billion at ₩320 billion in cash.
⑤ Made a loan of ₩200 billion to a supplier for 3 years.
⑥ Paid employees' salaries of ₩50 billion for 20×2 in cash.
⑦ Paid building rent of ₩40 billion for 20×2 in cash.
⑧ Paid interest of ₩30 billion on borrowings for 20×2 in cash.
⑨ Received interest of ₩20 billion on loans for 20×2 in cash.
⑩ Paid dividends of ₩15 billion in cash.
⑪ Paid income tax of ₩25 billion for 20×2 in cash.

1 Journal entries

〈Table 3-18〉 Journal entries

(Numbers in billions of ₩)

No.		Debit		Credit	
①		(Dr.) Cash	100	(Cr.) Share capital-common stock	100
②		(Dr.) Cash	90	(Cr.) Long-term borrowings	90
③		(Dr.) Merchandise	160	(Cr.) Cash	160
④	④a	(Dr.) Cash	320	(Cr.) Sales	320
	④b	(Dr.) Cost of goods sold	150	(Cr.) Merchandise	150
⑤		(Dr.) Long-term loans	200	(Cr.) Cash	200
⑥		(Dr.) Salaries expense	50	(Cr.) Cash	50
⑦		(Dr.) Rent expense	40	(Cr.) Cash	40
⑧		(Dr.) Interest expense	30	(Cr.) Cash	30
⑨		(Dr.) Cash	20	(Cr.) Interest revenue	20
⑩		(Dr.) Dividends	15	(Cr.) Cash	15
⑪		(Dr.) Income tax expense	25	(Cr.) Cash	25

All journal entries in 〈Table 3-18〉 are types of entries that are explained in 〈Illustration 3-3〉. Therefore, we omit any detailed explanations of the journal entries here.

2 Posting

In practice, all companies continuously use balance column ledger accounts from year to year, so that the posting of journal entries of 20×2 can be done without any additional work. But if we use T accounts or balance column T accounts (as in this book), we should set up new T accounts in each new year and we should record the beginning balance as shown in 〈Diagram 3-16〉 or 〈Diagram 3-17〉 before posting journal entries of 20×2. Beginning balances to be recorded are the balances of the statement of financial position accounts, which are shown, as in 〈Table 3-12〉, the post-closing trial balances at the end of 20×1.

〈Diagram 3-16〉 Recording beginning balance—in case of T account

Cash

Beginning 19	

〈Diagram 3-17〉 Recording beginning balance—in case of balance column T account

Cash

		Beginning 19 (Dr.)

or

Cash

Beginning		19 (Dr.)

〈Diagram 3-18〉, below, is the general ledger showing the journal entries in 〈Table 3-18〉 posted after recording beginning balances for the statement of financial position accounts.

⟨Diagram 3-18⟩ General ledger after posting

(Numbers in billions of ₩)

Cash

Debit	Credit	Balance
Beg.		19(Dr.)
① 100		119(Dr.)
② 90		209(Dr.)
	③ 160	49(Dr.)
④a 320		369(Dr.)
	⑤ 200	169(Dr.)
	⑥ 50	119(Dr.)
	⑦ 40	79(Dr.)
	⑧ 30	49(Dr.)
⑨ 20		69(Dr.)
	⑩ 15	54(Dr.)
	⑪ 25	29(Dr.)

Merchandise

Debit	Credit	Balance
Beg.		20(Dr.)
③ 160		180(Dr.)
	④b 150	30(Dr.)

Land

Debit	Credit	Balance
Beg.		220(Dr.)

Share capital-common stock

Debit	Credit	Balance
Beg.		100(Cr.)
	① 100	200(Cr.)

Long-term loans

Debit	Credit	Balance
Beg.		80(Dr.)
⑤ 200		280(Dr.)

Long-term borrowings

Debit	Credit	Balance
Beg.		200(Cr.)
	② 90	290(Cr.)

Retained earnings

Debit	Credit	Balance
Beg.		39(Cr.)

Dividends

Debit	Credit	Balance
⑩ 15		15(Dr.)

Sales

Debit	Credit	Balance
	④a 320	320(Cr.)

Interest revenue

Debit	Credit	Balance
	⑨ 20	20(Cr.)

Cost of goods sold

Debit	Credit	Balance
④b 150		150(Dr.)

Salaries expense

Debit	Credit	Balance
⑥ 50		50(Dr.)

Rent expense

Debit	Credit	Balance
⑦ 40		40(Dr.)

Interest expense

Debit	Credit	Balance
⑧ 30		30(Dr.)

Income tax expense

Debit	Credit	Balance
⑪ 25		25(Dr.)

3 Preparation of a trial balance

⟨Table 3-19⟩ Trial balance

SH Department Store December 31, 20×2 (Numbers in billions of ₩)

Debit	Account titles	Credit
29	Cash	
30	Merchandise	
280	Long-term loans	
220	Land	
	Long-term borrowings	290
	Share capital-common stock	200
	Retained earnings	39
15	Dividends	
	Sales	320
	Interest revenue	20
150	Cost of goods sold	
50	Salaries expense	
40	Rent expense	
30	Interest expense	
25	Income tax expense	
869	Total	869

4~6 Remaining steps

The remaining steps are Step 4 : Closing ; Step 5 : Preparing a post-closing trial balance ; and Step 6 : Preparing financial statements. These steps can be carried out by referencing ⟨Illustration 3-3⟩, that is, an accounting cycle(cash) when there is no beginning balance. Only three items are different from ⟨Illustration 3-3⟩. These differing items are 1) the number of outstanding common stock, information that is needed to compute earnings per share in the income statement, is increased from last year by the number of common stock issued in the current year, 2) there is cash at the beginning of the period in the statement of cash flows, and 3) there are beginning balances in share capital-common stock, and retained earnings in the statement of changes in equity.

IFRS references (http://www.kasb.or.kr)

[1] IAS 16 *Property, Plant and Equipment*, par. 30.
[2] *Ibid*, par. 31.
[3] IAS 7 *Statement of Cash Flows*, par. 31.

Key terms

Account (계정) : One of a series of accounting books in which increases and decreases in assets, liabilities, equity, revenue and expense are recorded via a mechanism of dividing them into debit and credit sides. (p.94)

Accounting cycle (회계순환과정) : A bookkeeping process that is repeated every accounting period to prepare financial statements. (p.102)

Acquisition cost principle (취득원가원칙) : A principle under which the assets reported in a statement of financial position should be valued at the acquisition cost ; that is, at the exchange price at the time of acquisition. (p.93)

Bookkeeping (부기) : Recoding transactions in accounting books. (p.84)

Closing journal entries (마감분개) : Journal entries that are required to close income statement accounts and dividends accounts (p.108)

Double-entry bookkeeping (복식부기) : A bookkeeping method under which each transaction is classified and recorded twice at two different angles, as in the case of a cash transaction for which a cash receipt or payment is recorded in the first time, and so is its cause in the second time. (p.86)

Historical cost principle (역사적 원가원칙) : Means acquisition cost principles, and it is called historical cost principle because acquisition cost is the cost in past (history). (p.93)

Income summary (집합손익) : A temporary account set up to summarize revenue and expense account balances when accounting books are closed. (p.108)

Journal entry (분개) : A recording order showing what account, what side (debit or credit), and what amount to be recorded for each transaction, per the bookkeeping rules. (p.97)

Post-closing trial balance (마감후시산표) : A trial balance prepared after closing journal entries are posted. (p.113)

Posting (전기) : Process of recording journal entries to ledger accounts. (p.98)

T account analysis (T 계정분석) : A task of identifiying causes of debit entries and credit entries of an account using T account. (p.118)

Transaction (거래) : An economic event affecting the financial position of a company, which can be measured. (p.84)

Trial balance (시산표): A table that lists the balances of all accounts and allows us to check whether the debit balance total and credit balance total are equal at the end of an accounting period, to help ensure the accuracy of accounting records. (p.106)

Exercises

1. Accounting equation ①

Compute the amount for the blanks in the following table.

(Numbers in billions of ₩)

Case	Beginning			Ending			Increase in contributed capital	Decrease in contributed capital	Revenues	expenses	Dividends
	Assets	Liabilities	Equity	Assets	Liabilities	Equity					
A	30	①	10	②	25	15	2	1	③	40	3
B	④	30	20	60	⑥	⑤	4	2	70	6	5

2. Accounting equation ②

Compute the amounts to fill in the blanks in the following table.

(Numbers in billions of ₩)

Case	Beginning equity	Ending equity	Increase in contributed capital	Decrease in contributed capital	Revenues	Expenses	Dividends
A	①	35	12	9	45	40	3
B	20	②	4	5	25	21	2
C	50	45	③	8	34	32	6
D	65	55	8	④	70	77	5
E	27	31	3	2	⑤	8	1
F	90	106	24	28	150	⑥	10
G	46	74	6	5	96	60	⑦

3. **Accounting equation ③**

Compute the amounts for the blanks in the following table. There is no increase in contributed capital, nor is there a decrease in contributed capital.

(Numbers in billions of ₩)

Case	Beginning assets	Beginning liabilities	Ending liabilities	Ending equity	Revenues	Expenses	Dividends
A	300	180	190	①	200	170	60
B	400	②	290	190	300	190	60
C	③	250	280	350	500	570	20
D	530	320	350	260	④	300	100
E	590	240	250	330	270	⑤	70
F	650	250	350	420	480	340	⑥

4. **Recording transaction using accounting equation**

The following are accounting transactions of Daehan Home Delivery for 20×1.

① Issued 10 million shares of common stock, with par value of ₩5,000, at par value at the beginning of 20×1 and received ₩50 billion in cash.
② Borrowed ₩30 billion from a bank for 5 years.
③ Rented an office and paid rent of ₩6 billion for 20×1.
④ Provided home delivery service and received ₩20 billion in cash.
⑤ Purchased land and paid ₩40 billion in cash.
⑥ Paid employees' salaries of ₩9 billion in cash for 20×1.
⑦ Paid interest of ₩1 billion in cash for 20×1 on the borrowing.

《Questions》

(1) Record the transactions in the accounting equation table.

(Numbers in billions of ₩)

	Assets			=	Liabilities	+	Equity								
									Retained earnings						
T. no.	Cash	+	Land	=	Long-term borrowings	+	Share capital—common stock	+	Service fees revenue	−	Salaries expense	−	Rent expense	−	Interest expense
①				=											
②				=											
③				=											
④				=											
⑤				=											
⑥				=											
⑦				=											
Total		+		=		+		+		−		−		−	

(2) Prepare an income statement of Daehan Home Delivery for 20×1.

(3) Prepare a statement of financial position of Daehan Home Delivery at the end of 20×1.

5. Analysis of transactions

The following are transactions of Korea Consulting for 20×1.

① Issued 100 million shares of common stock, with par value of ₩1,000, at the par value and received ₩100 billion in cash.
② Borrowed ₩170 billion from a bank for 5 years.
③ Rented an office and paid rent of ₩12 billion for 20×1.
④ Purchased land and paid ₩200 billion in cash.
⑤ Provided consulting services and received ₩90 billion in cash.
⑥ Purchased a building and paid ₩50 billion in cash.
⑦ Paid interest of ₩15 billion in cash for 20×1 on the borrowing.
⑧ Received advertising services and paid fees of ₩5 billion in cash.
⑨ Paid employees' salaries of ₩40 billion in cash for 20×1.

《Question》

Analyze the transactions above and complete the following table. (Start from Transaction ②, applying the same method used for Transaction ①, which is shown as an example.)

T. no.	Effects of transaction			
	Debit		Credit	
	Account titles	Increase or decrease	Account titles	Increases or decrease
①	Cash	Increase	Share capital-common stock	Increase
②				
③				
④				
⑤				
⑥				
⑦				
⑧				
⑨				

6. Preparation of a trial balance

The following is data gathered from the accounting books of Hankook Corp. at the end of 20×1.

(Numbers in billion of ₩)

Account titles	Amount	Account titles	Amount
Cash	6	Sales	65
Short-term loans	17	Interest revenue	4
Merchandise	26	Cost of goods sold	30
Land	37	Salaries expense	10
Short-term borrowings	15	Insurance expense	2
Long-term borrowings	8	Advertising expense	5
Share capital-common stock	20	Interest expense	1
Retained earnings	?	Income tax expense	3

《Question》

Prepare a trial balance for Hankook Corp. at the end of 20×1.

7. Preparation of financial statements using a trial balance

The following is a trial balance of Daehan Inc. at the end of 20×1.

Trial balance

Daehan Inc. December 31, 20×1 (Numbers in billion of ₩)

Debit	Account titles	Credit
17	Cash	
12	Short-term loans	
53	Merchandise	
300	Land	
	Short-term borrowings	34
	Long-term borrowings	80
	Share capital-common stock	150
	Retained earnings	55
2	Dividends	
	Sales	270
	Interest revenue	1
135	Cost of goods sold	
32	Salaries expense	
2	Advertising expense	
3	Insurance expense	
4	Interest expense	
30	Income tax expense	
590	Total	590

《Questions》

(1) Prepare an income statement of Daehan Inc. for 20×1. Number of outstanding common stock in 20×1 was 100 million shares.

(2) Prepare a statement of financial position of Daehan Inc. at the end of 20×1.

8. Preparing journal entries and posting

The following is the accounting transactions of Hankook Trading Inc. for 20×1.

① Issued 10 million shares of common stock, with par value of ₩5,000, at the par value and received ₩50 billion in cash.

② Borrowed ₩70 billion from a bank for 5 years.

③ Purchased merchandise at ₩50 billion in cash.

④ Sold merchandise costing ₩20 billion at ₩45 billion in cash.

⑤ Purchased land and paid ₩90 billion in cash.
⑥ Paid building rent of ₩6 billion for 20×1 in cash.
⑦ Sold merchandise costing ₩15 billion at ₩30 billion in cash.
⑧ Received advertising services and paid ₩12 billion in cash.
⑨ Paid employees' salaries of ₩20 billion in cash for 20×1.

《Questions》

(1) Prepare journal entries for the above transactions.
(2) Post the journal entries on balance column T accounts.

9. Guessing transactions ①

The following is data gathered from the general ledger of Daemyung Inc.

(Numbers in billions of ₩)

Cash

① 10		10(Dr.)
② 20		30(Dr.)
	③ 16	14(Dr.)
④a 25		39(Dr.)
	⑤ 15	24(Dr.)
	⑥ 8	16(Dr.)
	⑦ 4	12(Dr.)
	⑧ 1	11(Dr.)

Merchandise

③ 16		16(Dr.)
	④b 10	6(Dr.)

Land

⑤ 15		15(Dr.)

Long-term borrowings

	② 20	20(Cr.)

Share capital-common stock

	① 10	10(Cr.)

Sales

	④a 25	25(Cr.)

Cost of goods sold

④b 10		10(Dr.)

Salaries expense

⑥ 8		8(Dr.)

Rent expense

⑦ 4		4(Dr.)

Interest expense

⑧ 1		1(Dr.)

《Question》

For each transaction number, (1) prepare a journal entry and (2) describe the transaction.

10. Guessing transactions ②

The following is the journal of Korea Consulting.

(Numbers in billions of ₩)

①	(Dr.) Cash	20	(Cr.) Share capital-common stock	20
②	(Dr.) Cash	19	(Cr.) Service fees revenue	19
③	(Dr.) Land	10	(Cr.) Cash	10
④	(Dr.) Cash	15	(Cr.) Short-term borrowings	15
⑤	(Dr.) Rent expense	3	(Cr.) Cash	3
⑥	(Dr.) Interest expense	2	(Cr.) Cash	2
⑦	(Dr.) Salaries expense	8	(Cr.) Cash	8
⑧	(Dr.) Insurance expense	4	(Cr.) Cash	4

《Question》 For each transaction number, describe the transaction.

11. Closing journal entries—service company

The following is a summary of the trial balance of Masan Consulting at December 31, 20×1.

Summary of trial balance

(Numbers in billions of ₩)

Account titles	Amount	Account titles	Amount
Cash	2	Land	53
Short-term borrowings	10	Share capital-common stock	40
Dividends	1	Service fees revenue	56
Rent expense	12	Advertising expense	5
Salaries expense	25	Insurance expense	4
Interest expense	1	Income tax expense	3

Note : All account balances are normal balances.

《Question》 Prepare closing journal entries.

12. Closing journal entries—merchandising company

The following is a summary of the trial balance of Kwangju Trading Company at December 31, 20×1.

Summary of trial balance

(Numbers in billions of ₩)

Account titles	Amount	Account titles	Amount
Cash	2	Merchandise	80
Land	200	Long-term borrowings	150
Share capital-common stock	100	Dividends	6
Sales	410	Cost of goods sold	180
Rent expense	60	Salaries expense	80
Advertising expense	5	Insurance expense	4
Interest expense	12	Income tax expense	23

Note : All account balances are normal balances.

《Question》 Prepare closing journal entries.

13. Accounting cycle(cash)—a service company : When there is no beginning balance ①

The following are transactions of Hankook Consulting for 20×1.

① Issued 20 million shares of common stock, with par value of ₩1,000 at par value, at the beginning of 20×1 and received ₩20 billion in cash.
② Borrowed ₩10 billion from a bank for 1 year.
③ Acquired a piece of land and paid ₩27 billion in cash.
④ Rented an office and paid rent of ₩2 billion for 20×1 in cash.
⑤ Provided consulting service to a client and received ₩10 billion in cash.
⑥ Received advertising service and paid fees of ₩3 billion in cash.
⑦ Paid employees' salaries of ₩5 billion for 20×1 in cash.
⑧ Provided consulting service to a client and received ₩6 billion in cash.
⑨ Paid interest of ₩1 billion for 20×1 in cash.
⑩ Paid income tax expense of ₩3 billion for 20×1 in cash.
⑪ Paid dividends of ₩1 billion in cash.

13-1. Journalizing, posting, preparing a trial balance

《Questions》

(1) Prepare journal entries.
(2) Post the journal entries on balance column T accounts.
(3) Prepare a trial balance.

13-2. Preparing closing journal entries, posting, preparing a post-closing trial balance

The following is a summary of the trial balance.

Summary of trial balance

(Numbers in billions of ₩)

Account titles	Amount	Account titles	Amount
Cash	4	Land	27
Short-term borrowings	10	Share capital-common stock	20
Dividends	1	Service fees revenue	16
Rent expense	2	Advertising expense	3
Salaries expense	5	Interest expense	1
Income tax expense	3		

Note : All account balances are normal balances.

《Questions》

(1) Prepare closing journal entries.
(2) Post the closing journal entries.
(3) Prepare a post-closing trial balance.

13-3. Preparing financial statements

《Questions》

(1) Prepare an income statement.
(2) Prepare a statement of financial position.
(3) 1) Analyze the cash account and 2) Prepare a statement of cash flows.
(Assume that no exception is allowed in classifying reporting items.)
(4) 1) Conduct T account analysis for equity accounts and 2) Prepare a statement of changes in equity.

14. Accounting cycle(cash)—a merchandising company : When there is no beginning balance ②

The following are transactions of Hankook Department Store (HDS) for 20×1.

① Issued 100 million shares of common stock, with par value of ₩1,000, at par value at the beginning of 20×1 and received ₩100 billion in cash.
② Borrowed ₩150 billion from a bank for 5 years.
③ Rented a building and paid rent of ₩12 billion for 20×1 in cash.
④ Purchased merchandise and paid ₩100 billion in cash.
⑤ Sold merchandise costing ₩60 billion at ₩110 billion in cash.
⑥ Acquired a piece of land and paid ₩200 billion in cash.
⑦ Paid insurance premium of ₩4 billion for 20×1 in cash.
⑧ Received advertising services and paid ₩5 billion in cash.
⑨ Paid employees' salaries of ₩30 billion for 20×1 in cash.
⑩ Paid interest of ₩7 billion for 20×1 in cash.

14-1. Journalizing, posting, preparing a trial balance

《Questions》

(1) Prepare journal entries.
(2) Post the journal entries on balance column T accounts.
(3) Prepare a trial balance.

14-2. Preparing closing journal entries, posting, preparing a post-closing trial balance

The following is a summary of the trial balance.

Summary of trial balance

(Numbers in billions of ₩)

Account titles	Amount	Account titles	Amount
Cash	2	Merchandise	40
Land	200	Long-term borrowings	150
Share capital-common stock	100	Sales	110
Cost of goods sold	60	Salaries expense	30
Advertising expense	5	Insurance expense	4
Rent expense	12	Interest expense	7

Note : All account balances are normal balances.

《Questions》

(1) Prepare closing journal entries.
(2) Post the closing journal entries.
(3) Prepare a post-closing trial balance.

14-3. Preparing financial statements

《Questions》

(1) Prepare an income statement.
(2) Prepare a statement of financial position.
(3) 1) Analyze the cash account and 2) prepare a statement of cash flows. (Assume that no exception is allowed in classifying reporting items.)
(4) 1) Conduct T account analysis for equity accounts and 2) prepare a statement of changes in equity.

15. Accounting cycle(cash)—a merchandising company: When there are beginning balances

The followings are the statement of financial position of Chokook Department Store (CDS) at the end of 20×1 and its transactions in 20×2.

Statement of financial position

CDS As of December 31, 20×1 (Numbers in billions of ₩)

Account titles	Amount		Account titles	Amount	
Assets			Liability		
Current asset		4	Non-current liability		20
Cash	4		Cost financial liability:		
Non-current asset		30	Long-term borrowings	20	
Tangible asset:			Total liability		20
Land	30		Equity		
			Share capital		10
			Common stock	10	
			Retained earnings		4
			Total equity		14
Total assets		34	Total liability and equity		34

〈Transactions in 20×2〉

① Issued 20 million shares of common stock with par value of ₩1,000, at apr value at the beginning of 20×2 and received ₩20 billion in cash.
② Borrowed ₩25 billion from a bank for 10 years.
③ Purchased merchandise and paid ₩42 billion in cash.
④ Sold merchandise costing ₩27 billion at ₩55 billion in cash.
⑤ Acquired a piece of land and paid ₩29 billion in cash.
⑥ Made a loan of ₩10 billion to OS Mart for 10 months.
⑦ Rented a building and paid rent of ₩5 billion for 20×2 in cash.
⑧ Paid employees' salaries of ₩9 billion for 20×2 in cash.
⑨ Received interest of ₩1 billion for 20×2 in cash.
⑩ Paid interest of ₩3 billion for 20×2 in cash.
⑪ Paid income tax of ₩4 billion for 20×2 in cash.
⑫ Paid dividends of ₩2 billion in cash.

15-1. Journalizing, posting, preparing a trial balance

《Questions》

(1) Journalize transactions in 20×2.
(2) Set up balance column T accounts and record beginning balances and post journal entries of 20×2.
(3) Prepare a trial balance.

15-2. Preparing financial statements

The following is a summary of the trial balance.

Summary of trial balance

(Numbers in billions of ₩)

Account titles	Amount	Account titles	Amount
Cash	1	Short-term loans	10
Merchandise	15	Land	59
Long-term borrowings	45	Share capital-common stock	30
Retained earnings	4	Dividends	2
Sales	55	Interest revenue	1
Cost of goods sold	27	Rent expense	5
Salaries expense	9	Interest expense	3
Income tax expense	4		

Note : All account balances are normal balances.

《Questions》

(1) Prepare an income statement.
(2) Prepare a statement of financial position.
(3) 1) Analyze the cash account and 2) prepare a statement of cash flows (Assume that no exception is allowed in classifying reporting items.)
(4) 1) Conduct T account analysis for equity accounts and 2) prepare a statement of changes in equity.

Accrual Basis and Preparation of Financial Statements

Section 1 Measurement of income : Accrual basis and cash basis

Section 2 Recognition of revenue and expense under the accrual basis

Section 3 Adjusting journal entries

Section 4 Accounting cycle (accrual)

Chapter 4 Overview

In this chapter, we compare and explain (1) the accrual basis, which is the base of an income statement ; and (2) the cash basis, which is the base for a statement of cash flows. Next, we review the revenue and expense recognition principles under the accrual basis, as well as the reasons for which it is necessary to have adjusting journal entries at the end of the year if the accrual basis is applied. And then we examine the types of adjusting journal entries. Last, we explain an accounting cycle (accrual) that involves an application of the accrual basis.

Measurement of income : Accrual basis and cash basis

Income is a critical piece of information that shows a company's operational results. There are two income-measuring methods : the accrual basis (발생주의) and the cash basis (현금주의).

〈Box 4-1〉 What is recognition?

Recognition (인식), in accounting, means the act of recording transactions in the accounting books. To recognize a transaction, one must decide when the transaction should be recorded, and in what amount. In sum, recognition is the act of measuring a transaction in monetary units and classifying it as an asset, liability, equity, revenue, or expense ; recording it in the accounting books ; and, as a result, reporting it in the financial statements.

Under the accrual basis, revenues and expenses are recognized at the time when the causes of cash receipt and payment are incurred. Therefore, the accrual basis income is calculated by subtracting expenses from revenues recognized in this way. If the revenues are larger than the expenses, then net income (순이익) is reported. If the revenues are less than the expenses, net loss (순손실) is reported.

Under the cash basis, on the other hand, the cash basis income (or net operating cash flow) is calculated by subtracting cash payments from the cash receipts due to operating activities. If the cash receipts are greater than the cash payments, then a cash basis income (or net operating cash inflow) is reported. If the cash receipts are less than the cash payments, then a cash basis loss (or net operating cash outflow) is reported.

Which method, then, reports more meaningful income? We will explain this in the following illustration.

〈Illustration 4-1〉 Comparison of the accrual basis with the cash basis

Mr. Nara Kim works part time at a convenience store, and wishes to evaluate his own personal financial performance at this part time job. Mr. Kim's personal financial performance can be measured by subtracting the expenses that he has sacrificed for the job from the revenues earned from the job. Revenues from the job are calculated by multiplying the number of hours worked by his hourly wages. Expenses for the job include transportation expenses, food expenses, etc.

Mr. Kim receives his wages on the first day of the month that follows the month actually worked. Mr. Kim started his job in January. He worked 200 hours that month, and his hourly wage was ₩4,000. His expenses for the job totaled ₩200,000, and all of which he paid in cash in January.

Since revenue, under the accrual basis, is recognized at the point of inputting service for the job, the revenue for January is ₩800,000 (200 hours × ₩4,000). Under the cash basis, the cash receipt from the part-time job is not reported in January, because the cash is received on February 1. Because the expenses for the job, totaling ₩200,000, were incurred in January and paid in January, they are recognized as January expenses under the accrual basis, and as a cash payment in January under the cash basis. Therefore, under the accrual basis, performance for January is evaluated as a net income of ₩600,000 because revenue is ₩800,000 and expense is ₩200,000. Under the cash basis, January performance is evaluated as a net loss of ₩200,000 (that is, a net operating cash outflow) because only ₩200,000 of cash payment is reported. February performance under the cash basis, however, is evaluated as a net income of ₩800,000 (that is, a net operating cash inflow) because ₩800,000 of cash receipt is reported.

As can be seen in the above illustration, income under the accrual basis properly reflects the performance that is a result of the efforts provided, whereas income under the cash basis (that is, net operating cash flows) does not. Thus, income statements are prepared on the accrual basis these days. But the net operating cash flows is reported in the statement of cash flows because cash flow information is considered to be important as supplementary information.

In the next section, we will review the differences between the accrual basis and the cash basis for a merchandising company and a service rendering company. The above illustration shows only one type of difference between the accrual basis and the cash basis. In the next section, we classify the differences between the accrual basis and the cash basis into four different types, and explain each type in detail.

1.1 Merchandising company

In the case of a merchandising company, the accrual basis revenue is the sales amount (both cash sales and credit sales are included), and the expense is the purchase price of goods sold (cost of goods sold). (Sales are reviewed in detail in Chapter 6, and the cost of goods sold is reviewed in detail in Chapter 7). The cash receipt, on the other hand, is the cash amount received from selling products, whereas cash payment is the cash amount paid for merchandise purchased. This relationship is illustrated in 〈Diagram 4-1〉.

〈Diagram 4-1〉 Accrual basis and cash basis in a merchandising company

Description	January	February	March	April	At the end of April (Statement of financial position)
Economic events	Purchase of merchandise on credit 	Payment of trade payables 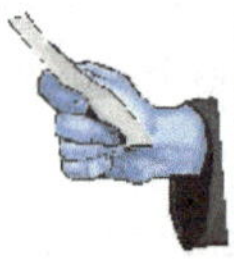	Sales of merchandise on credit 	Collection of trade receivables 	
Trade receivables			Sales : ₩12 billion	(-) ₩7 billion	₩5 billion
Merchandise	₩10 billion		Cost of goods sold : (-) ₩8 billion		₩2 billion
Trade payables	₩10 billion	(-) ₩6 billion			₩4 billion
Accrual basis (Income statement)			Revenue : ₩12 billion (Sales) Expense : ₩8 billion (Cost of goods sold)		
Cash basis (Statement of cash flows)		Payment : ₩6 billion (Cash outflows)		Receipt : ₩7 billion (Cash inflows)	

As seen in ⟨Diagram 4-1⟩, in January, ₩10 billion worth of merchandise was purchased on credit, so trade payables of ₩10 billion were recorded. In February, trade payables of ₩6 billion were paid. (Merchandise and trade payables are reviewed in detail in Chapter 7). In March, merchandise with a purchase price of ₩8 billion was sold on credit for ₩12 billion, so trade receivables of ₩12 billion were recorded. In April, trade receivables of ₩7 billion were collected. (Trade receivables are reviewed in detail in Chapter 6).

In this case, under the accrual basis, revenue and expense are not recognized in January, February or April. Only in March, in which sales were made, the sales of ₩12 billion and the cost of goods sold of ₩8 billion are recognized as revenue and expense respectively. Hence, a net income of ₩4 billion is reported in March. (The theories for recognizing revenue and for recognizing expense are reviewed in detail in Section 2, below).

Under the cash basis, cash receipts and payments are not reported in January and March, because there are no cash receipts and no cash payments. In February, there is no cash receipt but there is a cash payment of ₩6 billion, so a net operating cash outflow of ₩6 billion is reported. In April, there is no cash payment but there is a cash receipt of ₩7 billion, so a net operating cash inflow of ₩7 billion is reported.

1.2 Service company

⟨Illustration 4-2⟩, which follows, shows the difference between the accrual basis and the cash basis in a service company.

⟨Illustration 4-2⟩ Differences between the accrual basis and the cash basis in a service company.

Daehan Consulting Co., which was founded at the beginning of 20×1, rendered consulting services on credit in January for ₩14 billion. The consulting revenue collected in January was ₩8 billion. Hence, the uncollected consulting revenue at the end of January was ₩6 billion. In February the company rendered consulting services on credit for ₩15 billion. The consulting revenue collected in February was ₩18 billion. Uncollected consulting revenue at the end of February was ₩3 billion.

In ⟨Illustration 4-2⟩, the accrual basis service revenues and cash basis service revenues for the months of January and February are as in the following ⟨Table 4-1⟩.

⟨Table 4-1⟩ Accrual basis service revenues and cash basis service revenues

(Numbers in billions of ₩)

Description	Financial statement	January	February
Service revenue —(Accrual basis)	Income statement	14	15
Cash receipt —(Cash basis)	Statement of cash flows	8	18
Service fees receivable	Statement of financial position (at the end of month)	6	3

The accrual basis service revenues for January and February are the amount of services provided in each month, of ₩14 billion and ₩15 billion respectively. These amounts are reported in the income statements for each month as service revenues. (These are often reported as sales, in practice). Cash receipts, which are the cash basis service revenues for January and February, are the cash amounts collected of ₩8 billion and ₩18 billion, respectively. These amounts are reported in the statement of cash flows as 'cash inflows from operating activities.' The uncollected service revenues at the end of January and February are ₩6 billion and ₩3 billion, respectively. These amounts are reported in the statement of financial position at end of each month as an asset called service fees receivable. (In practice, this asset is often reported as trade receivable). (Service revenue and service fees receivable in service companies are accounted for in the same way as are sales and trade receivable in merchandising companies. The only difference is that there is no need to record the cost of goods sold in service companies).

Recognition of revenue and expense under the accrual basis

As noted, these days the accrual basis is used to recognize revenue and expense in accounting. By what standards, then, are revenue and expense recognized under the accrual basis? These standards play a very important role in deciding the amounts of revenue and of expense to be reported in the income statement. The standard for revenue recognition is called the revenue recognition principle, and the standard for expense recognition is called the revenue-expense matching principle.

2.1 Revenue recognition principle

In the accrual basis, revenue is recorded at the point when the cause for the revenue occurs in the operating activities. The standard by which this specific point in time is decided is called the revenue recognition principle (수익인식기준). According to IFRS[1], the following two conditions should be met to recognize revenue :

ⓐ Revenue amount can be reliably measured and

ⓑ the possibility of inflow of economic benefits associated with the transaction should be high.

In practice, the revenue recognition point is determined by applying the guideline that revenue is recognized when it is

① (a) 'realized' (실현되었거나) or (b) 'realizable' (실현 가능하고) and

② 'earned' (벌었을).

The first part of the guideline, being 'realized' in ① (a), means that there is an exchange between the seller and the buyer so that a cash inflow or right to claim cash, such as a trade receivable, is occurred. Being 'realizable,' as in ① (b), means that there is an active market so that the market price can be obtained at any time even there is no exchange between the seller and the buyer. In both cases, IFRS condition ⓐ—the amount of revenue can be measured reliably because there is an exchange price or a market price for the goods.

The second part of the guideline, being 'earned' in ②, means that almost all of the process of generating revenue is completed. As a result, IFRS condition ⓑ—it is very likely that an economic reward from revenue is to be received.

The process of generating revenue is a series of activities that a company carries out to earn revenue. Those of a merchandising company can be illustrated as in the following ⟨Diagram 4-2⟩.

⟨Diagram 4-2⟩ Revenue-generating process of a merchandising company

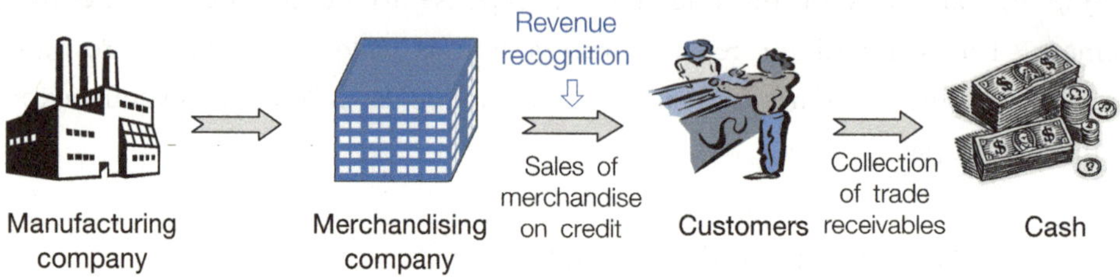

As can be seen in ⟨Diagram 4-2⟩, the revenue-generating process of a merchandising company consists of the activities of purchasing goods from a manufacturer, selling them to customers on credit, and collecting trade receivables. In general, merchandising companies recognize revenue when goods are sold as shown in ⟨Diagram 4-2⟩. This is because 1) there is an exchange price between a seller and a buyer, so that practice guideline ① (a) 'realized' is met and the amount of revenue can be measured reliably; and 2) important revenue generating activities, such as the activities of purchasing, displaying in the store and selling on credit are completed; thus, practice guideline ②, 'earned,' is met and the possibility of collecting proceeds from sales is high.

Although the selling point is a point in time when the proceeds of sales have not yet been collected, we consider that point as a point that meets the practice guideline of ②, 'earned'. This is because, in general, all those processes that lead up to selling merchandise on credit are important and the process of collecting sales proceeds is minimal in terms of the total earning process. If, on the other hand, the revenue was recognized at the point when sales proceeds were collected, then the revenue would not be reported when the important earning process was completed but would instead be reported at the time of cash collection. This would create a problem of reporting operational results with bias, as we showed above when we compared the accrual basis and the cash basis.

Can revenue be recognized when sales proceeds are received prior to the sale, as an advance from the customer? Revenue should be recognized after the merchandise is delivered to the customer. This is because 1) the act of delivering merchandise to the customer is an important part of the revenue-generating process and, until it has been provided, we cannot say it has been 'earned', 2) the advance received has to be returned to the customer if merchandise is not delivered, so we cannot say it has been ultimately received at this point.

Can revenue be recognized if merchandise is purchased and displayed in a store with a price tag attached? Revenue should be only recognized after the sale is made. This is because 1) the price on the price tag is not a reliable indicator of revenue because it can be adjusted by mark-down, and 2) making a sale to a customer is a significant part of the revenue-generating process, so we cannot say it has been 'earned' before the sale is made.

In the case above, selling merchandise on credit meets the practice guideline of ① (a), 'realized,' because there is an exchange between the seller and the buyer. Practice guideline ① (b), 'realizable,' is a case where revenue can be reliably measured even when there is no exchange. If there is an active market then the market price is available, enabling revenue to be measured reliably at the market price even though an exchange is not made. An example of revenue recognized in this way is the gain on valuation of fair value through profit of loss (FVPL) financial assets, which was briefly introduced in Chapter 2 and will be reviewed in detail in the Appendix. Although FVPL financial assets are not yet sold, revenue is recognized because the amount of revenue can be reliably measured via the market price (fair value) in an active market. (Industrial practice of recognizing revenue 〈At point of finishing production〉 in 〈Box 4-2〉 of 'Revenue recognition at points other than selling point' below is another example.)

〈Box 4-2〉 Revenue recognition at points other than selling point

Because of the characteristics of various industries, revenue can be recognized at points other than the point of sale, such as during production ; at the completion of production ; and at the point of cash receipt. These industry practices are likewise results of applying the general revenue recognition principles.

〈During production〉

In the case of long-term construction contracts, if we recognize revenue only when the construction is complete, there is a problem both of reporting no revenue for a period of many years, and of reporting the entire construction revenue in the year of completion. Therefore, if we can measure the percentage of completion reliably, we recognize this revenue during the construction. In the case of long-term construction, the total construction revenue is the contract price, which is predetermined. So if, as noted, we can measure the percentage of completion reliably, then we can also measure the construction revenue to be recognized each year reliably. One year's worth of construction is a significant part of the total revenue-generating process, and billing is based on the percentage of completion, so the possibility of inflow of revenue is high. Therefore, if we can measure the percentage of completion reliably, we recognize the construction revenue based on the percentage of completion. This is called the percentage of completion method. (IFRS[2])

If we cannot measure the percentage of completion or cost of construction reliably, we recognize the recoverable contract price by billing as revenue to the extent that no profit is reported. (IFRS[3])

〈At point of finishing production〉

In the industry of precious metal extraction, such as that of gold and silver, companies recognize revenue when the production process is finished. For example, in the case of a company that extracts gold ore and refines it, the market price for refined gold is readily available, so it is 'realizable' and the revenue can likewise be measured reliably. Also, the process of extracting and refining gold ore is a significant part of the revenue-generating process. Therefore, gold-mining companies recognize the revenue at the point of finishing the production process, which is at the point when the refining process is complete. (For the same reason, meat-processing companies that produce processed meats, for which market price is readily available and agricultural companies that deal in grains, for which the government purchase price is predetermined, recognize their revenue when production is finished.) (IFRS[4])

〈At point of cash receipt〉

Companies selling goods on a long-term installment plan recognize revenue at the point of cash receipt. In the case of the long-term installment sale, because the process of collecting sales proceeds is a critical part of the revenue generating process, one cannot say it is 'earned' when the long-term installment sale is made. In addition, the possibility of collecting sales proceeds at the point of sale is low. Therefore, we cannot recognize revenue at the point of sale; rather, we recognize revenue at the point of receiving sales proceeds. (IFRS[5])

Details of revenue recognition points other than the point of sale will be examined in Intermediate Accounting.

2.2 Revenue-expense matching principle : The expense recognition principle

The revenue-expense matching principle (수익 · 비용 대응기준) states that the expense incurred to create a specific revenue should be recognized in the accounting period within which that revenue is recognized. Assume, for instance, that Company A purchased some goods at ₩10 billion in cash in 20×1, sold them on credit at ₩15 billion in 20×2, and collected trade receivable in 20×3. In this case, ₩15 billion is recorded as sales revenue in 20×2 and, based on the revenue-expense matching principle, the ₩10 billion cost of goods that were provided to earn that sales revenue is recognized as the cost of goods sold in 20×2. As a result, a gross profit of ₩5 billion is reported in 20×2.

In the case of Company A, above, goods of ₩10 billion purchased in 20×1 are reported as merchandise inventory in the statement of financial position at the end of 20×1. Credit sales, in the amount of ₩15 billion in 20×2, are also reported as a trade receivable in the statement of financial position at the end of 20×2. As the revenue-expense matching principle is applied, an asset (or a liability) occurs as shown above. If an asset or liability, borne in this way, does not meet the definition of either asset or liability, which principle should be followed? In the past, when the income statement was considered most important, the revenue-expense matching principle was the prime principle. The IFRS[6] prioritizes the asset-liability valuation standard over the revenue-expense matching principle, however. This is the very reason for which IFRS[7] does not allow the LIFO (last-in, first-out) cost formula, because it does not reflect the real value of the inventory. (The various cost formulas including LIFO will be reviewed in Chapter 7).

There are six different ways to match expense against revenue as shown in ⟨Table 4-2⟩ : 1) As we saw in the case reviewed above, the cost of goods sold is reported as an expense because it directly matches specific revenue. Sales commission paid at a percentage of the sales amount is another example of this. 2) Because interest is incurred over time, it is reported as an expense as time elapses. This is called period matching. Rent expense is another example of this. 3)ⓐ In the case of supplies, they are reported as an expense when they are consumed. Travel and transportation expense, communication expense and utility expense are of this type. 3)ⓑ Payments for advertising and entertainment are directly reported as expenses when they occur (at the time of the advertising and entertainment), because their effects and the duration of said effects are uncertain. 4) Depreciation expense which is an expense of using a tangible asset for an accounting period is determined by allocating cost of the asset during the period the asset can be used. (This will be reviewed in Chapter 8). 5) If there is a decrease in value of an asset during a period, that decrease in value should be reported as an expense in the period the said decrease in value occurred. Bad debt expense is an example. (This will be reviewed in Chapter 6). 6) Income tax expense is a result of matching expense with income.

⟨Table 4-2⟩ Ways to match expenses

	Ways to match		Examples
1)	Matching with revenue		Cost of goods sold, Sales commissions (based on sales amount) expense
2)	Period matching		Interest expense, Rent expense
3)	Direct expensing	ⓐ Consumed or used	Supplies expense, Travel and transportation expense, Communication expense, Utility expense
		ⓑ Uncertainty	Advertising expense, Entertainment expense
4)	Allocation of cost		Depreciation expense
5)	Valuation of asset		Bad debts expense
6)	Matching with income		Income tax expense

Adjusting journal entries

3.1 Nature of adjusting journal entries

As reviewed above, the income statement and the statement of financial position are based on the accrual basis. Instead of applying the accrual basis every day, companies apply the following steps :

Step 1) Journalize and post the cash transactions (as reviewed in Chapter 3), as well as the transactions in which merchandise is purchased and sold on credit (this will be reviewed in detail in Chapters 6 and 7), up to the year's end.

Step 2) Prepare the adjusting journal entries to convert the outcomes of Step 1) into the accrual basis information at the year's end, and prepare financial statements.

In short, the adjusting journal entries are entries that convert cash basis information (including the purchase and sale of goods on credit) into accrual basis information (information to be reported in the income statement and the statement of financial position) at the year's end.

Because the general journal entries are prepared for cash transactions and transactions on credit, they can be prepared relatively easily, relying on objective documents such as cash receipt vouchers and cash payment vouchers or invoices. But to prepare adjusting journal entries, 1) we should identify items to be adjusted, and 2) we should obtain relevant information from documents such as agreements or contracts related to the items to be adjusted.

3.2 Types of adjusting journal entries

Because the adjusting journal entries are the ones that convert cash basis information into accrual basis information, they themselves mark the difference between the cash basis income (that is, the net operating cash) and the accrual basis income (that is, the net income reported in the income statement). The reason that we have differences between the net operating cash and the net income is that the time of cash flow is different from the time at which the revenue or expense is recognized. These differences are classified into four types, as shown in ⟨Table 4-3⟩. These four types are classified into those that are revenue-related and those that are expense-related. Next, they are categorized into a group where cash flow occurs 'after' the recognition of a revenue or expense ; and a group where cash flow occurs 'before' said recognition.

In the case of revenue, if cash flow occurs 'after' the recognition of revenue, then it is a later cash receipt and is classified as a 'later receipt.' If it occurs 'before' the recognition of revenue, then it is a cash receipt in advance and is classified as 'pre-receipt.' In the statement of financial position, items created by the former are accrued revenues and those created by the latter are unearned revenues.

In the case of an expense, in the same way as for revenue, if cash flow occurs 'after' the recognition of expense, that is a later cash payment and is classified as 'later payment.' If it occurs 'before' the recognition of expense, that is a cash receipt in advance and is classified as 'pre-payment'. In the statement of financial position, items created by the former are accrued expenses and those created by the latter are prepaid expenses.

To explain each type of adjusting journal entry, we introduce four illustrations from ⟨Illustration 4-3⟩ through ⟨Illustration 4-6⟩. These illustrations deal with interest revenue or interest expense, which are relatively easy to compute because they are recognized by a function of time.

⟨Table 4-3⟩ Types of adjusting journal entries

Descriptions	Cash flows 'after' recognition by accrual basis	Cash flows 'before' recognition by accrual basis
Revenue	'Later receipt'	'Pre-receipt'
	3.2.1 Accrued revenue ⟨Illustration 4-3⟩	3.2.2 Unearned revenue ⟨Illustration 4-4⟩
Expense	'Later payment'	'Pre-payment'
	3.2.3 Accrued expense ⟨Illustration 4-5⟩	3.2.4 Prepaid expense ⟨Illustration 4-6⟩

3.2.1 Accrued revenue

Accrued revenue means revenue that has been incurred by providing goods or services, but where cash has not yet been received. Accrued revenue implies a right to claim cash borne by an incurrence of revenue and is therefore classified as an asset. Trade receivables, service fees receivable (sometimes called accrued service revenue), interest receivable (sometimes called 'accrued interest revenue') and rent receivable (sometimes called 'accrued rent revenue') are examples. Here, we introduce an illustration of interest receivable, to explain adjusting journal entries that are associated with accrued revenue.

〈Illustration 4-3〉 Interest receivable

DH Trading Corp. loaned ₩240 billion to a supplier, AR Manufacturing Co. on June 1, 20×1. The loan period was one year, the interest rate was 20% per annum and the interest was a 'later receipt'. DH Trading Corp. thus received one year's interest, plus the principal amount on the maturity date. The company's fiscal year ends on December 31.

(1) Analysis of transactions

〈Diagram 4-3〉 below is prepared to analyze interest revenue and interest receipt transactions.

〈Diagram 4-3〉 Interest revenue, interest receivable and interest receipt

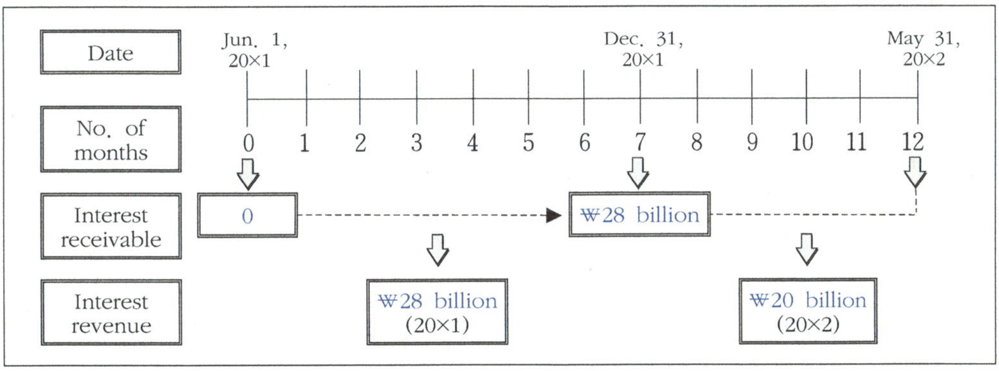

As shown in 〈Diagram 4-3〉 above, the accrual basis interest revenue is the interest earned as the loan period elapses. Thus, the interest revenue for 20×1 is ₩28 billion ; that is, interest for 7 months from June 1 to December 31 (₩240 billion × 20% × 7/12). Interest revenue for 20×2, meanwhile, is ₩20 billion ; that is, interest for 5 months from January 1 to May 31 (₩240 billion × 20% × 5/12). Each of these amounts is reported in income statements for 20×1 and 20×2 as an interest revenue. The interest receipt for 20×1 is none, while, for 20×2, it is ₩48 billion. This amount is reported in the statement of cash flows for 20×2 as 'cash inflows from investing activities.' Because the interest revenue of ₩28 billion for 20×1 had not yet been received in cash at the end of 20×1, it is reported as an asset, under the name of interest receivable, in the statement of financial position at the end of 20×1. The interest receivable of ₩28 billion is cleared when this amount and the interest revenue of ₩20 billion for 20×2 are received on May 31, 20×2. ⟨Table 4-4⟩ below gives a summary of this analysis.

⟨Table 4-4⟩ Summary of transaction analysis—interest receivable

(Numbers in billions of ₩)

Description	Financial statements	20×1	20×2
Interest earned (Accrual basis)	Income statement	28	20
Interest received (Cash basis)	Statement of cash flows	-	48
Interest receivable	Statement of financial position (at the end of the year)	28	

(2) Journal entries

We classify all journal entries in ⟨Illustration 4-3⟩ through ⟨Illustration 4-6⟩ into 1) journal entries prepared in 20×1 before an adjusting journal entry ; 2) an adjusting journal entry to be prepared at the end of 20×1 ; and 3) journal entries to be prepared in the next year, in 20×2. Numbers in all journal entries are in billions of ₩.

1) Journal entry in 20×1 before adjustment

Short-term loan of ₩240 billion made on June 1, 20×1 are journalized as below.

June 1, 20×1 :

(Dr.) Short-term loans	240	(Cr.) Cash	240

2) Adjusting journal entry

Interest revenue for 20×1 not yet received at the end of 20×1 is ₩28 billion. Therefore, the following adjusting journal entry should be prepared.

December 31, 20×1 :

(Dr.) Interest receivable	28	(Cr.) Interest revenue (20×1)	28

The interest revenue of ₩28 billion is closed to the income summary account in 20×1.

3) Journal entries in 20×2 (the following year)

Cash of ₩48 billion, which is the sum of the interest receivable of ₩28 billion and the interest revenue of ₩20 billion for 20×2, is received on May 31, 20×2. Short-term loan of ₩240 billion are collected on the same date. The following are journal entries for these transactions.

May 31, 20×2 :

(Dr.) Cash	48	(Cr.) Interest revenue (20×2)	20
		Interest receivable	28

(Dr.) Cash	240	(Cr.) Short-term loans	240

(Note : We can prepare a compound journal entry that combines these two entries and debits ₩288 billion into the cash account.)

〈Box 4-3〉 Reversing journal entry—accrued revenue

A reversing journal entry (It is also called a returning journal entry in Korean practice.) is a journal entry prepared by reversing debit side and credit side of a last year's adjusting entry. Reversing entries are prepared and posted in current year after closing last year's accounting books. Reversing journal entries are optional. That is, we do not always prepare them, although the reversing journal entries make the task of book keeping easy and convenient. Not all of the adjusting journal entries are subject to reversing journal entries. Only adjusting journal entries (accrued revenue and accrued expense) related with transactions recording cash received as a revenue and cash paid as an expense are subject to reversing journal entries. The adjusting journal entries (unearned revenue and prepaid expense) related with transactions recording cash received as a liability and cash paid as an asset should not be reversed.

A reversing journal entry to be prepared in 20×2 for interest receivable of DH Trading Inc. is as follows.

(Numbers in billions of ₩)

(Dr.) Interest revenue (20×2)	28	(Cr.) Interest receivable	28

The following journal entry should be prepared when interest of ₩48 billion was received on May 31, 20×2.

(Dr.) Cash	48	(Cr.) Interest revenue (20×2)	48

As we post two journal entries above, we obtain the same result that we obtain when we do not have the reversing journal entry, offsetting interest receivable of ₩28 billion and recognizing interest revenue of ₩20 billion for 20×2. When we do not have the reversing journal entry, we have to check the interest receivable to prepare a journal entry for cash received on May 31, 20×2. However, if we have the reversing journal entries, we do have a convenience of recording total cash receipt as interest revenue (20×2) without checking the interest receivable.

3.2.2 Unearned revenues

Unlike accrued revenue, unearned revenue (sometimes called deferred revenue) is cash that is received before goods or services are provided; that is, before revenue is recognized. Unearned revenue implies an obligation to provide goods or services, so it is classified as a liability. Unearned revenue is converted into revenue when the revenue actually occurs in the future. Examples of unearned revenue include advances from customers, unearned service fees (sometimes called deferred service fees), unearned interest (sometimes called deferred interest) and unearned rent (sometimes called deferred rent). An advance from customer is cash that is received from a customer in advance, prior to delivering goods. Unearned service fees is cash received from a customer in advance, before a service is rendered. These items are the opposite of the trade receivable and service fees receivable that are reviewed above, in terms of the timing of cash receipt. Here, unearned interest is reviewed as an example to explain adjusting journal entries associated with unearned revenue.

> ⟨Illustration 4-4⟩ Unearned interest
>
> DH Trading Corp. granted a loan of ₩300 billion to a supplier, ST Manufacturing Co., on October 1, 20×1. The loan period was one year, the interest rate was 20% per annum, and the interest was a 'pre-receipt'. Hence, DH Trading Corp. provided the net of the amount of the loan to the supplier, less one year's interest on the date of loan.

(1) Analysis of transactions

⟨Diagram 4-4⟩ below is prepared to analyze interest revenue and interest receipt transactions.

⟨Diagram 4-4⟩ Interest receipt, unearned interest and interest revenue

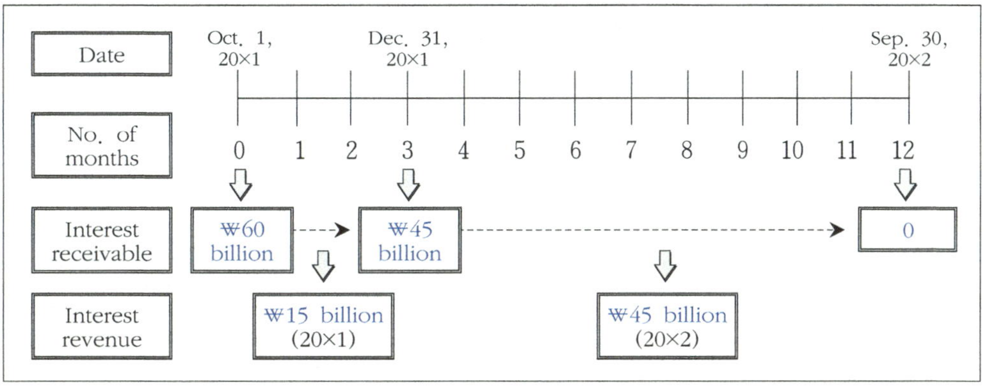

As shown in ⟨Diagram 4-4⟩ above, the accrual basis interest revenue is the interest earned as the loan period elapses. Thus, interest revenue for 20×1 is ₩15 billion ; that is, interest for 3 months from October 1 to December 31 (₩300 billion × 20% × 3/12). Interest revenue for 20×2 is ₩45 billion ; that is, interest for 9 months from January 1 to September 30 (₩300 billion × 20% × 9/12). Each of these amounts is reported in the income statements for 20×1 and 20×2 as interest revenue.

The interest receipt is ₩60 billion for 20×1 and none for 20×2. This amount is reported in the statement of cash flows as 'cash inflows from investing activities.' As of the end of 20×1, ₩15 billion, out of cash receipt of ₩60 billion, is interest revenue for 20×1. And the remaining ₩45 billion is interest revenue for 20×2, which is received in advance so it is reported as a liability under the name of unearned interest in the statement of financial position at the end of 20×1. This unearned interest is converted into interest revenue for 20×2, as the loan period matures. ⟨Table 4-5⟩ below gives a summary of this analysis.

⟨Table 4-5⟩ Summary of transaction analysis–unearned interest

(Numbers in billions of ₩)

Description	Financial statements	20×1	20×2
Interest revenue (Accrual basis)	Income statement	15	45
Cash received (Cash basis)	Statement of cash flows	60	–
Unearned interest	Statement of financial position (at the end of the year)	45	

(2) Journal entries

1) Journal entry in 20×1 before adjustment

Short-term loan of ₩300 billion made and unearned interest of ₩60 billion received, on October 1, 20×1, are journalized as below.

October 1, 20×1 :

(Dr.) Short-term loans	300	(Cr.) Cash	300

(Cr.) Cash	60	(Cr.) Unearned interest	60

(Note : We can prepare a compound journal entry that credits ₩240 billion to the cash account.)

2) Adjusting journal entry

The interest revenue for 20×1, from ₩60 billion of unearned interest, is ₩15 billion. Therefore, the following adjusting journal entry should be prepared.

December 31, 20×1 :

(Dr.) Unearned interest	15	(Cr.) Interest revenue (20×1)	15

The interest revenue of ₩15 billion is closed to the income summary account in 20×1.

3) Journal entries in 20×2 (the following year)

Unearned interest of ₩45 billion should be changed to interest revenue of 20×2, and short-term loan of ₩300 billion are collected on September 30, 20×2. The following are journal entries for these transactions.

September 30, 20×2 :

(Dr.) Unearned interest	45	(Cr.) Interest revenue (20×2)	45

(Dr.) Cash	300	(Cr.) Short-term loans	300

3.2.3 Accrued expense

Accrued expense means that the expense has occurred but has not yet been paid in cash. Because an accrued expense is an obligation to pay cash in the future, it is classified as a liability. Rent payable (sometimes called 'accrued rent expense'), salaries payable (sometimes called 'accrued salaries'), and interest payable (sometimes called 'accrued interest expense') are examples of accrued expense. Here, interest payable is reviewed as an example to explain adjusting journal entries associated with accrued expense.

〈Illustration 4-5〉 Interest payable

DH Trading Corp. borrowed ₩100 billion from AE Bank on May 1, 20×1. The borrowing period was one year, the interest rate was 12% per annum and the interest was a 'later payment.' Hence, the company paid one year's interest on the maturity date, along with the principal.

(1) Analysis of transactions

〈Diagram 4-5〉 below is prepared to analyze interest expense and interest payment transactions.

〈Diagram 4-5〉 Interest expense, interest payable and interest payment

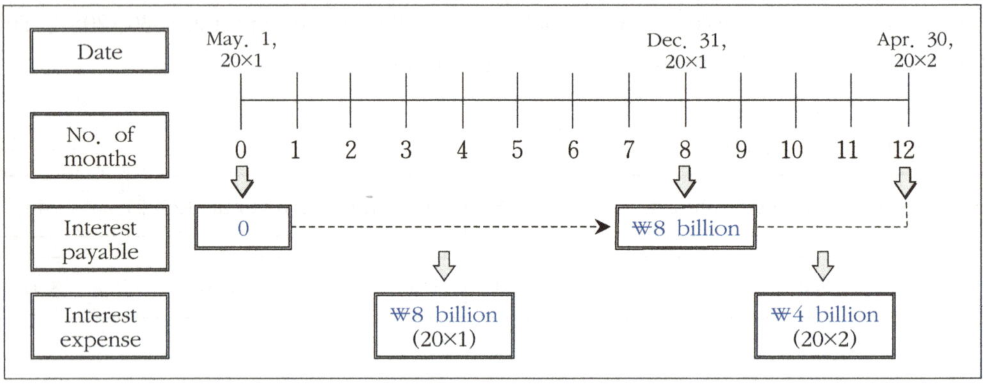

Because 〈Illustration 4-5〉 above is an illustration of a borrowing and 〈Illustration 4-3〉 examined above is an illustration of a loan, all terminology is symmetrical. Symmetrical terms include loan vs. borrowing ; interest revenue vs. interest expense ; interest receivable vs. interest payable ; and interest receipt vs. interest payment.

As shown in 〈Diagram 4-5〉 above, the accrual basis interest expense is the interest occurred as the borrowing period elapses. Thus, the interest expense for 20×1 is ₩8 billion ; that is, interest for 8 months, from May 1 to December 31 (₩100 billion × 12% × 8/12). Interest expense for 20×2 is ₩4 billion ; that is, interest for 4 months from January 1 to April 30 (₩100 billion × 12% × 4/12). Each of these amounts is reported in the income statements for 20×1 and 20×2 as an interest expense. No interest payment was made in 20×1, while interest of ₩12 billion was paid in 20×2. This amount is reported in the statement of cash flows as 'cash outflows from financing activities.' Because the interest expense of ₩8 billion for 20×1 had not yet been paid in cash at the end of 20×1, it is reported as a liability, under the name of interest payable, in the statement of financial position at the end of 20×1. This interest payable of ₩8 billion is cleared when this amount and the interest expense of ₩4 billion for 20×2 are paid on April 30, 20×2. ⟨Table 4-6⟩ below gives a summary of this analysis.

⟨Table 4-6⟩ Summary of transaction analysis—interest payable

(Numbers in billions of ₩)

Description	Financial statements	20×1	20×2
Interest expense (Accrual basis)	Income statement	8	4
Interest paid (Cash basis)	Statement of cash flows	-	12
Interest payable	Statement of financial position (at the end of the year)	8	

(2) Journal entries

1) Journal entry in 20×1 before adjustment

Short-term borrowing of ₩100 billion on May 1, 20×1 is journalized as the following.

May 1, 20×1 :

(Dr.) Cash	100	(Cr.) Short-term borrowings	100

2) Adjusting journal entry

Interest expense for 20×1, not yet paid at the end of 20×1, is ₩8 billion. Therefore, the following adjusting journal entry should be prepared.

December 31, 20×1 :

(Dr.) Interest expense (20×1)	8	(Cr.) Interest payable	8

The interest expense of ₩8 billion is closed to the income summary account in 20×1.

3) Journal entries in 20×2 (the following year)

Cash of ₩12 billion, which is an addition to the interest payable of ₩8 billion and the interest expense of ₩4 billion for 20×2, is paid on April 30, 20×2. Short-term borrowing of ₩100 billion is paid off on the same date. The following are journal entries for these transactions.

May 31, 20×2 :

(Dr.) Interest expense (20×2)	4	(Cr.) Cash	12
Interest payable	8		

(Dr.) Short-term borrowings	100	(Cr.) Cash	100

(Note : We can prepare a compound journal entry that credits ₩112 billion to the cash account.)

〈Box 4-4〉 Reversing journal entry—accrued expense

A reversing journal entry to be prepared in 20×2 for interest payable of DH Trading Inc. is as follows.

(Numbers in billions of ₩)

(Dr.) Interest payable (20×2)	8	(Cr.) Interest expense	8

The following journal entry should be prepared when interest of ₩12 billion was paid on April 30, 20×2.

(Dr.) Interest expense (20×2)	12	(Cr.) Cash	12

As we post two journal entries above, we obtain the same result that we obtain when we do not have the reversing journal entry, offsetting interest payable of ₩8 billion and recognizing interest expense of ₩4 billion for 20×2. When we do not have the reversing journal entry, we have to check the interest payable to prepare a journal entry for cash paid on April May 30, 20×2. However, if we have the reversing journal entry, we do have a convenience of recording total cash payment as interest expense (20×2) without checking the interest payable.

3.2.4 Prepaid expense

Opposite to accrued expense, prepaid expense is the expense which will occur in future that is paid in cash in advance. Prepaid expense is classified as an asset because it means a right to receive goods or services that are paid for in advance. Prepaid expense is cleared as the expense actually occurs later. Prepaid rent, prepaid insurance, and prepaid interest are examples of prepaid expense. Here, prepaid interest is reviewed as an example to explain adjusting journal entries associated with prepaid expense.

〈Illustration 4-6〉 Prepaid interest

DH Trading Corp. borrowed ₩80 billion from PE Bank on April 1, 20×1. The borrowing period was one year, the interest rate was 10% per annum, and the interest was a 'pre-payment.' Hence, the company received the net borrowed amount, less one year's interest, on the date of loan.

(1) Analysis of transactions

〈Diagram 4-6〉 below is prepared to analyze interest expense and interest payment transactions.

〈Diagram 4-6〉 Interest payment, prepaid interest and interest expense

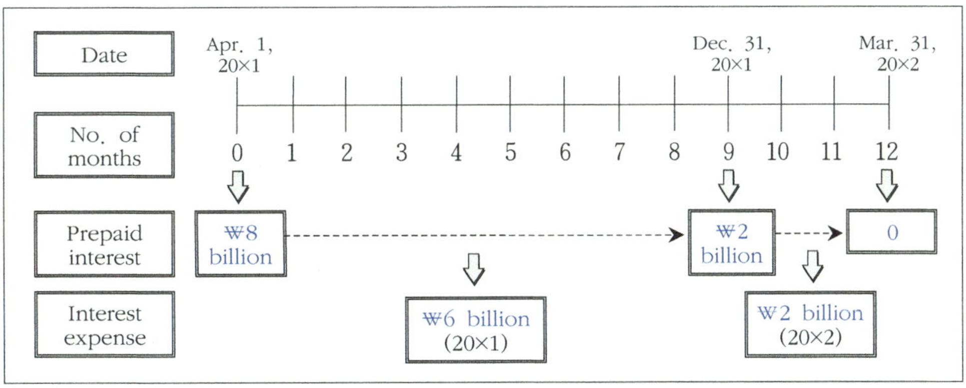

As 〈Illustration 4-5〉 interest payable and 〈Illustration 4-3〉 interest receivable are in symmetry, 〈Illustration 4-6〉 prepaid interest and 〈Illustration 4-4〉 unearned interest are likewise in symmetry.

As shown in ⟨Diagram 4-6⟩ above, the accrual basis interest expense is the interest that occurs as the borrowing period elapses. Thus, the interest expense for 20×1 is ₩6 billion for the 9 months from April 1 to December 31 (₩80 billion × 10% × 9/12), while the interest expense for 20×2 is ₩2 billion for the 3 months from January 1 to March 31 (₩80 billion × 10% × 3/12). Each of these amounts is reported in the income statement for 20×1 and 20×2 as an interest expense. The interest payment is ₩8 billion in 20×1, and none in 20×2. This amount is reported in the statement of cash flows in 20×1 as 'cash outflows from financing activities.' Because ₩2 billion out of ₩8 billion paid in 20×1 is the interest expense for 20×2, which was paid in advance, it is reported as an asset under the title of prepaid interest in the statement of financial position at the end of 20×1. The prepaid interest is converted into interest expense as the borrowing period elapses in 20×2. ⟨Table 4-7⟩ below gives a summary of this analysis.

⟨Table 4-7⟩ Summary of transaction analysis—prepaid interest

(Numbers in billions of ₩)

Description	Financial statement	20×1	20×2
Interest expense (Accrual basis)	Income statement	6	2
Interest paid (Cash basis)	Statement of cash flows	8	-
Prepaid interest	Statement of financial position (at the end of the year)	2	

(2) Journal entries

1) Journal entries in 20×1 before adjustment

Short-term borrowing of ₩80 billion and advance payment of interest of ₩8 billion on April 1, 20×1, are journalized as below.

April 1, 20×1 :

(Dr.) Cash	80	(Cr.) Short-term borrowings	80

(Dr.) Prepaid interest	8	(Cr.) Cash	8

(Note : We can prepare a compound journal entry that credits ₩72 billion to the cash account.)

2) Adjusting journal entry

The interest expense for 20×1, from prepaid interest of ₩8 billion, is ₩6 billion. Therefore, the following adjusting journal entry should be prepared.

December 31, 20×1 :

(Dr.) Interest expense (20×1)	6	(Cr.) Prepaid interest	6

The interest expense of ₩6 billion is closed to the income summary account in 20×1.

3) Journal entries in 20×2 (the following year)

The prepaid interest of ₩2 billion should be changed to an interest expense for 20×2, and the short-term borrowing of ₩80 billion is paid off on March 31, 20×2. The following are journal entries for these transactions.

March 31, 20×2 :

(Dr.) Interest expense (20×2)	2	(Cr.) Prepaid interest	2

(Dr.) Short-term borrowings	80	(Cr.) Cash	80

Accounting cycle (accrual)

The accounting cycle (accrual) ; when there are adjusting journal entries, as shown in ⟨Diagram 4-7⟩ below, has two more steps than does the accounting cycle (cash) when it includes no adjusting journal entries. These steps correspond to Steps 4 'preparing and posting adjusting journal entries' and Step 5 'preparing an adjusted trial balance.' Step 4 is the task of finding items to be adjusted after preparing a trial balance, journalizing them in the journal, and posting those entries on the accounts. Step 5 refers to the process of preparing a trial balance after the adjusting journal entries are posted. Therefore, here, we will review only from the Step 1 up to the Stop 5 which are related with the adjusting journal entries and omit explanation from the Step 6 to Step 8 which were examined in Chapter 3 the accounting cycle (cash). And only the income statement and the statement of financial position, which are affected by the adjusting journal entries, are reviewed. In additional material, the difference between the statement of cash flows information and the income statement are explained.

⟨Diagram 4-7⟩ Accounting cycle (accrual)

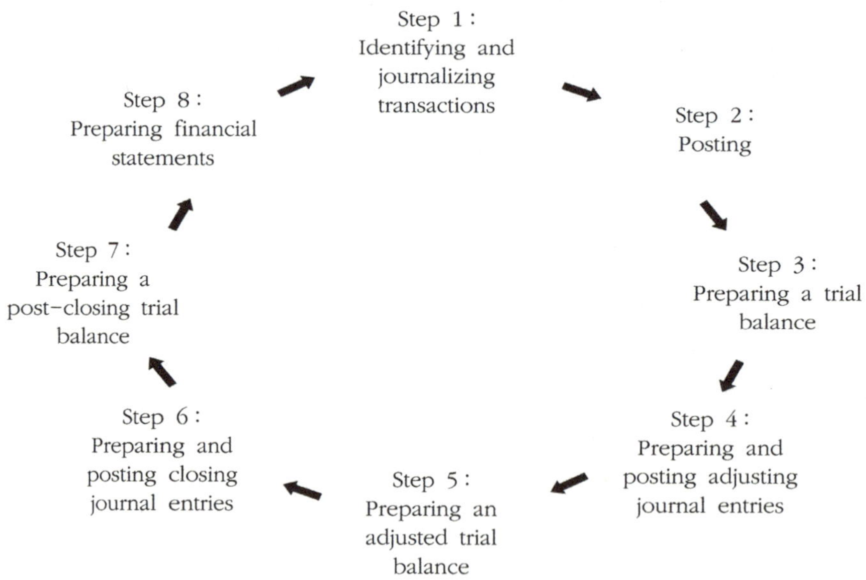

〈Illustration 4-7〉, below, deals with the accounting cycle (accrual) when there are no beginning balances but when there are adjusting journal entries. An accounting cycle (accrual) that includes both beginning balances and adjusting journal entries will later be reviewed in a comprehensive illustration in Chapter 5.

〈Illustration 4-7〉 Accounting cycle (accrual)—a service company: When there is no beginning balance

Korea Real Estate was founded in 20×1, and the following 〈Table 4-8〉 is a list of its transactions in 20×1.

〈Table 4-8〉 Transactions in 20×1

T. No.	Date	Transactions
①	January 2	Issued 10 million shares of common stock with par value of ₩5,000 and received ₩50 billion in cash.
②	February 1	Borrowed ₩100 billion from a bank for 1 year.
③	March 1	Rented an office building and paid rent of ₩120 billion in advance.
④	October 1	Rented out a part of an office building and rent of ₩240 billion was received in advance.
⑤	December 30	Paid employees' salaries of ₩80 billion for 20×1 in cash.

1 Identifying and journalizing transactions

⟨Table 4-9⟩ Journal entries

(Numbers in billions of ₩)

①	(Dr.) Cash	50	(Cr.) Share capital-common stock	50
②	(Dr.) Cash	100	(Cr.) Short-term borrowings	100
③	(Dr.) Prepaid rent	120	(Cr.) Cash	120
④	(Dr.) Cash	240	(Cr.) Unearned rent	240
⑤	(Dr.) Salaries expense	80	(Cr.) Cash	80

Journal entries for cash receipt and cash payment were reviewed above. Here we review only those types of transactions not previously reviewed in Chapter 3, namely : Transaction ③ and Transaction ④.

Transaction ③ involves renting a building and paying rent of ₩120 billion in advance. Due to this transaction, an asset (that is, prepaid rent) is increased. Because an increase in an asset should be recorded on the debit side, ₩120 billion is journalized on the debit side of the prepaid rent account.

Transaction ④ involves renting out an office and receiving rent of ₩240 billion in advance. Due to this transaction, a liability (that is, unearned rent) is increased. An increase in a liability is to be recorded on the credit side, so ₩240 billion is journalized on the credit side of the unearned rent account.

2 Posting

〈Diagram 4-8〉 General ledger after posting

(Numbers in billions of ₩)

Cash

Debit	Credit	Balance
① 50		50(Dr.)
② 100		150(Dr.)
	③ 120	30(Dr.)
④ 240		270(Dr.)
	⑤ 80	190(Dr.)

Prepaid rent

Debit	Credit	Balance
③ 120		120(Dr.)

Unearned rent

Debit	Credit	Balance
	④ 240	240(Cr.)

Short-term borrowings

Debit	Credit	Balance
	② 100	100(Cr.)

Share capital-common stock

Debit	Credit	Balance
	① 50	50(Dr.)

Salaries expense

Debit	Credit	Balance
⑤ 80		80(Dr.)

3 Preparing a trial balance

〈Table 4-10〉 Trial balance

Korea Real Estate December 31, 20×1 (Numbers in billions of ₩)

Debit	Account titles	Credit
190	Cash	
120	Prepaid rent	
	Unearned rent	240
	Short-term borrowings	100
	Share capital-common stock	50
80	Salaries expense	
390	Total	390

4 Preparing and posting adjusting journal entries

The information needed to prepare adjusting journal entries is different depending on whether the adjusting items are listed on the trial balance or not. Unearned revenue and prepaid expense appear in the trial balance ; therefore, there is no need to search for these items. Only we have to collect the information needed to adjust them. Accrued revenue and accrued expense do not appear on the trial balance. Therefore, the additional procedure of identifying items to be adjusted, based on a good understanding of revenue structure and expense structure, is needed. In most cases, as the adjusting journal entries are repeating every year, the adjusting journal entries of prior year can be a good reference in preparing these of current year.

The following 〈Table 4-11〉 gives a summary of the additional information collected to prepare adjusting journal entries.

〈Table 4-11〉 Additional information to prepare adjusting journal entries

	Additional information
ⓐ	Unearned rent revenue of ₩24 billion, recorded on October 1, was 1 year rent.
ⓑ	Prepaid rent expense of ₩12 billion, recorded on March 1, was 1 year rent.
ⓒ	Rented out a part of office building on May 1. Rental period was 1 year and 1 year rent of ₩240 billion is due on March 31 of 20×2.
ⓓ	Borrowing period of ₩100 billion, borrowed on February 1, was for 1 year; interest rate was 12% per annum; and interest would be paid on the maturity date of the debt.
ⓔ	Income tax for 20×1 was ₩8 billion and would be paid in 20×2.

In the case of the unearned rent of ⓐ and the prepaid rent of ⓑ in 〈Table 4-11〉, we should collect the information needed to adjust these items from the lease contracts. In the case of the rent receivable of ⓒ, first we should identify the possibility of having rent receivable by examining the revenue structure. Next, we should obtain detailed information by examining the related lease contract. In the case of interest payable of ⓓ, after recognizing that interest payable can be occurred due to short-term borrowing, we should collect detailed information from the related debt agreement. In the case of income tax payable of ⓔ, we should gather information about estimated income tax.

(1) Adjusting journal entries

Adjusting journal entries, based on the above additional information, are as below. All numbers in the journal entries are in billions of ₩.

1) Adjusting journal entry ⓐ—Unearned rent

〈Diagram 4-9〉 Rent receipt, unearned rent and rent revenue

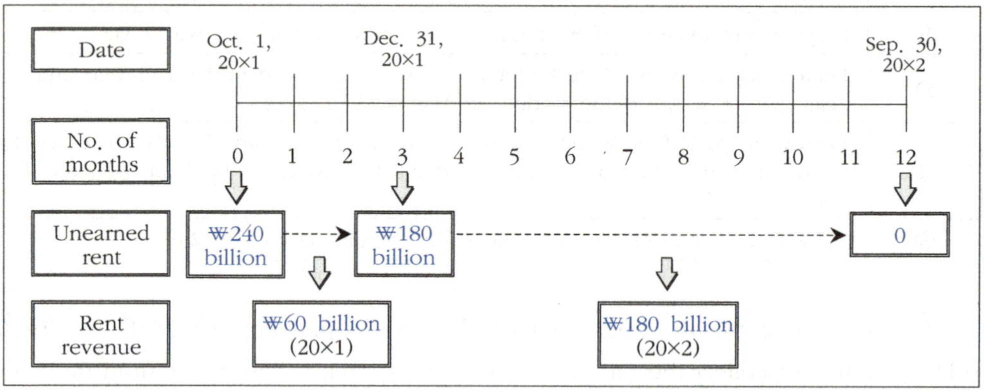

Rent revenue for 20×1, from unearned rent of ₩240 billion, is rent for 3 months (from October 1, 20×1 to December 31, 20×1) of ₩60 billion (₩240 billion × 3/12). Therefore, the following adjusting journal should be prepared.

ⓐ	(Dr.) Unearned rent	60	(Cr.) Rent revenue	60

2) Adjusting journal entry ⓑ—Prepaid rent

〈Diagram 4-10〉 Rent payment, prepaid rent and rent expense

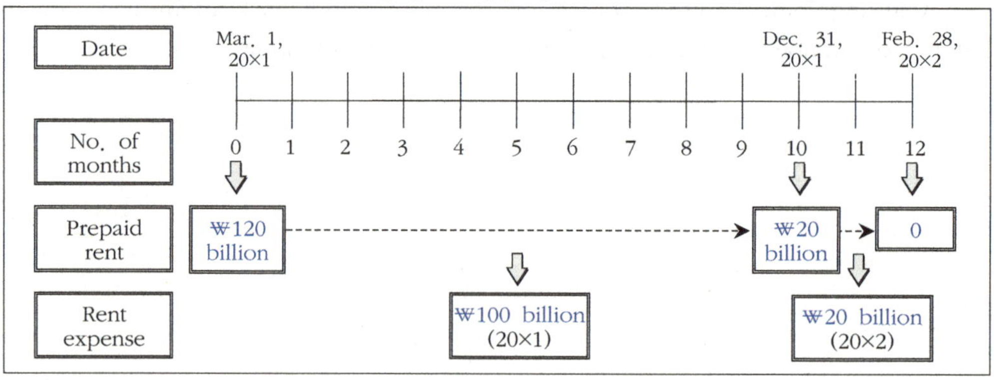

The 20×1 rent expense, from prepaid rent of ₩120 billion, represents the rent for 10 months (from March 1, 20×1 to December 31, 20×1) of ₩100 billion (₩120 billion × 10/12). Therefore, the following adjusting journal should be prepared.

ⓑ	(Dr.) Rent expense	100	(Cr.) Prepaid rent	100

3) Adjusting journal entry ⓒ—Rent receivable

〈Diagram 4-11〉 Rent revenue rent receivable

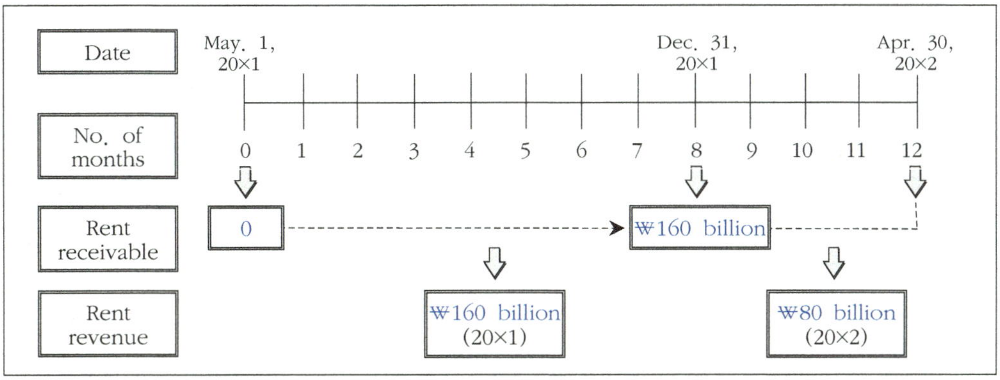

Rent revenue for 20×1, not yet received at the end of 20×1, is for 8 months' (from May 1, 20×1 to December 31, 20×1) rent of ₩160 billion (₩240 billion × 8/12). Therefore, the following adjusting journal entry should be prepared.

ⓒ	(Dr.) Rent receivable	160	(Cr.) Rent revenue	160

4) Adjusting journal entry ⓓ—Interest payable

〈Diagram 4-12〉 Interest expense and interest payable

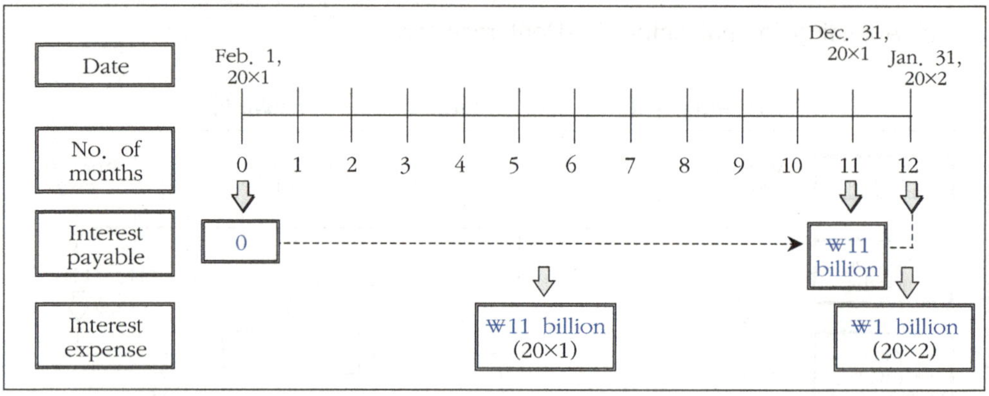

Interest expense for 20×1, not yet paid at the end of 20×1, are the interest for 11 months (from February 1, 20×1 to December 31, 20×1) of ₩11 billion (12 billion × 11/12). Therefore, the following adjusting journal entry should be prepared.

ⓓ	(Dr.) Interest expense	11	(Cr.) Interest payable	11

5) Adjusting journal entry ⓔ—Income tax payable

The income tax expense for 20×1 is estimated at ₩8 billion. Therefore, the following adjusting journal entry should be prepared. (Note : Because Chapter 3 deals with the accounting cycle (cash) without adjusting journal entries—by which accrued expenses such as income tax payable can be recorded—in that chapter it was assumed that all income tax expense was paid in cash in the current year).

ⓔ	(Dr.) Income tax expense	8	(Cr.) Income tax payable	8

The following 〈Table 4-12〉 gives a summary of the adjusting journal entries.

〈Table 4-12〉 Adjusting journal entries

(Numbers in billions of ₩)

ⓐ	(Dr.) Unearned rent	60	(Cr.) Rent revenue	60
ⓑ	(Dr.) Rent expense	100	(Cr.) Prepaid rent	100
ⓒ	(Dr.) Rent receivable	160	(Cr.) Rent revenue	160
ⓓ	(Dr.) Interest expense	11	(Cr.) Interest payable	11
ⓔ	(Dr.) Income tax expense	8	(Cr.) Income tax payable	8

(2) Posting adjusting journal entries

〈Diagram 4-13〉 General ledger after posting adjusting journal entries

(Numbers in billions of ₩)

Rent receivable

Debit	Credit	Balance
ⓒ 160		160(Dr.)

Prepaid rent

Debit	Credit	Balance
③ 120		120(Dr.)
	ⓑ 100	20(Dr.)

Interest payable

Debit	Credit	Balance
	ⓓ 11	11(Cr.)

Income tax payable

Debit	Credit	Balance
	ⓔ 8	8(Cr.)

Unearned rent

Debit	Credit	Balance
	④ 240	240(Cr.)
ⓐ 60		180(Cr.)

Rent revenue

Debit	Credit	Balance
	ⓐ 60	60(Cr.)
	ⓒ 160	220(Cr.)

Rent expense

Debit	Credit	Balance
ⓑ 100		100(Dr.)

Interest expense

Debit	Credit	Balance
ⓓ 11		11(Dr.)

Income tax expense

Debit	Credit	Balance
ⓔ 8		8(Dr.)

5 Preparing an adjusted trial balance

⟨Table 4-13⟩ Adjusted trial balance

Korea Real Estate December 31, 20×1 (Numbers in billions of ₩)

Dr.	Account titles	Cr.
190	Cash	
160	Rent receivable	
20	Prepaid rent	
	Interest payable	11
	Income tax payable	8
	Unearned rent	180
	Short-term borrowings	100
	Share capital-common stock	50
	Rent revenue	220
80	Salaries expense	
100	Rent expense	
11	Interest expense	
8	Income tax expense	
569	Total	569

6 Preparing an income statement and a statement of financial position

The following ⟨Table 4-14⟩ is the income statement prepared by using the adjusted trail balance.

⟨Table 4-14⟩ Income statement

Korea Real Estate From Jan. 1, 20×1 to Dec. 31, 20×1 (Numbers in billions of ₩)

Account titles	Amount	
Rent revenue		220
Operating expenses		(−)180
Salaries expense	(−)80	
Rent expense	(−)100	
Income from operations		40
Other expense		(−)11
Finance expense :		
Interest expense	(−)11	
Net income before income tax expense		29
Income tax expense		(−)8
Net income		21
Earnings per share*		₩2,100*

* ₩21 billion/10 million shares = ₩2,100

In general, the statement of financial position is prepared by using the post-closing trial balance. However, because the preparation of post-closing trial balance is omitted here, the following 〈Table 4-15〉 statement of financial position is prepared by using the adjusted trial balance and the income statement.

〈Table 4-15〉 Statement of financial position

Korea Real Estate As of December 31, 20×1 (Numbers in billion of ₩)

Account titles	Amount		Account titles	Amount	
Assets			**Liabilities**		
Current assets		370	**Current liabilities**		299
Cash	190		Interest payable	11	
Rent receivable	160		Income tax payable	8	
Prepaid rent	20		Unearned rent	180	
			Cost financial liability :		
			Short-term borrowings	100	
			Total liabilities		299
			Equity		
			Share capital		50
			Common stock	50	
			Retained earnings		21*
			Total equity		71
Total assets		370	**Total liabilities and equity**		370

* Net income in the income statement

◎ Section 4 Additional materials

Differences between statement of cash flows information and income statement information : When there is no beginning balance

1) Statement of cash flows

The following 〈Table 4-16〉 is an analysis of Korea Real Estate's cash account and 〈Table 4-17〉 is the statement of cash flows.

⟨Table 4-16⟩ Analysis of cash account

Cash (Numbers in billions of ₩)

T. No.	Activities	Opposite account	Amt.	T. No.	Activities	Opposite account	Amt.
①	Financing	Share capital-common stock	50	③	Operating	Prepaid rent	120
②	Financing	Short-term borrowings	100	⑥	Operating	Salaries expense	80
⑤	Operating	Unearned rent	240				

⟨Table 4-17⟩ Statement of cash flows

Korea Real Estate From Jan. 1, 20×1 to Dec. 31, 20×1 (Numbers in billions of ₩)

Description	Amount	
Cash flows from operating activities		
Cash receipts from customers	240	
Cash paid to suppliers and employees	(-)200	
Cash generated from operations	40	
Net cash from operating activities		40
Cash flows from financing activities		
Proceeds from issuing common stock	50	
Proceeds from short-term borrowings	100	
Net cash from financing activities		150
Net increase in cash		190
Cash at beginning of period		-
Cash at end of period		190

2) Differences between statement of cash flows information and income statement information : When there is no beginning balance

⟨Table 4-18⟩ shows the causes of the differences in information provided by the statement of cash flows and the income statement of Korean Real Estate in ⟨Illustration 4-7⟩.

〈Table 4-18〉 Differences between statement of cash flows information and income statement information : When there is no beginning balance

(Numbers in billions of ₩)

<table>
<tr><th colspan="3">Statement of cash flows</th><th colspan="2">Income statement</th><th colspan="2" rowspan="2">Difference Ⓐ－Ⓑ*</th><th>Cause of difference</th></tr>
<tr><th colspan="2">Description (T. No.)</th><th>Amount Ⓐ</th><th>Account titles</th><th>Amount Ⓑ</th><th>Account titles</th></tr>
<tr><td rowspan="2">Cash receipts from customers</td><td rowspan="2">Rent received ⑤</td><td rowspan="2">240</td><td rowspan="2">Rent revenue</td><td rowspan="2">220</td><td rowspan="2">20</td><td>(−)160</td><td>Rent receivable</td></tr>
<tr><td>180</td><td>Unearned rent</td></tr>
<tr><td rowspan="2">Cash paid to suppliers and employees</td><td>Rent paid ③</td><td>(−)120</td><td>Rent expense</td><td>(−)100</td><td colspan="2">(−)20</td><td>Prepaid rent</td></tr>
<tr><td>Salaries paid ⑥</td><td>(−)80</td><td>Salaries expense</td><td>(−)80</td><td colspan="2">-</td><td></td></tr>
<tr><td colspan="2">Income tax paid</td><td>-</td><td>Income tax expense</td><td>(−)8</td><td colspan="2">8</td><td>Income tax payable</td></tr>
<tr><td colspan="2">Interest paid</td><td>-</td><td>Interest expense</td><td>(−)11</td><td colspan="2">11</td><td>Interest payable</td></tr>
</table>

* If it is a minus, the cause of difference is an asset. If it is a plus, the cause of difference is a liability.

The cash receipt from customers of ₩240 billion, in the statement of cash flows, is different from the rent revenue of ₩220 billion in the income statement. This is because there is unearned rent of ₩180 billion (which was received in cash but not included in the 20×1 rent revenue) and rent receivable of ₩160 billion (which is included in the 20×1 rent revenue but has not yet been received in cash). These unearned rent and rent receivable are reported as a current liability and a current asset in the statement of financial position, respectively. Cash paid to suppliers and employees of ₩200 billion, in the statement of cash flows, is different from the operating expenses of ₩180 billion in the income statement. This is because there is prepaid rent of ₩20 billion, (which is paid in cash but not included in the 20×1 rent expense). This prepaid rent is reported as a current asset in the statement of financial position. Also, interest and income tax expenses are reported in the income statement, but interest paid and income tax paid are not reported in the statement of cash flows. This is because these interest and income tax expenses have not yet been paid at the end of 20×1. The interest payable and income tax payable are reported as current liabilities in the statement of financial position.

As in 〈Illustration 4-7〉, in the case of the founding year—when there is no beginning balance in the statement of financial position accounts—the differences between the statement of cash flows and the income statement appear as balances in accrued revenue, unearned revenue, accrued expense, and prepaid expense accounts. For the case of the years that follow the founding year—when there are beginning balances in the statement of financial position accounts—the differences between the statement of cash flows and the income statement will be reviewed in detail in Chapter 5, Section 1, under 'Additional materials.'

IFRS references (http://www.kasb.or.kr)

[1] *The Conceptual Framework for Financial Reporting*, par. 4.47.
[2] IFRS 15 *Revenue from Contracts with Customers*, par. 31, 35(b).
[3] *Ibid*, par. 45.
[4] IAS 2 *Inventories*, par. 3(a).
[5] IFRS 15 *op. cit.*, par. 9(e), 15.
[6] *The Conceptual Framework for Financial Reporting*, par. 4.50.
[7] IAS 2 *op. cit.*, par. BC9, 14.

Key terms

Accrual basis (발생주의) : An accounting method that computes net income or loss by recognizing revenue and expense when the causes occur. (p.140)

Accrued expense (미지급비용) : Expense that has occurred but not yet been paid, and is reported as a liability. (p.159)

Accrued revenue (미수수익) : Revenue that has incurred but not yet been received, and is reported as an asset. (p.152)

Adjusted trial balance (수정후시산표) : A trial balance that is prepared after adjusting journal entries are posted. (p.176)

Adjusting journal entries (수정분개) : Journal entries to adjust revenue, expense and the related assets and liabilities account balances, to the amount that should be reported on the accrual basis income statement and statement of financial position. (p.151)

Cash basis (현금주의) : An accounting method that computes net income or loss by recognizing revenue and expense at the points of cash inflow and cash outflow. (p.140)

Period matching (기간대응) : Recognizing expense based on the time elapsed, to match the current year's revenue. (p.149)

Prepaid expense (선급비용) : Cash that is paid before expense is recognized, and is reported as an asset. (p.163)

Recognition (인식) : An act of deciding when and by how much transactions are to be recorded on accounting books and reported in financial statements. (p.140)

Revenue recognition principle (수익인식기준) : A principle requiring that a revenue should be recognized when ⓐ the amount can be reliably measured, and ⓑ the possibility of inflow of economic benefits is high. (p.145)

Revenue-expense matching principle (수익 · 비용 대응기준) : A principle requiring that an expense that occurred to generate a certain revenue should be recognized during the period in which the revenue was recognized. (p.149)

Unearned revenue (선수수익) : Cash that is received before revenue is recognized, and is reported as a liability. (p.156)

Exercises

1. Cash basis and accrual basis

Daehan Consulting Company was founded on April 1, 20×1. The following is the information concerning the operating activities of Daehan Consulting Company for April 20×1.

① Consulting services provided in April were for ₩40 billion, and ₩35 billion of that was received in cash in April.

② Salaries for April were ₩15 billion, and ₩12 billion of that was paid in cash in April.

③ Rent expense for April was ₩6 billion, and this amount will be paid in May.

④ Insurance premium of ₩3 billion for April was paid on April 1, and insurance premium of ₩4 billion for May was prepaid at the end of April.

⑤ Cash paid for advertisement in April was ₩8 billion ; 25% was for April, and the remaining 75% was for May.

《Questions》

(1) Calculate accrual basis net income for April 20×1.

(2) Calculate cash basis net income for April 20×1.

2. Adjusting journal entries ①

The following are a part of the journal entries of Korea Realtor in 20×1. Korea Realtor's fiscal year ends on December 31.

(Numbers in billions of ₩)

T No.	Date	Dr.		Cr.	
①	April 1	Prepaid insurance	6	Cash	6
②	June 1	Cash	48	Unearned rent	48

(Additional information)

(a) Insurance premium for building, paid on March 1 by transaction ①, was for 1 year, from March 1 to February 28 of the following year.

(b) Building rent, received on June 1 by transaction ②, was for 1 year from June 1 to May 31 of next year.

(c) Made a loan of ₩100 billion on July 1 at an interest rate of 12% per annum. Interest will be received on June 30 of next year, the maturity date of the loan.

(d) Borrowed ₩200 billion on October 1 at an interest rate of 10% per annum. Interest will be paid on September 30 of next year, the maturity date of the borrowing.

《Question》 List adjusting journal entries that Korea Realtor should prepare on December 31, 20×1.

3. Adjusting journal entries ②

The fiscal year of all the companies shown below ends December 31.

(1) Hankook Company rented an office building on April 1, 20×1 and paid 1 year rent of ₩36 billion in advance. The company recorded the rent paid on its prepaid rent account.

(2) Daehan Company leased its building on May 1, 20×1 and received one year's rent of ₩12 billion in advance. The company recorded the rent received on its unearned rent account.

(3) Korea Company borrowed ₩240 billion on June 1, 20×1 for 1 year. The interest rate is 10% per annum and the interest is to be paid on the maturity date of the borrowing.

(4) Namhan Company made a loan of ₩480 billion on August 1, 20×1 for 1 year. Interest rate is 10% per annum and interest is to be received on the maturity date of the loan.

《Question》

Write down journal entries that each company should prepare on the dates listed below.

(1) Hankook Company
- 1) April 1, 20×1　　2) December 31, 20×1 (adjustment)

(2) Daehan Company
- 1) May 1, 20×1　　2) December 31, 20×1 (adjustment)

(3) Korea Company
- 1) June 1, 20×1　　2) December 31, 20×1 (adjustment)
- 3) May 31, 20×2

(4) Namhan Company
- 1) August 1, 20×1　　2) December 31, 20×1 (adjustment)
- 3) July 31, 20×2

4. Guessing adjusting journal entries

The following are the trial balance, income statement, and statement of financial position of Woojoo Mart for 20×1.

Trial balance

Woojoo Mart　　December 31, 20×1　　(Numbers in billions of ₩)

Dr.	Account titles	Cr.
12	Cash	
23	Trade receivables	
40	Short-term loans	
9	Prepaid insurance	
11	Merchandise	
80	Land	
	Trade payables	26
	Unearned rent	10
	Short-term borrowings	20
	Share capital-common stock	55
	Retained earnings	49
	Sales	82
46	Cost of goods sold	
15	Salaries expense	
6	Advertising expense	
242	Total	242

Income statement

Woojoo Mart From Jan. 1, 20×1 to Dec. 31, 20×1 (Numbers in billions of ₩)

Account titles	Amount	
Sales		82
Cost of goods sold		(−)46
Gross profit		36
Operating expenses		(−)25
Salaries expense	(−)15	
Advertising expense	(−)6	
Insurance expense	(−)4	
Other operating revenue		4
Rent revenue	4	
Income from operations		15
Other revenue		3
Interest revenue	3	
Other expense		(−)2
Finance expense :		
Interest expense	(−)2	
Net Income		16
Earnings per share		₩1,600

Statement of financial position

Woojoo Mart As of December 31, 20×1 (Numbers in billions of ₩)

Account titles	Amount		Account titles	Amount	
Assets			Liabilities		
Current assets		94	Current liabilities		54
Cash	12		Trade payables	26	
Trade receivables	23		Interest payable	2	
Interest receivable	3		Unearned rent	6	
Cost financial assets :			Cost financial liabilities :		
Short-term loans	40		Short-term borrowings	20	
Prepaid insurance	5		Total liabilities		54
Inventory :			Equity		
Merchandise	11		Share capital		55
Non-current asset		80	Common stock	55	
Tangible asset :			Retained earnings		65
Land	80		Total equity		120
Total assets		174	Total liabilities and equity		174

《Question》

Guess the adjusting journal entries of Woojoo Mart for 20×1.

5. Preparing adjusting journal entries and financial statements

The following is Hankook Realtor's trial balance at the end of 20×1.

Trial balance

Hankook Realtor December 31, 20×1 (Numbers in billions of ₩)

Dr.	Account titles	Cr.
78	Cash	
350	Prepaid rent	
	Unearned rent	100
	Short-term borrowings	120
	Share capital-common stock	190
	Rent revenue	140
110	Salaries expense	
12	Advertising expense	
550	Total	550

Additional information needed to prepare adjusting journal entries is as below.

ⓐ Interest payable at the end of 20×1 is ₩22 billion.

ⓑ Prepaid rent to be recognized as expense is ₩120 billion.

ⓒ Rent receivable at the end of 20×1 is ₩200 billion.

ⓓ Unearned rent to be recognized as revenue is ₩40 billion.

《Questions》

(1) Prepare adjusting journal entries.

(2) Prepare an adjusted trial balance.

(3) Prepare an income statement.

(4) Prepare a statement of financial position.

6. Accounting cycle (accrual)—a service company : When there is no beginning balance

Ohsung Consulting was established in 20×1. The following are the accounting transactions of Ohsung Consulting in 20×1.

Date	Transactions
Jan. 2	Issued 100 million shares of common stock at par value of ₩1,000 and received ₩100 billion in cash.
Mar. 1	Rented a building for 1 year and received one year's rent of ₩12 billion in advance.
Apr. 15	Provided consulting services for 2 months from February 15 and received service fees of the ₩20 billion in cash.
Apr. 20	Purchased a piece of land and paid ₩40 billion in cash.
Apr. 30	Made a loan of ₩50 billion to Seoul Industry, Inc., for 3 years. The interest rate is 12% per annum, and Ohsung Consulting received one year's interest of ₩6 billion in advance.
May 1	Signed an advertising contract with Daehan Broadcasting Company for one year. Annual advertising fee is ₩6 billion and it is to be paid on April 30, 20×2.
Nov. 1	Signed a contract with Bada Chemical Inc. to provide management consulting services for the next 3 months. Consulting fees of ₩12 billion are to be received on January 31, 20×2. Two-thirds of the total services were provided in 20×1.
Dec. 31	Paid employees' salaries of ₩9 billion for 20×1 in cash.

6-1. Journalizing, posting, preparing a trial balance

《Questions》

(1) Journalize the above transaction.

(2) Post journal entries on balance column T accounts.

(3) Prepare a trial balance.

6-2. Preparing adjusting journal entries, posting, preparing an adjusted trial balance

The following is a summary of the trial balance.

Summary of trial balance

(Numbers in billions of ₩)

Account titles	Amount	Account titles	Amount
Cash	15	Prepaid rent	12
Long-term borrowings	50	Land	40
Unearned interest	6	Share capital-common stock	100
Service fees revenue	20	Salaries expense	9

Note : All account balances are normal balances.

《Questions》

(1) Find the adjusting items and journalize them. Note that the income tax expense for 20×1 is estimated to be ₩3 billion and it will be paid in the next year, 20×2.
(2) Post the adjusting journal entries.
(3) Prepare an adjusted trail balance.

6-3. Preparing an income statement and a statement of financial position

The following is a summary of the adjusted trial balance.

Summary of adjusted trial balance

(Numbers in billions of ₩)

Account titles	Amount	Account titles	Amount
Cash	15	Service fees receivable	8
Prepaid rent	2	Long-term loans	50
Land	40	Advertising fees payable	4
Income tax payable	3	Unearned interest	2
Share capital-common stock	100	Service fees revenue	28
Interest revenue	4	Salaries expense	9
Rent expense	10	Advertising expense	4
Income tax expense	3		

Note : All account balances are normal balances.

《Questions》

(1) Prepare an income statement.
(2) Prepare a statement of financial position.

6-4. Differences between the statement of cash flows information and income statement information

《Questions》

(1) 1) Analyse the cash account and 2) prepare a statement of cash flows. (Assume that no exception is allowed in classifying items reported in the statement of cash flows).
(2) Compute the differences between the statement of cash flows information and income statement information, and describe the causes of these differences using the statement of financial position accounts.*

* The level of difficulty is high.

Comprehensive Illustration of Preparing and Using Financial Statements

Section 1 A comprehensive illustration of preparing financial statements

Section 2 A comprehensive illustration of using financial statements

Chapter 5 Overview

In this chapter, the process of preparing financial statements when there are beginning balances and adjusting journal entries to be prepared is examined using a comprehensive illustration. After financial statements are prepared, the differences between the information in the statement of cash flows and in the income statement are examined according to the types of adjusting journal entries. Next, we explain the basic financial ratios by which we can analyze financial statements.

A comprehensive illustration of preparing financial statements

As summarized in ⟨Table 5-1⟩ below, in Chapter 3, we reviewed accounting cycles (cash) without adjusting journal entries of various types. These included a service company, (when there was no beginning balance); merchandising companies (when there was no beginning balances and when there were beginning balances). In Chapter 4, we mainly reviewed adjusting entries for a service company (when there was no beginning balance). In this chapter, we will review the accounting cycle (accrual) of a merchandising company, where adjusting journal entries are required (when there are beginning balances). The financial statements to be reviewed are the income statement and the statement of financial position, which are affected by the adjusting journal entries. In addition, we will explain the causes of the differences between the information shown in the statement of cash flows and the income statement, according to the types of adjusting journal entries.

⟨Table 5-1⟩ Types reviewed

<table>
<tr><th colspan="4">Service company</th></tr>
<tr><th colspan="2" rowspan="3">Types</th><th colspan="2">Adjusting journal entries</th></tr>
<tr><th>-</th><th>Added</th></tr>
<tr><th>Accounting cycle (cash)</th><th>Accounting cycle (accrual)</th></tr>
<tr><td rowspan="2">Beginning balances</td><td>No</td><td>Chapter 3</td><td>Chapter 4</td></tr>
<tr><td>Yes</td><td>-</td><td>-</td></tr>
<tr><th colspan="4">Merchandising company</th></tr>
<tr><th colspan="2" rowspan="3">Types</th><th colspan="2">Adjusting journal entries</th></tr>
<tr><th>-</th><th>Added</th></tr>
<tr><th>Accounting cycle (cash)</th><th>Accounting cycle (accrual)</th></tr>
<tr><td rowspan="2">Beginning balances</td><td>No</td><td>Chapter 3</td><td>-</td></tr>
<tr><td>Yes</td><td>Chapter 3</td><td>This chapter</td></tr>
</table>

〈Illustration 5-1〉 Accounting cycle (accrual)—a merchandising company : When there are beginning balances

The following 〈Table 5-2〉 and 〈Table 5-3〉 are a statement of financial position of Hankook Department Store (HDS) at the end of 20×1 and a summary of transactions occurred in 20×2, respectively. HDS issued 10 million shares of common stock with par value of ₩5,000 at the beginning of 20×1, its founding year.

〈Table 5-2〉 Statement of financial position

HDS As of December 31 20×1 (Numbers in billions of ₩)

Account titles	Amount		Account titles	Amount	
Assets			**Liabilities**		
Current assets		42	**Current liabilities**		37
Cash	6		Trade payables	15	
Trade receivables	22		Interest payable	10	
Interest receivable	2		Income taxes payable	6	
Prepaid rent	2		Unearned rent	6	
Inventory :			**Non-current liability**		100
Merchandise	10		**Cost financial liability :**		
Non-current assets		160	Long-term borrowings	100	
Cost financial asset :			**Total liabilities**		137
Long-term loans	40		**Equity**		
Tangible asset :			**Share capital**		50
Land	120		Common stock	50	
			Retained earnings		15
			Total equity		65
Total assets		202	**Total liabilities and equity**		202

〈Table 5-3〉 Summary of transactions

T. No.	Dates	Transactions
①	Feb. 1	Purchased merchandise at ₩172 billion on credit.
②	Feb. 10	Sold merchandise costing ₩100 billion at ₩150 billion in cash.
③	Feb. 20	Purchased merchandise at ₩70 billion in cash.
④	Feb. 28	For ₩100 billion borrowing from A Bank, paid interest of ₩12 billion for 1 year from March 1, 20×1 in cash. Interest payable of ₩10 billion was recorded at the end of 20×1.
⑤	Mar. 1	Prepaid store rent of ₩18 billion for 1 year starting from March 1, 20×2.
⑥	Mar. 2	Sold merchandise costing ₩140 billion at ₩160 billion on credit.
⑦	Apr. 15	Paid income tax of ₩6 billion for 20×1 in cash.
⑧	Apr. 16	Paid dividends of ₩2 billion in cash. (₩200 per share of common stock × 10 million shares)
⑨	Apr. 30	Collected trade receivables of ₩143 billion in cash.
⑩	May. 15	Paid trade payables of ₩165 billion.
⑪	Jun. 30	For long-term loan of ₩40 billion to P Supplier, received interest of ₩4 billion for 1 year starting from July 1, 20×1. Interest receivable of ₩2 billion was recorded at the end of 20×1.
⑫	Jul. 1	Made a loan of ₩20 billion to Q Supplier for 5 years.
⑬	Jul. 1	Borrowed ₩20 billion from B Bank for 5 years.
⑭	Oct. 1	Received in advance rent of ₩12 billion for 1 year, starting from October 1, 20×2.
⑮	Oct. 30	Purchased a piece of land and paid ₩10 billion in cash.
⑯	Dec. 30	Paid employees' salaries of ₩25 billion for 20×2 in cash.

1 Journal entries

〈Table 5-4〉 Journal entries

(Numbers in billions of ₩)

①		(Dr.) Merchandise	172	(Cr.) Trade payables	172
②	②a	(Dr.) Cash	150	(Cr.) Sales	150
②	②b	(Dr.) Cost of goods sold	100	(Cr.) Merchandise	100
③		(Dr.) Merchandise	70	(Cr.) Cash	70
④		(Dr.) Interest payable Interest expense	10 2	(Cr.) Cash	12
⑤		(Dr.) Prepaid rent	18	(Cr.) Cash	18
⑥	⑥a	(Dr.) Trade receivables	160	(Cr.) Sales	160
⑥	⑥b	(Dr.) Cost of goods sold	140	(Cr.) Merchandise	140
⑦		(Dr.) Income tax payable	6	(Cr.) Cash	6
⑧		(Dr.) Dividends	2	(Cr.) Cash	2
⑨		(Dr.) Cash	143	(Cr.) Trade receivables	143
⑩		(Dr.) Trade payables	165	(Cr.) Cash	165
⑪		(Dr.) Cash	4	(Cr.) Interest receivable Interest revenue	2 2
⑫		(Dr.) Long-term loans	20	(Cr.) Cash	20
⑬		(Dr.) Cash	20	(Cr.) Long-term borrowings	20
⑭		(Dr.) Cash	12	(Cr.) Unearned rent	12
⑮		(Dr.) Land	10	(Cr.) Cash	10
⑯		(Dr.) Salaries expense	25	(Cr.) Cash	25

Types of transactions not reviewed in Chapter 4 are Transaction ① (purchase of merchandise on credit), Transaction ⑩ (payment of trade payables), Transaction ⑥ (sales of merchandise on credit), Transaction ⑨ (collection of trade receivables), Transaction ④ (payment of interest payable), Transaction ⑪ (receipt of interest receivable), and Transaction ⑦ (payment of income tax payable).

Transactions ① and ⑩ are transactions with trade payables, carried out by purchasing merchandise on credit and paying off that trade payables. The trade payables in these transactions are liabilities with the same characteristics of an accrued expense. An increase in liability should be recorded on the credit side and a decrease should be recorded on the debit side. (Trade payables will be reviewed in detail in Chapter 7).

Transactions ⑥ and ⑨ are transactions with trade receivables, carried out by selling merchandise on credit and collecting those trade receivables. The trade receivables in these transactions are an asset, with the same characteristics as accrued revenue. An increase in asset should be recorded on the debit side and a decrease should be recorded on the credit side. (Trade receivables will be reviewed in detail in Chapter 6).

Transaction ④ is a transaction paying 1 year's interest of ₩12 billion, from March 1, 20×1 to February 28, 20×2, on a debt of ₩100 billion borrowed from A Bank. Out of ₩12 billion interest paid, the interest of ₩10 billion for 10 months, from March 1, 20×1 to December 31, 20×1, was the interest expense for 20×1. As such, it was reported as an interest payable in the statement of financial position at the end of 20×1. Out of the ₩12 billion interest paid, 2 months' interest of ₩2 billion from January 1, 20×2 to February 28, 20×2 was the interest expense for 20×2. In sum, interest of ₩12 billion was paid for an interest payable of ₩10 billion and an interest expense of ₩2 billion for 20×2. Therefore, ₩10 billion should be recorded on the debit side of the interest payable account and ₩2 billion should be recorded on the debit side of the interest expense account.

Transaction ⑪ is a transaction receiving 1 year's interest of ₩4 billion, from July 1, 20×1 to June 30, 20×2, for a loan of ₩40 billion to P Supplier. Out of ₩4 billion of interest received, the interest of ₩2 billion for 6 months (from July 1, 20×1 to December 31, 20×1) was interest revenue for 20×1 and was reported as an interest receivable in the statement of financial position at the end 20×1. Out of ₩4 billion in interest paid, 6 months' interest of ₩2 billion from January 1, 20×2 to June 30, 20×2 was interest revenue for 20×2. In sum, interest of ₩4 billion was received for an interest receivable of ₩2 billion and an interest revenue of ₩2 billion for 20×2. Therefore, ₩2 billion should be recorded on the credit side of the interest receivable account and ₩2 billion should be recorded on the credit side of the interest revenue account.

Transaction ⑦ is that of paying income tax of ₩6 billion for 20×1. Income tax for 20×1 was reported as an income tax payable in the statement of financial position at the end of 20×1. Therefore, ₩6 billion should be recorded on the debit side of the income tax payable account.

2 Posting

⟨Diagram 5-1⟩ Posting journal entries

(Numbers in billions of ₩)

Cash

Debit	Credit	Balance
Beginning		6(Dr.)
②a 150		156(Dr.)
	③ 70	86(Dr.)
	④ 12	74(Dr.)
	⑤ 18	56(Dr.)
	⑦ 6	50(Dr.)
	⑧ 2	48(Dr.)
⑨ 143		191(Dr.)
	⑩ 165	26(Dr.)
⑪ 4		30(Dr.)
	⑫ 20	10(Dr.)
⑬ 20		30(Dr.)
⑭ 12		42(Dr.)
	⑮ 10	32(Dr.)
	⑯ 25	7(Dr.)

Trade receivables

Debit	Credit	Balance
Beginning		22(Dr.)
⑥a 160		182(Dr.)
	⑨ 143	39(Dr.)

Interest receivable

Debit	Credit	Balance
Beginning		2(Dr.)
	⑪ 2	–

Prepaid rent

Debit	Credit	Balance
Beginning		2(Dr.)
⑤ 18		20(Dr.)

Merchandise

Debit	Credit	Balance
Beginning		10(Dr.)
① 172		182(Dr.)
	②b 100	82(Dr.)
③ 70		152(Dr.)
	⑥b 140	12(Dr.)

Long-term loans

Debit	Credit	Balance
Beginning		40(Dr.)
⑫ 20		60(Dr.)

Land

Debit	Credit	Balance
Beginning		120(Dr.)
⑮ 10		130(Dr.)

Trade payables

Debit	Credit	Balance
Beginning		15(Cr.)
	① 172	187(Cr.)
⑩ 165		22(Cr.)

Interest payable

Debit	Credit	Balance
Beginning		10(Cr.)
④ 10		–

Income tax payable

Beginning		6(Cr.)
	⑦ 6	–

Unearned rent

Beginning		6(Cr.)
	⑭ 12	18(Cr.)

Long-term borrowings

Beginning		100(Cr.)
	⑬ 20	120(Cr.)

Share capital-common stock

Beginning		50(Cr.)

Retained earnings

Beginning		15(Cr.)

Dividends

⑧ 2		2(Dr.)

Sales

	②a 150	150(Cr.)
	⑥a 160	310(Cr.)

Interest revenue

	⑪ 2	2(Cr.)

Cost of goods sold

②b 100		100(Dr.)
⑥b 140		240(Dr.)

Salaries expense

⑯ 25		25(Dr.)

Interest expense

④ 2		2(Dr.)

3 Preparing a trial balance

〈Table 5-5〉 Trial balance

HDS December 31, 20×2 (Numbers in billions of ₩)

Debit	Account titles	Credit
7	Cash	
39	Trade receivables	
20	Prepaid rent	
12	Merchandise	
60	Long-term loans	
130	Land	
	Trade payables	22
	Unearned rent	18
	Long-term borrowings	120
	Share capital-common stock	50
	Retained earnings	15
2	Dividends	
	Sales	310
	Interest revenue	2
240	Cost of goods sold	
25	Salaries expense	
2	Interest expense	
537	Total	537

4 Adjusting journal entries and posting

(1) Adjusting journal entries

The following 〈Table 5-6〉 is a summary of items requiring additional information to prepare adjusting journal entries.

〈Table 5-6〉 Items requiring additional information to prepare adjusting journal entries

	Items requiring additional information
ⓐ	Rent expense from prepaid rent of ₩20 billion.
ⓑ	Interest payable from long-term borrowings of ₩120 billion.
ⓒ	Interest receivable from long-term loans of ₩60 billion.
ⓓ	Rent revenue from unearned rent of ₩18 billion.
ⓔ	Income tax expense for 20×2.

1) Adjusting journal entry ⓐ : Prepaid rent

(Additional information)

Prepaid rent of ₩20 billion, reported in the trial balance, was composed of the balance at the end of 20×1 of ₩2 billion and ₩18 billion paid on March 1, 20×2. The balance, at the end of 20×1, of ₩2 billion was 2 months' rent from January 1, 20×2 to February 28, 20×2, out of ₩12 billion prepaid on March 1, 20×1. Rent of ₩18 billion, paid on March 1, 20×2, was 1 year's rent from March 1, 20×2 to February 28, 20×3.

(Computation of rent expense)

Rent expense for 20×2—computed based on the rent period—is ₩17 billion, as shown in 〈Table 5-7〉 below.

⟨Table 5-7⟩ Computation of rent expense

(Numbers in billions of ₩)

Prepaid rent before adjustment		Rent period	Rent expense for 20×2		
At end of 20×1	2	2 months (Jan. 1, 20×2 ~ Feb. 28, 20×2)	2 months (Same as left column)	2	2
Paid on March 1, 20×2	18	12 months (Mar. 1, 20×2 ~ Feb. 28, 20×3)	10 months (Mar. 1, 20×2 ~ Dec. 31, 20×2)	18×10/12	15
Total	20				17

(Adjusting Journal entry)

Therefore, the following adjusting journal entry should be prepared.

ⓐ	(Dr.) Rent expense	17	(Cr.) Prepaid rent	17

2) Adjusting journal entry ⓑ : Interest payable

(Additional information)

Long-term borrowings reported in the trial balance was ₩100 billion from A Bank and ₩20 billion from B Bank, for a total of ₩120 billion. The maturity date of the borrowing from A Bank was February 28, 20×6. The interest rate was 12% per annum, and interest for 1 year (from March 1 of the current year to February 28 of the following year) was to be paid on February 28 of the following year, each year. The maturity date of the borrowing from B Bank was June 30, 20×7. The interest rate was 10% per annum, and interest for 1 year (from July 1 of the current year to June 30 of the following year) was to be paid on June 30 of the following year, each year.

〈Table 5-8〉 Computation of interest payable

(Numbers in billions of ₩)

Long-term borrowings		Period of interest accrued	Interest payable at end of 20×2	
A Bank	100	10 months (Mar. 1, 20×2 ~ Dec. 31, 20×2)	100 × 12% × 10/12	10
B Bank	20	6 months (Jul. 1, 20×2 ~ Dec. 31, 20×3)	20 × 10% × 6/12	1
Total	120			11

(Adjusting journal entry)

ⓑ	(Dr.) Interest expense	11	(Cr.) Interest payable	11

3) Adjusting journal entry ⓒ : Interest receivable

(Additional information)

Long-term loans reported in the trial balance were ₩40 billion to P Supplier and ₩20 billion to Q Supplier, for a total of ₩60 billion. The maturity date of the loan to P Supplier was June 30, 20×6 and that of Q Supplier was June 30, 20×7. The interest rate on both was 10% per annum and interest for 1 year (from July 1 of current year to June 30 of the following year) was to be paid on June 30 of the following year, each year.

〈Table 5-9〉 Computation of interest receivable

(Numbers in billions of ₩)

Long-term loans		Period interest accrued	Interest receivable at end of 20×2	
P Supplier	40	6 months (Jul. 1, 20×2 ~ Dec. 31, 20×2)	40 × 10% × 6/12	2
Q Supplier	20	6 months (Jul. 1, 20×2 ~ Dec. 31, 20×2)	20 × 10% × 6/12	1
Total	60			3

(Adjusting journal entry)

ⓒ	(Dr.) Interest receivable	3	(Cr.) Interest revenue	3

4) Adjusting journal entry ⓓ : Unearned rent

(Additional information)

The unearned rent of ₩18 billion, reported in the trial balance, was composed of the balance at the end of 20×1 of ₩6 billion and ₩12 billion received on October 1, 20×2. The balance at the end of 20×1 of ₩6 billion was 9 months' rent (from January 1, 20×2 to September 30, 20×2) out of ₩8 billion pre-received on October 1, 20×1. Rent of ₩12 billion, received on October 1, 20×2, was 1 year's rent from October 1, 20×2 to September 30, 20×3.

〈Table 5-10〉 Computation of rent revenue

(Numbers in billions of ₩)

Unearned rent		Rent period	Rent revenue for 20×2		
At end of 20×1	6	9 months (Jan. 1, 20×2 ~ Sep. 30, 20×2)	9 months (Same as left column)	6	6
Received on October 1, 20×2	12	12 months (Oct. 1, 20×2 ~ Sep. 30, 20×3)	3 months (Oct. 1, 20×2 ~ Dec. 31, 20×2)	12 × 3/12	3
Total	18				9

(Adjusting Journal entry)

ⓓ	(Dr.) Unearned revenue	9	(Cr.) Rent revenue	9

5) Adjusting journal entry ⓔ : Income tax payable

(Additional information)

Income tax for 20×2 was estimated at ₩7 billion and will be paid in 20×3.

(Adjusting Journal entry)

ⓔ	(Dr.) Income tax expense	7	(Cr.) Income tax payable	7

The following ⟨Table 5-11⟩ is a summary of the above adjusting journal entries.

⟨Table 5-11⟩ Adjusting journal entries

(Numbers in billions of ₩)

ⓐ	(Dr.) Rent expense	17	(Cr.) Prepaid rent	17
ⓑ	(Dr.) Interest expense	11	(Cr.) Interest payable	11
ⓒ	(Dr.) Interest receivable	3	(Cr.) Interest revenue	3
ⓓ	(Dr.) Unearned rent	9	(Cr.) Rent revenue	9
ⓔ	(Dr.) Income tax expense	7	(Cr.) Income tax payable	7

⟨Box 5-1⟩ Adjusting journal entry when we initially record a prepaid expense as an expense

In general, when an expense is prepaid, we record it in prepaid expense account and adjust expense for the current year at the end of the year. But if almost of all of prepaid amount is expired during the current year, we record it in expense account rather than prepaid expense account. Only if unexpired portion is material at the end of the year, we prepare an adjusting journal entry to record it as a prepaid expense.

Supplies shown below could be a good example. In general, if we purchase supplies, we consume almost all of them so almost nothing left. Therefore, when we purchase supplies, we record on supplies expense account rather than supplies account. And when amount of supplies unused and remained on hand is immaterial (in most cases), we omit adjusting journal entry. Only if amount of supplies remained on hand is material, we prepare an adjusting entry to recognize those supplies.

In practice, when we pay a great number of **short-term insurance premium** (1~3 months) or a great number of **short-term rent** (1~3 months) in advance, we record them as expenses rather than as prepaid expenses same as we do for supplies. Because of the same reason, we record the revenue received in advance as revenue rather than as unearned revenue. A great number of short-term rent (1~3 months) or a great number of short-term service fees (1~3 months) received in advance are good examples of this kind.

⟨Example : Supplies⟩

(1) When we record purchase of supplies on supplies expense account

AB Co.'s 20×2 beginning supplies inventory was ₩1 billion. And AB Co. purchased supplies and paid ₩24 billion in 20×2.

(1.1) Assuming that the beginning supplies inventory remains on hand at the end of 20×2

The company anticipated that the supplies inventory remained on hand and all purchased supplies would be consumed and prepared the following journal entry.

① Recording purchase of supplies

(Numbers in billions of ₩)

(Dr.) Supplies expense	24	(Cr.) Cash	24

As a result of an examination of physical inventory of supplies at the end of 20×2, it was found that supplies inventory on hand was ₩3 billion.

⟨Table 5-12⟩ below shows that the supplies account and supplies expense account balances before adjustment ; the balances after the adjustment (amount to be reported in financial statements) ; and the difference between these balances, which are the amounts of the adjustment.

⟨Table 5-12⟩ Analysis of transactions—assuming (1) and (1.1)

(Numbers in billions of ₩)

Account titles	Balance before adjustment	Balance after adjustment	Adjustment
Supplies expense (Income statement)	24(Dr.)	22(Dr.)*	2(Cr.)
Supplies (Statement of financial position)	1(Dr.)	3(Dr.)	2(Dr.)

* 1 billion (beginning inventory) + 24 billion (purchase) − 3 billion (ending inventory) = ₩22 billion

② Adjusting journal entry

An adjusting journal entry to be prepared at the end of 20×2 is as follows.

December 31, 20×2 :

(Dr.) Supplies	2	(Cr.) Supplies expense	2

(1.2) Assuming the beginning supplies inventory will be consumed in 20×2

The company anticipated that the supplies inventory and all purchased supplies would be consumed and prepared the following two journal entries.

① Recoding consumption of the beginning supplies inventory

(Numbers in billions of ₩)

(Dr.) Supplies expense	1	(Cr.) Supplies	1

② Recording purchases of supplies

(Dr.) Supplies expense	24	(Cr.) Cash	24

〈Table 5-13〉 Analysis of transactions—assuming (1) and (1.2)

(Numbers in billions of ₩)

Account titles	Balance before adjustment	Balance after adjustment	Adjustment
Supplies expense (Income statement)	25(Dr.)*	22(Dr.)	3(Cr.)
Supplies (Statement of financial position)	-	3(Dr.)	3(Dr.)

* 1 billion (beginning inventory) + 24 billion (purchase) = ₩25 billion

③ Adjusting journal entries

December 31, 20×2 :

(Dr.) Supplies	3	(Cr.) Supplies expense	3

Journal entry ① above is a journal entry reversing an adjusting journal entry prepared at the end of 20×1. We explained the reversing journal entry in Chapter 4 〈Box 4-3〉 'Reversing journal entry—accrued revenue' and 〈Box 4-4〉 'Reversing journal entry—accrued expense.' At the beginning of 20×3, a journal entry reversing adjusting journal entry ③ should be prepared. If we prepare a reversing journal entry like this, it becomes easy to prepare the year end adjusting journal entry. [In case (1.2) of preparing the reversing journal entry, there is no need to check the beginning supplies inventory when we prepare the adjusting journal entry at the end of the year. However, in case (1.1) of not preparing the reversing journal entry, we must check the beginning supplies inventory when we prepare the adjusting journal entry at the end of the year.]

(2) When we record purchase of supplies on supplies account

The company recorded purchase of supplies on supplies account as shown below because the level of the ending supplies inventory is considered to be significant and tight control over supplies inventory is needed.

(Recording purchase of supplies)

(Numbers in billions of ₩)

(Dr.) Supplies	24	(Cr.) Cash	24

〈Table 5-14〉 Analysis of transactions–assuming (2)

(Numbers in billions of ₩)

Description	Balance before adjustment	Balance after adjustment	Adjustment
Supplies expense (Income statement)	–	22(Dr.)*	22(Dr.)
Supplies (Statement of financial position)	25(Dr.)*	3(Dr.)	22(Cr.)

* 1 billion (beginning inventory) + 24 billion (purchase) = ₩25 billion

(Adjusting journal entry)

December 31, 20×2 :

(Dr.) Supplies expense	22	(Cr.) Supplies	22

(2) Posting adjusting journal entries

⟨Diagram 5-2⟩ Posting adjusting journal entries

(Numbers in billions of ₩)

Interest receivable

Beginning		2(Dr.)
	⑪ 2	–
ⓒ 3		3(Dr.)

Prepaid rent

Beginning		2(Dr.)
⑤ 18		20(Dr.)
	ⓐ 17	3(Dr.)

Interest payable

Beginning		10(Cr.)
④ 10		–
	ⓑ 11	11(Cr.)

Income tax payable

Beginning		6(Cr.)
⑦ 6		–
	ⓔ 7	7(Cr.)

Unearned rent

Beginning		6(Cr.)
	⑭ 12	18(Cr.)
ⓓ 9		9(Cr.)

Rent revenue

	ⓓ 9	9(Cr.)

Interest revenue

	⑪ 2	2(Cr.)
	ⓒ 3	5(Cr.)

Rent expense

ⓐ 17		17(Dr.)

Interest expense

④ 2		2(Dr.)
ⓑ 11		13(Dr.)

Income tax expense

ⓔ 7		7(Dr.)

5 Preparing an adjusted trial balance

〈Table 5-15〉 Adjusted trial balance

KDS December 31, 20×2 (Numbers in billions of ₩)

Debit	Account titles	Credit
7	Cash	
39	Trade receivables	
3	Interest receivable	
3	Prepaid rent	
12	Merchandise	
60	Long-term loans	
130	Land	
	Trade payables	22
	Interest payable	11
	Income taxes payable	7
	Unearned rent	9
	Long-term borrowings	120
	Share capital-common stock	50
	Retained earnings	15
2	Dividends	
	Sales	310
	Rent revenue	9
	Interest revenue	5
240	Cost of goods sold	
25	Salaries expense	
17	Rent expense	
13	Interest expense	
7	Income tax expense	
558	Total	558

6 Preparing an income statement and a statement of financial position

The following ⟨Table 5-16⟩ is the income statement prepared by using the adjusted trial balance.

⟨Table 5-16⟩ Income statement

HDS From Jan. 1, 20×2 to Dec. 31 20×2 (Numbers in billions of ₩)

Account titles	Amount	
Sales		310
Cost of goods sold		(−)240
Gross profit		70
Operating expenses		(−)42
Salaries expense	(−)25	
Rent expense	(−)17	
Other operating revenue		9
Rent revenue	9	
Income from operations		37
Other revenue		5
Interest revenue	5	
Other expense		(−)13
Finance expense :		
Interest expense	(−)13	
Net income before income tax expense		29
Income tax expense		(−)7
Net income		22
Earnings per share		₩2,200*

* 22 billion / 10 million shares = ₩2,200

In general, the statement of financial position is prepared by using the post-closing trial balance. However, because the preparation of post-closing trial balance is omitted here, the following ⟨Table 5-17⟩ statement of financial position is prepared by using the adjusted trial balance and the income statement.

⟨Table 5-17⟩ Statement of financial position

HDS As of December 31, 20×2 (Numbers in billions of ₩)

Account titles	Amount		Account titles	Amount	
Assets			**Liabilities**		
Current assets		64	**Current liabilities**		49
Cash	7		Trade payables	22	
Trade receivables	39		Interest payable	11	
Interest receivable	3		Income taxes payable	7	
Prepaid rent	3		Unearned rent	9	
Inventory :			**Non-current liability**		120
Merchandise	12		**Cost financial liability :**		
Non-current assets		190	Long-term borrowings	120	
Cost financial asset :			**Total liabilities**		169
Long-term loans	60		**Equity**		
Tangible asset :			**Share capital**		50
Land	130		Common stock	50	
			Retained earnings		35*
			Total equity		85
Total assets		254	**Total liabilities and equity**		254

* Beginning balance + Net income − Dividends = 15 billion + 22 billion − 2 billion = ₩35 billion

◎ Section 1 Additional materials

Differences between the information shown in the statement of cash flows and the income statement—classification by types : When there are beginning balances

1. Statement of cash flows

The following 〈Table 5-18〉 is an analysis of cash account of Hankook Department store and 〈Table 5-19〉 is the statement of cash flows.

〈Table 5-18〉 Analysis of cash account

Cash

(Numbers in billions of ₩)

T. No.	Activities	Opposite account	Amt.	T. No.	Activities	Opposite account	Amt.
②	Operating	Sales	150	③	Operating	Merchandise	70
⑨	Operating	Trade receivables	143	④	Financing	Interest payable	10
						Interest expense	2
⑪	Investing	Interest revenue	2	⑤	Operating	Prepaid rent	18
		Interest receivable	2				
⑬	Financing	Long-term borrowings	20	⑦	Operating	Income tax payable	6
⑭	Operating	Unearned rent	12	⑧	Financing	Dividends	2
				⑩	Operating	Trade payables	165
				⑫	Investing	Long-term loans	20
				⑮	Investing	Land	10
				⑯	Operating	Salaries expense	25

〈Table 5-19〉 Statement of cash flows

HDS From Jan. 1, 20×2 to Dec. 31, 20×2 (Numbers in billions of ₩)

Description	Amount	
Cash flows from operating activities		
Cash receipts from customers	305	
Cash paid to suppliers and employees	(−)278	
Cash generated from operations	27	
Individually reporting item :		
Income tax paid	(−)6	
Net cash from operating activities		21
Cash flows from investing activities		
Individually reporting item :		
Interest received	4	
Acquisition of land	(−)10	
Long-term loans made	(−)20	
Net cash used for investing activities		(−)26
Cash flows from financing activities		
Proceeds from long-term borrowing	20	
Individually reporting items :		
Interest paid	(−)12	
Dividends paid	(−)2	
Net cash from financing activities		6
Net increase in cash		1
Cash at beginning of period		6
Cash at end of period		7

2. Differences between the statement of cash flows information and the income statement information—classification by types : When there are beginning balances

The following 〈Table 5-20〉 shows a summary of the differences between the information shown in the statement of cash flows and in the income statement of Hankook Department Store. We can classify these differences into four types. Here we explain the causes for each type of difference by conducting the T account analyses.

〈Table 5-20〉 Differences between the statement of cash flows information and the income statement information : When there are beginning balances

(Numbers in billions of ₩)

<table>
<tr><th colspan="3">Statement of cash flows</th><th colspan="2">Income statement</th><th colspan="2" rowspan="2">Difference
Ⓐ − Ⓑ*</th><th colspan="2">Cause of differences</th></tr>
<tr><th colspan="2">Description (T. No.)</th><th>Amount
Ⓐ</th><th>Account titles</th><th>Amount
Ⓑ</th><th>Changes in account balance</th><th>Types</th></tr>
<tr><td rowspan="2">Cash receipts from customers</td><td>Sales of merchandise—cash received ②⑨</td><td>293</td><td>Sales</td><td>310</td><td colspan="2">(−)17</td><td>Increase in trade receivables</td><td>(1)</td></tr>
<tr><td>Rent received ⑭</td><td>12</td><td>Rent revenue</td><td>9</td><td colspan="2">3</td><td>Increase in unearned rent</td><td>(2)</td></tr>
<tr><td rowspan="4">Cash paid to suppliers and employees</td><td rowspan="2">Purchases of merchandise—cash paid ③⑩</td><td rowspan="2">(−)235</td><td rowspan="2">Cost of goods sold</td><td rowspan="2">(−)240</td><td rowspan="2">5</td><td>7</td><td>Increase in trade payables</td><td>(3)</td></tr>
<tr><td>(−)2</td><td>Increase in merchandise</td><td>(4)</td></tr>
<tr><td>Rent paid ⑤</td><td>(−)18</td><td>Rent expense</td><td>(−)17</td><td colspan="2">(−)1</td><td>Increase in prepaid rent</td><td>(4)</td></tr>
<tr><td>Salaries paid ⑯</td><td>(−)25</td><td>Salaries expense</td><td>(−)25</td><td colspan="2">−</td><td></td><td></td></tr>
<tr><td colspan="2">Income tax paid ⑦</td><td>(−)6</td><td>Income tax expense</td><td>(−)7</td><td colspan="2">1</td><td>Increase in income tax payable</td><td>(3)</td></tr>
<tr><td colspan="2">Interest received ⑪</td><td>4</td><td>Interest revenue</td><td>5</td><td colspan="2">(−)1</td><td>Increase in interest receivable</td><td>(1)</td></tr>
<tr><td colspan="2">Interest paid ④</td><td>(−)12</td><td>Interest expense</td><td>(−)13</td><td colspan="2">1</td><td>Increase in interest payable</td><td>(3)</td></tr>
</table>

* If it is a minus, the cause of the difference is an increase in an asset or a decrease in a liability. If it is a plus, the cause of the difference is a decrease in an asset or an increase in a liability.

(1) Accrued revenue—Type (1)

1) Cash receipt and revenue when accrued revenue is reported.

Hankook Department Store's interest receivable at the beginning of 20×2 was ₩2 billion. In 20×2, transactions in the following ⟨Table 5-21⟩ were made.

⟨Table 5-21⟩ Transactions related with interest receivable

T No.	Transactions
⑪	Received interest of ₩4 billion in cash.
ⓒ	Interest receivable at the end of 20×1 was ₩3 billion.

Therefore, journal entries in the following ⟨Table 5-22⟩ were prepared. For the sake of analysis, transaction ⑪ is divided into the collection of interest receivable (⑪-1) and the interest revenue received in cash (⑪-2).

⟨Table 5-22⟩ Journal entries related with interest receivable

(Numbers in billions of ₩)

⑪-1	(Dr.)	Cash	2	(Cr.)	Interest receivable	2
⑪-2	(Dr.)	Cash	2	(Cr.)	Interest revenue	2
ⓒ	(Dr.)	Interest receivable	3	(Cr.)	Interest revenue	3

The following ⟨Diagram 5-3⟩ is the interest receivable account after recording the beginning balance and posting journal entries of ⑪-1 and ⓑ.

⟨Diagram 5-3⟩ Interest receivable

		Beginning 2(Dr.)
	⑪-1 Interest received 2	–
ⓒ Interest revenue 3		Ending 3(Dr.)

The contents of the interest receivable account can be summarized as the following.

Beg. interest receivable	−	Interest received	+	Interest revenue	=	End. interest receivable
2	−	2	+	3	=	3

If interest revenue received in cash of ₩2 billion from journal entry ⑪-2 is added to the above equation, the following equation can be made.

Beg. interest receivable	−	Interest received	+	Interest revenue	=	End. interest receivable
2	−	(2 + 2)	+	(3 + 2)	=	3
2	−	4	+	5	=	3

The above equation can be rearranged as an equation to compute cash inflow, as shown below.

Interest received	=	Interest revenue	−	(End. interest receivable	−	Beg. interest receivable)
4	=	5	−	(3	−	2)

If the difference between the ending balance and beginning balance of interest receivable is converted as an increase in interest receivable, the following equation can be obtained.

Interest received	=	Interest revenue	−	Increase in interest receivable
4	=	5	−	1

When interest receivable decreases, the following equation is made.

Interest received = Interest revenue + Decrease in interest receivable

2) Cash receipts from sales of merchandise and sales

The difference of ₩17 billion between cash receipts from sales of merchandise of ₩293 billion (Transaction ② ₩150 billion + Transaction ⑨ ₩143 billion), which was included in cash receipts from customers in the statement of cash flows and sales of ₩310 billion in the income statement, was caused by an increase in trade receivables. The relationship among these items can be classified as Type (1) in the following equation, treating trade receivables as accrued revenue.

Cash receipts from sales of merchandise	=	Sales	−	Increase in trade receivables
2,930	=	3,100	−	170

When trade receivables decrease, the following equation is made.

Cash receipts from sales of merchandise = Sales + Decrease in trade receivables

(2) Unearned revenue—Type (2)

1) Rent received and rent revenue when unearned rent is reported

Hankook Department Store's unearned rent at the beginning of 20×2 was ₩6 billion. During 20×2, transactions in the following ⟨Table 5-23⟩ were made.

⟨Table 5-23⟩ Transactions related with unearned rent

T No.	Transactions
⑭	Received rent of ₩12 billion in cash in advance.
ⓓ	Unearned rent to be recognized as rent revenue was ₩9 billion.

Therefore, journal entries in the following ⟨Table 5-24⟩ were prepared.

⟨Table 5-24⟩ Journal entries related with unearned rent

(Numbers in billions of ₩)

⑭	(Dr.)	Cash	12	(Cr.)	Unearned rent	12
ⓓ	(Dr.)	Unearned rent	9	(Cr.)	Rent revenue	9

The following ⟨Diagram 5-4⟩ is the unearned rent account after recording the beginning balance and posting the above journal entries.

⟨Diagram 5-4⟩ Unearned rent

		Beginning 6(Cr.)
	⑭ Rent received 12	18(Cr.)
ⓓ Rent revenue 9		Ending 9(Cr.)

The contents of the unearned rent account can be summarized as the following.

Beg. unearned rent + Rent received − Rent revenue = End. unearned rent
6 + 12 − 9 = 9

The above equation can be rearranged as an equation to compute cash inflows, as shown below.

Rent received = Rent revenue + (End. unearned rent − Beg. unearned rent)
12 = 9 + (9 − 6)

If the difference between the ending balance and the ending balance of unearned rent is converted as an increase in unearned rent, the following equation can be obtained.

Rent received = Rent revenue + Increase in unearned rent
12 = 9 + 3

When unearned rent decreases, the following equation is made.

Rent received = Rent revenue − Decrease in unearned rent

(3) Accrued expense—Type (3)

1) Interest paid and interest expense when interest payable is reported.

Hankook Department Store's interest payable at the beginning of 20×2 was ₩10 billion. In 20×2, transactions in the following ⟨Table 5-25⟩ were made.

⟨Table 5-25⟩ Transaction related with interest payable

T No.	Transactions
④	Paid interest of ₩12 billion in cash.
ⓑ	Interest payable at the end of 20×1 was ₩11billion.

Therefore, journal entries in the following ⟨Table 5-26⟩ were prepared. For the sake of analysis, transaction ④ is divided into payment of interest payable (④-1) and interest expense paid in cash (④-2).

⟨Table 5-26⟩ Journal entries related with interest payable

(Numbers in billions of ₩)

④-1	(Dr.)	Interest payable	10	(Cr.)	Cash	10
④-2	(Dr.)	Interest expense	2	(Cr.)	Cash	2
ⓑ	(Dr.)	Interest expense	11	(Cr.)	Interest payable	11

The following ⟨Diagram 5-5⟩ is the interest payable account after recording the beginning balance and posting the above entries of ④-1 and ⓑ.

⟨Diagram 5-5⟩ Interest payable

(Numbers in billions of ₩)

		Beginning 10(Cr.)
④-1 Interest paid 10		–
	ⓑ Interest expense 11	Ending 11(Cr.)

The contents of the interest payable account can be summarized as the following.

Beg. interest payable	−	Interest paid	+	Interest expense	=	End. interest payable
10	−	10	+	11	=	11

If the interest expense paid in cash of ₩2 billion, from journal entry ④-2, is added to the above equation, the following equation can be made.

Beg. interest payable	−	Interest paid	+	Interest expense	=	End. interest payable
10	−	(10 + 2)	+	(11 + 2)	=	11
10	−	12	+	13	=	11

The above equation can be rearranged as an equation to compute cash outflows, as shown below.

Interest paid	=	Interest expense	−	(End. interest payable	−	Beg. interest payable)
12	=	13	−	(11	−	10)

If the difference between the ending balance and the beginning balance of interest payable is converted as a decrease in interest payable, the following equation can be obtained.

Interest paid	=	Interest expense	−	Increase in interest payable
12	=	13	−	1

When interest payable increases, the following equation is made.

Interest paid = Interest expense + Decrease in interest payable

2) Income tax paid and income tax expense, when income tax payable is reported

Income tax payable is an accrued expense. Therefore, the difference of ₩1 billion between the income tax paid of ₩6 billion, in the statement of cash flows, and the income tax expense of ₩7 billion, in the income statement, can be expressed as the following.

Income tax paid	=	Income tax expense	−	Increase in income tax payable
6	=	7	−	1

When income tax payable increases, the following equation is made.

Income tax paid = Income tax expense + Decrease in income tax payable

(4) Prepaid expense—Type (4)

1) Rent paid and rent expense when prepaid rent is reported

Hankook Department Store's prepaid rent at the beginning of 20×2 was ₩2 billion. During 20×2, transactions in the following ⟨Table 5-27⟩ were made.

⟨Table 5-27⟩ Transactions related with prepaid rent

T No.	Transactions
①	Paid rent of ₩18 billion in cash in advance.
②	Prepaid rent to be recognized as rent expense was ₩17 billion.

Therefore, journal entries in the following ⟨Table 5-28⟩ were prepared.

⟨Table 5-28⟩ Journal entries related with prepaid rent

(Numbers in billions of ₩)

①	(Dr.)	Prepaid rent	18	(Cr.)	Cash	18
②	(Dr.)	Rent expense	17	(Cr.)	Prepaid rent	17

The following ⟨Diagram 5-6⟩ is the prepaid rent account after recording the beginning balance and posting the above journal entries.

〈Diagram 5-6〉 Prepaid rent

		Beginning 2(Dr.)
⑤ Rent paid 18		20(Dr.)
	ⓐ Rent expense 17	Ending 3(Dr.)

The contents of the prepaid rent account can be summarized as the following.

Beg. prepaid rent	+	Rent paid	−	Rent expense	=	End. prepaid rent
2	+	18	−	17	=	3

The above equation can be rearranged as an equation to compute cash outflows, as shown below.

Rent paid	=	Rent expense	+	(End. prepaid rent	−	Beg. prepaid rent)
18	=	17	+	(3	−	2)

If the difference between the ending balance and the beginning balance of prepaid rent is converted as an increase in prepaid rent, the following equation can be obtained.

Rent paid	=	Rent expense	+	Increase in prepaid rent
18	=	17	+	1

When prepaid rent decreases, the following equation is made.

Rent paid = Rent expense − Decrease in prepaid rent

(5) Combination of trade payables—Type (3) and merchandise inventory—Type (4)

1) Difference between cash paid for merchandise purchase and cost of goods sold

As shown in the following 〈Table 5-29〉 the difference between cash paid of ₩235 billion (Transaction ③ ₩70 billion and Transaction ⑩ ₩165 billion) to purchase merchandise—which was included in cash paid to suppliers and employees—and the cost of goods sold of ₩240 billion in the income statement, can be segregated into two parts using the merchandise purchase of ₩242 billion (Transaction ① ₩172 billion and Transaction ③ ₩70 billion) as an intermediary. The first difference (a) is the difference between cash paid for a merchandise purchase of ₩235 billion and a merchandise purchase of ₩242 billion. The second difference (b) is the difference between a merchandise purchase of ₩242 billion and the cost of goods sold at ₩240 billion.

〈Table 5-29〉 Difference between cash paid for merchandise purchase and cost of goods sold

(Numbers in billions of ₩)

Statement of cash flows			Income statement	Difference (Type)		
(a)	Cash paid for merchandise purchase 235 = ③ 70 + ⑩ 165	Purchases of merchandise 242 = ① 172 + ③ 70		7	Increase in trade payables	(3)
(b)		Purchases of merchandise 242 = ① 172 + ③ 70	Cost of goods sold 240	2	Increase in merchandise	(4)

(a) Difference between cash paid for merchandise purchase of ₩235 billion and merchandise purchase of ₩242 billion is explained by an increase in trade payables, as shown in (Equation ①). The relationship among items in (Equation ①) can be classified as Type (3), considering trade payables as merchandise purchase payable.

Cash paid for merchandise purchase	=	Merchandise purchase	−	Increase in trade payables	······ (Equation ①)
235	=	242	−	7	

(b) The difference between the merchandise purchase of 242 billion and the cost of goods sold of ₩240 billion is explained by an increase in the merchandise inventory of ₩2 billion, as shown in (Equation ②). The relationship among items in (Equation ②) can be classified as Type (4), considering the cost of goods sold as an expense and the merchandise inventory as the prepaid cost of goods sold.

Merchandise purchase	=	Cost of goods sold	+	Increase in merchandise	······ (Equation ②)
242	=	240	+	2	

If the merchandise purchase in (Equation ①) is substituted by (Equation ②), the following (Equation ③) is obtained.

Cash paid for merchandise purchase	=	Cost of goods sold	−	Increase in trade payables	+	Increase in merchandise	··· (Equation ③)
235	=	240	−	7	+	2	

When trade payable decreases and merchandise inventory decreases, the following equation can be obtained.

Cash paid for merchandise purchase	=	Cost of goods sold	+	Decrease in trade payables	−	Decrease in merchandise

3. Differences between cash flows information and revenue and expense information by type

The following ⟨Table 5-30⟩ summarizes the differences between the statement of cash flows information and the income statement information by type.

⟨Table 5-30⟩ Differences between cash flows information and revenue and expense information by type

Types		Formula	
(1)	Accrued revenue	Cash received = Revenue − Increase in accrued revenue	Cash received = Revenue + Decrease in accrued revenue
(2)	Unearned revenue	Cash received = Revenue + Increase in unearned revenue	Cash receipt = Revenue − Decrease in unearned revenue
(3)	Accrued expense	Cash paid = Expense − Increase in accrued expense	Cash paid = Expense + Decrease in accrued expense
(4)	Prepaid expense	Cash paid = Expense + Increase in prepaid expense	Cash paid = Expense − Decrease in prepaid expense

A comprehensive illustration of using financial statements

In Section 1 of this chapter, we studied a process for preparing financial statements. In this section, we will explain the fundamental financial ratios that are used to analyze the financial statements prepared above. Financial ratios are ratios between items included in financial statements. They are mostly used by investors to help forecast the stock price of a firm, by creditors when they evaluate a firm's credit to decide whether to give the firm a loan, and by managers when they analyze a firm's operating performance.

Evaluation using financial ratios is not absolute but relative. There is no desirable absolute value for each ratio. Each ratio should instead be evaluated by comparing it with that of the previous year, with that of competing companies, or with the industry average.

2.1 Financial ratios evaluating profitability

There are a few profitability ratios by which one can evaluate how much income is generated by a firm. The basic ones are profit margin on sales, return on assets, return on equity, and earnings per share.

(1) Profit margin on sales

Profit margin on sales is a ratio of net income on sales, as shown below.

$$\text{Profit margin on sales} = \frac{\text{Net income}}{\text{Sales}}$$

This ratio shows the amount of net income on every sale of ₩1. In Korea, this ratio is called the net income to sales ratio. It is also called the profit margin (이익마진).

(Ratio of Hankook Department Store)

$$\text{Profit margin on sales} = \frac{22 \text{ billion}}{310 \text{ billion}} = 7.1\%$$

This ratio of 7.1% means that Hankook Department Store earned roughly ₩7 on every sale of ₩100. If a competing company's profit margin on sales is 5%, then Hankook Department Store may at first glance be evaluated to have higher profitability than the competing company. Yet, when we use this ratio, we should consider many other factors along with it. For example, if the competing company sells what we call middle to low price products with high turnover and Hankook Department Store sells high price products providing a large margin with low turnover, it is problematic to use only this profit margin on sales ratio to evaluate profitability. (Refer to (3) 'Return on assets' and (4) 'Return on equity' below.)

(2) Operating income to sales ratio

The operating income to sales ratio is the ratio of income from operations to sales, as shown below.

$$\textbf{Operating income to sales ratio} = \frac{\textbf{Income from operations}}{\textbf{Sales}}$$

This ratio shows how much income from operations has been generated in relation to ₩1 of sales.

(Ratio of Hankook Department Store)

$$\text{Operating income to sales ratio} = \frac{37 \text{ billion}}{310 \text{ billion}} = 11.94\%$$

According to this ratio, we know that Hankook Department Store has generated income of roughly ₩12 on every ₩100 of sales through its operating activities alone. If we compare this ratio with the profit margin on sales, we can find out whether a company's net income is generated from operating activities or from investing or financing activities.

(3) Return on assets

Return on assets is the ratio of net income to equity, as shown below.

$$\text{Return on assets (ROA)} = \frac{\text{Net income}}{\text{Average total assets}} = \frac{\text{Net income}}{(\text{Beg. total assets} + \text{End. total assets}) / 2}$$

This ratio shows how much net income is generated on every ₩1 of total assets. This return on assets is called ROA (총자산이익률) and is categorized as one type of ROI (return on investment : 투자이익률). The return on investment is the ratio of investment income to the investment. If total assets are considered a company's investment, then ROA is the ROI.

(Ratio of Hankook Department Store)

$$\text{ROA} = \frac{\text{22 billion}}{(\text{202 billion} + \text{254 billion}) / 2} = 9.65\%$$

This ratio of 9.65% means that Hankook Department Store earned roughly ₩10 of income on every ₩100 of total assets for 1 year. This ratio can be used effectively when companies of different sizes are compared and evaluated. For example, if only net income is used to evaluate profitability, then in general a large company with large investments, that is large total assets will be evaluated more favorably. But because the ROA incorporates investment size when evaluating profitability, this kind of problem can be solved.

ROA can be expressed as a multiplication of two ratios, as shown blow.

$$\text{ROA} = \frac{\text{Net income}}{\text{Average total assets}} = \frac{\text{Net income}}{\text{Sales}} \times \frac{\text{Sales}}{\text{Average total assets}}$$

$$= \underset{\text{(Profitability)}}{\text{Profit margin on sales}} \times \underset{\text{(Activity)}}{\text{Total assets turnover}}$$

The above formula shows that ROA is a multiplication of the profit margin on sales (by which the profitability of a firm can be evaluated) and the total assets turnover (which will be reviewed in 2.3 'Financial ratio evaluating activity,' below, and by which the activity of a firm can be evaluated). The method of breaking down a ratio into other ratios like this can provide a great deal of insight to users of financial statements, since it helps them evaluate a firm by observing the detailed factors that comprise the ratio. For example, if the ROA is below our expectations, we can apply this approach to discover whether this problem is caused by the profitability of the firm or by its activities. Hankook Department Store's ROA can be broken down as below.

$$\text{ROA} = \frac{22 \text{ billion}}{310 \text{ billion}} \times \frac{310 \text{ billion}}{228 \text{ billion}} = 7.1\% \times 1.36 = 9.65\%$$

As seen above, Hankook Department Store's ROA can be computed by multiplying its profit margin on sales of 7.1% and its total assets turnover of 1.36. If Hankook Department Store's profit margin on sales is higher than the industry average and its total assets turnover is lower than the industry average, then Hankook Department Store must search for an alternative to utilize its assets more efficiently.

(4) Return on equity

Return on equity is the ratio of net income to equity, as shown below.

$$\textbf{Return on equity (ROE)} = \frac{\textbf{Net income}}{\textbf{Average equity}} = \frac{\textbf{Net income}}{\textbf{(Beg. equity + End. equity) / 2}}$$

This ratio is used to evaluate profitability on equity, and thus represents a firm's profitability ratio from the perspective of its stockholders. It is called ROE (return on equity : 자기자본이익률). ROA is an index by which profitability on total assets—that is, the sum of both equity and liabilities—can be evaluated. ROE, in contrast, is an index by which profitability on equity is evaluated. This is a return on investment(ROI) that considers equity as an investment.

(Ratio of Hankook Department Store)

$$\text{ROE} = \frac{\text{22 billion}}{\text{(65 billion + 85 billion) / 2}} = 29.33\%$$

This ratio of 29.33% means that Hankook Department Store has earned roughly ₩29 of income on every ₩100 of equity for 1 year. Like the ROA, this ROE can be used effectively when companies of different amounts of equity are compared and evaluated.

ROE can be expressed as a multiplication of three ratios, as shown below.

$$\text{ROE} = \frac{\text{Net income}}{\text{Average equity}} = \frac{\text{Net income}}{\text{Sales}} \times \frac{\text{Sales}}{\text{Average total assets}} \times \frac{\text{Average total assets}}{\text{Average equity}}$$

$$= \text{Profit margin on sales (Profitability)} \times \text{Total assets turnover (Activity)} \times \frac{1}{\text{Equity ratio (Safety)}}$$

As can be seen in the above formula, ROE is a composite ratio. It is, in turn, composed of the profit margin on sales (by which profitability can be evaluated) ; of the total assets turnover ratio (by which the activity of a firm can be evaluated) ; and by the reversal of equity ratio (by which the financial safety of a firm can be evaluated). (Note : The total assets turnover ratio will be reviewed in 2.3 'Financial ratios evaluating activity.' The year-end equity ratio will be reviewed in 2.4 'Financial ratios evaluating safety (financial),' below. Here, the year-average equity ratio is used.). If we rewrite this ratio, it can be expressed as the following.

$$\textbf{ROE} = \textbf{ROA (Profitability)} \times \frac{\textbf{1}}{\textbf{Equity ratio (Safety)}}$$

From the above formula, we can understand that the ROE can be computed by multiplying the ROA by the reciprocal of the equity ratio (year-average).

In the case of Hankook Department Store, if the return on equity is expressed with its detailed components, it is a multiplication of the profit margin on sales of 7.1%, the total assets turnover of 1.36, and the reciprocal of equity ratio (year-average) of 304%.

$$\text{ROE} = \frac{22\ \text{billion}}{310\ \text{billion}} \times \frac{310\ \text{billion}}{228\ \text{billion}} \times \frac{228\ \text{billion}}{75\ \text{billion}} = 7.1\% \times 1.36 \times 304\% = 29.35\%$$

If we rewrite this ratio by the second formula above, it can be expressed as a multiplication of the return on assets of 9.56% and the reciprocal of equity ratio (year-average) of 304%.

$$\text{ROE} = \frac{22\ \text{billion}}{228\ \text{billion}} \times \frac{228\ \text{billion}}{75\ \text{billion}} = 9.65\% \times 304\% = 29.34\%$$

Given a constant ROA in the above formula, if equity takes up a larger portion of total assets, the ROE gets lower and equity takes up a smaller portion of total assets, then the ROE gets higher. This is what we call 'the leverage effect (레버리지효과).'

(5) Earnings per share

Earnings per share (EPS : 주당이익) is an outcome of computing the net income per share of common stock outstanding, as below :

$$\text{EPS} = \frac{\text{Net income} - \text{Preferred stock dividends}}{\text{Weighted average common shares outstanding}}$$

Preferred stock dividends are paid before common stock dividends. Therefore, earnings belongs to common stock holders are net income after preferred stock dividends. The weighted average common shares outstanding refers to the number of shares computed with different weights for the different time lengths during which said shares have been outstanding. For example, if 1,000 shares are issued on April 1, then the weighted average number of shares outstanding is 750 shares (1,000 shares × 9/12). Since, in the case of Hankook Department Store, shares were issued only once at the beginning of 20×1 (when the company was founded), the weighted average number of shares outstanding is the same as the total number of shares issued. Since Hankook Department Store did not issue preferred stock, there were no preferred stock dividends. EPS is computed to be ₩2,200, as below :

$$\text{EPS} = \frac{\text{22 billion}}{\text{10 million shares}} = ₩2{,}200$$

This EPS constitutes a piece of accounting information that is most often used in the stock market.

2.2 Financial ratios evaluating growth

As the value of a company is affected by its expected future growth, the task of evaluating its growth is very important when forecasting the company's value. Key financial ratios by which the growth of a company can be evaluated include: sales growth rate, total assets growth rate, operating income growth rate, and net income growth rate.

To compute growth rates, we must also have the prior year's income statement information. It is assumed that Hankook Department Store had sales of ₩280 billion, income from operations of ₩32 billion, and net income of ₩19 billion for 20×1.

(1) Sales growth rate

The sales growth rate is the ratio of sales increased for the current period over sales in a prior period, as shown below.

$$\text{Sales growth rate} = \frac{\text{Sales for current period} - \text{Sales for prior period}}{\text{Sales in prior period}}$$

This rate shows how much sales have grown. To have growth in profitability for a long period, sales must be grown continuously by exploring new markets and developing new products. This rate is an index by which one can evaluate whether the growth strategy of a company is established and implemented properly.

Operating income growth rate and net income growth rate, which will be reviewed below, may fluctuate a lot. Therefore, when the long-term growth rate of a company is to be projected, the sales growth rate or total assets growth rate is used. Of these two, the sales growth rate is used more often, because the correlation of the profitability of a company with its sales growth is high.

(Rate of Hankook Department Store)

$$\text{Sales growth rate} = \frac{310 \text{ billion} - 280 \text{ billion}^{*}}{280 \text{ billion}^{*}} = 10.71\%$$

* Amount assumed.

(2) Total asset growth rate

The total asset growth rate is the rate of the total assets increased in the current period over the total assets at the end of the prior period, as shown below.

$$\textbf{Total asset growth rate} = \frac{\text{(Total assets at the end of current period} - \text{Total assets at the end of prior period)}}{\text{Total assets at the end of prior period}}$$

This rate shows how much total assets have grown. Assets are the results of the investing activities of a company, so this rate is an index by which one can see how actively the company carries out its investing activities.

(Rate of Hankook Department Store)

$$\text{Total asset growth rate} = \frac{254 \text{ billion} - 202 \text{ billion}}{202 \text{ billion}} = 25.74\%$$

(3) Operating income growth rate

The operating income growth rate is the rate of income from operations increased for the current period over the income from operations for a prior period, as shown below.

$$\textbf{Operating income growth rate} = \frac{\text{(Income from operations for current period} - \text{Income from operations for prior period)}}{\text{Income from operations for prior period}}$$

Income from operations is income which is generated from the operating activities of a company. This rate shows how much income from operating activities of a company has grown.

(Rate of Hankook Department Store)

$$\text{Operating income growth rate} = \frac{37\text{ billion} - 32\text{ billion}^*}{32\text{ billion}^*} = 15.63\%$$

* Amount assumed.

(4) Net income growth rate

The net income growth rate is the rate of net income increased for the current period over the net income for a prior period, as shown below.

$$\textbf{Net income growth rate} = \frac{\textbf{(Net income for current period} - \textbf{Net income for prior period)}}{\textbf{Net income for prior period}}$$

Net income is income generated from all operating activities, investing activities, and financing activities of a company. This rate shows how much the net income of a company has grown, due not only to its operating activities but also to its investing and financing activities.

(Rate of Hankook Department Store)

$$\text{Net income growth rate} = \frac{22\text{ billion} - 19\text{ billion}^*}{19\text{ billion}^*} = 15.79\%$$

* Amount assumed.

2.3 Financial ratios evaluating activity

The most basic activity ratio by which we can evaluate how efficiently assets are utilized is the total assets turnover.

(1) Total assets turnover

The total assets turnover is the ratio of sales to total assets, as below.

$$\text{Total assets turnover} = \frac{\text{Sales}}{\text{Average total assets}} = \frac{\text{Sales}}{\text{(Beg. total assets + End. total assets) / 2}}$$

The total assets turnover shows the amount of sales generated per ₩1 of asset for 1 year. It is called turnover because this ratio shows how many times total assets are used to generate sales in a year. The higher this ratio is, the better utilization of assets has been made.

(Ratio of Hankook Department Store)

$$\text{Total assets turnover} = \frac{\text{310 billion}}{\text{228 billion}} = \text{1.36 times}$$

2.4 Financial ratios evaluating safety (financial)

The most important of financial ratios by which we can evaluate whether a company can pay back its liabilities and stay in business as a going concern (financial saftey) are the debt ratio and the equity ratio.

(1) Debt ratio

The debt ratio is the ratio of liabilities to equity, as shown below.

$$\text{Debt ratio} = \frac{\text{Liabilities}}{\text{Equity}}$$

This ratio is used to evaluate a company's financial soundness. If its debt ratio is high, a firm's risk of going into a bankruptcy is likewise high because the proportion of principal and interest to be paid are elevated.

(Ratio of Hankook Department Store)

$$\text{Debt ratio} = \frac{169 \text{ billion}}{85 \text{ billion}} = 198.82\%$$

When we had a foreign exchange crisis in 1977, Korean government recommended that companies keep their debt ratios below 200% to raise their financial soundness. Hankook Department Store's debt ratio is very much up to this 200% guideline.

(2) Equity ratio

The equity ratio is the ratio of equity to total assets, as shown below. This ratio shows what proportion of the firm's total assets is contributed by stockholders.

$$\textbf{Equity ratio} = \frac{\textbf{Equity}}{\textbf{Total assets}}$$

This ratio has a reversal relationship with the debt ratio. That is, if the debt ratio is high, then the equity ratio is low and vice versa. The relationship between the debt and equity ratios is as below.

$$\textbf{Equity ratio} = \frac{\textbf{1}}{\textbf{(1 + Debt ratio)}}$$

(Ratio of Hankook Department Store)

$$\text{Equity ratio} = \frac{85 \text{ billion}}{254 \text{ billion}} = \frac{1}{(1 + 1.99)} = 33.44\%$$

(3) Quick ratio

The quick ratio is the ratio of quick assets to current liabilities, as shown below.

$$\text{Quick ratio} = \frac{\text{Quick assets}}{\text{Current liabilities}}$$

Quick assets are current assets, excluding inventory. This ratio is an index that compares a firm's quick assets with its current liabilities (short-term debts).

(Ratio of Hankook Department Store)

$$\text{Quick ratio} = \frac{\text{52 billion}}{\text{49 billion}} = 106.12\%$$

(4) Current ratio

The current ratio is the ratio of current assets to current liabilities.

$$\text{Current ratio} = \frac{\text{Current assets}}{\text{Current liabilities}}$$

This ratio shows the quantity of current assets (short-term assets) held by a company, in comparison with its current liabilities (short-term debts).

(Ratio of Hankook Department Store)

$$\text{Current ratio} = \frac{\text{64 billion}}{\text{49 billion}} = 130.61\%$$

(5) Net working capital

Net working capital, sometimes called working capital or working fund, is computed by subtracting current liabilities from current assets, as shown below.

Net working capital = Current assets − Current liabilities

This index shows the amount of current assets (short-term assets) remaining after paying current liabilities (short-term debts). This index is called as (net amount) working capital because this index shows the amount of additional funds that are spent for an efficient operation after investing in production facilities.

(Ratio of Hankook Department Store)

Net working capital = 64 billion − 49 billion = ₩15 billion

The quick ratio, current ratio, and net working capital are all indexes by which we can evaluate a company's ability to pay off short-term debts, that is, its short-term liquidity. Reliance on these indexes is diminishing in these days because it is more effective to examine what constitutes a firm's current assets and current liabilities rather than simply comparing these indexes.

2.5 Price multiple

(1) Price earnings ratio

Price earnings ratio (PER : 주가이익비율) is a ratio between the price of common stock and the earnings per share (EPS), as shown below.

$$\text{PER} = \frac{\text{Price of common stock}}{\text{EPS}}$$

This ratio shows price of common stock at the market is formed how many times of EPS. In general, a company with high growth potential in the future has a larger price earnings ratio than does a company with low growth potential. If the stock price of HK Department Store is ₩12,000, its PER is 5.45 times, as follows.

$$\text{PER} = \frac{12{,}000}{2{,}200} = 5.45 \text{ times}$$

This ratio is frequently used to predict future stock price. For example, if HK Department Store's EPS for 20×3 is forecasted to be ₩2,500 and its PER is forecasted upward to be 8 times, then its stock price for 20×3 is predicted at ₩20,000 (₩2,500 × 8).

All key financial ratios introduced in this textbook. are summarized in Appendix 2 ⟨Table B-1⟩ at the end of this book. The basic financial ratios using the statement of financial position and the income statement are reviewed in this chapter. (These are the ratios in the column of 'Text' in ⟨Table B-1⟩ that are shaded). Ratios that use more detailed information and cash flow information are additionally explained from Chapter 6 to Chapter 11 (These are the ratios in the column of 'Text' in ⟨Table B-1⟩ that are not shaded).

Exercises

1. Accounting for supplies ①

Busan Trading Co.'s supplies inventory at the beginning of 20×1 was ₩2 billion, purchases of supplies during 20×1 was ₩30 billion and supplies inventory at the end of 20×1 was ₩3 billion.

《Questions》

(1) How much is supplies expense for 20×1?

(2) In each of the following cases of 1), 2-1) and 2-2) prepare adjusting journal entries at the end of the year.

1) When purchases of supplies was recorded on supplies account

2) When purchases of supplies were recorded on supplies expense account

2-1) Assume that the beginning inventory remained on supplies account

2-2) Assume that the beginning inventory was used and recorded on supplies expense account

2. Accounting for supplies ②

The following is data concerning supplies for 20×1.

(Numbers in billions of ₩)

Beginning inventory	Purchases	Ending inventory	Supplies expense
10	200	25	(1)
(2)	40	1	46
20	300	(3)	305
8	(4)	7	150

《Question》 Calculate the blanks in the above table.

3. Converting cash basis data into accrual basis Information

Mr. Kim, Hankook, who is operating Nara Consulting, is currently studying accounting at H University. The following is a trial balance of Nara Consulting at the end of 20×1, the year of the firm's foundation. It was one that Mr. Kim prepared after preparing journal entries for cash inflows and outflows and posting them.

Trial balance

Nara Consulting　　December 31, 20×1　　(Numbers in billions of ₩)

Dr.	Account titles	Cr.
3	Cash	
80	Short-term loans	
	Long-term borrowings	20
	Share capital-common stock	50
	Rent revenue	80
	Interest revenue	6
44	Rent expense	
27	Salaries expense	
2	Interest expense	
156	Total	156

Mr. Lee Kwangbok, a CPA who is auditing Nara Consulting, found the following items.

ⓐ Service fees receivable is ₩10 billion at the end of 20×1
ⓑ Unearned interest is ₩2 billion at the end of 20×1
ⓒ Prepaid rent is ₩5 billion at the end of 20×1
ⓓ Salaries payable are ₩8 billion at the end of 20×1

《Questions》

(1) Prepare adjusting journal entries.
(2) Prepare an adjusted trial balance.
(3) Prepare an income statement
(4) Prepare a statement of financial position,

4. Accrual basis and cash flow ①

The following is information gathered from the financial statements of Korea Company for 20×1.

(Numbers in billions of ₩)

Statement of financial position			Income statement	
Account titles	Amount		Account titles	Amount
	Beginning	Ending		
Prepaid insurance	10	15	Insurance expense	20
Interest receivable	26	30	Interest revenue	40
Salaries payable	5	6	Salaries expense	65
Unearned rent	77	85	Rent revenue	90

《Question》 Calculate the following.

(1) Insurance premium paid in cash in 20×1
(2) Interest received in cash in 20×1
(3) Salaries paid in cash in 20×1
(4) Rent received in cash in 20×1

5. Accrual basis and cash flow ②

Compute the amounts that should be in the blanks of the following table.

(Numbers in billions of ₩)

Description	Amount	Description	Amount
Beginning prepaid rent	50	Beginning unearned interest	4
Rent paid in cash	350	Interest received in cash	(2)
Rent expense	(1)	Interest revenue	15
Ending prepaid rent	80	Ending unearned interest	1

Description	Amount	Description	Amount
Beginning rent receivable	(3)	Beginning salaries payable	40
Rent received in cash	70	Salaries paid in cash	180
Rent revenue	75	Salaries expense	150
Ending rent receivable	20	Ending salaries payable	(4)

6. Accounting cycle (accrual)—a merchandising company : When there is no beginning balance

Namhan Department Store (NDS) was established in 20×1. Its fiscal year ends on December 31. The following are transactions that occurred in 20×1.

T. no.	Date	Description of transaction
①	Jan. 2	Issued 20 million shares of common stock at par value of ₩5,000 and received ₩100 billion in cash.
②	Jan. 10	Purchased merchandise and paid ₩65 billion in cash.
③	Feb. 1	Rented a building and paid rent of ₩24 billion in advance.
④	Feb. 15	Sold merchandise costing ₩35 billion at ₩60 billion in cash.
⑤	Mar. 1	Borrowed ₩150 billion from a bank for 4 years.
⑥	Mar. 20	Purchased a piece of land and paid ₩200 billion in cash.
⑦	Mar. 25	Purchased merchandise of ₩50 billion on credit.
⑧	Apr. 1	Signed a casualty insurance contract and paid insurance premium of ₩12 billion in advance.
⑨	Apr. 12	Sold merchandise costing ₩45 billion at ₩70 billion on credit.
⑩	May. 14	Collected trade receivables of ₩65 billion.
⑪	Jun. 21	Paid trade payables of ₩44 billion.
⑫	Jul. 16	Made a TV commercial advertising the company and paid fees of ₩14 billion.
⑬	Sep. 1	Rented a part of the building and received rent of ₩6 billion in advance.
⑭	Dec. 30	Paid employees' salaries of ₩17 billion for 20×1 in cash.

6-1. Journalizing, posting, preparing a trial balance

《Questions》

(1) Journalize transactions.
(2) Set up balance column T accounts and post the journal entries.
(3) Prepare a trial balance.

6-2. Preparing adjusting journal entries, posting, preparing an adjusted trial balance

The following is a summary of the trial balance.

Summary of trial balance

(Numbers in billions of ₩)

Account titles	Amount	Account titles	Amount
Cash	5	Trade receivables	5
Prepaid rent	24	Prepaid insurance	12
Merchandise	35	Land	200
Trade payables	6	Unearned rent	6
Long-term borrowings	150	Share capital-common stock	100
Sales	130	Cost of goods sold	80
Salaries expense	17	Advertising expense	14

Note : All account balances are normal balances.

《Questions》

(1) Prepare the adjusting journal entries using the following additional information.

No.	Additional information
ⓐ	Rent of ₩24 billion, paid in advance on February 1, was for 1 year from February 1, 20×1 to January 31, 20×2.
ⓑ	Interest rate on ₩150 billion, borrowed on March 1 for 4 years, is 12% per annum and interest is to be paid at the end of February every year.
ⓒ	Insurance premium of ₩12 billion, paid on April 1, was for 1 year from April 1, 20×1 to March 31, 20×2.
ⓓ	Rent of ₩6 billion, received in advance on September 1, was for 1 year from September 1, 20×1 to August 31, 20×2.

(2) Post the adjusting journal entries.

(3) Prepare an adjusted trial balance.

6-3. Preparing an income statement and a statement of financial position

The following is a summary of the adjusted trial balance.

Summary of adjusted trial balance

(Numbers in billions of ₩)

Account titles	Amount	Account titles	Amount
Cash	5	Trade receivables	5
Prepaid rent	2	Prepaid insurance	3
Merchandise	35	Land	200
Trade payables	6	Interest payable	15
Unearned rent	4	Long-term borrowings	150
Share capital-common stock	100	Sales	130
Rent revenue	2	Cost of goods sold	80
Salaries expense	17	Advertising expense	14
Rent expense	22	Insurance expense	9
Interest expense	15		

Note : All account balances are normal balances.

《Questions》

(1) Prepare an income statement.
(2) Prepare a statement of financial position.

6-4. Computing financial ratios

The following is a summary of data gathered from the income statement and the statement of financial position.

(Numbers in billions of ₩)

Description	Amount	Description	Amount
Sales	130	Liabilities	175
Loss from operations	(-)10	Equity	75
Net loss	(-)25	Current assets	50
Total assets	250	Current liabilities	25

《Question》

Compute the following financial ratios. (Use the balance at year-end for the ratios requiring an average balance.)

(1) Profit margin on sales
(2) Operating income to sales ratio
(3) Return on assets (ROA)
(4) Return on equity (ROE)
(5) Total assets turnover
(6) Debt ratio
(7) Equity ratio
(8) Current ratio
(9) Net working capital

6-5. The differences between the statement of cash flows information and the income statement information

《Questions》

(1) 1) analyse the cash account and 2) prepare a statement of cash flows. (Assume that no exception is allowed in classifying items reported in the statement of cash flows.)

(2) Compute the differences between the statement of cash flows information and the income statement information, and describe the causes of the differences using the statement of financial position accounts.*

* The level of difficulty is high.

7. Accounting cycle (accrual)—a merchandising company : When there are beginning balances

The following is the statement of financial position of Korea Department Store (KDS) at the end of 20×1.

Statement of financial position

KDS As of December 31 20×1 (Numbers in billions of ₩)

Account titles	Amount		Account titles	Amount	
Assets			**Liabilities**		
Current assets		69	**Current liabilities**		47
Cash	3		Trade payables	30	
Trade receivables	23		Interest payable	10	
Interest receivable	1		Income taxes payable	3	
Cost financial assets :			Unearned rent	4	
Short-term loans	20		**Non-current liability**		100
Prepaid insurance	3		**Cost financial liability :**		
Prepaid rent	2		Long-term borrowings	100	
Inventory :			**Total liabilities**		147
Merchandise	17		**Equity**		
Non-current asset		140	**Share capital**		50
Tangible asset			Common stock	50	
Land	140		**Retained earnings**		12
			Total equity		62
Total assets		209	**Total liabilities and equity**		209

The following are transactions of KDS for 20×2.

T. no.	Date	Description of transaction
①	Jan. 2	Purchased merchandise of ₩90 billion on credit.
②	Jan. 12	Sold merchandise costing ₩40 billion at ₩90 billion on credit.
③	Feb. 15	Collected trade receivables of ₩60 billion in cash.
④	Feb. 20	Paid trade payables of ₩50 billion in cash.
⑤	Feb. 25	Sold merchandise costing ₩55 billion at ₩115 billion in cash.
⑥	Feb. 28	Paid interest of ₩12 billion on long-term borrowing for 1 year (from March 1, 20×1 to February 28, 20×2) in cash. Interest payable of ₩10 billion was recorded at the end of 20×1.
⑦	Feb. 28	Paid off, early, the long-term borrowing of ₩20 billion in cash.
⑧	Mar. 1	Paid building rent of ₩18 billion in advance.
⑨	Mar. 2	Paid dividends of ₩5 billion in cash.
⑩	Mar. 10	Purchased a piece of land and paid ₩40 billion in cash.
⑪	Mar. 15	Collected trade receivables of ₩50 billion in cash.
⑫	Mar. 30	Purchased merchandise of ₩30 billion on credit.
⑬	Apr. 1	Issued 2 million shares of common stock at par value of ₩5,000 and received ₩10 billion in cash.
⑭	Apr. 1	Paid casualty insurance premium of ₩16 billion in advance.
⑮	Apr. 10	Paid income taxes payable of ₩3 billion in cash.
⑯	Apr. 30	Sold merchandise costing ₩28 billion at ₩50 billion on credit.
⑰	Jun. 15	Paid trade payables of ₩50 billion in cash.
⑱	Jun. 30	Collected short-term loans of ₩20 billion and interest of ₩2 billion for 1 year (from July 1, 20×1 to June 30, 20×2) in cash. Interest receivable of ₩1 billion was recorded at the end of 20×1.
⑲	Sep. 1	Made a loan of ₩30 billion to Korea Trading Co. for 1 year.
⑲	Sep. 1	Received building rent of ₩9 billion in cash in advance.
㉑	Dec. 29	Paid employees' salaries of ₩20 billion for 20×2 in cash.

7-1. Journalizing, posting, preparing a trial balance

《Questions》

(1) Journalize transactions.

(2) Set up balance column T accounts, and record beginning balances and post the journal entries.

(3) Prepare a trial balance.

7-2. Preparing adjusting journal entries, posting, preparing an adjusted trial balance
The following is a summary of the trial balance.

Summary of trial balance

(Numbers in billions of ₩)

Account titles	Amount	Account titles	Amount
Cash	5	Trade receivables	53
Short-term loans	30	Prepaid insurance	19
Prepaid rent	20	Merchandise	14
Land	180	Trade payables	50
Unearned rent	13	Long-term borrowings	80
Share capital-common stock	60	Retained earnings	12
Dividends	5	Sales	255
Interest revenue	1	Cost of goods sold	123
Salaries expense	20	Interest expense	2

Note : All account balances are normal balances.

《Questions》

(1) Prepare the adjusting journal entries, using the following information.

Number	Additional Information
ⓐ	Rent of ₩18 billion paid in advance on March 1 was for 1 year from March 1, 20×2 to February 28, 20×3. One year rent of ₩12 billion was also paid in advance on March 1, 20×1.
ⓑ	Long-term borrowings interest rate is 12 % per annum and interest is to be paid on February 28 every year.
ⓒ	Insurance premium of ₩16 billion, paid in advance on April 1, was for 1 year from April 1, 20×2 to March 31, 20×3. One year insurance premium of ₩12 billion was also paid in advance on February 1, 20×1.
ⓓ	Interest rate on ₩30 billion short-term loan, made on September 1, was 10% per annum and interest is to be received on loan maturity date of August 31, 20×3.
ⓔ	Rent of ₩9 billion, received in advance on September 1, was for 1 year from September 1, 20×2 to August 31, 20×3. One year rent of ₩6 billion was also received in advance on September 1, 20×1.
ⓕ	Income taxes expense for 20×2 was estimated to be ₩18 billion and will be paid in 20×3.

(2) Post the adjusting journal entries.

(3) Prepare an adjusted trial balance.

7-3. Preparing an income statement and a statement of financial position

The following is a summary of the adjusted trial balance.

Summary of adjusted trial balance

(Numbers in billions of ₩)

Account titles	Amount	Account titles	Amount
Cash	5	Trade receivables	53
Interest receivable	1	Short-term loans	30
Prepaid insurance	4	Prepaid rent	3
Merchandise	14	Land	180
Trade payables	50	Interest payable	8
Income tax payable	18	Unearned rent	6
Long-term borrowings	80	Share capital-common stock	60
Retained earnings	12	Dividends	5
Sales	255	Rent revenue	7
Interest revenue	2	Cost of goods sold	123
Salaries expense	20	Rent expense	17
Insurance expense	15	Interest expense	10
Income tax expense	18		

Note : All account balances are normal balances.

《Questions》

(1) Prepare an income statement.

(2) Prepare a statement of financial position.

7-4. Computing financial ratios

The following is a summary of data gathered from the income statements for 20×1 and 20×2, and the statement of financial position as of December 31, 20×2.

(Numbers in billions of ₩)

Description	Amount	
	20×2	20×1
Sales	255	210
Income from operations	87	73
Net income	61	55

(Numbers in billions of ₩)

Description	Amount	Description	Amount
	Dec. 31, 20×2		Dec. 31, 20×2
Liabilities	162	Current assets	110
Equity	128	Current liabilities	82
Total assets	290		

《Question》

Compute the following financial ratios. (Stock price of KDS common stock at the end of 20×2 was ₩40,000.)

(1) Profit margin on sales
(2) Operating income to sales ratio
(3) Return on assets (ROA)
(4) Return on equity (ROE)
(5) Sales growth rate
(6) Total assets growth rate
(7) Operating income growth rate
(8) Net income growth rate
(9) Total assets turnover
(10) Debt ratio
(11) Equity ratio
(12) Current ratio
(13) Net working capital
(14) Price earnings ratio (PER)

7-5. The differences between the statement of cash flows information and the income statement information

《Questions》

(1) 1) Analyse the cash account and 2) prepare a statement of cash flows. (Assume that no exception is allowed in classifying items reported in the statement of cash flows.)

(2) Compute the differences between the statement of cash flows information and the income statement information, and describe the causes of the differences using the statement of financial position accounts.*

* The level of difficulty is high.

Case Financial Statements of Daehan Department Store

I. Financial statements

II. Footnotes

Case Overview

Case of Daehan Department Store introduced here are financial statements composed of statement of financial position, comprehensive income statement, statement of cash flows, and statement of changes in equity and footnotes thereto. This case is financial statements and footnotes prepared for this book so that the readers can study while enjoying actual field-like experience. This book will show where and how the subjects covered in each chapter after Chapter 6 are actually shown in the financial statement.

I. Financial statements

Statement of financial position (Ft. 2.ⓐ)

As of December 31, 20×2

DDS As of December 31, 20×1 (Numbers in billions of ₩)

Account titles	December 31, 20×2		December 31, 20×1	
Assets				
Current assets				
Cash and cash equivalents(Ft. 4)		45		41
Trade receivables(Ft. 3ⓑ)	30		20	
Allowance for uncollectibe accounts (Ft. 3ⓑ, 5)	(-)4	26	(-)2	18
Inventory :				
Merchandise (Ft. 3ⓒ)		43		23
Total current assets		**114**		**82**
Non-current assets				
FVOCI financial asset (Ft. 3ⓓ, 6)		13		10
Investment in associate (Ft. 3ⓔ, 7)		24		-
Tangible assets (Ft. 8) :				
Land(Ft. 3ⓕ)		96		90
Plant assets (Ft. 3ⓕ, 16)	310		160	
Accumulated depreciation(Ft. 3ⓕ)	(-)13	297	(-)3	157
Intangible asset (Ft. 3ⓖ) :				
Industrial property right (Ft. 8)		9		-
Total non-current assets		**439**		**257**
Total assets		**553**		**339**
Liabilities				
Current liabilities				
Trade payables		42		18
Interest payable		5		4
Salaries payable		2		3
Income tax payable		14		5
Cost financial liabilities (Ft. 3ⓘ) :		38		48
Short-term borrowings (Ft. 9ⓐ)	10		30	
Current portion of long-term borrowings (Ft. 9ⓑ)	28		18	
Provision :				
Provision for refunds (Ft. 3ⓗ, 11)		3		2
Total current liabilities		**104**		**80**
Non-current liabilities				
Cost financial liability (Ft. 3ⓘ) :		126		112
Long-term borrowings (Ft. 9ⓑ)	84		72	
Amortized cost financial liability (Ft. 3ⓘ) :				
Bonds payable (Ft. 10)	42		40	
Total non-current liabilities		**126**		**112**
Total Liabilities		**230**		**192**

Equity				
Share capital				
Common stock (Ft. 13, 16)		150		100
Share premium				
Common stock (Ft. 16)		60		10
Accumulated other comprehensive income		**20**		**11**
Accumulated gain on valuation of FVOCI* financial asset (Ft. 3ⓓ, 6)	4		1	
Land revaluation surplus (Ft. 3ⓕ, 8)	16		10	
Retained earnings (Ft. 3ⓘ, 15)		**93**		**26**
Total equity		**323**		**147**
Total liabilities and equity		**553**		**339**

* FVOCI : Fair value through other comprehensive income

Comprehensive income statement (Ft. 2ⓑ)

From Jan. 1, 20×2 to Dec. 31, 20×2

DDS From Jan. 1, 20×1 to Dec. 31, 20×1 (Numbers in billions of ₩)

Account titles	20×2		20×1	
Sales (Ft. 3ⓐ)		430		220
Cost of goods sold		(−)230		(−)118
Gross profit		200		102
Operating expenses :		(−)85		(−)50
Salaries expense	(−)43		(−)26	
Bad debts expense (Ft. 3ⓑ)	(−)4		(−)2	
Depreciation expense (Ft. 3ⓕ)	(−)10		(−)3	
Rent expense	(−)24		(−)12	
Other operating expenses	(−)4		(−)7	
Income from operations		115		52
Other revenue		6		−
Equity income from associate (Ft. 7)	6		−	
Other expenses		(−)19		(−)14
Finance expense (Ft. 2ⓑ) :				
Interest expense	(−)19		(−)13	
Loss on disposal of tangible assets (Ft. 8)	−		(−)1	
Net income before income tax expense		102		38
Income tax expense		(−)30		(−)12
Net income		72		26
Other comprehensive income :		9		11
Items that will not be reclassified to profit or loss :				
Gain on revaluation of land (Ft. 3ⓕ, 8)	6		10	
Items that may be reclassified subsequently to profit or loss :				
Gain on valuation of FVOCI financial asset (Ft. 3ⓓ, 6)	3		1	
Total comprehensive income		81		37
Earnings per share (Ft. 12)		₩2,880		₩1,733

Statement of cash-flows (Ft. 2ⓒ)

From Jan. 1, 20×2 to Dec. 31, 20×2

DDS From Jan. 1, 20×1 to Dec. 31, 20×1 (Numbers in billions of ₩)

Description	20×2		20×1	
Cash flows from operating activities				
Net income before income tax expense (NIBITE)		**102**		**38**
Adjustments (Ft. 2ⓒ):				
NIBITE expense related with individually reporting item				
Interest expense		**19**		**13**
Gain and loss from non-operating activities		**(−)6**		**1**
Loss on disposal of tangible assets (Ft. 8)	−		1	
Equity income from associate (Ft. 7)	(−)6		−	
Operating expense without cash outflows				
Depreciation expense		**10**		**3**
Changes in assets and liabilities due to operating activities:		**(−)4**		**(−)18**
Increase in trade receivables	(−)8		(−)18	
Increase in merchandise	(−)20		(−)23	
Increase in trade payables	24		18	
Increase (decrease) in salaries payable	(−)1		3	
Increase in provision for refunds (Ft. 11)	1		2	
Cash generated from operations		**121**		**37**
Individually reporting item:				
Income tax paid (Ft. 2ⓒ)		**(−)21**		**(−)7**
Net cash from operating activities		**100**		**30**
Cash flows from investing activities				
Proceeds from sales of land (Ft. 8)	−		39	
Individually reporting item:				
Dividends received (Ft. 7)	2			
Purchase of FVOCI financial asset (Ft. 6)	−		(−)9	
Purchase of stock of associate (Ft. 7)	(−)20		−	
Purchase of land (Ft. 8)	−		(−)120	
Purchase of plant assets (Ft. 8)	(−)150		(−)100	
Purchase of intangible assets (Ft. 8)	(−)9		−	
Net cash used in investing activities		**(−)177**		**(−)190**
Cash flows from financing activities				
Proceeds from short-term borrowings (Ft. 9ⓐ)	10		30	
Proceeds from long-term borrowings (Ft. 9ⓑ)	40		90	
Proceeds from issuing bonds (Ft. 10)	−		39	
Proceeds from issuing common stock (Ft. 13)	100		50	
Retirement of short-term borrowings (Ft. 9ⓐ)	(−)30		−	
Retirement of current portion of long-term borrowings (Ft. 9ⓑ)	(−)18		−	
Individually reporting items:				
Interest paid (Ft. 2ⓒ)	(−)16		(−)8	
Dividends paid (Ft. 2ⓒ, 14)	(−)5		−	

Net cash from financing activities		81		201
Net increase in cash and cash equivalents		4		41
Cash and cash equivalents at beginning of period(Ft. 4)		41		–
Cash and cash equivalents at end of period		45		41

Statement of changes in equity (ft. 2ⓓ)

From Jan. 1, 20×2 to Dec. 31, 20×2

DDS From Jan. 1, 20×1 to Dec. 31, 20×1 (Numbers in billions of ₩)

Description	Share capital	Share premium	Retained earnings	Accumulated other comprehensive income		Total
	Common stock	Common stock		Accumulated gain on valuation of FVOCI financial asset	Land revaluation surplus	
Balance as of January 1, 20×1	–	–	–	–	–	–
Changes in 20×1 :						
Issuance of common stock (Ft. 13)	100	10				110
Total comprehensive income (Ft. 3ⓓ, 3ⓕ, 6, 8)			26	1	10	37
Balance as of December 31, 20×1	100	10	26	1	10	147
Changes in 20×2 :						
Issuance of common stock (Ft. 13)	50	50				100
Cash dividends (Ft. 14)			(−)5			(−)5
Total comprehensive income (Ft. 3ⓓ, 3ⓕ, 6, 8)			72	3	6	81
Balance as of December 31, 20×2	150	60	93	4	16	323

II. Footnotes

1. Company overview

DH Department Store was established on January 1, 20×1 by issuing 10 million shares of common stock with par value of ₩5,000 at ₩5,000 per share. Mr. Song Kyungsung, the founder, owns 75% of the equity ; his wife owns 10% ; and each of his three children owns 5%. The company's head office and store are in Sukchon-dong, Songpa-ku, Seoul, and it conducts merchandising business.

2. Formats of financial statements

The company reports two years (last year's and current year's) comparative financial statements : statement of financial position, comprehensive income statement, statement of cash flows, and statement of changes in equity. Formats of these financial statements are as follow.

ⓐ Format of statement of financial position

The company classifies assets and liabilities into current and non-current based on the one-year standard, and reports them in order of liquidity, as well as reporting equity after liabilities.

ⓑ Format of comprehensive income statement

The company combines its income statement and its statement of reporting other comprehensive income, and prepares only one comprehensive income statement. The company also classifies expenses by function, and it reports multistep comprehensive income statement, reporting each step of gross profit, income from operations, income before income tax expense, net income, and total comprehensive income. And it reports finance expense separately.

ⓒ Format of statement of cash flows

The company prepares its statement of cash flows using the indirect method. It classifies adjustments made to income before income tax expense (NIBITE), to compute cash generated from operations into : NIBITE revenue and expense related with individually reporting items ; gain and loss from non-operating activities ; operating expense without cash outflows ; and changes in assets and liabilities due to operating activities. The company also classifies income tax paid as an operating activity, dividends received as an investing activity, and interest paid and dividends paid as financing activities, and reports these items individually.

ⓓ Format of statement of changes in equity

In the statement of changes in equity, the company reports its total comprehensive income by reconciling each item of 'other comprehensive income' with the corresponding 'accumulated other comprehensive income.'

3. Important accounting policies

Financial statements were prepared in accordance with K-IFRS (Korean International Financial Reporting Standards). Important accounting policies of the company are as follow.

ⓐ Revenue recognition

The company recognizes revenue when the amount can be measured reliably and when it is probable that the economic benefits will flow into the company. More specifically, the company's 'revenue recognition time' is the time at which the company transfers (sells) goods to customers.

ⓑ Valuation of trade receivables

The company issued credit card to customers after reviewing customers' credit standing. The trade receivables are the company-issued credit card sales amount not yet collected in cash at the end of the year. Trade receivables are reported in a format by which the net amount is computed by subtracting the allowance for uncollectible accounts from the gross amount. The allowance for uncollectible accounts is estimated by classifying past due accounts by age, and by applying bad debt rates based on past experience.

ⓒ Valuation of inventory

Inventory is composed of merchandise, the number of units of which is verified by a physical inventory taken at the end of each year. Jewelries and foodstuffs are valued at their aquisition cost, determined by the specific identification method and by the 'first-in first-out' cost formula, respectively. The remaining merchandise inventory is valued via the retail inventory method.

ⓓ Classification of financial assets

Financial assets are classified into cost financial assets, amortized cost financial assets, fair value through profit or loss (FVPL) financial assets, and fair value through other comprehensive income (FVOCI) financial assets. The amortized cost is cost after amortizing premium (discount) on financial assets by the effective interest method. (The company reports no amortized cost financial assets and FVPL financial assets as of December 31, 20×1 and 20×2). Because valuation gains on FVOCI financial assets may be reclassified to profit or loss when these assets are sold, it is reported as an 'item that may be reclassified subsequently to profit or loss.' And the accumulated sum of these gains are reported as 'accumulated gain on valuation of FVOCI financial assets,' in the equity section of the statement of financial position.

ⓔ Valuation of investment in associate

When the company invests in more than 20% of another company's stock, with voting right, and can thus influence the investee company significantly, that investment is reported as an 'investment in associate.' Investment in associate is valued by the equity method, and equity income is reported as 'other income' in the comprehensive income statement.

ⓕ Aquisition cost, depreciation methods, and revaluation of tangible assets

(1) Plant assets are composed of buildings and structures, and are reported in a format of subtracting accumulated depreciation from acquisition cost. The acquisition cost includes expenditures that are directly attributable to the acquisition. The plant assets are depreciated by the straight-line method. It is estimated that the useful life of buildings is 40 years and the useful life of structures is 10 years, and there is no residual value for either asset. The company checks whether the depreciation expense reflects the reduction in real value of the asset at the end of every year. If it doesn't, then the company reviews and changes the depreciation method, useful life, and residual value.

(2) Capital expenditures, such as large repair costs that improve the efficiency of an asset or extend its useful life, are added to the balance of that asset. Revenue expenditure, such as repair and maintenance cost that is necessary to recover and maintain an asset's current condition, is recorded as a current period expense. The gain or loss on the disposal of plant assets is the difference between the sales proceeds and the book value of the asset, and is reported in the comprehensive income statement as other income or loss.

(3) Land is revaluated at an appraisal value, which is determined by an external and independent appraiser, every 3 years or whenever there is a large change in fair value. The gain on revaluation, that is, the amount of increase in the book value of the asset due to the revaluation, is an item in other comprehensive income in the comprehensive income statement. This gain on revaluation is reported as an 'item that will not be reclassified to profit or loss.' Accumulated gain on revaluation is reported as revaluation surplus, in the equity section of the statement of financial position.

ⓖ Amortization of intangible assets

Intangible assets are composed of industrial property rights (patents). They are amortized by the straight-line method, during their estimated useful life of 10 years, with no residual value

ⓗ Setting up provisions and contingent liabilities

Among liabilities for which the timing of payment and amount are not yet known, a liability for which 1) the possibility of its incurrence is more than 50%, and 2) its amount can be reliably estimated, is reported as a provision. Any liability that meets only one of the two above conditions is reported as a contingent liability. (The company reports provision for refunds and no contingent liability as of December 31, 20×1 and 20×2).

ⓘ Classification of financial liabilities

Financial liabilities are classified into cost financial liabilities, amortized cost financial liabilities, and fair value through profit or loss (FVPL) financial liabilities. Amortized cost means the cost after amortizing premium (discount) on issuance of financial liabilities by the effective interest method. (The company reports no FVPL financial liabilities as of December 31, 20×1 and 20×2).

ⓙ Reporting appropriated retained earnings and unappropriated retained earnings

In the statement of financial position, the company reports the total amount of appropriated retained earnings and unappropriated retained earnings as retained earnings. It reports them separately only in the statement of retained earnings (a proposal), which is disclosed in the footnotes.

4. Cash and cash equivalents

Cash and cash equivalents include cash on hand and bank deposits, as well as financial instruments that can be readily convertible to a known amount of cash and that are subject to an insignificant risk of change in value because they are matured less than 3 months from their acquisition date. Cash equivalents are valued at the quoted price on the active market. 'Cash and cash equivalents' in the statement of financial position is the same as 'cash and cash equivalent' in the statement of cash flows.

5. Allowance for uncollectible accounts

The following reconciliation of the allowance for uncollectible accounts shows the changes in the allowance account during each year.

Reconciliation of allowance for uncollectible accounts

(Numbers in billions of ₩)

Description	20×2	20×1
Beginning balance	2	-
Write-off	(-)2	(-)1
Bad debts expense	4	3
Ending balance	4	2

6. Fair value through other comprehensive income (FVOCI) financial asset

The company purchased the following stock for long-term investment purpose and decided to classify this investment in stock as a FVOCI financial asset on the acquisition day. They are valued at the quoted price (market price).

(Numbers in billions of ₩)

<table>
<tr><th>Investment in stock</th><th>Acquisition date</th><th>Number of shares</th><th colspan="2">Base price per share</th><th>Year-end market price per share</th><th>Valuation gain</th></tr>
<tr><td rowspan="2">KM-Mart</td><td rowspan="2">Nov. 1, 20×1</td><td rowspan="2">1 million share</td><td>20×1</td><td>₩9,000 (Acquisition cost)</td><td>₩10,000</td><td>₩1,000 × 1 million share = 1</td></tr>
<tr><td>20×2</td><td>₩10,000 (Market price at beginning of the year)</td><td>₩13,000</td><td>₩3,000 × 1 million share = 3</td></tr>
</table>

7. Investment in associate

Shown below is the content of investment in associate and the reconciliation of the investment in associate account, revealing changes in that account.

Composition of investment in associate

Associate	Aquisition date	Number of shares	Equity
Sohan Inc.	January 2, 20×2	20,000 shares	20%

Reconciliation of investment in associate

(Numbers in billions of ₩)

Balance at the beginning of 20×2	Changes in 20×2			Balance at the end of 20×2
	Investment	Add : Equity income	Less : Dividends received	
–	20	6	2	24

8. Aquisition and disposal of tangible and intangible assets

The acquisition and disposal of tangible and intangible assets for each year are as follow.

(Numbers in billions of ₩)

Description		Land	Plant assets	Intangible assets
20×1	Beginning balance	–	–	–
	Acquisition in cash	120	100	–
	Acquisition by issuing stock	–	60	–
	Disposal	(–)40*	–	–
	Gain on revaluation	10		
	Ending balance	90	160	–
20×2	Acquisition in cash	–	150	9**
	Gain on revaluation	6		
	Ending balance	96	310	9

* Proceeds from sales were ₩39 billion.
** An industrial property right (patent) acquired at the end of 20×2.

9. Compositions of short-term and long-term borrowings

ⓐ Short-term borrowings

The company borrowed the following in short term to use as working capital.

(Numbers in billions of ₩)

Date of borrowing	Lender	Interest rate	Amount of borrowing	Terms
Apr. 1 20×1	Seoul Bank	10% per annum	30	Matured in 1 year (Interest : after every 6 months)
Apr. 1 20×2	Busan Bank	10% per annum	10	Matured in 1 year (Interest : after every 6 months)

ⓑ Long-term borrowings

(1) Composition of long-term borrowings : Long-term borrowings at the end of 20×2 and 20×1 are shown below :

(Numbers in billions of ₩)

Date of borrowing	Lender	Interest rate	Remaining balance		Terms
			At end of 20×2	At end of 20×1	
Mar. 1, 20×1	Daehan Capital	12% per annum	72	90	5 years installments (Interest : after every 6 months)
May 1, 20×2.	IBK	12% per annum	40	-	4 years installments (Interest : after every year)
Total			112	90	

(2) Retirement schedule : The long-term borrowing retirement schedule for each year is as below.

(Numbers in billions of ₩)

Year	Retirement amount
20×2	18
20×3	28
20×4	28
20×5	28
20×6	28

(3) Current portion of long-term borrowings : The company reclassified ₩28 billion and ₩18 billion of long-term borrowings into the current portion of long-term borrowings at the end of 20×2 and 20×1, respectively per the above retirement schedule.

(Numbers in billions of ₩)

Classification	Account titles	At end of 20×2	At end of 20×1
Current liability	Current portion of long-term borrowings	28	18
Non-Current liability	Long-term borrowings	84	72
Total		112	90

10. Bonds payable

Bonds payable at the end of 20×2 and 20×1 are as follow.

(Numbers in billions of ₩)

Type	Issuance date	Maturity date	Face interest rate	Face value	Issuance price
Debenture bonds	July 1, 20×1	June 30, 20×6	6% per annum	50	39

Interest is paid after every 6 months. Effective interest rate is 12% per annum.

11. Provision for refunds

The following reconciliation schedule shows changes in provision for refunds.

Reconciliation of provision for refunds

(Numbers in billions of ₩)

Description		Provision for refunds
20×1	Beginning balance	-
	Actual refunds made	(-)1
	Estimated refunds	3*
	Ending balance	2
20×2	Actual refunds made	(-)2
	Estimated refunds	3*
	Ending balance	3

* Merchandise returned for a refund is scraped and the estimated amount of refunds is deducted from sales.

12. Earnings per share

Earnings per share for each year are as follow.

(Numbers in billions of ₩)

Year	Net income (1)	Weighted average outstanding shares (2)	Earnings per share [(1)/(2)]
20×2	72	25 million shares**	₩2,880
20×1	26	15 million shares*	₩1,733

* 10 million shares (issued on January 1) × 12/12 + 10 million shares (issued on July 1) × 6/12 = 15 million shares

** 20 million shares (as of January 1) × 12/12 + 10 million shares (issued on July 1) × 6/12 = 25 million shares

13. Share capital

The composition of share capital at the end of each year is as follow.

Year end	Type of stock	Par value	Number of share issued
20×2	Common stock	₩5,000	30 million shares
20×1	Common stock	₩5,000	20 million shares

14. Dividends

Computations of dividends and payout ratio for each year are as follow.

(Numbers in billions of ₩)

Year	Type of stock	Number shares subject to dividends	Par value dividend rate	Amount of dividends
20×2	Common stock	30 million shares	10%	15
20×1	Common stock	20 million shares	5%	5

* The same dividend rate is applied to all stock outstanding at the end of the year regardless of the issuance date of stock per the company's charter.

(Numbers in billions of ₩)

Year	Amount of dividends (1)	Net income (2)	Payout ratio [(1)/(2)]
20×2	15*	72	20.83%
20×1	5**	26	19.23%

* This represents the dividend payment plan of the management. If the plan is finalized by ballot at the stockholders meeting to be held on March 15, 20×3, they will be paid on March 22, 20×3.

** This was finalized by ballot at the stockholders meeting on March 14, 20×2 and paid on March 21, 20×2.

15. Appropriation of retained earnings

The appropriation of retained earnings (a proposal) for each year is as below.

Statement of retained earnings (a proposal)

From Jan. 1, 20×2 to Dec. 31, 20×2

DDS From Jan. 1, 20×1 to Dec. 31, 20×1 (Numbers in billions of ₩)

Description	Retained earnings			
	Legally appropriated	Discretionary appropriated	Unappropriated	Total
	Income	For business expansion		
Balance at beginning of 20×1	–	–	–	–
Changes in retained earnings in 20×1 :				
Net income			26	26
Appropriation per commercial codes**	1		(−)1	
Appropriation for business expansion**		2	(−)2	
Cash dividends**			(−)5	(−)5
Balance at end of 20×1	1	2	18	21
Changes in retained earnings in 20×2 :				
Net income			72	72
Appropriation per commercial codes***	2		(−)2	
Appropriation for business expansion***		4	(−)4	
Cash dividends***			(−)15	(−)15
Balance at end of 20×2	3	6	69	78

* Appropriate more than 10% of each year's dividends until it reaches 1/2 of share capital.

** Finalized by ballot at the stockholders meeting on March 14, 20×2.

*** This is the management's plan and will be finalized by ballot at the stockholders meeting, which will be held on March 16, 20×3.

16. Statement of cash flows : non-cash transactions

Significant non-cash financing and investing transactions for each year are as follow.

(Numbers in billions of ₩)

Description	Amount	
	20×2	20×1
Acquisition of plant assets by issuing stock	–	60*

* It was the cash selling price of plant assets acquired. The company issued and distributed 10 million shares of common stock with par value of ₩5,000 on July 1, 20×1 to the seller.

Operating Activities—Sales and Trade Receivables

Section 1 Sales and trade receivables

Section 2 Trade receivables and bad debts

Section 3 Trade receivables and cash flows

Section 4 Related financial ratios

Chapter 6 ~ Chapter 10 Overview

In Chapters 6 through 10, we explain key transactions incurred from operating, investing, and financial activities. We also examine how to present accounts related to these transactions on the statement of financial position, the comprehensive income statement, and the statement of changes in equity. We present the financial statement of Daehan Department Store at the start of each chapter, to show which part of the financial statement (shaded area) is relevant to the contents of that particular chapter. In addition, we present the corresponding footnotes.

Chapter 6 Overview

In this chapter, we study sales and trade receivables. First, we review the concept of sales revenue and the methods for recording it. Next we study the trade receivables, allowance for uncollectible accounts, and bad debts expense that may be incurred from selling products on credit. Last, we examine how to use trade receivables and bad debt related information.

Case of Daehan Department Store

Statement of financial position (Ft. 2.ⓐ)

DDS As of December 31, 20×2
As of December 31, 20×1 (Numbers in billions of ₩)

Account titles	December 31, 20×2		December 31, 20×1	
Assets				
Current assets				
Cash and cash equivalents(Ft. 4)		45		41
Trade receivables(Ft. 3ⓑ)	30		20	
Allowance for uncollectibe accounts (Ft. 3ⓑ, 5)	(−)4	26	(−)2	18
Inventory :				
Merchandise (Ft. 3ⓒ)		43		23
Total current assets		**114**		**82**
Non-current assets				
FVOCI financial asset (Ft. 3ⓓ, 6)		13		10
Investment in associate (Ft. 3ⓔ, 7)		24		−
Tangible assets (Ft. 8) :				
Land(Ft. 3ⓕ)		96		90
Plant assets (Ft. 3ⓕ, 16)	310		160	
Accumulated depreciation(Ft. 3ⓕ)	(−)13	297	(−)3	157
Intangible asset (Ft. 3ⓖ) :				
Industrial property right (Ft. 8)		9		−
Total non-current assets		**439**		**257**
Total assets		**553**		**339**
Liabilities				
Current liabilities				
Trade payables		42		18
Interest payable		5		4
Salaries payable		2		3
Income tax payable		14		5
Cost financial liabilities (Ft. 3ⓘ) :		38		48
Short-term borrowings (Ft. 9ⓐ)	10		30	
Current portion of long-term borrowings (Ft. 9ⓑ)	28		18	
Provision :				
Provision for refunds (Ft. 3ⓗ, 11)		3		2
Total current liabilities		**104**		**80**
Non-current liabilities				
Cost financial liability (Ft. 3ⓘ) :		126		112
Long-term borrowings (Ft. 9ⓑ)	84		72	
Amortized cost financial liability (Ft. 3ⓘ) :				
Bonds payable (Ft. 10)	42		40	
Total non-current liabilities		**126**		**112**
Total Liabilities		**230**		**192**

Equity				
Share capital				
Common stock (Ft. 13, 16)		150		100
Share premium				
Common stock (Ft. 16)		60		10
Accumulated other comprehensive income		20		11
Accumulated gain on valuation of FVOCI financial asset* (Ft. 3ⓓ, 6)	4		1	
Land revaluation surplus (Ft. 3ⓕ, 8)	16		10	
Retained earnings (Ft. 3ⓛ, 15)		93		26
Total equity		323		147
Total liabilities and equity		553		339

* FVOCI : Fair value through other comprehensive income

Comprehensive income statement (Ft. 2ⓑ)

From Jan. 1, 20×2 to Dec. 31, 20×2

DDS From Jan. 1, 20×1 to Dec. 31, 20×1 (Numbers in billions of ₩)

Account titles	20×2		20×1	
Sales (Ft. 3ⓐ)		430		220
Cost of goods sold		(−)230		(−)118
Gross profit		200		102
Operating expenses :		(−)85		(−)50
Salaries expense	(−)43		(−)26	
Bad debts expense (Ft. 3ⓑ)	(−)4		(−)2	
Depreciation expense (Ft. 3ⓕ)	(−)10		(−)3	
Rent expense	(−)24		(−)12	
Other operating expenses	(−)4		(−)7	
Income from operations		115		52
Other revenue		6		–
Equity income from associate (Ft. 7)	6		–	
Other expenses		(−)19		(−)14
Finance expense (Ft. 2ⓑ) :				
Interest expense	(−)19		(−)13	
Loss on disposal of tangible assets (Ft. 8)	–		(−)1	
Net income before income tax expense		102		38
Income tax expense		(−)30		(−)12
Net income		72		26
Other comprehensive income :		9		11
Item that will not be reclassified to profit or loss :				
Gain on revaluation of land (Ft. 3ⓕ, 8)	6		10	
Item that may be reclassified subsequently to profit or loss :				
Gain on valuation of FVOCI financial asset (Ft. 3ⓓ, 6)	3		1	
Total comprehensive income		81		37
Earnings per share (Ft. 12)		₩2,880		₩1,733

〈Footnotes〉

3. Important accounting policies

ⓐ Revenue recognition

The company recognizes revenue when the amount can be measured reliably and when it is probable that the economic benefits will flow into the company. More specifically, the company's 'revenue recognition time' is the time at which the company transfers (sells) goods to customers.

ⓑ Valuation of trade receivables

The company issued credit card to customers after reviewing customers' credit standing. The trade receivables are the company-issued credit card sales amount not yet collected in cash at the end of the year. Trade receivables are reported in a format by which the net amount is computed by subtracting the allowance for uncollectible accounts from the gross amount. The allowance for uncollectible accounts is estimated by classifying past due accounts by age, and by applying bad debt rates based on past experience.

5. Allowance for uncollectible accounts

The following reconciliation of the allowance for uncollectibe accounts shows the changes in the allowance account during each year.

Reconciliation of allowance for uncollectibe accounts

(Numbers in billions of ₩)

Description	20×2	20×1
Beginning balance	2	-
Write-off	(-)2	(-)1
Bad debts expense	4	3
Ending balance	4	2

Explanation of case financial statements

▪ Note : Number in superscripts are main text page numbers where the corresponding subjects are explained.

The accounts related to this chapter are trade receivables and the allowance for uncollectible accounts—which are reported as current assets in the statement of financial position—as well as sales and bad debts expense, which are reported in the comprehensive income statement. Footnote 3, ⓑ explains that trade receivables are a portion of the company-issued credit card sales not yet collected in cash, as of fiscal year-end.[288] It also shows that trade receivables are reported in the statement of financial position, in a format that computes the net amount by subtracting the allowance for uncollectible accounts from the gross amount.[274] In addition, it shows that the allowance for uncollectible accounts is estimated by classifying past due accounts by age, and applying bad debt rates based on past experience.[276]

Here, the case explanation is mainly focused on the year 20×2 and detailed discussion of the year 20×1 is omitted to avoid explaining the same items twice. According to the statement of financial position, the total trade receivables are ₩30 billion as of December 31, 20×2. The allowance for uncollectible accounts, of ₩4 billion, is the estimated amount of trade receivables that are thought to be uncollectible. Hence, net trade receivables that are estimated to be collectible are reported at ₩26 billion.[274]

Footnote 5 provides a reconciliation schedule showing changes in the allowance for uncollectible accounts. According to this schedule, the allowance for uncollectible accounts balance was decreased by ₩2 billion because of bad debts that were written off, and was increased by ₩4 billion because of bad debts expense reported in the comprehensive income statement.[278]

According to the comprehensive income statement, sales for 20×2—that is, the total amount of sales of merchandise for the year—are ₩430 billion. Footnote 3, ⓐ informs us that the sales revenue is reported at the point of sales that is, at the point when the goods are delivered to the customers.[270] According to the comprehensive income statement, bad debts expense of ₩4 billion was reported as one of the operating expenses for 20×2.[272]

Sales and trade receivables

The money that companies receive by selling merchandise is called sales revenue (or, for short, 'sales' or 'sales amount'). Because sales are the source of a company's profit, the amount and the changing trend of sales are important barometers to evaluate the company's profitability and its future profit-generating capability. In general, sales refer to the sales revenue earned by selling merchandise. Yet services revenue—that is, returns generated by providing services in the service industry—is also called 'sales' in practice.

1.1 Recording sales and cost of goods sold

Sales can be made in cash or on credit. If a sale is made in cash, the sales proceeds are received in cash at the time of sale. If a sale is made on credit, trade receivables are incurred. A trade receivable (매출채권) is the right to receive sales proceeds from the sale of merchandise on account. When a company sells merchandise on an account, depending on the customer's credit standing, sometimes the company receives a promissory note, and sometimes it receives nothing. The promissory note is a 'document showing a promise to pay the amount owed on the promised date.' The right incurred when a note is received is called 'notes receivable' (받을어음) the right incurred when no note is received is called 'accounts receivable' (외상매출금). Both types of receivables uncollected are reported as trade receivables in the statement of financial position.

⟨Box 6-1⟩ A note receivable

A note that will be received? A note by which cash will be received?

Some students think that a note receivable is 'a note that will be received in the future.' A note receivable is an account where we record credit sales receiving a promissory note. Thus, if a company reports ₩1 billion of note receivable, it means that the company has a note by which the company can receive cash of ₩1 billion in the future.

If we sell merchandise, the merchandise inventory decreases. The amount of purchase (cost) of the merchandise, decreased by sales (sold), is called the cost of goods sold. The systems for recording the cost of goods sold include: (1) the perpetual inventory system, which records the cost of goods sold every time a sale is made and (2) the periodic inventory system, which takes a physical inventory at the end of the fiscal year and indirectly computes and reports the cost of goods sold. In Chapter 3 and Chapter 5, we studied how to record sales and cost of goods sold, assuming that the case company uses the perpetual inventory system. In this chapter, we will study how to record sales if the case company uses the periodic inventory system. The method by which cost of goods sold is recorded under the periodic inventory system will be examined in Chapter 7.

⟨Box 6-2⟩ Sale returns, sales allowance, and sales discounts

If the merchandise sold is returned due to a defect, it is called as a **sales return**. A reduction in the sales amount that is made due to a defect in merchandise sold is called as a **sales allowance**. Although this seldom happens in Korea, as a means to collect trade receivables early, some companies in other countries allow a discount on the credit sales amount if customers pay the amount owed within a specified period. This is called a **sales discount**.

The sales amount after subtracting sales returns, sales allowance, and sales discounts from gross sales, that are total amount of sales, is called '**net sales**.' Some companies set up separate accounts to tightly control sales returns, sales allowance, and sales discounts. But these items are not reported and only net sales are reported in the externally reported comprehensive income statement. This book, mainly examining the externally reported financial statements, assumes that all of these items are reflected on the sales account.

Trade receivables and bad debts

When companies sell on credit, rather than exclusively selling in cash, it can increase their sales revenue. However, by doing so they must take on the risk of not collecting trade receivables. It is because some customers who bought merchandise on credit may not be able to pay the amount owed. This is similar to making a personal loan to a friend and being unable to collect the principal amount of the loan.

2.1 Uncollectible accounts and bad debt expense

2.1.1 Bad debts expense

Trade receivables that are estimated to be impossible to collect are called uncollectible accounts. The credit sales amount that cannot be collected from customers is an expense that the company must bear, as a side effect of selling merchandise on credit. This expense is called the 'bad debts expense.'

2.1.2 Bad debts expense recording methods

There are two methods for recording bad debts expense : the direct write-off method (직접상각법) and the allowance method (충당금법). Here we examine the differences between the direct write-off method and the allowance method, by applying these two methods to ⟨Illustration 6-1⟩ below.

〈Illustration 6-1〉 Comparison of the direct write-off method with the allowance method

Suwon Department Store's sales on credit for 20×1 were ₩950 billion. Trade receivables at end of 20×1 were ₩200 billion and the company estimated that ₩4 billion of trade receivables would be uncollectible. In 20×2, trade receivables of ₩1 billion were determined as a bad debt and written off. (Numbers in journal entries are in billions of ₩.)

(1) Direct write-off method

Under the direct write-off method, bad debts expense is not reported in 20×1. In 20×2, ₩1 billion of trade receivables are determined to be uncollectible and written off from the accounting books. That amount is reported as bad debts expense in 20×2. This is journalized as below.

(Dr.) Bad debts expense (20×2)	1	(Cr.) Trade receivables	1

If the revenue-expense matching principle is strictly applied, then ₩1 billion of uncollectible trade receivables should be recorded as an expense for 20×1, because they were a part of 20×1 sales even though they were finalized as uncollectible in 20×2. As can be seen in the above journal entry, the direct write-off method poses two problems : it records ₩1 billion of bad debts expense as an expense in 20×2, and it overstates trade receivables above the expected future cash flow of ₩196 billion.

(2) The allowance method

Under the allowance method, we deduct the estimated uncollectible amount of ₩ 4 billion from the trade receivables of ₩200 billion at the end of 20×1, and we record that amount as a bad debts expense in 20×1. The deduction from the trade receivables is done through the allowance for uncollectible accounts, which is a contra account (see 〈Box 6-3〉 below) to the trade receivables account. This method is called the allowance method because it uses an allowance account. If we apply the allowance method, the following journal entry should be prepared.

(Dr.) Bad debts expense (20×1) 4	(Cr.) Allowance for uncollectible accounts 4

〈Box 6-3〉 Contra account

A contra account is one that offsets the balance in another account, with which it is paired. The allowance of uncollectible accounts is a contra account to the trade receivables. The accumulated depreciation, which will be reviewed in Chapter 8, is a contra account to the plant assets.

Due to the above journal entry, ₩4 billion of estimated uncollectible accounts from trade receivables of ₩200 billion at the end of 20×1 is recorded as an expense of 20×1. This expense is one that occurred because they sold merchandise at ₩950 billion on credit in 20×1. We can say that the allowance method is one that properly matches expense against revenue, because ₩4 billion of expense, which occurred due to sales on credit, was recorded as an expense in 20×1, the same year in which the sales revenue was recorded.

There are two methods for reporting trade receivables in the statement of financial position : the gross method and the net method. Under the gross method, first, the gross trade receivables of ₩200 billion are reported and the allowance for uncollectible accounts of ₩4 billion is deducted, as shown in 〈Table 6-1〉 below. Then the net trade receivables of ₩196 billion are reported.

〈Table 6-1〉 Statement of financial position—Gross method

(Numbers in billions of ₩)

Account titles	Amount	
Assets		
Current assets		
Trade receivables	200	
Allowance for uncollectible accounts	(−)4	196

Under the net method, only the net trade receivables of ₩196 billion are reported in the statement of financial position, as shown in 〈Table 6-2〉 below.

〈Table 6-2〉 Statement of financial position–Net method

(Numbers in billions of ₩)

Account titles	Amount	
Assets		
Current assets		
Trade receivables		196

As seen, trade receivables are not overstated in either the gross method or the net method because the trade receivables are reported at the expected future cash flow of ₩196 billion in both methods. IFRS[1] allows only the allowance method as a bad debt expense recording method. It allows both of the gross method and the net method of reporting trade receivables in the statement of financial position. Whatever reporting method is used, a reconciliation schedule must be disclosed, showing the changes in allowance for uncollectible accounts.

2.2 Methods of estimating uncollectible accounts

There are two methods for estimating uncollectible accounts : the individual estimating method and the group estimating method. Under the individual estimating method, trade receivables at the end of the year are classified by customer, and uncollectible receivables are estimated individually by each customer as well. Under the group estimating method, trade receivables at the end of the year are classified by customers, and they are grouped by similarity of credit risk. Uncollectible receivables are estimated for each group.

The individual estimating method is used when a company has a small number of major customers. If they are corporate customers, then the factors to be considered include : delinquency in the interest or principal amount of other loans, lowering interest rates or principal amounts of other loans through refinancing, possibility of default, possibility of workout (revival through creditors' management), possibility of court receivership, possibility of bankruptcy, etc. If a corporate customer is bankrupt, the applicable trade receivables are usually written off. If, on the other hand, customers are individuals, the following factors should be considered : delinquency in interest or principal amount of other loans, possibility of default, possibility of financial recovery, possibility of bankruptcy, etc. Usually if a customer is bankrupt, or if the residence of the customer is unknown due to escape, the applicable trade receivables are written off.

The group estimating method is used when there are a large number of minor customers, in which case the application of the individual estimating method is unrealistic and unjustified. In addition, this method should be used when the company does not have reasonable and supportable information that is available to estimate bad debts on an individual customer basis (IFRS[2]). Under this method, customers with similar levels of credit risk are formed into groups. A statistical method (for example: the 'aging method', shown below) is then applied to each group, based on historical experience. After trade receivables are past due by a certain number of days (for example: 180 days), they are usually written off.

IFRS[3] demonstrates the 'aging method,' under which uncollectible trade receivables are estimated by customer groups with similar credit risk. It also provides examples of different customer groups, such as sales regions, types of merchandise, credit ratings of customers, and customer types like wholesalers and retailers.

Here, we examine the aging method with 〈Illustration 6-2〉.

〈Illustration 6-2〉 Estimating uncollectible receivables using the aging method

Trade receivables of Suwon Department Store at end of 20×1 were ₩400 billion. The following 〈Table 6-3〉 shows uncollectible trade receivables, which are estimated by analyzing ages of trade receivables.

〈Table 6-3〉 Aging method

(Numbers in billions of ₩)

Past due	Amount of receivables	Loss rate (based on historical experience)	Estimated uncollectible receivables
Current	294	0.41%	1.2
1~30	60	2%	1.2
31~60	40	3%	1.2
61~90	4	6%	0.24
Over 91 days	2	8%	0.16
Total	400		4

As seen in 〈Illustration 6-2〉 above, under the aging method, the uncollectible trade receivables are estimated by applying a higher loss rate to groups with older trade receivables. The loss rate is computed by adjusting historical statistical data for accounts with similar credit risk.

〈Box 6-4〉 Bad debt accounting when trade receivables contain interest

Trade receivables may contain an interest component because the trade receivables possess certain characteristics of a loan. Per IFRS[4], the interest included in trade receivables is called a financing component. This is shown as the difference between the cash selling price and the contract amount.

In the following cases, IFRS[5] allows companies to treat the trade receivables with a financing component same as the trade receivable without a financing component when they account for bad debts.

(1) Although there is a financing component, the credit period is shorter than one year ; or,
(2) Although there is a financing component, the company decides to account for bad debts as there is no financing component.

Although there is a financing component with credit terms over one year in trade receivables, the company may not fulfill requirement (2) above. In that case, as per IFRS[6] the company should account for bad debts by considering the trade receivable as an amortized cost financial asset, as shown below.

When there is a significant increase in the risk of bad debts (e.g., more than 30 days past due), the company should report the allowance for uncollectible accounts at an amount equal to the bad debts expected for a period equal to the whole contract period of related trade receivables (the lifetime expected bad debts). (Note that this method is the same method used when there is no financing component in trade receivables.) When there is no significant increase in the risk of bad debts, the company should report the allowance at an amount equal to the bad debts expected for the 12-month period, calculated from the date of statement of financial position (the 12-month expected bad debts). The aging method can be used for both the lifetime expected bad debts and the 12-month expected bad debts. (Detailed accounting treatments for the credit loss on amortized cost financial assets will be reviewed in the Intermediate Accounting course.)

2.3 Accounting for bad debts by the allowance method

〈Illustration 6-3〉, below, examines how to account for bad debts under the allowance method.

〈Illustration 6-3〉 Accounting for bad debts by the allowance method

Suwon Department Store' allowance for uncollectible accounts at end of 20×1 was ₩4 billion. And trade receivables found to be bad and written off in 20×2 and as well as estimated uncollectible trade receivables at end of 20×2, are as shown in 〈Table 6-4〉 below.

〈Table 6-4〉 Data to record bad debts

(Numbers in billions of ₩)

Case number		Allowance for uncollectible accounts balance at end of 20×1	Trade receivables written off in 20×2	Estimated uncollectible trade receivables at end of 20×2
(1)	(1.1)	4	2	5
	(1.2)	4	2	1
(2)		4	5	3

(Case 1) When trade receivables written off are less than the allowance for uncollectible accounts balance at the beginning of the year

When trade receivables written off are less than the allowance for uncollectible accounts balance at the beginning of the year, there could be two different cases. These include (Case 1.1), where we must set up more allowance for uncollectible accounts at the end of the year and (Case 1.2), where we must recover the allowance for uncollectible accounts at the end of the year.

(Case 1.1) When additional allowance for uncollectible accounts should be set up

1) Recording determined bad debts

In (Case 1.1), when ₩2 billion is determined to be bad debts in 20×2, the following entry should be prepared.

(Dr.) Allowance for uncollectible accounts 2	(Cr.) Trade receivables 2

Through the journal entry above, the trade receivables determined to be bad debts are written off from the accounting books by posting ₩2 billion on the credit side of the trade receivables account. The allowance for uncollectible accounts balance is also reduced by posting ₩2 billion on the debit side of the allowance for uncollectible accounts.

2) Setting up the allowance for the uncollectible accounts at the end of the year

The estimated uncollectible trade receivables at the end of 20×2 are ₩5 billion. The allowance for the uncollectible accounts balance is ₩2 billion : the balance at the end of 20×1 of ₩4 billion, less bad debts written off during 20×2 of ₩2 billion. To convert the allowance for the uncollectible accounts balance of ₩2 billion into the estimated uncollectible trade receivables of ₩5 billion, ₩3 billion should be recorded on the credit side of the allowance for uncollectible accounts. To achieve this, the following journal entry should be made.

(Dr.) Bad debts expense 3	(Cr.) Allowance for uncollectible accounts 3

As can be seen in the journal entry above, the bad debts expense is recorded at ₩3 billion, even though the estimated uncollectible trade receivables at year-end are ₩5 billion. This is because, while the allowance for uncollectible accounts balance at the beginning of the year was ₩4 billion, only ₩ 2 billion of trade receivables was written off during the year, leaving the difference of ₩2 billion as the balance of the allowance for uncollectible accounts.

(Case 1.2) When the allowance for uncollectible accounts should be recovered

Although it seldom happens, sometimes, due to changes in the economic situation the customers' credit standing improves so that the allowance for uncollectible accounts to be set up at end of year can be less than the allowance for uncollectible accounts balance before the set up. In that case, the allowance for uncollectible accounts balance in excess of amount to be set up is recorded as profit from reversal of allowance for uncollectible accounts.

1) Recording determined bad debts

For (Case 1.2), above, the following journal entry to record determined bad debts of ₩2 billion should be prepared.

(Dr.) Allowance for uncollectible accounts 2	(Cr.) Trade receivables 2

2) Recovery of allowance for uncollectible accounts

In (Case 1.2), above, ₩1 billion of allowance for uncollectible accounts to be set up at end of year is less by ₩1 billion than the ₩2 billion of allowance for uncollectible accounts balance, after recording bad debts (₩4 billion of allowance for uncollectible accounts balance at beginning of year - ₩2 billion of bad debts recorded). Therefore, the following journal entry should be prepared to reduce the allowance for uncollectible accounts balance and to recognize profit from the reversal of the allowance for uncollectible accounts of ₩1 billion.

(Dr.) Allowance of uncollectible accounts 1	(Cr.) Profit from reversal of allowance for uncollectible accounts 1

(Case 2) When trade receivables written off are greater than the allowance for uncollectible accounts balance at the beginning of the year

There are two methods for recording bad debts—the traditional method and the summary method—which can be used when the trade receivables determined to be uncollectible are greater than the allowance for uncollectible accounts balance at the beginning of the year.

(Case 2.1) Traditional method

This is a traditional accounting method for bad debts when reporting on tax in Korea. (Refer to 〈Box 6-5〉 'Effects of tax accounting.') Under this method, we first set the allowance for uncollectible accounts to '0' with the amount of bad debts to be written off. We then record any excess of bad debts over the allowance as a bad debts expense. The allowance for uncollectible accounts at the year end is set at the amount of estimated bad debts, and this amount should also be recorded as a bad debts expense.

⟨Box 6-5⟩ Effects of tax accounting

In past, companies used to accounting not for external reporting (financial accounting) but for tax reporting (tax accounting). Some accounting conventions in tax accounting are still observed in financial accounting. One of example is the traditional method of accounting bad debts.

Korean tax codes allow that a certain percentage (e.g., 1% in general, but 2% for financial institutions) of the year end trade receivables be recognized as a bad debts expense, and set up as an allowance for uncollectible accounts. In tax accounting, we show the amount allowed by the tax codes as a separate journal entry. To do this, the allowance for uncollectible accounts balance should be first set to '0.'

When the bad debts to be written off is less than the allowance for uncollectible accounts balance at the beginning of the year—(Case 1.1) and (Case 1.2) in the main text

In tax accounting, if there is a balance remaining in the allowance for uncollectible accounts after recording the total bad debts to be written off, this remaining balance is recorded as profit from the reversal of the allowance and set the allowance account balance to '0.' Then the total amount of estimated bad debts at the year end is set up as an allowance for uncollectible accounts, and that amount is recorded as a bad debts expense. This method is rejected in financial accounting because it reports the profit from the reversal of allowance and bad debts expense together. Instead, the method of reporting the net amount of these two figures is adopted.

When bad debts to be written off is more than the allowance for uncollectible accounts balance at the beginning of the year—(Case 2) in the main text

The balance for the allowance for uncollectible accounts is first set to '0' with the amount of bad debts to be written off, and the amount in excess of the allowance is then recorded as a bad debts expense. Then the amount of estimated bad debts at year end is set as an allowance for uncollectible accounts, and this amount is recorded as an additional bad debts expense. This method is still in use in financial accounting, as it reports the correct amount for both the bad debts expense and the allowance for uncollectible accounts.

1) Recording determined bad debts

In (Case 2), the determined bad debts amount in 20×2 of ₩5 billion is ₩1 billion greater than the allowance for uncollectible accounts balance at the beginning of the year, of ₩4 billion. Therefore, ₩1 billion is recorded as bad debts expense, as below.

(Dr.)		(Cr.)	
Allowance for uncollectible accounts	4	Trade receivables	5
Bad debts expense	1		

2) Setting up the allowance for uncollectible accounts at the end of the year

Because there is no balance remaining in the allowance for uncollectible accounts, after the determined bad debts of ₩5 billion are recorded, the following journal entry should be prepared to set up ₩3 billion of allowance for uncollectible accounts.

(Dr.)		(Cr.)	
Bad debts expense	3	Allowance for uncollectible accounts	3

(Case 2.2) Summary method

Under this method, we use the allowance for uncollectible accounts as an account summarizing all bad debt-related transactions. Through an adjusting journal entry at the year's end, we change the allowance for uncollectible accounts balance to the balance that it should have, and we recognize the total bad debts expense for the current year.

1) Recording determined bad debts

Using the allowance for uncollectible accounts as a summary account, bad debts of ₩5 billion, to be written off in (Case 2), should be journalized as below.

(Dr.)		(Cr.)	
Allowance for uncollectible accounts	5	Trade receivables	5

2) Setting up the allowance for uncollectible accounts at the end of the year

As a result of the above journal entry for bad debts, the allowance for uncollectible accounts balance becomes a debit balance of ₩1 billion. To convert the allowance account balance into a credit balance of ₩3 billion, we should prepare the following journal entry.

(Dr.)		(Cr.)	
Bad debts expense	4	Allowance for uncollectible accounts	4

Usually bad debts are written off many times throughout the year. Under this method, there is no need to check the balance of allowance for uncollectible accounts every time we write off bad debts. This method is also consistent with (Case 1.1) and (Case 1.2) above. Because of its practical usefulness and consistency in recording bad debt transactions, this method is used in the U.S.

The following ⟨Table 6-5⟩ is a summary of the journal entries for ⟨Illustration 6-3⟩.

⟨Table 6-5⟩ Journal entries for ⟨Illustration 6-3⟩

(Numbers in billions of ₩)

Year	Case No.	Journal entries	
20×2	(1.1)	(Dr.) Allowance for uncollectible accounts 2	(Cr.) Trade receivables 2
		(Dr.) Bad debts expense 3	(Cr.) Allowance for uncollectible accounts 3
	(1.2)	(Dr.) Allowance for uncollectible accounts 2	(Cr.) Trade receivables 2
		(Dr.) Allowance for uncollectible accounts 1	(Cr.) Profit from reversal of allowance for uncollectible accounts 1
	(2.1) TM	(Dr.) Allowance for uncollectible accounts 4 (Dr.) Bad debts expense 1	(Cr.) Trade receivables 5
		(Dr.) Bad debts expense 3	(Cr.) Allowance for uncollectible accounts 3
	(2.2) SM	(Dr.) Allowance for uncollectible accounts 5	(Cr.) Trade receivables 5
		(Dr.) Bad debts expense 4	(Cr.) Allowance for uncollectible accounts 4

TM : Traditional method, SM : Summary method

(Case 3) Accounting for trade receivables collected after they were written off

Sometimes a company collects trade receivables that were previously written off from the books because they were determined to be bad debts. In such cases, first, both trade receivables that were written off from the books and the reduced amount of allowance for uncollectible accounts should be recovered. Then, the collection of the recovered trade receivables should be recorded. For instance, if in ⟨Illustration 6-3⟩, ₩1 billion is collected in 20×2 from trade receivables written off, it is journalized as :

① (Dr.) Trade receivables	1	(Cr.) Allowance for uncollectible accounts	1

② (Dr.) Cash	1	(Cr.) Trade receivables	1

The above journal entry ① is to recover the trade receivables that were written off, and ② is to record the collection of the recovered trade receivables. The reason for going through the trade receivables account, here, is to leave a trail in that account. This recording method is more effective when trade receivables are recorded and managed by individual customers.

If trade receivables that were previously written off are collected in 〈Illustration 6-3〉, as shown above, then the amounts in the year-end adjusting journal entries should be changed as follows. In the case of (Case 1.1) and (Case 2), the amount in the journal entry, to set up the allowance for uncollectible accounts at year-end, should be reduced by ₩1 billion. In the case of (Case 2), the profit from the reversal of the allowance for uncollectible accounts to be recognized at year-end should be increased by ₩1 billion.

〈Box 6-6〉 Accounting for bad debts should be applied prospectively

The allowance for uncollectible accounts is set up according to the management's **estimate**. Since this estimate, by nature, attempts to foresee events that will take place in the future, it will in most cases differ from the actual amount of uncollectible accounts. If this estimate is **retrospectively** adjusted every time the estimated amount and the real amount prove to be different, then the **credibility** of the accounting information will be hampered. As a recognition of the basic nature of estimates, if the actual amount is different from the estimated amount, then accounting records are not retrospectively adjusted. Instead, they are **prospectively** reflect the difference in the current period.

Because of this reason, in bad debt accounting, when we write off trade receivables and set up the allowance for uncollectible accounts, bad debts are accounted for prospectively. Thus, when we account for bad debts, we do not differentiate the year in which the applicable trade receivables occurred, or whether they were included in the allowance for uncollectible accounts at the beginning of the year. IFRS[7] requires **prospective** accounting for bad debts.

Trade receivables and cash flows

If trade receivables are not collected after selling goods on credit, then this may cause a shortage of cash even if profit is reported in the income statement. Therefore, the greater the amount of trade receivables that remain uncollected after sales are made on credit, the worse a company's cash position may be.

3.1 Credit sales and cash flow

Let's review the relationship between profit and cash flow, when goods are sold on credit, by examining the following illustration.

> 〈Illustration 6-4〉 Trade receivables and cash flows
>
> Shinchon Trading Company's total sales on credit in 20×1 were ₩30 billion. Trade receivables on January 1, and December 31, 20×1 were ₩3 billion and ₩4 billion, respectively. Total operating expense in 20×1 was ₩25 billion (including cost of goods sold of ₩10 billion), and all of it was paid in cash.

3.1.1 Computing net income

Net income is computed by subtracting expense from revenue, as shown in 〈Table 6-6〉 below. In 〈Illustration 6-4〉 above, net income is ₩5 billion that was computed by subtracting total operating expenses from sales.

⟨Table 6-6⟩ Income statement

(Numbers in billions of ₩)

Account titles	Amount
Sales	30
Operating expenses	(−)25
Net income	5

3.1.2 Computing cash flows from operating activities

Cash flows from operating activities is computed by subtracting cash paid for operating expenses from cash received from selling goods (that is : trade receivables collected in cash) as shown in ⟨Table 6-7⟩ below.

⟨Table 6-7⟩ Cash flows from operating activities

(Numbers in billions of ₩)

Description	Amount
Trade receivables collected in cash	29
Cash paid for operating expenses	(−)25
Net cash from operating activities	4

Shinchon Trading Company's cash collection of trade receivables in 20×1 was ₩29 billion and cash paid for operating expenses was ₩25 billion, so cash was increased by ₩4 billion from operating activities. The amount of cash collected from trade receivables can be easily calculated through an analysis of the trade receivables T account, as shown in ⟨Diagram 6-1⟩ below.

⟨Diagram 6-1⟩ T account analysis—Trade receivables

(Numbers in billions of ₩)

		Beginning 3(Dr.)
Sales on credit 30		33(Dr.)
	Cash collected 29	Ending 4(Dr.)

The reason that the trade receivables balance increased by ₩1 billion—from the beginning (January 1) balance of ₩3 billion to the ending (December 31) balance of ₩4 billion—is that only ₩29 billion out of ₩30 billion in credit sales was collected in cash. The credit sales of ₩1 billion was not collected in cash, assuming the beginning balance of trade receivables was not collected at all. Thus, net income was ₩5 billion but net cash from operating activities was ₩4 billion, so the cash position was not good in comparison to the profit.

In Chapter 5, we examined the causes for the difference between net income and operating cash flows by classifying them into four types. Here, we have reviewed the same issue through a T account analysis of trade receivable account and we will reexamine it using the double-entry bookkeeping mechanism in Chapter 11, which introduces methods for preparing the statement of cash flows.

3.2 Early conversion of trade receivables into cash

As explained above, trade receivables can cause a company to have a poor cash position. Here we examine methods to resolve this problem, including ways in which we can convert the accounts receivable and notes receivable—of which trade receivables are comprised—into cash ahead of time.

3.2.1 Transfer of accounts receivable

If a company has sold its merchandise on credit, the company's cash position can be poor because the money is tied up in accounts receivable until it is collected. A method that allows us to convert accounts receivable into cash early, so that it can be used for operation is the transfer of accounts receivable. This method is to transfer a company's accounts receivable to a financial institution to which it pays commission fees. This is called a 'factoring (팩토링).' If a company transfers its accounts receivable, it receives the cash amount of the accounts receivable transferred, less the commission fee. Some transfers of accounts receivable actually transfer the risk, benefit, and control of said accounts to the financial institution, and some do not. The former is considered a sale of accounts receivable, while the latter is considered a borrowing with accounts receivable as collateral per IFRS[8].

If, after a sale of accounts receivable, some or all of the accounts turn out to be uncollectible, the financial institution may have the right to recourse from the company. When a financial institution has the recourse right against a company, then the company must estimate the uncollectible amount from the accounts receivable sold, and set up that estimated amount as a liability. However, if there is no right to recourse, nothing is done by the company for the uncollectible accounts receivable.

3.2.2 Transfer with endorsement and discount of notes receivable

Notes receivable are collected in cash only when the due date arrives. However, by transferring the notes receivable with an endorsement prior to the due date, we can use them as a means of settlement for liability, in lieu of cash. Early cash conversion of notes receivable is also possible, by discounting said notes to financial institutions. In this case, a specific rate of commission must be paid to the financial institutions, which is called the discount rate.

A promissory note carries the risk that the issuer may not be able to pay the amount of the note on the maturity date, which is the risk of default. In the case of a transfer with endorsement or discount of notes receivable, whether the risk, benefit and control are transferred or not depends on the issuer's possibility of default. If the probability of default is above 50%, it is regarded as borrowing with the note receivable as collateral per IFRS[9]. However, if the probability is below 50%, then it is regarded as a sale and it should be disclosed in a footnote as a contingent liability (우발부채). Here, contingent liability refers to a liability with less than a 50% possibility that the company will be responsible, depending on future events. It is not reported as a liability on the statement of financial position, but it is instead disclosed in the footnote. However, if the probability is very low, it is not considered contingent liability, so there is no need to disclose it in the footnote.

3.2.3 Sales with credit card

In addition to cash sales and credit sales, companies can make sales with credit cards that are issued by credit card companies. (Sales made with credit cards that are issued by the company itself are considered sales on credit). Accounting for credit card sales can differ, based on the length of time that elapses in collecting cash from the credit card company.

When a company submits sales slips to the credit card company, then the company receives cash in the amount of sales, less fees. If cash is received a long time after the sales slips are turned in to the credit card company, then we record credit card sales as trade receivables until cash is received. If cash is received as soon as the sales slips are turned in, then we record credit card sales as cash sales.

⟨Box 6-7⟩ Recording value-added tax and sales revenue

Korea runs the value-added tax system. Therefore, when customers purchase products, value-added tax of 10% of selling price is added to the sales price. Value-added tax is paid by customers, but the tax is received by the selling companies and they pay it to the Office of National Tax Administration on behalf of the customers.

The value-added tax that companies received from customers is the tax to be paid to the Office of National Tax Administration, so it is a liability from perspective of the company. Thus, this is recorded in a liability account called 'value-added tax collected in advance.' For example, if merchandise that has selling price of ₩10 billion is sold in cash, ₩11 billion of cash received from customer, that includes value-added tax, is journalized as following. (Numbers in journal entry are in billions of ₩.)

(Dr.) Cash	11	(Cr.) Sales	10
		Value-added tax collected in advance	1

And when the value-added tax received by customers is paid to the tax office, then it is journalized as following.

(Dr.) Value-added tax collected in advance	1	(Cr.) Cash	1

Related financial ratios

Financial ratios that use sales and trade receivables include trade receivables turnover and days' sales in trade receivables (by which one can evaluate a company's activities), as well as trade receivables uncollectibility risk (by which one can evaluate a company's financial safety).

4.1 Financial ratios evaluating activity

(1) Trade receivables turnover

The trade receivables turnover is an index that measures how many times, on average, trade receivables are collected in cash in a year. It is calculated by dividing sales by the average trade receivables amount. The average trade receivables amount is the average between the beginning trade receivables and the ending trade receivables. For practical convenience, and because there are no beginning trade receivables in the first year of operation, ending trade receivables can be used instead of the average trade receivables.

$$\text{Trade receivables turnover} = \frac{\text{Sales}}{\text{Average trade receivables}} = \frac{\text{Sales}}{(\text{Beginning trade receivables} + \text{Ending trade receivables}) / 2}$$

The speed at which trade receivables are collected greatly affects a company's cash position. If the receivables turnover is 6 times, it means that trade receivables are collected in cash an average of 6 times in a year. To raise the receivables turnover, we should lower the trade receivables balances by collecting the trade receivables earlier. A higher receivables turnover is better. It is because a company's working capital condition can be improved.

(Ratio of Daehan Department Store)

$$20\times2 : \frac{430\text{ billion}}{(20\text{ billion} + 30\text{ billion})/2} = 17.2\text{ times}$$

$$20\times1 : \frac{220\text{ billion}}{20\text{ billion}^{*}} = 11\text{ times}$$

* Ending trade receivables were used as the denominator because there were no beginning trade receivables 20×1, the year of fundation. In practice, ending trade receivables are used as the denominator for convinience's sake.

Daehan Department Store's receivable turnover is increased by 6.2 times from 20×1 to 20×2. This means that the store's efficiency at managing trade receivables has improved.

(2) Days' sales in trade receivables

Days' sales in trade receivables is defined as the average number of days it takes to collect trade receivables. This is calculated by dividing 365 days by the trade receivables turnover. Days' sales in trade receivables gets lower as trade receivables turnover gets higher.

$$\textbf{Days' sales in trade receivables} = \frac{\textbf{365}}{\textbf{Trade receivables turnover}}$$

If the days' sales in trade receivables of a company decrease, compared to that of the prior year, it can be understood that money tied up in trade receivables is reduced.

(Ratio of Daehan Department Store)

$$20\times2 : \frac{365}{17.2} = 21.22\text{ days}$$

$$20\times1 : \frac{365}{11.0} = 33.18\text{ days}$$

Daehan Department Store's days' sales in trade receivables is reduced by 12 days, from 20×1 to 20×2. This can be understood that the money tied up in trade receivables was reduced from 20×1 to 20×2, so Daehan Department Store's working capital condition has improved.

4.2 Financial ratio evaluating safety (financial)

(1) Trade receivables uncollectibility risk

The trade receivables uncollectibility risk is an index that represents how much of the ending trade receivables is uncollectible. This is calculated by dividing the allowance for uncollectible accounts balance by the trade receivables.

$$\textbf{Trade receivables uncollectibility risk} = \frac{\textbf{Allowance for uncollectible accounts}}{\textbf{Trade receivables}}$$

Because the allowance for uncollectible accounts is an estimated amount of uncollectible trade receivables, the higher the allowance, the higher the risk of trade receivables uncollected.

(Ratio of Daehan Department Store)

$$20\times2: \quad \frac{4 \text{ billion}}{30 \text{ billion}} = 13.33\%$$

$$20\times1: \quad \frac{2 \text{ billion}}{20 \text{ billion}} = 10\%$$

If this ratio is relatively high in comparison to other department stores, then it can be understood that Daehan Department Store may have a problem managing its trade receivables.

- Note : Financial ratios reviewed in this chapter are summarized in Appendix 2 〈Table B-1〉 'Key financial ratios' at the end of this book.

IFRS references (http://www.kasb.or.kr)

[1] IFRS 9 *Financial Instruments*, par. 5.5.1.
IFRS 7 *Financial Instruments : Disclosures*, par. 16.
[2] IFRS 9 *op. cit.*, par. B5.5.4.
[3] IFRS 9 *op. cit.*, par. 5.5.15, B5.5.35.
[4] IFRS 15 *Revenue from Contracts with Customers*, par. 61.
[5] IFRS 9 *op. cit.*, par. 5.5.15(a)(i)(ii).
[6] IFRS 9 *op. cit.*, par. 5.5.3, 5.5.5, 5.5.11, B5.5.1~5.5.6.
[7] IAS 8 *Accounting Policies, Changes in Accounting Estimates and Errors*, par. 36
[8] IFRS 9 *op. cit.*, par. 3.2.6.
[9] IAS 37 *Provisions, Contingent Liabilities and Contingent Assets*, par. 28.

Key terms

Accounts receivable (외상매출금) : Receivable that has not yet been collected in cash, among receivable arising from the sales of merchandise made purely on the credit of customers. (p.270)

Allowance for uncollectible accounts (대손충당금) : Estimated uncollectible amount in the trade receivables at the end of the year. (p.273)

Allowance method (충당금법) : The method of estimating the uncollectible amount from trade receivables at year-end, and reporting it as bad debt expense and an allowance for uncollectible accounts in financial statements. (p.272)

Bad debts expense (대손상각비) : Expense occurred because trade receivables are not collected. (p.272)

Direct write-off method (직접상각법) : The method of recognizing a bad debts expense and directly writing it off from trade receivables in the same period during which a specific trade receivable is determined to be uncollectible. (p.272)

Notes receivable (받을어음) : Promissory notes that have not yet been collected in cash, among those notes received as a consideration from selling merchandise on credit. (p.270)

Promissory note (약속어음) : A document of debt agreement specifying the amount to be paid and date of payment (the maturity date). (p.270)

Sales revenue (매출수익) : The revenue that companies generate by selling merchandise and also it is simply called sales. (p.270)

Trade receivables (매출채권) : The receivables from selling merchandise on credit, meaning the right to receive cash in future and consist of accounts receivable and notes receivable. (p.270)

Exercises

▪ Note: Assume that the periodic inventory system is used by the company in all exercises.

1. Recording sales and trade receivables

The following are the transactions of Wooam Trading Company for 20×1 and 20×2. Wooam Trading Company uses accounts receivable account and notes receivable account.

〈20×1〉

① Jan. 5: Sold goods for ₩20 billion in cash to Daejin Trading Company.

② Jun. 9: Sold goods for ₩10 billion on credit to Youngsin Trading Company.

③ Oct. 25: Sold goods for ₩15 billion to Daegu Trading Company and received cash of ₩5 billion and received a 3-month promissory note for remaining balance of ₩10 billion.

④ Nov. 25: Received cash of ₩10 billion from Youngsin Trading Company for accounts receivable of June 9, 20×1.

⑤ Dec. 1: Sold goods for ₩25 billion to Daejeon Trading Company and received ₩10 billion in cash and left ₩15 billion on an account.

〈20×2〉

⑥ Jan. 15: Received cash of ₩15 billion from Daejeon Trading Company for accounts receivable of December 1, 20×1.

⑦ Jan. 25: Received cash of ₩10 billion from Daegu Trading Company for the promissory note of October 25, 20×1.

《Questions》

(1) Journalize each transaction.

(2) Compute the trade receivables to be reported in Wooam Trading company's statement of financial position as of December 31, 20×1.

2. Accounting for bad debts

Daejun Inc.'s trade receivables at the end of 20×1 were ₩400 billion, and ₩8 billion was estimated to be uncollectible, based on an analysis of the ages of trade receivables. During 20×2, trade receivables of ₩5 billion was written off as bad debts because they were 180 days over due. Trade receivables at the end of 20×2 were ₩500 billion, and ₩15 billion was estimated to be uncollectible, based on an analysis of the ages of trade receivables.

《Questions》

(1) How much is the allowance for uncollectible accounts to be reported in the statement of financial position at end of 20×2?
(2) How much is the bad debts expense for 20×2?
(3) How should the trade receivables be reported in the statement of financial position at the end of 20×2?
(4) Compute the trade receivables uncollectibility risk at the end of 20×2.

3. Collecting trade receivables previously written off

The following is part of the statement of financial position of Seocho Inc., as of December 31, 20×1.

(Numbers in billions of ₩)

Account titles	Amount	
Trade receivables	200	
Allowance of uncollectible accounts	(−)5	195

Transactions that occurred in 20×2, in relation to the above financial statement, are the following.

① Feb. 1 : ₩6 billion of trade receivables were written off as bad debts, due to the bankruptcy of the customer.
② Sep. 1 : ₩4 billion of the trade receivables previously written off as bad debts were collected.

《Questions》

(1) Journalize the above transactions under each of the traditional method and the summary method.
(2) It is estimated that uncollectible trade receivables, on December 31, 20×2, were ₩9 billion. Prepare an adjusting journal entry under each of the traditional method and the summary method.

4. Estimating uncollectible accounts

The following is the result of an analysis of the ages of trade receivables, of Hanil Trading Company, as of December 31, 20×1. The allowance for uncollectible accounts in the trial balance shows a credit balance of ₩3 billion.

(Numbers in billions of ₩)

Past due	Amount	Estimated bad debt rate
Current	709	0.1%
1 ~ 30 days	20	1%
31 ~ 60 days	10	10%
61 ~ 90 days	6	30%
91 ~ 120 days	3	50%
Over 121 days	2	70%
Total	750	

《Questions》

(1) Estimate the amount of Hanil Trading Company's uncollectible accounts, by the aging method.
(2) Prepare a journal entry to record the estimated uncollectible accounts.

5. Bad debt accounting (comprehensive)

The following are the transactions related to trade receivables of Daeduk Trading Company.

〈20×1〉

① Dec. 31 : ₩75 billion of trade receivables balance is estimated to be uncollectible, as a result of analysing the ages of ending balance of trade receivables. The allowance for uncollectible accounts in the trial balance shows a credit balance of ₩15 billion.

〈20×2〉

① Mar. 10 : Trade receivables of ₩12 billion were determined to be uncollectible and written off as bad debts.
② May 15 : Trade receivables of ₩5 billion were determined to be uncollectible and written off as bad debts.
③ Jun. 11 : Trade receivables of ₩30 billion were determined to be uncollectible and written off as bad debts.
④ Jun. 22 : Trade receivables of ₩15 billion, previously written off as bad debts, were collected in cash.
⑤ Jul. 18 : Trade receivables of ₩25 billion were determined to be uncollectible and written off as bad debts.
⑥ Sep. 20 : Trade receivables of ₩5 billion were determined to be uncollectible and written off as bad debts.
⑦ Dec. 31 : The trade receivables balance of ₩90 billion was estimated to be uncollectible.

〈20×3〉

① Mar. 15 : Trade receivables of ₩45 billion were determined to be uncollectible and written off as bad debts.

② May 25 : Trade receivables of ₩40 billion were determined to be uncollectible and written off as bad debts.

③ Jul. 18 : Trade receivables of ₩25 billion, previously written off as bad debts, were collected in cash.

④ Nov. 20 : Trade receivables of ₩60 billion was determined to be uncollectible and written off as bad debts.

⑤ Dec. 31 : The trade receivables balance of ₩60 billion was estimated to be uncollectible.

《Question》

Journalize each transaction above. For transactions ④ and ⑤ in 20×3, prepare journal entries under each of the traditional method and the summary method.

6. Guessing bad debt transactions

The following are journal entries (traditional method) concerning bad debts.

(Numbers in billions of ₩)

T. No.	Journal entries	
①	(Dr.) Bad debts expense 45	(Cr.) Allowance for uncollectible accounts 45
②	(Dr.) Bad debts expense 75	(Cr.) Allowance for uncollectible accounts 75
③	(Dr.) Allowance for uncollectible accounts 30	(Cr.) Trade receivables 30
④	(Dr.) Allowance for uncollectible accounts 65	(Cr.) Profit from reversal of allowance for uncollectible accounts 65
⑤	(Dr.) Allowance for uncollectible accounts 40 Bad debts expense 30	(Cr.) Trade receivables 70
⑥	(Dr.) Trade receivables 55 Cash 55	(Cr.) Allowance for uncollectible accounts 55 Trade receivables 55
⑦	(Dr.) Trade receivables 80 Cash 80	(Cr.) Bad debts expense 80 Trade receivables 80

《Question》

Guess what transaction caused each of the journal entries above. (Each entry is independent from the others).

7. Trade receivables and cash flows ①

Koryo Trading Company's beginning (January 1) balance of the trade receivables was ₩3 billion and its ending (December 31) balance was ₩4 billion. The trade receivables collected in cash in 20×1 were ₩40 billion.

《Question》 How much were the total credit sales for 20×1?

8. Trade receivables and cash flows ②

Daesung Company's beginning (January 1) balance of the trade receivable was ₩46 billion and its ending (December 31) balance decreased to ₩39 billion in 20×1. The company's total sales for 20×1 were ₩274 billion. Its operating expenses were ₩250 billion, all of which were paid in cash. All merchandise was sold on credit.

《Questions》

(1) How much was the net income for 20×1?
(2) How much of trade receivables were collected in cash in 20×1?
(3) Compute cash flows from operating activities in 20×1.
(4) Compute the trade receivables turnover and the days' sales in trade receivables for 20×1.

9. Trade receivables, advance from customers, and cash flow

The following is the data related to Dukmyung Trading Company's sales for 20×1.

(Numbers in billions of ₩)

Account titles	Beginning (January 1)	Ending (December 31)
Advance from customers	15	20
Trade receivables	45	30

《Question》

If sales for 20×1 was ₩120 billion, how much were total cash receipts from customers?

10. Computing net sales, gross profit, and cash flows

The following is the data related with the sales of Dongku Trading Company for 20×1.

(Numbers in billions of ₩)

Description	Amount	Description	Amount
Trade receivables (beginning)	50	Trade receivables (ending)	30
Sales	360	Cost of goods sold	175
Sales allowance	5	Sales returns	15
Sales discounts	10		

《Questions》

(1) How much were the net sales for 20×1?
(2) How much was the gross profit for 20×1?
(3) How much cash was received through merchandise sales in 20×1? (All sales were made on credit).

11. Accounting for credit card sales

Hangdo Electronic Land sold ₩200 billion merchandise on credit cards on December 30, 20×1. Credit card sales proceeds are paid by the bank 3 days after the sales (January 2, 20×2), after deducting 3%(₩6 billion) in fees.

《Questions》

(1) How much was the sales revenue of Hangdo Electronic Land by this transaction?
(2) Journalize this transaction.

12. Accounting for value-added tax

Daegu Department Store sold merchandise and received the sales amount of ₩150 billion, plus value-added tax of ₩15 billion in cash, in April, 20×1. Value-added tax is paid to the tax office in cash on July 25, 20×1.

《Questions》

(1) How much was Daegu Department Store's sales revenue by this transaction?
(2) Prepare a journal entry for the transaction in April, 20×1.
(3) Prepare a journal entry for the transaction on July 25, 20×1.

Operating Activities—Cost of Goods Sold, Inventory, and Trade Payables

Chapter 7 Overview

This chapter examines the purchases, trade payables, cost of goods sold, and inventory. More specifically, first we examine the method for recording purchases of merchandise. Next, we explain the method for recording the cost of goods sold (that is, the purchased cost of goods sold). And we explain the methods for correcting inventory errors and the methods for valuing merchandise inventory left at the end of the accounting period. In addition, we study how to use accounting information such as trade payables, cost of goods sold, and inventory.

Case of Daehan Department Store

Statement of financial position (Ft. 2.ⓐ)

As of December 31, 20×2
DDS As of December 31, 20×1 (Numbers in billions of ₩)

Account titles	December 31, 20×2		December 31, 20×1	
Assets				
Current assets				
Cash and cash equivalents(Ft. 4)		45		41
Trade receivables(Ft. 3ⓑ)	30		20	
Allowance for uncollectibe accounts (Ft. 3ⓑ, 5)	(−)4	26	(−)2	18
Inventory :				
Merchandise (Ft. 3ⓒ)		43		23
Total current assets		**114**		**82**
Non-current assets				
FVOCI financial asset (Ft. 3ⓓ, 6)		13		10
Investment in associate (Ft. 3ⓔ, 7)		24		-
Tangible assets (Ft. 8) :				
Land(Ft. 3ⓕ)		96		90
Plant assets (Ft. 3ⓕ, 16)	310		160	
Accumulated depreciation(Ft. 3ⓕ)	(−)13	297	(−)3	157
Intangible asset (Ft. 3ⓖ) :				
Industrial property right (Ft. 8)		9		-
Total non-current assets		**439**		**257**
Total assets		**553**		**339**
Liabilities				
Current liabilities				
Trade payables		42		18
Interest payable		5		4
Salaries payable		2		3
Income tax payable		14		5
Cost financial liabilities (Ft. 3ⓘ) :		38		48
Short-term borrowings (Ft. 9ⓐ)	10		30	
Current portion of long-term borrowings (Ft. 9ⓑ)	28		18	
Provision :				
Provision for refunds (Ft. 3ⓗ, 11)		3		2
Total current liabilities		**104**		**80**
Non-current liabilities				
Cost financial liability (Ft. 3ⓘ) :		126		112
Long-term borrowings (Ft. 9ⓑ)	84		72	
Amortized cost financial liability (Ft. 3ⓘ) :				
Bonds payable (Ft. 10)	42		40	
Total non-current liabilities		**126**		**112**
Total Liabilities		**230**		**192**

Equity				
Share capital				
Common stock (Ft. 13, 16)		150		100
Share premium				
Common stock (Ft. 16)		60		10
Accumulated other comprehensive income		20		11
Accumulated gain on valuation of FVOCI financial asset* (Ft. 3ⓓ, 6)	4		1	
Land revaluation surplus (Ft. 3ⓕ, 8)	16		10	
Retained earnings (Ft. 3ⓙ, 15)		93		26
Total equity		323		147
Total liabilities and equity		553		339

* FVOCI : Fair value through other comprehensive income

Comprehensive income statement (Ft. 2ⓑ)

From Jan. 1, 20×2 to Dec. 31, 20×2

DDS From Jan. 1, 20×1 to Dec. 31, 20×1 (Numbers in billions of ₩)

Account titles	20×2		20×1	
Sales (Ft. 3ⓐ)		430		220
Cost of goods sold		(−)230		(−)118
Gross profit		200		102
Operating expenses :		(−)85		(−)50
Salaries expense	(−)43		(−)26	
Bad debts expense (Ft. 3ⓑ)	(−)4		(−)2	
Depreciation expense (Ft. 3ⓕ)	(−)10		(−)3	
Rent expense	(−)24		(−)12	
Other operating expenses	(−)4		(−)7	
Income from operations		115		52
Other revenue		6		−
Equity income from associate (Ft. 7)	6		−	
Other expenses		(−)19		(−)14
Finance expense (Ft. 2ⓑ) :				
Interest expense	(−)19		(−)13	
Loss on disposal of tangible assets (Ft. 8)	−		(−)1	
Net income before income tax expense		102		38
Income tax expense		(−)30		(−)12
Net income		72		26
Other comprehensive income :		9		11
Item that will not be reclassified to profit or loss :				
Gain on revaluation of land (Ft. 3ⓕ, 8)	6		10	
Item that may be reclassified subsequently to profit or loss :				
Gain on valuation of FVOCI financial asset (Ft. 3ⓓ, 6)	3		1	
Total comprehensive income		81		37
Earnings per share (Ft. 12)		₩2,880		₩1,733

〈Footnotes〉

2. Formats of financial statements

ⓑ Format of comprehensive income statement

……. The company also classifies expenses by function, and it reports multistep comprehensive income statement, reporting each step of gross profit, income from operations, income before income tax expense, net income, and total comprehensive income. ……

3. Important accounting policies

ⓒ Valuation of inventory

Inventory is composed of merchandise, the number of units of which is verified by a physical inventory taken at the end of each year. Jewelries and foodstuffs are valued at their aquisition cost, determined by the specific identification method and by the 'first-in first-out' cost formula, respectively. The remaining merchandise inventory is valued via the retail inventory method.

Explanation of case financial statements

■ Note : Numbers in superscripts are main text page numbers where the corresponding subjects are explained.

Accounts related to this chapter are inventory (classified as current assets), trade payables (classified as current liabilities) in the statement of financial position, and cost of goods sold (reported in the comprehensive income statement). Inventory,[306] in the statement of financial position of Daehan Department Store, is only one merchandise account, and it stands at ₩43 billion at the end of 20×2 and ₩23 billion at the end of 20×1.

It is understood that Daehan Department Store has selected a comprehensive income statement format, classifying expenses by function and reporting the cost of goods sold and gross profit[313] as explained in Footnote 2, ⓑ. According to Footnote 2, ⓒ, it is understood that Daehan Department Store verifies the number of units of merchandise left at the end of every year by taking a physical inventory. It values jewelry at acquisition cost, determined by the specific identification method[326]; foodstuffs, by the first-in first-out cost formula[328]; and remaining merchandise inventory by the retail method.[335]

Trade payables,[306] which are merchandise purchased on credit but not yet paid and thus reported as a current liability, are ₩42 billion at the end of 20×2 and ₩18 billion at the end of 20×1. The cost of goods sold,[306] reported in the comprehensive income statement, is ₩230 billion in 20×2 and ₩118 billion in 20×1.

Cost of goods sold, inventory, and trade payables

When the company sells merchandise to customers, sales are recorded and the original purchase price (acquisition cost) of the merchandise sold to customers is recorded as the cost of goods sold. Assets that are held by the companies for sale are called inventory. Inventory that is held by merchandising companies is called 'merchandise inventory' or simply 'merchandise.' Merchandise is classified in current assets, because it is expected to be sold within one year. The company may purchase the merchandise on credit rather than in cash. If merchandise is purchased on credit, the company may issue a promissory note or may not. In case of the former the purchased amount is recorded on notes payable (지급어음) account and in case of the later it is recorded on accounts payable (외상매입금) account. In the statement of financial position, an addition of notes payable and accounts payable is reported as trade payables (매입채무). Trade payables are classified as current liabilities because they are expected to be paid within one year.

〈Box 7-1〉 Composition of manufacturing cost of finished goods

- **Direct material cost**: Cost of materials that are identified with finished goods.
- **Direct labor cost**: Cost of labor directly assigned to the production of finished goods.
- **Manufacturing overhead**: includes
  (1) Cost of indirect materials such as supplies that are not identified with finished goods.
  (2) Cost of indirect labor such as salaries paid to the employees in departments that support the production.
  (3) Expenses that are not identified with finished goods, such as factory rent and factory utility expense.

〈Box 7-2〉 Goods in transit (FOB shipping point and FOB destination)

Merchandise purchase contracts can be classified into **FOB (free on board : 인도기준)** shipping point and FOB destination depending on timing of the ownership transfer. Under the terms of **FOB shipping point (선적지인도기준)** the ownership of the goods is transferred to the buyer at point in time when the seller ships the goods. Under the terms of **FOB destination (목적지인도기준)** the ownership of the merchandise is transferred to the buyer at point in time when the buyer receives the goods. If the goods are sold FOB shipping point, the buyer take responsibility for delivering the goods and they should be included in the buyer's inventory even they are in transit. These goods are called '**goods in transit**.' On the other hand, if goods are sold FOB destination, the goods can be part of the buyer's inventory only when these goods are received by the buyer.

For example, assume that A Co. purchases the merchandises at a FOB shipping point on December 28, 20×1, and that these goods are in transit as of December 31, 20×1. In this case, A Co. records this purchase transaction on December 28, 20×1. This is because A Co. has the ownership of these goods even though they have not yet arrived. Therefore, A Co. reports these goods in its statement of financial position as merchandise inventory (more specifically, as '**goods in transit**') on December 31, 20×1.

What happen, if A Co. purchases the merchandises FOB destination on December 28, 20×1 and these goods are in transit as of December 31, 20×1? In that case, these purchased goods should not be included in A Co.'s merchandise inventory because these goods have not arrived so A Co. likewise does not yet have ownership of the goods.

Recording cost of goods sold

The operating activities of merchandising companies can be described as a repetition of a cycle of 'purchase-store-sell.' If goods are sold, sales revenue is incurred and, at the same time, the merchandise is decreased. As noted, the cost of goods decreased (sold) is called the cost of goods sold. The cost of goods sold is the expense that is incurred in order to gain sales revenue. It is one of the most significant expense items in the income statement. There are two systems for recording the cost of goods sold : the perpetual inventory system and the periodic inventory system (which is sometimes called the physical inventory system).

2.1 Perpetual inventory system

The perpetual inventory system is the method by which the cost of goods sold is recorded whenever sales are made. In the perpetual inventory system, the company records the number of units and unit costs on the 'inventory in and out journal' (or 'merchandise in and out journal') whenever merchandise is purchased, and computes and records the cost of goods sold by multiplying the number of units sold with the unit cost whenever goods are sold. The merchandise inventory account balance is therefore automatically identified, because all merchandise increases and decreases from purchases and sales are continuously recorded. In the comprehensive examples in Chapter 5, this perpetual inventory system was explained.

The perpetual inventory system is complex and may have a high cost of record-keeping because the company has to record cost of goods sold everytime a sale is made. Therefore, it may be appropriate for companies that sell high-priced goods with a relatively low frequency of transactions. However, it may not be an expensive system because the information regarding purchases (the number of units and unit cost) and sales (the number of units sold and the unit selling price) are automatically updated by computers if bar codes (바코드) are used. Recent trends show that the number of companies using the perpetual inventory system is increasing. It is expected that more companies will use the perpetual inventory system as the RF (radio frequency) ID chip is more utilized, so that the whereabouts of goods can be automatically traced. If the perpetual inventory system is used, the book balance of merchandise inventory can be identified on a real-time basis. Yet, without a physical inventory examination, there is no way to be sure whether the actual merchandise inventory on hand is up to the level of the book balance. Therefore, even when the perpetual inventory system is used, a physical inventory count should periodically be carried out, and should be compared with the book balance to control inventory effectively.

2.2 Periodic inventory system

Under the periodic inventory system we record only sales revenues when sales occur. We do not record purchases on the merchandise account, rather, we record on the separate purchases account. (Purchases mean 'purchases of merchandise for the current period,' and numerous purchases are made during the accounting period. Using the purchases account, we can keep the merchandise account simple like other asset accounts.) Then we compute the cost of goods sold indirectly, using the following formula, after taking a physical count of merchandise inventory that remains at the end of the period.

Beginning merchandise + Purchases − Ending merchandise* = Cost of goods sold

* Ending merchandise is the amount determined by physical counting at the end of the period.

The cost of goods sold, as computed as above, is recorded by the following adjusting entry made at the end of the period.

(Dr.) Cost of goods sold	xxx	(Dr.) Purchases	xxx
Merchandise (ending)	xxx	Merchandise (beginning)	xxx

The periodic inventory system has the advantage of being relatively simple and having a lower cost of record-keeping, because under this system we do not need to compute and record the cost of goods sold each time sales are made. Therefore, it is used by companies that sell low-priced merchandise (such as necessities, food, and general merchandise) to large numbers of customers, so they have a high frequency of transactions. Under the periodic inventory system, it is assumed that all goods available for sale during the current period are sold, except for the ending inventory that is verified by a physical count taken at the end of the period. Therefore, lost or stolen goods are assumed to be sold and might be unintentionally included in the cost of goods sold. In this way, the cost of goods sold may be computed as higher than the real cost. Due to these problems, companies using the periodic inventory system usually keep an inventory in and out journal to record the units of the inflow and outflow of merchandise and the units of the merchandise that remains. In this way, we can tightly control inventory, since we can identify inventory shortages by comparing the quantities in the journal with the physical count.

2.3 Illustration of the perpetual inventory system with the periodic inventory System

Let's compare the perpetual inventory system with the periodic inventory system in detail with 〈Illustration 7-1〉.

〈Illustration 7-1〉 Application of the perpetual inventory system with the periodic inventory system

Purchases and sales during January 20×2 of Hanbat Co. are as shown in 〈Table 7-1〉 below. All purchases and sales are made in cash and the unit cost of merchandise is ₩10 and the selling price per unit is ₩30. Inventory as of January 1 was 10 units and the physical count of goods remaining in store as of January 31 was 30 units.

〈Table 7-1〉 Purchases and sales

Date	Number of units purchased	Number of units sold
January 8	20	
January 14		20
January 19	30	
January 24		30
January 29	40	
January 31		20

(1) Perpetual inventory system

To use the perpetual inventory system, we should record information concerning the purchase and sale of merchandise continuously, in the 'merchandise in and out journal' as shown in ⟨Table 7-2⟩ below. We should record the number of units, unit costs, and amount in the merchandise in and out journal every time merchandise comes into the store or leaves the store. We should record this information (number of units, unit cost, and amount of merchandise inventory remaining) also in the inventory column, as shown in ⟨Table 7-2⟩ below.

⟨Table 7-2⟩ Merchandise in and out journal

(Numbers in ₩)

Date	In			Out			Inventory		
	No. of units	Unit cost	Amount	No. of units	Unit cost	Amount	No. of units	Unit cost	Amount
Jan. 1	10	10	100				10	10	100
Jan. 8	20	10	200				30	10	300
Jan. 14				20	10	200	10	10	100
Jan. 19	30	10	300				40	10	400
Jan. 24				30	10	300	10	10	100
Jan. 29	40	10	400				50	10	500
Jan. 31				20	10	200	30	10	300
Total	100		1,000	70		700			

The following ⟨Table 7-3⟩ are journal entries for these transactions in the merchandise in and out journal.

⟨Table 7-3⟩ Journal entries under the perpetual inventory system

(Numbers in ₩)

Date	Journal entries			
Jan. 8	(Dr.) Merchandise	200	(Cr.) Cash	200
Jan. 14	(Dr.) Cash Cost of goods sold	600 200	(Cr.) Sales Merchandise	600 200
Jan. 19	(Dr.) Merchandise	300	(Cr.) Cash	300
Jan. 24	(Dr.) Cash Cost of goods sold	900 300	(Cr.) Sales Merchandise	900 300
Jan. 29	(Dr.) Merchandise	400	(Cr.) Cash	400
Jan. 31	(Dr.) Cash Cost of goods sold	600 200	(Cr.) Sales Merchandise	600 200

After the above entries are posted on each account, the sales account balance is ₩2,100, and the cost of goods sold account balance is ₩700. The merchandise account balance is ₩300.

(2) Periodic inventory system

The journal entries required under the periodic inventory system are as shown in 〈Table 7-4〉 below.

〈Table 7-4〉 Journal entries under the periodic inventory system

(Numbers in ₩)

<table>
<tr><th>Date</th><th colspan="4">Journal entries</th></tr>
<tr><td>Jan. 8</td><td>(Dr.) Purchases</td><td>200</td><td>(Cr.) Cash</td><td>200</td></tr>
<tr><td>Jan. 14</td><td>(Dr.) Cash</td><td>600</td><td>(Cr.) Sales</td><td>600</td></tr>
<tr><td>Jan. 19</td><td>(Dr.) Purchases</td><td>300</td><td>(Cr.) Cash</td><td>300</td></tr>
<tr><td>Jan. 24</td><td>(Dr.) Cash</td><td>900</td><td>(Cr.) Sales</td><td>900</td></tr>
<tr><td>Jan. 29</td><td>(Dr.) Purchases</td><td>400</td><td>(Cr.) Cash</td><td>400</td></tr>
<tr><td>Jan. 31</td><td>(Dr.) Cash</td><td>600</td><td>(Cr.) Sales</td><td>600</td></tr>
<tr><td rowspan="3">Adjusting journal entries</td><td>(Dr.) Cost of good sold
Cost of goods sold
Merchandise(ending)</td><td>100
900
300</td><td>(Cr.) Merchandise(beginning)
Purchases
Cost of goods sold</td><td>100
900
300</td></tr>
<tr><td colspan="4">or</td></tr>
<tr><td>(Dr.) Cost of good sold
Merchandise(ending)</td><td>700
300</td><td>(Cr.) Purchases
Merchandise(beginning)</td><td>900
100</td></tr>
</table>

Under the periodic inventory system, we record the purchases on the purchase account when we make purchases as explained above. Yet, when we make sales we record only the sales ; we do not record the cost of goods sold. Therefore, we should compute the cost of goods sold indirectly only after taking a physical inventory identifying how many units remain on hand at the end of the accounting period.

In 〈Illustration 7-1〉, above, first we should identify the quantity of ending inventory (30 units) by taking a physical inventory. Then we should identify the unit cost (₩10) and multiply by the quantity of ending inventory (30 units). As a result, the monetary value of ending inventory (₩300) is determined. The cost of goods sold (₩700) can be computed by adding the beginning inventory (₩100) and purchases (₩900), and deducting the ending inventory (₩300), as below.

Beginning merchandise (₩100) + Purchase (₩900) − Ending merchandise (₩300) = Cost of goods sold (₩700)

As explained above, the cost of goods sold is recorded by adjusting journal entries. The adjusting journal entries include three entries. The first entry is made with the assumption that all the beginning inventory was sold. This entry gets rid of the beginning inventory by recording it on the credit side of the merchandise account while also recording it on the debit side of the cost of goods sold account. The second entry is made with the assumption that all purchases during the period are sold. It gets rid of the purchases by recording them on the credit side of the purchases account and recording them also on the debit side of the cost of goods sold account. The third entry is to record the unsold ending inventory on hand, on the debit side of the merchandise account, while reducing the cost of goods sold by recording it on the credit side of the cost of goods sold account. These three entries can be aggregated. Together, we can record ₩700 on the debit side of the cost of goods sold account, ₩300 on the debit side of the merchandise (ending) account, ₩900 on the credit side of the purchases account, and ₩100 on the credit side of the merchandise (beginning) account by one journal entry.

〈Box 7-3〉 Methods of presenting inventory related expense (cost of goods sold)

IFRS[1] provides two methods of presenting expenses. One presents expenses by their **function** and the other presents them by their **nature**. A typical expense related with inventory is the cost of goods sold. The method of identifying and presenting the cost of goods sold is the functional classification method. If the method of classifying by nature is adopted, then the purchased amount of merchandise and changes in inventory are presented so the cost of goods sold is presented indirectly. If the formula showing the relationship among beginning inventory, purchases, ending inventory, and cost of goods sold is redefined, it is as follows :

(Formula 1) Beginning inventory + Purchases − Ending inventory = Cost of goods sold (Formula 2) Purchases − Changes in inventory = Cost of goods sold (Changes in inventory = Ending inventory − Beginning inventory)

If expenses in the income statement are classified by their function, as shown in Formula (1) above, the cost of goods sold is presented by adding beginning inventory with purchases to show goods available for sale and deducting ending inventory from it. On the contrary, if expenses in the income statement are classified by their nature, as shown in Formula (2) above, the cost of goods sold is presented indirectly by showing purchases and changes in inventory.

For example, Seoul Mart's 20×1 sales are ₩15,000 and its beginning merchandise inventory is ₩1,000. Its purchases are ₩10,000 and its ending merchandise inventory is ₩2,000. Its operating expenses are composed of salaries expense of ₩2,200 and rent expense of ₩1,300.

Seoul Mart's income statement, classified by function, for 20×1 is as shown in ⟨Table 7-5⟩ below:

⟨Table 7-5⟩ Income statement (classified by function)

Seoul Mart From Jan. 1, 20×1 to Dec. 31, 20×1 (Numbers in ₩)

Account titles	Amount
Sales	15,000
Cost of goods sold	(−)9,000*
Gross profit	6,000
Operating expenses	(−)3,500**
Net income	2,500

* Cost of goods sold: 1,000 (Beginning inventory) + 10,000 (Purchases) − 2,000 (Ending inventory) = ₩9,000

** Operating expenses: 2,200 (Salaries expense) + 1,300 (Rent expense) = ₩3,500

Seoul Mart's income statement, classified by nature, for 20×1 is as shown in ⟨Table 7-6⟩ below:

⟨Table 7-6⟩ Income statement (classified by nature)

Seoul Mart From Jan. 1, 20×1 to Dec. 31, 20×1 (Numbers in ₩)

Account titles	Amount
Sales	15,000
Purchases of merchandise	(−)10,000
Changes in merchandise inventory	1,000*
Salaries expense	(−)2,200
Rent expense	(−)1,300
Net income	2,500

* Changes in merchandise inventory: 2,000 (Ending inventory) − 1,000 (Beginning inventory) = ₩1,000

〈Box 7-4〉 Freight-in, purchase returns, purchase allowance, and purchase discounts

Typical items that can be incurred with purchases of merchandise under the periodic inventory system are freight-in, purchase returns, purchase allowance, and purchase discounts.

(1) Freight-in

The acquisition cost of merchandise includes all costs incurred to have the merchandise delivered to the store. Therefore, the acquisition cost of merchandise includes the cost of purchase and of **freight-in**, which is the freight cost incurred to have merchandise delivered to the store. But freight-out, which is incurred to ship goods to customers, is included in the selling expense.

(2) Purchase returns, purchase allowance, and purchase discounts

Purchase returns refer to merchandise returned to the seller because of defects. The seller may reduce the amount of the purchase because some of the purchased merchandise has a slight defect. This is called the **purchase allowance**. As mentioned in Chapter 6, although it is seldom observed in Korea, in other countries a discount of a fixed-percentage of purchase amount is sometimes given when the purchase amount on credit is paid within a given period. This is called a **purchase discount**.

(3) Delivered cost of net purchases

The amount of purchases—plus fright-in and less purchase returns, purchase allowance, and purchase discounts—is called the '**delivered cost of net purchases**.' The freight-in, purchase returns, purchase allowance, and purchase discounts accounts can be set up for internal reporting purposes. But they are not presented in the comprehensive income statement reported externally. Most companies present only the cost of goods sold in their externally reporting comprehensive income statement, as is seen in Daehan Department Store's comprehensive income statement (illustrated in front of Chapter 6). This book mainly examining the externally reporting financial statements assumes that all of these items are reflected on the purchases account thus having a balance equal to the delivered cost of net purchases.

Correction of inventory errors

We may sometimes make computational mistakes, such as errors of excluding of some of the inventory or those of including merchandise already sold when we value the inventory. How can we correct these errors? Here we examine ways to correct inventory errors.

3.1 Income statement effects of inventory errors

〈Table 7-7〉, below, shows the effects of inventory errors on the cost of goods sold and net income. If the ending merchandise inventory is overstated due to an error, then the net income before income tax expense, the income tax expense and the net income are also overstated because the cost of goods sold is understated. The ending merchandise inventory of the current year becomes the beginning merchandise inventory of the next year. If the beginning merchandise inventory of the next year is overstated, then the effects of the income statement are the exact opposite of those we see when the ending inventory of the current year is overstated. Therefore, the income statement effects of the current year's inventory error are automatically offset in the next year. This type of error is called a self-balancing error.

〈Table 7-7〉 Income statement effects of inventory errors

Account titles	Overstated(O)		Understated(U)	
	Next year	Current year	Next year	Current year
Sales				
Beginning merchandise	O		U	
Purchases				
Goods available for sale				
(−)Ending merchandise		O		U
Cost of goods sold	O	U	U	O
Net income before income tax expense*	U	O	O	U
Income tax expense**	U	O	O	U
Net income	U	O	O	U

* We assume that there are no operating expenses, other revenues and other expenses.
** We assume that income tax expense is a fixed percentage of the net income before income tax expense.

3.2 Comprehensive illustration of correction of inventory errors

〈Illustration 7-2〉 Correction of inventory errors.

The following SM Department store's three illustrated errors in 〈Table 7-8〉 are independent of each other. The correction of these errors is accepted as either revenue or expense in tax accounting. The income tax rate is 30% and all of the current year's income tax is paid in the following year.

〈Table 7-8〉 Inventory errors

	Year	Ending merchandise inventory valuation errors
1.	20×3 (current year)	₩30 billion understated
2.	20×2	₩10 billion overstated
3.	20×1	₩20 billion overstated

3.2.1 Adjusting journal entry

(1) When the merchandise inventory at the end of 20×3 was understated by ₩30 billion

Because 20×3 is current year, we should prepare the following adjusting journal entry. (All numbers in adjusting journal entry are in billions of ₩).

Ⓐ When income statement accounts are not closed

Because we can still use income statement accounts and income summary account, we prepare the following journal entry.

(Dr.)			(Cr.)		
(Dr.)	Merchandise	30	(Cr.)	Cost of goods sold*	30
	Income tax expense	9		Income tax payable	9

* Income summary account, if cost of goods sold account is not used,

Ⓑ When income statement accounts are closed

Because we cannot use the temporary accounts, the income statement effects of the error are journalized directly in the retained earnings account, as follows.

(Dr.)			(Cr.)		
(Dr.)	Merchandise	30	(Cr.)	Retained earnings	21
				Income tax payable	9

(2) When ending merchandise inventory of 20×2 was ₩10 billion overstated

There is no need to prepare an adjusting journal entry, because 20×2 error is offset in 20×3.

(3) When ending merchandise inventory of 20×1 was ₩20 billion overstated

There is no need to prepare an adjusting journal entry, because 20×1 error is offset in 20×2.

〈Box 7-5〉 Restating comparative financial statements and disclosing information when there are inventory errors

The following 〈Table 7-9〉, 〈Table 7-10〉 and 〈Table 7-11〉 are SM Department Store's (〈Illustration 7-2〉) comparative income statements and comparative partial statements of changes in equity for 20×3 and 20×2, as well as its comparative partial statements of financial position at the end of 20×3 and at the end of 20×2, respectively, There are no operating expenses, other revenues, other expenses or dividends. Net income and income tax expense for 20×1 were ₩35 billion and ₩15 billion, respectively.

〈Table 7-9〉 Income statement

SM Department Store (Numbers in billions of ₩)

Account titles	20×3		20×2	
Sales		530		300
Beginning merchandise	180		160	
Purchases	300		200	
Goods available for sale	480		360	
Ending merchandise	(−)200		(−)180	
Cost of goods sold		(−)280		(−)180
Net income before income tax expense		250		120
Income tax expense		(−)75		(−)36
Net income		175		84

〈Table 7-10〉 Partial statement of changes in equity

SM Department Store (Numbers in billions of ₩)

Description	20×3	20×2
Beginning retained earnings	184	100
Net income	175	84
Ending retained earnings	359	184

〈Table 7-11〉 Partial statement of financial position

SM Department Store (Numbers in billions of ₩)

Account titles	Dec. 31, 20×3	Dec. 31, 20×2
Merchandise	200	180
Income tax payable	75	36
Retained earnings	359	184

For each of inventory errors in 〈Illustration 7-2〉 the comparative financial statements should be restated as follow.

(Current year's error)

1. When ending merchandise inventory of 20×3 was ₩30 billion understated

1) Correcting comparative financial statements

The year of 20×3 is current year. When there is an inventory error in current year, the current year's error-corrected financial statements should be presented with past year's financial statements for comparison, as follows. (Corrected amounts are in **Bold letters**.)

〈Table 7-12〉 Corrected income statement—Current year's error

SM Department Store (Numbers in billions of ₩)

Account titles	20×3		20×2	
Sales		530		300
Beginning merchandise	180		160	
Purchases	300		200	
Goods available for sale	480		360	
Ending merchandise	**(−)230**		(−)180	
Cost of goods sold		**(−)250**		(−)180
Net income before income tax expense		**280**		120
Income tax expense		**(−)84**		(−)36
Net income		**196**		84

⟨Table 7-13⟩ Corrected partial statement of changes in equity —Current year's error

SM Department Store (Numbers in billions of ₩)

Description	20×3	20×2
Beginning retained earnings	184	100
Net income	196	84
Ending retained earnings	380	184

⟨Table 7-14⟩ Corrected partial statement of financial position —Current year's error

SM Department Store (Numbers in billions of ₩)

Account titles	Dec. 31, 20×3	Dec. 31, 20×2
Merchandise	230	180
Income tax payable	84	36
Retained earnings	380	184

(Prior year's errors)

IFRS[2] requires us to adjust the prior year's error and disclose the relevant information, as shown in ⟨Table 7-15⟩ below, depending upon whether the error occurs during or prior to the years for which the comparative financial statements are presented (comparison years hereafter).

⟨Table 7-15⟩ Correction of prior year's errors

	Timing of error's occurrence	Adjustments
Ⓧ	During comparison years	1) Retrospectively adjust error and restate comparative financial statements. 2) Disclose effects of error on comparative financial statement items.
Ⓨ	Before comparison years	Restate the beginning balances of assets, liabilities and equity for the earliest comparison year.

2. When ending merchandise inventory of 20×2 was ₩10 billion overstated

SM Department Store presents its financial statements for the two years, 20×3 and 20×2, in comparison. Because the year 20×2 is a comparison year, we should adjust and disclose the error shown as Ⓧ in ⟨Table 7-15⟩, above.

1) Restating comparative financial statements

For the current year of 20×3, we prepare financial statements reporting error-corrected the ending merchandise inventory of 20×2 as the beginning merchandise inventory. For the prior year of 20×2, we restate financial statements retrospectively adjusting the error as shown below. (Restated amounts are in **Bold letters**.)

⟨Table 7-16⟩ Restated income statement—Comparison year's error

SM Department Store (Numbers in billions of ₩)

Account titles	20×3		20×2	
Sales		530		300
Beginning merchandise	**170**		160	
Purchases	300		200	
Goods available for sale	**470**		360	
Ending merchandise	(−)200		**(−)170**	
Cost of goods sold		**(−)270**		**(−)190**
Net income before income tax expense		**260**		**110**
Income tax expense		**(−)78**		**(−)33**
Net income		**182**		**77**

⟨Table 7-17⟩ Restated partial statement of changes in equity —Comparison year's error

SM Department Store (Numbers in billions of ₩)

Description	20×3	20×2
Beginning retained earnings	**177**	100
Net income	**182**	**77**
Ending retained earnings	359	**177**

⟨Table 7-18⟩ Restated partial statement of financial position —Comparison year's error

SM Department Store (Numbers in billions of ₩)

Account titles	Dec. 31, 20×3	Dec. 31, 20×2
Merchandise	200	**170**
Income tax payable	**78**	**33**
Retained earnings	359	**177**

2) Effects of error on prior year's financial statements

The effects of error on prior year's financial statements should be disclosed in the footnotes. The effects of error on the financial statements of SM Department Store for the prior year of 20×2 are as shown in the following ⟨Table 7-19⟩.

⟨Table 7-19⟩ Error's effects on financial statements for 20×2

SM Department Store (Numbers in billions of ₩)

Account titles	Before adjustments	Adjustments	After adjustments
Income statement			
Cost of goods sold	(-)180	(-)10	(-)190
Income tax expense	(-)36	3	(-)33
Net income	84	(-)7	77
Statement of financial position			
Merchandise	180	(-)10	170
Income tax payable	36	(-)3	33
Retained earnings	184	(-)7	177

3. When ending merchandise inventory of 20×1 was ₩20 billion overstated

The ending merchandise of 20×1 is the beginning merchandise of 20×2. Because 20×2 is a comparison year, we should adjust the error and disclose the information required by Ⓧ in ⟨Table 7-15⟩, above. Since 20×1 is the year prior to the comparison years, we should also disclose the information required by Ⓨ in ⟨Table 7-15⟩, above.

1) Restating comparative financial statements

We should use the error-corrected ending merchandise of 20×1 as the beginning merchandise of 20×2 and restate the comprehensive income statement for 20×2 as follows. (Restated amounts are in Bold letters.)

⟨Table 7-20⟩ Restated income statement —Error before comparison years

SM Department Store (Numbers in billions of ₩)

Account titles	20×3		20×2	
Sales		530		300
Beginning merchandise	180		140	
Purchases	300		200	
Goods available for sale	480		340	
Ending merchandise	(−)200		(−)180	
Cost of goods sold		(−)280		(−)160
Net income before income tax expense		250		140
Income tax expense		(−)75		(−)42
Net income		175		98

We should prepare a statement of changes in equity for 20×2, with the beginning balance of retained earnings adjusted for 20×1 error (after the income tax effect) as follows.

⟨Table 7-21⟩ Restated partial statement of changes in equity —Error before comparison years

SM Department Store (Numbers in billions of ₩)

Description	20×3	20×2
Beginning retained earnings	184	100
Prior year adjustment	−	(−)14
Net income	175	98
Ending retained earnings	359	184

There is no need to restate the statements of financial position because the error is self-balanced at the end of 20×2.

2) Effects of error on prior year's financial statements

The prior year's financial statement that is affected by the error is the income statement for 20×2. Therefore, information shown in the following ⟨Table 7-22⟩ should be disclosed in the footnotes.

〈Table 7-22〉 Error's effects on income statement for 20×2

SM Department Store (Numbers in billions of ₩)

Account titles	Before adjustments	Adjustments	After adjustments
Cost of goods sold	(−)180	20	(−)160
Income tax expense	(−)36	(−)6	(−)42
Net income	84	14	98

3) Beginning balance of asset, liability and equity for the earliest comparison year

Asset (merchandise), liability (income tax payable) and equity (retained earnings) at the beginning of year of 20×2, the earliest comparison year, are as shown in 〈Table 7-23〉 below.

〈Table 7-23〉 Account balances on January 1, 20×2

SM Department Store (Numbers in billions of ₩)

Account titles	Before adjustments	Adjustments	After adjustments
Merchandise	160	(−)20	140
Income tax payable	15	(−)6	9
Retained earnings	100	(−)14	86

Inventory valuation methods

If we purchase identical goods many different times, the unit cost may be different. For example, let's assume that we purchase 1,000 sets of soccer uniforms at the unit cost of ₩15,000 once, and we purchase 1,000 identical sets at the unit cost of ₩20,000 the second time around. If we sell 800 sets, then should we say that 800 sets with the unit cost of ₩15,000 are sold? Or that sets with the unit cost of ₩20,000 are sold? Or should we say that goods with the unit cost of ₩15,000 and those with the unit cost of ₩20,000 are sold evenly?

One of the inventory valuation methods is to tag each uniform with its unit cost (₩15,000 or ₩20,000) and to identify the tag every time a uniform is sold. In this way, we can identify the unit cost of uniforms that are sold and the unit cost of the inventory that remains. This inventory valuation method is called the specific identification method (개별법).

But it is not easy to identify merchandise one by one. For example, let's think about gas stations and rice stores. Every time we purchase gas and we purchase rice, the unit purchase costs can be different. And if we sell them continuously, it may be impossible to identify the unit cost of gas or rice sold. Even when it is possible to identify the merchandise one by one, the handling cost can be high if there are a lot of different kinds of inventory to keep track of.

Under the specific identification method, managers may be able to discretionarily manipulate the cost of goods sold. For example, if managers want to report more profit, they may insist that the sale of goods with low unit costs was made. On the other hand, if managers want to report less profit, they may insist that the sale of goods with high unit costs was made. Because of this problem, K-IFRS[3] prohibits the use of the specific identification method for inventories that are exchangeable (example : when identical inventory can be purchased at different costs). The only companies using the specific identification method are jewelry stores, dealing in non-exchangeable and expensive gems ; and companies in the construction and ship building industries, which construct buildings or ships by job order.

If goods are exchangeable, then a cost flow assumption should be made, regardless of the actual physical movement of the goods, to determine which goods are sold and which goods remain as inventory. As the cost flow assumptions we have : FIFO (first-in first-out : 선입선출) ; LIFO (last-in first-out : 후입선출) ; and the weighted average.

IFRS[4] calls these cost flow assumptions the 'cost formulas (원가계산식),' and allows only FIFO and the weighted average. LIFO is not allowed. (Refer to 〈Box 7-6〉—'IFRS does not allow LIFO'). It is also required that inventories with similar nature and similar use is to be valued with the same cost formula.

Let's examine ways to compute the cost of goods sold and ending inventory, under FIFO, LIFO, and the weighted average, in 〈Illustration 7-3〉.

〈Illustration 7-3〉 Inventory cost formulas

The following 〈Table 7-24〉 are details of purchase and sale of goods of Kwangduk Trading Co. during January 20×1. The ending inventory was 15 units per the physical inventory count.

〈Table 7-24〉 Merchandise purchases and sales

(Numbers in ₩)

Purchase Date	No. of units purchased	Unit cost	Amount	No. of units sold
Beginning inventory	10	180	1,800	
Purchases :				
Jan. 4	20	190	3,800	
Jan. 8				20
Jan. 10	10	200	2,000	
Jan. 15	30	210	6,300	
Jan. 18				30
Jan. 20	30	230	6,900	
Jan. 25	10	240	2,400	
Jan. 28				45
Total purchases	100		21,400	
Goods available for sale	110		23,200	

4.1 First-in first-out (FIFO) cost formula

FIFO assumes that the goods purchased earliest are also sold first. This cost flow assumption often reflects the actual physical flow of merchandise, because companies generally do sell the first units purchased earlier. Under this cost formula, ending inventories are valued at the unit cost of the most recent purchase, because the goods purchased most recently are those that remain as the ending inventory. In ⟨Illustration 7-3⟩, the ending inventory is valued under FIFO as shown in ⟨Table 7-25⟩ below.

⟨Table 7-25⟩ Inventory valuation—FIFO

(Numbers in ₩)

Description	No. of units	Unit cost	Amount
Jan. 25 Purchase	10	240	2,400
Jan. 20 Purchase	5	230	1,150
Ending inventory	15		3,550

The ending inventory of 15 units is more than the 10 units purchased most recently, on January 25. The inventory is valued in two steps : 1) 10 units out of the 15 units of the ending inventory are valued at the unit cost of ₩240, which was the unit cost of the January 25 purchase. 2) The remaining 5 units of the ending inventory are valued at the unit cost of ₩230, which is the unit cost of the second most recent purchase, on January 20. Therefore, the ending inventory is ₩3,550.

4.2 Last-in first-out (LIFO) cost formula

LIFO, in contrast to FIFO, assumes that the goods purchased last are sold first. Because this cost formula assumes that inventory purchased long ago continuously remains as inventory, it rarely reflects the actual physical flow of goods. Under this formula, the ending inventory is valued at the unit cost of the earliest purchase, because the goods purchased earliest remain in the ending inventory. In ⟨Illustration 7-3⟩, the ending merchandise inventory is valued under LIFO as shown in ⟨Table 7-26⟩ below.

⟨Table 7-26⟩ Inventory valuation–LIFO

(Numbers in ₩)

Description	No. of units	Unit cost	Amount
Beginning inventory	10	180	1,800
Jan. 4 Purchase	5	190	950
Ending inventory	15		2,750

Because the 15 units counted in the ending inventory are more than the 10 units of the beginning inventory, the ending inventory is valued in two steps : 1) 10 units out of the 15 units of the ending inventory are valued at a unit cost of ₩180, which is the unit cost of the beginning inventory. 2) 5 units out of the 15 units of the ending inventory are valued at a unit cost of ₩190, that is the unit cost of the earliest purchase on January 4. Therefore, the ending merchandise inventory is ₩2,750.

4.3 Weighted average cost formula

The weighted average cost formula assumes that the goods purchased at different costs are sold evenly. Under this formula, the weighted average cost is computed by dividing the total cost of goods available for sale by the total number of goods available for sale. In Korean, it is called the total average (총평균), because the total cost is divided by total number of units. The ending merchandise inventory is computed by multiplying this weighted average cost with the number of units remaining in the ending inventory. In English, this formula is called the weighted average (가중평균) cost formula, because we compute the average by assigning different weights of the number of units purchased to each unit cost.

In ⟨Illustration 7-3⟩, under the weighted average cost formula, the ending merchandise inventory is valued as shown in ⟨Table 7-27⟩ below.

⟨Table 7-27⟩ Inventory valuation–Weighted average

(Numbers in ₩)

Description	No. of units	Unit cost	Amount
Ending inventory	15	211*	3,165

* Weighted average : Cost of goods available for sale/Number of units available for sale
23,200 / 110 = ₩211

Under the weighted average cost formula, the ending merchandise inventory is valued at ₩3,165 by multiplying the weighted average (₩211) by the number of units in the ending inventory (15 units). The weighted average (₩211) is computed by dividing the cost of goods available for sale (₩23,200) by the number of goods available for sale (110 units).

〈Box 7-6〉 Moving average cost formula

The moving average cost formula is the formula under which we compute the cost of goods sold and merchandise inventory applying the weighted average cost formula every time a sale is made. In 〈Illustration 7-3〉, when 20 units were sold on January 8, the weighted average is ₩186.67 [(1,800 + 3,800) / 30]. This represents the weighted average of the beginning inventory of 10 units with the unit cost of ₩180, and the purchase of 20 units at the unit cost of ₩190 on January 4. On January 8, when 20 units were sold, the cost of goods sold was ₩3,733 [(186.67 × 20)] and the merchandise inventory was ₩1,867 [(186.67 × 10)]. On January 18, when 30 units were sold, the weighted average was ₩203.34 [(1,867 + 2,000 + 6,300) / 50], that is, the weighted average of 10 units of inventory with a unit cost of ₩186.67 ; 10 units purchased on January 10 at a unit cost of ₩200 ; and 30 units purchased on January 16 at a unit cost of ₩210. On January 18, when 30 units were sold, the cost of goods sold was ₩6,100 [(203.34 × 30)] and the merchandise inventory was ₩4,067 [(203.34 × 20)].

Under the moving average cost formula, the cost of goods sold and inventory is computed every time a sale is made. Therefore, to use this formula it is necessary to apply the perpetual inventory system, in which the number of units and unit cost are continuously recorded every time a purchase or sale is made. This formula is used to compute the cost of investment in stock, when one listed company's stock is purchased and sold continuously. It is, practically speaking, nearly impossible for retailing companies and manufacturing companies with a lot of different inventories and high turnover to use this formula to evaluate their inventories. Nonetheless, many Korean firms disclose, in the footnotes to their financial statements, that they use the moving average cost formula to value their inventories. As 'moving average,' these companies are referring to a system of monthly weighted average, under which a weighted average is computed every month so that the average is moving 12 times a year. (The weighted average of 〈Illustration 7-3〉, in the main text, is the monthly weighted average for the month of January).

IFRS[5] allows companies to decide the computing frequency of moving averages. Therefore, both and the monthly weighted average (under which the weighted average is computed every month) and the weighted average (under which the weighted average is computed once in a year) are allowed.

4.4 Comparison of inventory cost formulas

When merchandise is purchased at different unit costs, the ending merchandise inventory and cost of goods sold are different depending on whether FIFO, LIFO, or the weighted average cost formula is used. If these various formulas are used for tax reporting purposes, then taxes to be paid are also different. During a period in which the cost of merchandise is continuously increasing, the cost of goods sold will be the highest under LIFO, among the three formulas. Under LIFO, the income subject to income tax will be the lowest, and the lowest income tax will be paid. LIFO was developed to minimize income tax in this way. (Refer to 〈Box 7-7〉 'IFRS does not allow LIFO,' below). 〈Illustration 7-3〉 shows a period of rising unit costs. The cost of goods sold and the ending merchandise inventory, under each of these cost formulas, are compared and summarized as shown in 〈Table 7-28〉 below.

〈Table 7-28〉 Comparison of inventory cost formulas

(Numbers in ₩)

Description	Cost formulas		
	FIFO	LIFO	Weighted average
Available for sale	23,200	23,200	23,200
Ending inventory	(-)3,550	(-)2,750	(-)3,165
Cost of goods sold	19,650	20,450	20,035

As shown above, the ending merchandise inventories are in descending order of FIFO (₩3,550) ; the weighted average (₩3,165) ; and LIFO (₩2,750). The costs of goods sold are in descending order of LIFO (₩20,450) ; the weighted average (₩20,035) ; and FIFO (₩19,650).

〈Box 7-7〉 IFRS doses not allow LIFO

IFRS[6] does not allow the **LIFO** as an inventory cost formula. The reason is that it is not appropriate for financial reporting purpose, because it was developed to **minimize taxes** during periods of increasing cost of goods. It also rarely reflects the real flow of inventory, so it may distort the financial position and operating performance of the company.

In the United States, 50~60% of listed companies use LIFO and if this cost formula is used for financial reporting purposes, it should also be used for tax reporting purposes. In Korea, only two refineries, SK Corporation and S-Oil, used LIFO among all listed companies (as of 2009) before K-IFRS was adopted.

Estimating cost of ending merchandise inventory

Sometimes companies estimate the cost of ending merchandise inventory without identifying the number of units in the ending merchandise inventory, or without examining documents showing the actual unit costs, one by one. The gross profit method and the retail inventory method are typical methods of estimating the cost of ending merchandise inventory.

5.1 Gross profit method

The gross profit method (매출총이익률법) uses the gross profit percentage obtained from income statements of past years, to estimate the cost of the ending merchandise inventory. First, we should estimate the gross profit by multiplying the gross profit percentage by the current year's sales, and estimate the cost of goods sold by subtracting this gross profit from the sales. Next, the cost of ending inventory can be estimated by subtracting the estimated cost of goods sold from the cost of goods available for sale (beginning merchandise inventory + purchases). This method is used to prepare performance reports for internal use, as well as in estimating inventory destroyed by fire. Let's examine the gross profit method with 〈Illustration 7-4〉.

〈Illustration 7-4〉 Gross profit method

The following 〈Table 7-29〉 is information concerning merchandise of Buyngjin Mart during the period from January 1, 20×1 to June 30, 20×1 :

〈Table 7-29〉 Data related with merchandise

(Numbers in billions of ₩)

Account titles	Amount	
Beginning merchandise inventory	2	
Purchases	10	
Goods available for sale	12	
Sales		15

(Buyngjin Mart's average gross profit percentage on sales for the past 3 years is 40%.)

Under the gross profit method, the cost of ending merchandise inventory is estimated as follows :

Estimated gross profit : 15 billion × 40% = ₩6 billion
Estimated cost of goods sold : 15 billion − 6 billion or
15 billion × (1 − 40%) = ₩9 billion
Goods available for sale : 2 billion + 10 billion = ₩12 billion
Estimated ending merchandise inventory : 12 billion − 9 billion = ₩3 billion

In 〈Illustration 7-4〉, Buyngjin Mart's gross profit percentage on sales for the past 3 years is 40%, so the gross profit for 6 months (from January 1, 20×1 to June 30, 20×1) is estimated to be ₩6 billion. The cost of goods sold is thus estimated at ₩9 billion. The cost of the ending merchandise inventory is estimated to be ₩3 billion, by subtracting the estimated cost of goods sold of ₩9 billion from the cost of goods available for sale of ₩12 billion (which is an addition of the beginning merchandise inventory of ₩2 billion and purchases of ₩10 billion). Under the gross profit method, the ending inventory is not verified by a physical inventory count and is instead roughly estimated with the past gross profit rate. It may, therefore, be quite different from real inventory. Thus the gross profit method is not allowed in preparing externally disclosed annual financial statements.

5.2 Retail inventory method

Another method of estimating ending merchandise inventory is the retail inventory method (소매재고법). This method is usually applied by retail companies, such as department stores or discount stores, where they generally sell the merchandise at the price listed on the price tag. Under this method, we estimate the cost of inventory using the retail price of the ending merchandise inventory.

To use this method, it is necessary to compute the ratio of the cost to the retail price of the goods available for sale ; that is, the cost-to-retail ratio. To compute this ratio, we need the cost and retail price of the beginning inventory, the cost and retail price of the goods purchased during the year, and the amount of mark-down during the year. The cost of the beginning merchandise inventory and the cost of goods purchased are on the merchandise and purchase ledger accounts. We should obtain additional information in the following ways. 1) Retail price of goods purchased during the year : We should record separately retail price recorded on the price tag when purchased goods are displayed in the store. 2) Retail price of beginning merchandise inventory : Use retail price of ending inventory of previous year recorded separately. 3) Amount of mark-downs : We should record separately mark-downs given during the bargain sales periods. Using this data, we compute the cost-to-retail ratio, that is ratio of cost of goods available for sale to the retail price of goods available for sale as follows :

$$\text{Cost-to-retail ratio} = \frac{\text{Cost of goods available for sale}}{\text{Retail price of goods available for sale}}$$

$$= \frac{\text{Cost of beginning merchandise inventory} + \text{Cost of goods purchased}}{\text{Retail price of beginning merchandise inventory} + \text{Retail price of goods purchased} - \text{Mark-downs}}$$

After computing the cost-to-retail ratio, we compute the retail price of the ending inventory by subtracting sales from the retail price of goods available for sale. We estimate the cost of the ending inventory by multiplying the cost-to-retail ratio with the retail price of the ending inventory.

The following ⟨Illustration 7-5⟩ shows the procedures for estimating the cost of the ending inventory, under the retail inventory method.

〈Illustration 7-5〉 Retail inventory method

Y-Mart uses the retail inventory method to estimate the cost of the ending merchandise inventory. The following 〈Table 7-30〉 is data related with Y-Mart's merchandise.

〈Table 7-30〉 Data related with merchandise

(Numbers in billions of ₩)

Description	Cost	Retail Price
Beginning merchandise inventory	3	4
Purchases	417	607
Mark-downs		(-)11
Goods available for sale	420	600
Sales		(-)590
Ending merchandise inventory		10

The cost of the ending merchandise inventory is estimated using these data as follows :

$$\text{Cost-to-retail ratio} : \frac{\text{Cost of goods available for sale}}{\text{Retail price of goods available for sale}} = \frac{420}{600} = 70\%$$

(1) Retail price of the ending merchandise inventory
: Retail price of goods available for sale − Sales
= 600 billion − 590 billion = ₩10 billion

(2) Cost of the ending merchandise inventory
: (1) × Cost-to-retail ratio
= 10 billion × 70% = ₩7 billion

(3) Cost of goods sold
: Cost of goods available for sale − (2)
= 420 billion − 7 billion = ₩413 billion

In 〈Illustration 7-5〉, the cost-to-retail ratio is 70%. Retail price of the ending merchandise inventory is computed to be ₩10 billion, by subtracting sales of ₩590 billion from the retail price of goods available for sale of ₩600 billion. The cost of the ending merchandise inventory is estimated to be ₩7 billion by multiplying the cost-to-retail ratio of 70% to the retail price of the ending merchandise inventory of

₩10 billion. The cost of goods sold is computed to be ₩413 billion, by subtracting the cost of the ending merchandise inventory of ₩7 billion from the cost of goods available for sale of ₩420 billion.

The retail inventory method has the merit of not examining tax receipts or invoices one by one to identify the unit cost of merchandise inventory, because a physical examination of the ending merchandise inventory can be made by using the retail price on the price tag and verify the estimated ending merchandise inventory at retail price. But if the cost ratios are different among different inventory items, then inventory valuation might be biased. IFRS[7] allows the retail inventory method only when the cost ratios are similar among inventory items and when the inventory turnover is high, so that using other inventory valuation methods is practically unrealistic. It additionally recommends that we should apply this method by each department with a similar cost ratio, for example in case of a department store, each of electronic home appliance, furniture, men's clothing, women's clothing, cosmetics department, etc.

Inventory shortage loss and valuation loss

6.1 Inventory shortage loss

There may be a difference between the number of units on the perpetual inventory record and the number of units verified by physical inventory counts at the end of the year. Unless no mistake is made in the perpetual inventory record, the number of units, according to the physical inventory, is usually smaller than that in the perpetual record. This shortage may be due to items that are stolen, lost, or subject to natural evaporation, decay, etc. Loss from shortage in the number of units in inventory is called 'inventory shortage loss.'

As explained above, under the periodic inventory system inventory shortage cannot be detected so any lost or stolen merchandise is treated as sold. The periodic inventory system is therefore unable to properly control inventory. Yet if the perpetual inventory system is run together (In practice, the perpetual inventory system recording unit only is used a lot.), inventory shortage can be identified so that more efficient inventory control can be made.

Inventory shortage loss from inventory shortages incurred in the normal operating activities of a company (a certain level of inventory is expected to be lost, evaporated, spoiled, etc.) should be added to the cost of goods sold. Per IFRS[8], loss from abnormal inventory shortage should be reported as an expense of the current year.

〈Illustration 7-6〉 Inventory shortage loss

Daehan Inc.'s beginning merchandise inventory was 100 units (₩2,000 thousand) and purchases were 1,000 units (₩20,000 thousand) in 20×1. The number of ending merchandise inventory at the end of 20×1 per perpetual inventory record was 200 units after considering the normal shortage. But the number of units of ending merchandise inventory, verified by a physical inventory taken at the end of the year, was 180 units. The cost to be applied to ending merchandise inventory was ₩20 thousand per unit. The following journal entry should be prepared to report the inventory shortage loss.

(Numbers in thousands of ₩)

(Dr.) Inventory shortage loss	400*	(Cr.) Merchandise	400

* (200 − 180) × 20 thousand = ₩400 thousand

The cost of goods sold of ₩18,000 thousand (2,000 thousand + 20,000 thousand − 4,000 thousand) and inventory shortage loss of ₩400 thousand [(200 − 180) × 20 thousand] are reported as expenses in Daehan Inc.'s 20×1 income statement. Merchandise inventory reported on the statement of financial position at the end of 20×1 is ₩3,600 thousand (4,000 thousand − 400 thousand), which is the amount after reflecting inventory shortage loss. The ending merchandise inventory used in computing the cost of goods sold is the acquisition cost of ₩4,000 thousand (200 × 20 thousand). The reason is that, if ₩3,600 thousand is used, then the inventory shortage is included in the cost of goods sold, and is thus reported twice.

6.2 Inventory valuation loss

The inventory value of high technology goods or high fashion goods can be drastically lowered, due to new technology developed or changes in fashion. If the selling price of the inventory falls so that it is impossible to recover the cost, then inventory should be lowered to the amount to be recovered. This valuation method is based on the principle that inventory should not be valued higher than the amount that can be obtained by selling it. The amount that can be obtained by selling inventory is called net realizable value (NRV : 순실현가치). NRV is the expected selling price, less the expected selling expense. Valuing inventory at the lower cost or NRV, is called LCNRV(lower cost or NRV : 저가법).

IFRS[9] allows companies to apply LCNRV to individual inventory items or to groups of similar inventory items. When NRV is lower than cost, we should report the difference between the two as an inventory valuation loss. After the inventory valuation loss is reported, the NRV can be recovered. In this case, we should recognize the recovered amount, not exceeding the inventory valuation loss recorded in previous years, as a reduction to the cost of goods sold. We should also disclose the amounts of and reasons for reversal of inventory valuation loss, reported as a reduction to the cost of goods sold in footnotes.

〈Illustration 7-7-1〉 Inventory valuation loss

Daehan Telecom Inc. retails G-Smart Phone. The number of G-Smart Phone remaining as inventory at end of 20×1 is 100 units and unit cost was ₩330 thousand. Early in December 20×1, the management of the company decided to lower the unit selling price of the G-Smart Phone to ₩300 thousand from ₩400 thousand because I-Smart Phone, which was functionally better and cheaper than G-Smart Phone, was introduced into the market. The expected selling expense per unit is ₩30 thousand. Daehan Telecom Inc.'s decline in selling price of G-Smart Phone should be accounted for as follows :

(Numbers in thousands of ₩)

(Dr.) Inventory valuation loss 6,000*	(Cr.) Merchandise 6,000

* Computation of inventory valuation loss :
Cost : 100 × 330 thousand = ₩33,000 thousand
NRV : 100 × (300 thousand − 30 thousand) = ₩27,000 thousand
Inventory valuation loss : 33,000 thousand − 27,000 thousand
= ₩6,000 thousand

In 〈Illustration 7-7-1〉 merchandise inventory should be reported at ₩27,000 thousand in the statement of financial position at the end of 20×1. But the ending inventory used to compute the cost of goods sold should be ₩33,000 thousand.

〈Illustration 7-7-2〉 Reversal of inventory valuation loss

In 20×2, Daehan Telecom Inc. sold 90 units of the G-Smart Phone, and the remaining 10 units were continuously held as inventory at end of the year. Because the market conditions were more favorable than expected, the net realizable value of the G-Smart Phone was recovered from ₩270 thousand to ₩310 thousand. In this case, the following journal entry should be prepared.

(Numbers in thousands of ₩)

(Dr.) Merchandise	400*	(Cr.) Cost of goods sold	400

* ① Inventory valuation gain :
10 × (310 thousand − 270 thousand) = ₩400 thousand
② Maximum amount of reversal that can be recognized :
10/100 × 6,000 thousand = ₩600 thousand
③ Reversal of inventory valuation loss : ① ₩400 thousand (It is because ① is less than ②.)

In 〈Illustration 7-7-2〉 10 units of the G-Smart Phone that remained in inventory at the end of 20×2 are reported at ₩3,100 thousand in the statement of financial position. But the ending inventory should be ₩2,700 thousand when the cost of goods sold is computed in 20×2. And we should disclose the details and reasons for the reversal of inventory valuation in footnotes.

Cost of goods sold and cash flows

It is said that cash position becomes unfavorable if inventory is increased. It is also said that cash position becomes favorable if trade payables are increased. What are the reasons for this? Let's identify the reasons in the following 〈Illustration 7-8-1〉 and 〈Illustration 7-8-2〉.

〈Illustration 7-8-1〉 Cash flows and cost of goods sold —when merchandise inventory is increased

Hanbat Trading Co. sells printers. All purchases and sales are made in cash. During the founding year of 20×1, the company purchased 100 units of printers at ₩80 thousand per unit and sold 90 units at ₩120 thousand per unit. 10 units remained in inventory. If there are no other expenses, cash outflows and cost of goods sold, and operating cash flows and net income of Hanbat Trading Co. for 20×1 are as follow.

(Numbers in thousands of ₩)

- Operating cash flows
  (1) Cash inflows : 90 units × 120 = 10,800
  (2) Cash outflows : 100 units × 80 = 8,000
  (3) Operating cash flows : (1) − (2) = 2,800
- Net income
  (1) Sales : 90 units × 120 = 10,800
  (2) Cost of goods sold : 90 units × 80 = 7,200
  (3) Net income : (1) − (2) = 3,600
- Difference between cash outflows and cost of goods sold :
  8,000 − 7,200 = 800 or Increase in merchandise inventory (800)
- Difference between operating cash flows and net income :
  2,800 − 3,600 = −800 or Increase in merchandise inventory (−800)

In ⟨Illustration 7-8-1⟩, cash outflows are more than the cost of goods sold by ₩800 thousand. This is because the cost of goods sold includes the cost of 90 units of merchandise sold, and the cash outflows include the cost of 100 units (that is, 90 units sold plus an additional 10 units of merchandise inventory). If merchandise inventory increases, as in this illustration, the cash outflows are higher than the cost of goods sold. If cash outflows are higher then, on the contrary, operating cash flows are lower. Therefore, operating cash flows are less than net income. The reason that an excessive merchandise inventory becomes a burden on the cash flows of a company is that an increase in merchandise inventory negatively affects cash flows as shown above.

On the contrary, when merchandise inventory is decreased because all goods purchased during the current period and some of the beginning merchandise inventory are sold, cash outflows will be lower than the cost of goods sold. If cash outflows are lower, then operating cash flows are higher. Therefore, operating cash flows are higher than net income. If merchandise inventory is decreased through efficient inventory control, then the cash position of the company can improve for this reason.

⟨Illustration 7-8-2⟩ Cash flows and cost of goods sold —when trade payables are increased

All items are the same as ⟨Illustration 7-8-1⟩. Only the following items are different : 1) All merchandise purchased was sold so there was no ending merchandise inventory, and 2) All purchases were made on credit and trade payables at the end of the year were ₩200 thousand. The difference between cash outflows and cost of goods sold and the difference between operating cash flows and net income are as follow :

(Numbers in thousands of ₩)

- Operating cash flows
  - (1) Cash inflows : 100 units × 120 = 12,000
  - (2) Cash outflows : 100 units × 80 − 200 = 7,800
  - (3) Operating cash flows : (1) − (2) = 4,200
- Net income
  - (1) Sales : 100units × 120 = 12,000
  - (2) Cost of goods sold : 100 units × 80 = 8,000
  - (3) Net income : (1) − (2) = 4,000

- Difference between cash outflows and cost of goods sold:
  7,800 − 8,000 = −200 or Increase in trade payables (−200)
- Difference between operating cash flows and net income:
  4,200 − 4,000 = 200 or Increase in trade payables (200)

In ⟨Illustration 7-8-2⟩ cash outflows are less than the cost of goods sold by ₩200 thousand. This is because the cost of goods sold includes ₩8,000 thousand; the cost of 100 units of merchandise sold and cash outflows include only ₩7,800 thousand, cost of 100 units of ₩8,000 thousand less ₩200 thousand trade payables. If trade payables increase, as in this illustration, the cash outflows will be lower than the cost of goods sold. If cash outflows are lower, then, on the contrary, operating cash flows are higher. Therefore, operating cash flows are higher than net income. The reason for which trade payables are called 'working capital provided by suppliers' is that an increase in trade payables affects cash flows positively as shown above.

On the contrary, when trade payables are decreased because all purchases made during the current period are paid and some of the beginning trade payables are additionally paid off, then cash outflows will be higher than the cost of goods sold. If cash outflows are higher, then, on the contrary operating cash flows are lower. Therefore, operating cash flows are lower than net income. If a company wants to decrease trade payables by paying them off early, the company will need a lot of funds for this reason.

The effects of an increase or decrease in merchandise inventory and an increase or decrease in trade payables on cash flows can be summarized as shown in ⟨Table 7-31⟩ below:

⟨Table 7-31⟩ Effects of increase or decrease in merchandise inventory and increase or decrease in trade payable on cash flows

(1) When merchandise inventory is increased: Cost of goods sold + Increase in merchandise inventory = Cash outflows Net income − Increase in merchandise inventory = Operating cash flows
(2) When merchandise inventory is decreased: Cost of goods sold − Decrease in merchandise inventory = Cash outflows Net income + Decrease in merchandise inventory = Operating cash flows

(3) When trade payables are increased : Cost of goods sold − Increase in trade payables = Cash outflows Net income + Increase in trade payables = Operating cash flows
(4) When trade payables are decreased : Cost of goods sold + Decrease in trade payables = Cash outflows Net income − Decrease in trade payables = Operating cash flows

The above formulas show that an increase in merchandise inventory causes more cash outflows than the cost of goods sold, and causes less operating cash flows than net income. An increase in trade payables causes less cash outflows than cost of goods sold, and causes more operating cash flows than net income. Decreases in merchandise inventory and trade payables cause the exact opposite effects on cash flows.

In Chapter 5, we explained the causes for the difference between net income and operating cash flows by classifying them into four types. Here we reviewed the same issue conceptually, and will reexamine it using the double-entry bookkeeping mechanism in Chapter 11, where methods of preparing the statement of cash flows are introduced.

Related financial ratios

Financial ratios that are related with merchandise inventory and trade payables are the inventory turnover and days' sales in inventory ; the trade payables turnover and days' sales in trade payables ; and the operating cycle and cash operating cycle.

8.1 Financial ratios evaluating activity

(1) Inventory turnover

How much inventory do companies carry? Generally, companies must carry an inventory that is just enough to meet customer demand. If companies hold excessive inventory, they may bear extra expenses, such as carrying expense, financing expense for the borrowing to buy inventory, and obsolescence (out-of-date merchandise) expense. Excess inventory may also worsen a company's cash position, as we reviewed in Section 7. To check whether a company holds adequate inventory and efficiently uses its inventory, the inventory turnover ratio is used. Inventory turnover can be computed as follows.

$$\text{Inventory turnover} = \frac{\text{Cost of goods sold}}{\text{Average inventory}} = \frac{\text{Cost of goods sold}}{(\text{Beginning inventory} + \text{Ending inventory}) / 2}$$

Inventory turnover measures how many times inventory is are sold during the year. It is understood that the higher the inventory turnover is, the more efficiently inventory is utilized.

(Daehan Department Store's ratio)

$$20\times2: \frac{230 \text{ billion}}{(23 \text{ billion} + 43 \text{ billion})/2} = 6.97 \text{ times}$$

$$20\times1: \frac{118 \text{ billion}}{23 \text{ billion}} = 5.13 \text{ times}^{*}$$

* Ending merchandise inventory was used as the denominator because there was no beginning merchandise inventory in 20×1, the year of foundation. In practice ending inventory is used as the denominator for convenience's sake.

Daehan Department Store's inventory turnover for 20×1 was 5.13 times. It was 6.97 times for 20×2, so we know that the inventory is being managed more efficiently than last year.

(2) Days' sales in inventory

The days' sales in inventory is computed by dividing the inventory turnover into 365 days as follows. If the inventory turnover is 10, it means that, on average, inventory was sold 10 times over the year. In other words, the period from the purchase of merchandise to the sale of merchandise, or the average selling period of inventory, is roughly 37 days (365/10).

$$\textbf{Days' sales in inventory} = \frac{\textbf{365 days}}{\textbf{Inventory turnover}}$$

(Daehan Department Store's ratio)

$$20\times2: \frac{365 \text{ days}}{6.97} = 52.37 \text{ days}$$

$$20\times1: \frac{365 \text{ days}}{5.13} = 71.15 \text{ days}$$

Daehan Department Store's days' sales in inventory was shortened significantly, from 71.15 days in 20×1 to 52.37 days in 20×2. If days' sales in inventory is shortened like this, then funds tied up with inventory are reduced.

(3) Trade payables turnover

As explained above, if companies delay the payment of trade payables, then the cash position of the company can be improved. The trade payables turnover shows, on average, how many times trade payables were paid in a year. It is computed as follows.

$$\text{Trade payables turnover} = \frac{\text{Purchases}^{*}}{\text{Average trade payables}} = \frac{\text{Purchases}^{*}}{(\text{Beginning T/P} + \text{Ending T/P}) / 2}$$

* In practice cost of goods sold is used instead of purchases for convenience's sake.
Purchases = Cost of goods sold + Increase in inventory

The higher this turnover is, the worse the cash position of the company may be.

(Daehan Department Store's ratio)

$$20\times2: \frac{230 \text{ billion} + (43 \text{ billion} - 23 \text{ billion})}{(18 \text{ billion} + 42 \text{ billion}) / 2} = 8.33 \text{ times}$$

$$20\times1: \frac{118 \text{ billion} + 23 \text{ billion}}{18 \text{ billion}} = 7.83 \text{ times}^{*}$$

* Ending trade payables were used as the denominator because there were no beginning trade payables in 20×1, the year of foundation. In practice ending trade payables are used as the denominator for convenience's sake.

Daehan Department Store's trade payables turnover was slightly increased from 7.83 times for 20×1, to 8.33 times for 20×2.

(4) Days' sales in trade payables

Days' sales in trade payables is computed as follows.

$$\text{Days' sales in trade payables} = \frac{\text{365 Days}}{\text{Trade payables turnover}}$$

If the trade payables turnover is 12, it means that, on average, the trade payables were paid 12 times in a year. It also means that the trade payable is paid after roughly 30 days (365/12) have passed from the day on which merchandise was purchased on credit. In other words, it means that the trade payables payment period is 30 days.

(Daehan Department Store's ratio)

$$20\times2 : \frac{365 \text{ days}}{8.33} = 43.82 \text{ days}$$

$$20\times1 : \frac{365 \text{ days}}{7.83} = 46.62 \text{ days}$$

Daehan Department Store's days' sales in trade payables was slightly decreased from 46.62 days for 20×1, to 43.82 days for 20×2.

(5) Operating cycle

The operating cycle (영업주기) is the period required to sell merchandise inventory on credit and to collect trade receivables after the purchases of merchandise. This is computed as follows, by adding days' sales in inventory and days' sales in trade receivables, which were reviewed in Chapter 6.

Operating cycle = Days' sales in trade receivables + Days' sales in inventory

(Daehan Department Store's ratio)

20×2 : 21.22* + 52.37 = 73.59 days
20×1 : 33.18* + 71.15 = 104.33 days

* Refer to Chapter 6, Section 4, for days' sales in trade receivables.

Daehan Department Store's operating cycle was reduced significantly, from 104.33 days for 20×1 to 73.59 days for 20×2.

(6) Cash operating cycle

The cash operating cycle (현금영업주기) is defined as the time period from the time of cash payment for the purchase of merchandise to the time of cash receipt from sales of merchandise. The cash operating cycle is computed as follows.

Cash operating cycle = Days' sales in trade receivables + Days' sales in inventory − Days' sales in trade payables

If inventory is purchased on credit, then cash outflow is not incurred until trade payables are paid off. Therefore, the period from the time of cash outflow for purchasing the goods to the time of cash inflow from the collection of trade receivables can be computed by the operating cycle, which was reviewed above, minus days' sales in trade payables. This is called the cash operating cycle. Companies must finance working capital during the cash operating cycle. The more the cash operating cycle is shortened, the less working capital must be financed. If we want to shorten the cash operating cycle, we should decrease days' sales in inventory or days' sales in trade receivable, or increase days' sales in trade payables.

In practice, companies compute their working capital by multiplying average daily sales with the cash operating cycle when they ask for loans to finance working capital from financial institutions. (If a company wants to maintain working capital conservatively enough, the company computes its working capital by multiplying average daily sales with the operating cycle instead of the cash operating cycle.)

(Daehan Department Store's ratio)

20×2 : 21.22 + 52.37 − 43.82 = 29.77 days 20×1 : 33.18 + 71.15 − 46.62 = 57.71 days

Daehan Department Store's cash operating cycle is significantly reduced from 57.71 days for 20×1, to 29.77 days for 20×2. If the cash operating cycle is reduced in this way, then the company's financial burden is lessened because the demand for working capital is lowered.

■ Note : Financial ratios reviewed in this chapter are summarized in Appendix 2 〈Table B-1〉 'Key financial ratios' at the end of this book.

IFRS references (http://www.kasb.or.kr)

[1] IAS 1 *Presentation of Financial Statements*, par. 99.
[2] IAS 8 *Accounting Policies, Changes in Accounting Estimates and Errors*, par. 42, 49.
[3] IAS 2 *Inventories*, par. 23, 25.
[4] *Ibid*, par. 25.
[5] *Ibid*, par. 27.
[6] *Ibid*, par. BC9, 10, 11, 12, 13.
[7] *Ibid*, par. 22.
[8] *Ibid*, par. 16(a).
[9] *Ibid*, par. 34, 36(e), (f), (g).

Key terms

Accounts payable (외상매입금) : Payable that has not yet been paid in cash, among payable arising from the purchases of merchandise made on purely on credit. (p.306)

Cost of goods sold (매출원가) : The acquisition cost of merchandise sold during the current period ; this is an expense to generate sales revenue. (p.308)

FIFO (first-in first-out : 선입선출) : An inventory cost formula for exchangeable goods, involving an assumption that goods acquired earlier are the first to be sold. (p.327)

FOB destination (목적지인도기준) : A sales term in which the legal title to the goods passes to the buyer when the carrier delivers the goods to the buyer. (p.307)

FOB shipping point (선적지인도기준) : A sales term in which the title of the goods passes to the buyer when the goods are loaded for shipping at the seller's place of operations. (p.307)

Gross profit method (매출총이익률법) : A method of estimating the cost of the ending inventory by, first, estimating the cost of goods sold by applying the past gross profit percentage to sales for the current period and, next, subtracting the estimated cost of goods sold from the cost of goods available for sale. (p.333)

LIFO (last-in first-out : 후입선출) : An inventory cost formula for exchangeable goods, involving an assumption that the most recently acquired goods are the first to be sold. (p.327)

Lower cost or NRV (net realizable value) : LCNRV (저가법) : An inventory valuation method under which inventory is valued at acquisition cost or net realizable value, whichever is lower. (p.339)

Moving average (이동평균) : An inventory cost formula for exchangeable goods, under which merchandise inventory is valued using the weighted average every time a sale is made. (p.330)

Net realizable value (NRV : 순실현가능가치) : Value that can be obtained from selling a certain asset ; this is the projected selling price, less the estimated selling expense. (p.339)

Notes payable (지급어음) : Promissory notes that have not yet been paid in cash, among these notes issued as a consideration from purchasing merchandise on credit. (p.306)

Periodic inventory system (실사법) : An inventory recording system in which purchases of merchandise are recorded on the debit side of the purchase account and the cost of goods sold is computed by taking the physical inventory at the end of period and valuing the cost of the ending inventory, then subtracting this cost from the cost of goods available for sales. (p.309)

Perpetual inventory system (계속기록법) : An inventory recording system under which 1) the purchased amount is recorded on the debit side of the merchandise account when a purchase of merchandise is made, and 2) the cost of goods sold is recorded on the debit side of the cost of goods sold account and the credit side of merchandise account, when a sale of merchandise is made. (p.308)

Retail inventory method (소매재고법) : An inventory estimation method used by retailers, such as department stores, in which the cost of ending inventory is estimated by applying a cost-to-retail ratio of goods available for sales to the ending inventory at retail price. (p.335)

Specific identification method (개별법) : A method of computing cost of goods sold and evaluating inventory by identifying which items that were purchased at a specific price are sold, and which items that were purchased at a specific price remain in inventory, per the actual flow of inventory. (p.326)

Trade payable (매입채무) : The payables from purchasing merchandise on credit, meaning the obligation to pay cash in future and consist of accounts payable and notes payable. (p.306)

Weighted average (가중평균) : An inventory cost formula for exchangeable goods, involving an assumption that the beginning inventory and purchases goods are sold at an evenly weighted average unit cost and it is called total average (총평균) in Korean. (p.329)

Exercises

1. Purchases of merchandise

Hanbat Telecom Co. which was founded on December 5, 20×1, and imports and sells the parts of smart phone. The following are merchandise purchase transactions of Hanbat Telecom Co. for the month of December 20×1.

① December 8 : Purchased in cash part X (500 units, ₩10 thousand per unit) from a domestic manufacturer. ② December 12 : Purchased in cash part Y (500 units, ₩20 thousand per unit) from a domestic manufacturer. ③ December 20 : The company imported part Z (400 units, ₩50 thousand per unit) FOB shipping point (the shipping date was December 23, 20×1 and the arrival date was January 5, 20×2). ④ December 25 : The company imported part W (500 units, ₩80 thousand per unit) FOB destination (the shipping date was December 29, 20×1 and the arrival date was January 10, 20×2).

《Question》

Compute the total amount of merchandise purchases of Hanbat Telecom Co. for the month of December.

2. Recording purchases and sales of merchandise—perpetual inventory system and periodic inventory system

The following are data concerning the purchases and sales of Mapo Trading Co. for the month of January 20×1. All purchases and sales were made in cash. Unit purchase cost was ₩20 and unit selling price was ₩40. There was no beginning inventory. Ending merchandise inventory was 40 units, per the physical inventory taken on January 31.

Date	Number units purchased	Number of units sold
January 8	20	
January 12	40	
January 15		30
January 20	60	
January 28		50

《Questions》

(1) Prepare journal entries to record purchases and sales of merchandise under the perpetual inventory system.
(2) Prepare journal entries to record purchases and sales of merchandise under the periodic inventory system.

3. Merchandise inventory, purchases and cost of goods sold

Daejeon Trading Co.'s cost of goods sold was ₩365 billion, purchases were ₩343 billion, freight-in was ₩25 billion, purchase returns and allowance were ₩11 billion for the year of 20×1, and ending merchandise inventory was ₩49 billion per the physical inventory taken.

《Questions》

(1) How much were Daejeon Trading Co.'s delivered cost of net purchases for the year of 20×1?
(2) How much was Daejeon Trading Co.'s beginning merchandise inventory?

4. Correcting inventory errors

The following are SS Department Store's inventory errors. The income tax rate is 30%, and all of the current year's income tax is paid in the following year. All inventory errors introduced here are independent of each other, and corrections of these errors are accepted as revenue or expense in tax accounting.

Inventory errors

	Year	Ending merchandise inventory valuation errors
1.	20×3 (current year)	₩10 billion overstated
2.	20×2	₩20 billion overstated
3.	20×1	₩30 billion understated

4-1. Adjusting journal entries

《Questions》

Answer the following questions for each inventory error.

(1) Prepare an adjusting journal entry to correct the error when income statement accounts are not closed. The company uses the cost of goods sold account.
(2) Prepare an adjusting journal entry to correct the error when income statement accounts are closed.

4-2.* **Restating comparative financial statements**

The following are SS Department Store's comparative income statements and comparative partial statements of changes in equity for 20×3 and 20×2, as well as its comparative partial statements of financial position at the ends of both 20×3 and 20×2. There are no operating expenses, other revenues, other expenses or dividends.

Income statement

SS Department Store (Numbers in billions of ₩)

Account titles	20×3		20×2	
Sales		430		350
Beginning merchandise	180		150	
Purchases	240		200	
Goods available for sale	420		350	
Ending merchandise	(−)200		(−)180	
Cost of goods sold		(−)220		(−)170
Net income before income tax expense		210		180
Income tax expense		(−)63		(−)54
Net income		147		128

Partial statement of changes in equity

SS Department Store (Numbers in billions of ₩)

Description	20×3	20×2
Beginning retained earnings	226	100
Net income	147	126
Ending retained earnings	373	226

Partial statement of financial position

SS Department Store (Numbers in billions of ₩)

Account titles	Dec. 31, 20×3	Dec. 31, 20×2
Merchandise	200	180
Income tax payable	63	54
Retained earnings	373	226

《Question》

Restate the following comparative financial statements for each inventory error.

(1) Income statement

(2) Partial statement of changes in equity, showing changes in retained earnings

(3) Partial statement of financial position, showing merchandise, income tax payable and retained earnings

* The level of difficulty is high.

5. Inventory cost formulas—periodic inventory system

The following are data concerning Product X of Gangchon Trading Co. for July 20×1. The company used the periodic inventory system and the ending merchandise inventory was 250 units per the physical inventory taken at the end of July.

(Numbers in ₩)

Description	Quantity (units)	Unit cost	Amount
Beginning inventory	200	5	1,000
July 13 purchase	400	6	2,400
July 25 purchase	500	7	3,500
Total	1,100		6,900

《Questions》

(1) Compute the ending inventory and cost of goods sold by FIFO.
(2) Compute the ending inventory and cost of goods sold by LIFO.
(3) Compute the ending inventory and cost of goods sold by weighted average.
(4) Which cost formula reports the highest cost of goods sold? why?

6. Inventory cost formulas—periodic inventory system and perpetual inventory system

The following are detail transactions concerning Product Y of Hyunam Mart for October 20×1. The ending merchandise inventory was 250 units per the physical inventory taken on October 31.

(Numbers in ₩)

Date	Purchases			Sales		
	Quantity (units)	Unit cost	Amount	Quantity (units)	Unit price	Amount
Beg. Inv.	200	10	2,000			
Oct. 5	300	15	4,500			
Oct. 10				350	30	10,500
Oct. 15	200	20	4,000			
Oct. 20				100	30	3,000
Oct. 25	200	22	4,400			
Oct. 30				200	30	6,000
Total	900		14,900	650		19,500

《Questions》

(1) Compute gross profit for October 20×1 when inventory is valued under FIFO.
  1) Under the periodic inventory system
  2) Under the perpetual inventory system

(2) Compute gross profit for October 20×1 when inventory is valued under LIFO.
  1) Under the periodic inventory system
  2) Under the perpetual inventory system

(3) Compute gross profit for October 20×1 when inventory is valued by weighted average.

(4) Compute gross profit for October 20×1 when inventory is valued by moving average.

7. **FIFO and LIFO**

The following are the beginning and ending merchandise inventory and gross profit of Gana Electronics and Dami Electronics applying FIFO and LIFO.

(Numbers in billions of ₩)

	Beginning inventory		Ending inventory		Gross profit	
	FIFO	LIFO	FIFO	LIFO	FIFO	LIFO
Gana Electronics	24	20	28	20	18	(1)
Dami Electronics	29	26	19	13	(2)	24

《Question》 Compute (1) and (2) in the above table.

8. **Gross profit method**

K-Mart is a small retail store. The management of the company wanted to know its merchandise inventory at the end of first quarter of 20×1. The following is information for the first quarter of 20×1.

(Numbers in billions of ₩)

Description	Amount
Beginning merchandise inventory	16
Purchases	42
Freight-in	4
Sales	106
Sales returns	6

《Question》

Estimate ending merchandise inventory of the first quarter by the gross profit method. Gross profit to net sales was 20% for past three years.

9. **Retail inventory method**

Daesin Bookstore is a retailor of books and stationaries. The following are the data of Daesin Bookstore for 20×1.

(Numbers in billions of ₩)

Description	Cost	Retail
Beginning merchandise inventory	6	8
Purchases	30	42
Mark-downs		2
Sales		36
Ending merchandise inventory		12

《Questions》

(1) Calculate the cost-to-retail ratio (cost ratio) of merchandise for 20×1.

(2) Estimate the cost of ending inventory using the ratio calculated in (1).

10. Inventory shortage loss

Daehan Food Co. hold 200 units (₩9,000) as a beginning inventory of 20×1. Purchase for 20×1 is 2,000 units (₩100,000). Under the perpetual inventory system, the number of units at December 31, 20×1 was 300 units after considering normal shortage loss. However, as a result of the physical inventory count, the actual number of units was 270 units. The unit cost to be applied to the ending merchandise inventory was ₩50.

《Question》

Prepare a journal entry to record the loss from inventory shortage.

11. Inventory valuation loss

Hanbat Fashion Inc. sells women's fashion dresses. The cost of ending merchandise inventory at the end of 20×1, by FIFO and under the periodic inventory system, was ₩8,800 thousand (20 dresses × ₩440 thousand). The management of the company projected that the selling price per dress should be lowered from ₩600 thousand to ₩400 thousand, to sell merchandise inventory, because of changes in fashion. Estimated disposal costs is ₩50 thousand per dress.

《Question》

Prepare a journal entry to record the valuation loss from the decline in selling price of the merchandise inventory.

12. Inventory turnover and days' sales in inventory

The following is the accounting information of X-Mart for 20×1, 20×2, and 20×3.

(Numbers in billions of ₩)

Description	20×1	20×2	20×3
Beginning merchandise inventory	40	60	80
Ending merchandise inventory	60	80	100
Cost of goods sold	170	224	240
Sales	240	320	380

《Question》

Compute inventory turnover and days' sale in inventory for each year.

13. Inventory turnover and days' sales in inventory, trade payables and days' sales in trade payables

The following are the data of Sogang Bookstore for 20×1.

(Numbers in billions of ₩)

Description	Amount	Description	Amount
Beginning merchandise inventory	5	Beginning trade payables	4
Ending merchandise inventory	6	Ending trade payables	5
Purchases	15		

《Questions》

(1) Compute cost of goods sold.
(2) Compute inventory turnover and days' sales in inventory.
(3) Compute trade payables turnover and days' sales in trade payables.

14. Operating cycle and cash operating cycle

The following are data gathered from the financial statements of 20×1 of Cheonan Trading Co. which was founded on January 1, 20×1.

(Numbers in billions of ₩)

Account titles	Amount	Account titles	Amount
Sales	200	Cost of goods sold	120
Purchases	180	Trade receivables	10
Merchandise	12	Trade payables	15

《Questions》

(1) Compute days' sales in trade receivables, days' sales in trade payables, Days' sales in inventory. (Use the ending balance rather than the average for trade receivables, and trade payables and merchandise inventory).
(2) Compute operating cycle and cash operating cycle.

Investing Activities–
Non-current Assets

Chapter 8 Overview

In this chapter we explore how we record tangible and intangible assets and present in the statement of financial position. More specifically, we explain how to determine the cost of tangible assets ; what kinds of depreciation methods are available for plant assets, which are a part of tangible assets ; how to account for repair and maintenance of plant assets, disposal of tangible assets, and impairment of tangible assets. We also briefly review the characteristics and types of intangible assets. Last, we explain methods for using accounting information that is related to non-current assets.

Case of Daehan Department Store

Statement of financial position (Ft. 2.ⓐ)

As of December 31, 20×2
DDS As of December 31, 20×1 (Numbers in billions of ₩)

Account titles	December 31, 20×2		December 31, 20×1	
Assets				
Current assets				
Cash and cash equivalents(Ft. 4)		45		41
Trade receivables(Ft. 3ⓑ)	30		20	
Allowance for uncollectibe accounts (Ft. 3ⓑ, 5)	(−)4	26	(−)2	18
Inventory :				
Merchandise (Ft. 3ⓒ)		43		23
Total current assets		**114**		**82**
Non-current assets				
FVOCI financial asset (Ft. 3ⓓ, 6)		13		10
Investment in associate (Ft. 3ⓔ, 7)		24		-
Tangible assets (Ft. 8) :				
Land(Ft. 3ⓕ)		96		90
Plant assets (Ft. 3ⓕ, 16)	310		160	
Accumulated depreciation(Ft. 3ⓕ)	(−)13	297	(−)3	157
Intangible asset (Ft. 3ⓖ) :				
Industrial property right (Ft. 8)		9		-
Total non-current assets		**439**		**257**
Total assets		**553**		**339**
Liabilities				
Current liabilities				
Trade payables		42		18
Interest payable		5		4
Salaries payable		2		3
Income tax payable		14		5
Cost financial liabilities (Ft. 3ⓘ) :		38		48
Short-term borrowings (Ft. 9ⓐ)	10		30	
Current portion of long-term borrowings (Ft. 9ⓑ)	28		18	
Provision :				
Provision for refunds (Ft. 3ⓗ, 11)		3		2
Total current liabilities		**104**		**80**
Non-current liabilities				
Cost financial liability (Ft. 3ⓘ) :		126		112
Long-term borrowings (Ft. 9ⓑ)	84		72	
Amortized cost financial liability (Ft. 3ⓘ) :				
Bonds payable (Ft. 10)	42		40	
Total non-current liabilities		**126**		**112**
Total Liabilities		**230**		**192**

Equity				
Share capital				
Common stock(Ft. 13, 16)		150		100
Share premium				
Common stock(Ft. 16)		60		10
Accumulated other comprehensive income		20		11
Accumulated gain on valuation of FVOCI financial asset* (Ft. 3ⓓ, 6)	4		1	
Land revaluation surplus (Ft. 3ⓕ, 8)	16		10	
Retained earnings (Ft. 3ⓛ, 15)		93		26
Total equity		323		147
Total liabilities and equity		553		339

* FVOCI : Fair value through other comprehensive income

Comprehensive income statement (Ft. 2ⓑ)

From Jan. 1, 20×2 to Dec. 31, 20×2

DDS From Jan. 1, 20×1 to Dec. 31, 20×1 (Numbers in billions of ₩)

Account titles	20×2		20×1	
Sales (Ft. 3ⓐ)		430		220
Cost of goods sold		(−)230		(−)118
Gross profit		200		102
Operating expenses :		(−)85		(−)50
Salaries expense	(−)43		(−)26	
Bad debts expense (Ft. 3ⓑ)	(−)4		(−)2	
Depreciation expense (Ft. 3ⓕ)	(−)10		(−)3	
Rent expense	(−)24		(−)12	
Other operating expenses	(−)4		(−)7	
Income from operations		115		52
Other revenue		6		−
Equity income from associate (Ft. 7)	6		−	
Other expenses		(−)19		(−)14
Finance expense (Ft. 2ⓑ) :				
Interest expense	(−)19		(−)13	
Loss on disposal of tangible assets (Ft. 8)	−		(−)1	
Net income before income tax expense		102		38
Income tax expense		(−)30		(−)12
Net income		72		26
Other comprehensive income :		9		11
Item that will not be reclassified to profit or loss :				
Gain on revaluation of land (Ft. 3ⓕ, 8)	6		10	
Item that may be reclassified subsequently to profit or loss :				
Gain on valuation of FVOCI financial asset (Ft. 3ⓓ, 6)	3		1	
Total comprehensive income		81		37
Earnings per share (Ft. 12)		₩2,880		₩1,733

〈Footnotes〉

3. Important accounting policies

ⓕ Aquisition cost, depreciation methods, and revaluation of tangible assets

(1) Plant assets are composed of buildings and structures, and are reported in a format of subtracting accumulated depreciation from acquisition cost. The acquisition cost includes expenditures that are directly attributable to the acquisition. The plant assets are depreciated by the straight-line method. It is estimated that the useful life of buildings is 40 years and the useful life of structures is 10 years, and there is no residual value for either asset. The company checks whether the depreciation expense reflects the reduction in real value of the asset at the end of every year. If it doesn't, then the company reviews and changes the depreciation method, useful life, and residual value.

(2) Capital expenditures, such as large repair costs that improve the efficiency of an asset or extend its useful life, are added to the balance of that asset. Revenue expenditure, such as repair and maintenance cost that is necessary to recover and maintain an asset's current condition, is recorded as a current period expense. The gain or loss on the disposal of plant assets is the difference between the sales proceeds and the book value of the asset, and is reported in the comprehensive income statement as other income or loss.

ⓖ Amortization of intangible assets

Intangible assets are composed of industrial property rights (patents). They are amortized by the straight-line method, during their estimated useful life of 10 years, with no residual value

8. Aquisition and disposal of tangible and intangible assets

The acquisition and disposal of tangible and intangible assets for each year are as follow.

(Numbers in billions of ₩)

Description		Land	Plant assets	Intangible assets
20×1	Beginning balance	–	–	–
	Acquisition in cash	120	100	–
	Acquisition by issuing stock	–	60	–
	Disposal	(–)40*	–	–
	Gain on revaluation	10		
	Ending balance	90	160	–
20×2	Acquisition in cash	–	150	9**
	Gain on revaluation	6		
	Ending balance	96	310	9

* Proceeds from sales were ₩39 billion.
** An industrial property right (patent) acquired at the end of 20×2.

Explanation of case financial statements

- Note : Numbers in superscripts are main text page numbers where the corresponding subjects are explained.

The statement of financial position accounts that are related to this chapter include land and plant assets ; accumulated depreciation expense of plant assets, which are parts of non-current assets that are classified as tangible assets ; and industrial property rights, which are classified as intangible assets. Comprehensive income statement accounts also include depreciation expense and loss on the disposal of tangible assets. At the end of 20×2, Daehan Department Store reported land of ₩96 billion, plant assets of ₩297 billion, and industrial property rights of ₩9 billion, in its statement of financial position. Plant assets were presented with the acquisition cost[367] of ₩310 billion, less accumulated depreciation expense of ₩13 billion.[376] Per Footnote 3 ⓕ (2), the company adds capital expenditures to the balance of the affected asset and records revenue expenditure as a current period expense.[380] Per Footnote 8, the industrial property right[386], which was reported as an intangible asset, refers to a patent. There was no amortization expense[385] because it was purchased at the year's end.

Depreciation expense[371] of ₩10 billion was reported in 20×2 as an operating expense in the comprehensive income statement. Per Footnote 3 ⓕ (1), this depreciation expense was for plant assets such as buildings and structures. These assets had no residual value[371] and the useful lives[371] of the building and structure were estimated at 40 years and 10 years respectively. These assets were depreciated by the straight-line method.[372] The company checks whether the depreciation expense reflects the reduction in real value of the asset at the end of every year. If it does not reflect this reduction, the company reviews and changes the depreciation method, residual value, and useful life at the end of every year. The company reported 'loss on disposal of tangible asset'[382] of ₩1 billion, in its comprehensive income statement for 20×1. Per Footnote 8, this loss resulted from selling a piece of land with book value of ₩40 billion at ₩39 billion.

Acquisition cost of tangible assets

1.1 Determination of acquisition cost of tangible assets

Tangible assets, like other assets, are also recorded at acquisition cost. The acquisition cost of tangible assets includes all expenditures necessary to acquire the asset and to get it into the proper place and condition for its intended use. Therefore, in addition to purchase price, acquisition cost includes incidental costs such as acquisition tax and registration tax for land and buildings ; and freight, installation, and trial run cost for machinery. We will examine the concept of acquisition cost through ⟨Illustration 8-1⟩ and ⟨Illustration 8-2⟩.

⟨Illustration 8-1⟩ Acquisition cost of tangible assets—acquisition tax and registration tax

Company A purchased a piece of land at ₩100 billion on January 1, 20×1. Acquisition tax and registration tax to be paid to the district municipal office were 5% of the purchase price. The acquisition cost of the land is computed as follows.

Purchase price	₩100 billion
Acquisition tax and registration tax (100 billion × 5%)	5 billion
Acquisition cost	₩105 billion

In ⟨Illustration 8-1⟩, the acquisition cost of land is ₩105 billion ; that is, the total amount of the purchase price of ₩100 billion and the incidental costs of ₩5 billion such as acquisition tax and registration tax.

〈Illustration 8-2〉 Acquisition cost of tangible assets—freight, installation cost, trial run cost

Company B purchased semi-conductor testing equipment for ₩100 billion on January 1, 20×1. Freight, installation cost, and trial run cost for this equipment were ₩2 billion, ₩3 billion, and ₩5 billion respectively. The cost of this equipment is computed as follows :

Purchase price	₩100 billion
Incidental cost*	10 billion
Acquisition cost	₩110 billion

* Freight + Installation cost + Trial run cost = 2 billion + 3 billion + 5 billion = ₩10 billion

In 〈Illustration 8-2〉, the acquisition cost of semi-conductor testing equipment, to be reported as a plant asset, is ₩110 billion. This includes the total purchase price of the equipment, at ₩100 billion, and incidental costs of ₩10 billion such as freight, installation cost, and trial run cost.

1.2 Lump-sum purchase

When we acquire a building, we generally acquire the building and land together and pay a single lump-sum price. Not because a building is just different from land in nature, but also because we do not depreciate land, we can not report the two together as 'land and building.' How, then, can we separate the costs for land and for building? We proportionally allocate the total cost between the land and building, based on their relative fair market value. 〈Illustration 8-3〉, below, shows how the cost is allocated when assets are purchased at a lump-sum price.

〈Illustration 8-3〉 Allocation of lump-sum cost

Shinil Ltd. acquired a building and land together at ₩30 billion on July 1, 20×1. At the time of the acquisition fair market value of building and land were ₩24 billion and ₩12 billion respectively. In this case the acquisition costs of building and of land are computed as follows :

Acquisition cost of building :
30 billion × [24 billion/(24 billion + 12 billion)] = ₩20 billion
Acquisition cost of land :
30 billion × [24 billion/(24 billion + 12 billion)] = ₩10 billion

In 〈Illustration 8-3〉, the cost of the building is computed as ₩20 billion. This is calculated by multiplying a ratio of the fair market value of the building to the total fair market value of building (₩24 billion) and land (₩12 billion) of ₩36 billion, which is a ratio of 2/3 (24 billion/36 billion), to the lump-sum price of ₩30 billion. The cost of the land is computed as ₩10 billion by multiplying a ratio of the fair market value of the building to total fair market value, which is 1/3 (12 billion/36 billion) to the lump-sum price of ₩30 billion.

〈Box 8-1〉 Acquisition on a long-term installment plan

If Company A purchases a machine in cash, it must pay ₩30 billion. But if the company purchases on a long-term installment plan, it must pay ₩1 billion every month for 36 months for a grand total of ₩36 billion. In the case of a long-term installment plan purchase, what is the acquisition cost? The fair market value of the machine on the acquisition date was ₩30 billion, which means that the company purchased an asset worth ₩30 billion. Therefore, the acquisition cost should be ₩30 billion. If that is the case, then how do we classify the ₩6 billion in total installment payments of ₩36 billion over 36 months? That is an **interest charge** on a liability occurred due to the long-term installment plan.

⟨Box 8-2⟩ Capitalization of finance cost

A company may construct tangible assets by itself. A **construction in progress** is one of those self-constructing assets that is not completed yet, so is not in use. The cost of construction in progress includes all expenditures made during the construction period. **Interest cost** is one of those expenditures. In the case of getting a loan to construct an asset and paying interest during the construction period, that interest should be included in the acquisition cost. This is called the **capitalization of finance costs**.

Depreciation methods

If we use plant assets, such as building, equipment, and machinery, for operation, we should report the expense of using those assets. If we use plant assets, the value of that asset decreases. It is technically very difficult to measure the decrease in the value of plant assets every year. Therefore, we systematically allocate the cost of plant assets during the time period which it is possible to use these assets (the useful lives of the assets) and report as a depreciation expense. In summary, the depreciation expense means the expense of using the asset, the decrease in its value, and the allocation of its cost.

Depreciation methods include the straight-line method, the diminishing balance method, and the units of production method. To compute the depreciation of a plant asset, we need three pieces of basic information : the acquisition cost of the plant asset, its estimated useful life, and its estimated residual value (its expected value after its useful life is over).

IFRS[1] requires that the company should select a depreciation method that produces a depreciation expense reflecting the real decrease in economic value of the asset. It also requires that, at the end of every year, the company checks whether the depreciation expense reflects the economic reality. If not, it should change the depreciation method. Furthermore, it requires that the company review the estimated useful lives and residual values and, if they are different from the expected values, the company should adjust them.

We will explain the straight-line method, the diminishing balance method, and the units of production method, using 〈Illustration 8-4〉.

〈Illustration 8-4〉 Depreciation methods

B Semi-conductor Ltd. purchased semi-conductor testing equipment for ₩110 billion on January 1, 20×1. It is estimated that the useful life of this equipment was 10 years and the residual value was ₩10 billion. The total estimated useful machine hours of this semi-conductor testing equipment were 100,000 hours and actual machine hours used in 20×1 and 20×2 were 8,000 hours and 12,000 hours respectively.

2.1 Straight-line method

The straight-line method (정액법) is a method under which the depreciation expense is computed evenly for each year over the estimated useful life of the asset. Depreciation expense under the straight-line method is computed as follows.

$$\text{Depreciation expense} = \frac{\text{Acquisition cost} - \text{Residual value}}{\text{Useful life}}$$

In ⟨Illustration 8-4⟩, the depreciation expense under the straight-line method for 20×1 and 20×2 are computed as shown in ⟨Table 8-1⟩ below.

⟨Table 8-1⟩ Depreciation expense—straight-line method

Depreciation method	20×1	20×2
Straight-line method	(110 billion - 10 billion)/10 = ₩10 billion	(110 billion - 10 billion)/10 = ₩10 billion

Under the straight-line method the acquisition cost (₩110 billion), minus the residual value (₩10 billion), which is the depreciable cost (₩100 billion), is divided by the useful life (10 years) so that the same amount of depreciation expense (₩10 billion) is computed for every year.

2.2 Diminishing balance method

The diminishing balance method (체감잔액법) is a method under which the depreciation expense is computed by multiplying a fixed rate by the book value at the beginning of the year, that is diminishing every year. A typical example of the diminishing balance method is the fixed rate on diminishing balance method. There are the double declining method (one of the diminishing balance methods) and the sum-of-the-years'-digits method (not a diminishing balance method) that provide a pattern of depreciation expense similar to that under the fixed rate on diminishing balance method. These two methods are used quite a bit in the United States because they are simple to use. Here we review only the fixed rate on diminishing balance method. The double declining balance method and the sum-of-the-years'-digits method are introduced in the ⟨Box 8-3⟩ below.

The depreciation expense under the fixed rate on diminishing balance method (정률법) is computed as follows.

Depreciation expense = Book value at beginning of year × constant rate*

* Constant rate is computes as follows :

$$\text{Constant rate} = \sqrt[n]{\frac{\text{Residual value}}{\text{Acquisition cost}}}$$

where, n is the useful life

Depreciation expense under the fixed rate on diminishing balance method is computed by multiplying a fixed rate by the book value at the beginning of every year. The first year depreciation expense is computed by multiplying the fixed rate by the acquisition cost, which is the book value at the beginning of the year. The second year depreciation expense is computed by multiplying the fixed rate by the amount obtained from deducting the depreciation expense for the prior year from the acquisition cost, that is, the book value (or undepreciated cost) at the beginning of the second year.

In ⟨Illustration 8-4⟩, the depreciation expense for each year under the fixed rate on diminishing balance method is computed as shown in ⟨Table 8-2⟩ below. It is assumed that the fixed rate is computed as 21%.

⟨Table 8-2⟩ Depreciation expense—fixed rate on diminishing balance method

Depreciation method	20×1	20×2
Fixed rate on diminishing balance method	110 billion × 21% = ₩23.1 billion	(110 billion − 23.1 billion) × 21% ≒ ₩18.2 billion

The depreciation expense for the first year (₩23.1 billion) is obtained by multiplying the acquisition cost (₩110 billion) by the constant rate (21%). The depreciation expense for the second year (₩18.2 billion) is obtained by multiplying the book value at the beginning of the year (₩86.9 billion), which is the acquisition cost (₩110 billion), less the amount already depreciated (₩23.1 billion) by the constant depreciation rate (21%). In this way, under the fixed rate on diminishing balance method, depreciation expense decreases as the years go by because depreciation expense is computed by multiplying the fixed rate to the diminishing beginning book value. Depreciation expense for the last year of the useful life is ₩3.2 billion that converts the book value into the residual value.

〈Box 8-3〉 The double declining balance method and the sum-of-the-years'-digits method

Two other depreciation methods that provide more depreciation in the early years and gradually less in later years, like the fixed rate on diminishing balance method, are the double declining balance method and the sum-of-the-years'-digits method. These methods were developed as alternatives to the fixed rate on diminishing balance method, because it is very difficult to compute and apply the fixed rate.

First, the **double declining balance method (이중체감법)** is a simple method under which the fixed rate is not computed by a complex formula, as under the fixed rate on diminishing balance method. The depreciation rate is just **double the straight-line depreciation rate** [if the useful life is 10 years, it is double 1/10 (or 10%) ; that is, 20%].

Under the **sum-of-the-years'-digits method (연수합계법)**, we compute the depreciation expense in the following way. If the asset's useful life is 10 years, then we compute the depreciation expense by the ratio of the sum of numbers from 1 to the useful life of 10 as the denominator, and numbers in order from 10 to 1 as the numerator every year. In this case, the denominator of depreciation rate is 55. So we compute the depreciation expense by multiplying the ratio of 10/55, 9/55, ⋯, 1/55 each year to the depreciable cost, which is the acquisition cost less residual value.

2.3 Units of production method

The units of production method (생산량비례법) is a method under which the depreciation expense is computed by a ratio of the units of production (or consumption) in the current year over the total possible units of production. Depreciation expense under this method is computed as follows.

$$\text{Depreciation expense} = (\text{Acquisition cost} - \text{Residual value}) \times \frac{\text{Units of production for current year.}}{\text{Total possible units of production}}$$

In 〈Illustration 8-4〉, the depreciation expense for each year under the units of production method is computed as shown in 〈Table 8-3〉 below.

〈Table 8-3〉 Depreciation expense—units of production method

Depreciation method	20×1	20×2
Units of production method	$(110 \text{ billion} - 10 \text{ billion}) \times \frac{8,000}{100,000} =$ ₩8 billion	$(110 \text{ billion} - 10 \text{ billion}) \times \frac{12,000}{100,000} =$ ₩12 billion

Depreciation expense for 20×1 is ₩8 billion. which is applicable to 8,000 machine hours used out of the total possible machine hours of 100,000 hours. The depreciation expense for 20×2 is ₩12 billion, which is applicable to 12,000 machine hours used.

2.4 Recording depreciation expense

Depreciation expense can be recorded by either the direct or the indirect method. The difference between these two methods is using, or not using, the accumulated depreciation account, which is an account contra to the plant asset account.

(1) Direct method

The direct method is a method under which the depreciation expense is directly recorded in the plant asset account. Under the direct method, the straight-line depreciation expense of ₩10 billion for 20×1 in 〈Illustration 8-4〉 is journalized as follows.

(Numbers in billions of ₩)

(Dr.) Depreciation expense	10	(Cr.) Machinery	10

As shown above, because the depreciation expense is directly deducted from the plant asset account under the direct method, the acquisition cost of the plant asset is not maintained and accumulated depreciation is not recorded.

(2) Indirect method

Under the indirect method, we do not directly subtract the depreciation expense from the plant asset account. Rather, we indirectly record it in the accumulated depreciation account. Under the indirect method, the straight-line depreciation expense of ₩10 billion for 20×1, in 〈Illustration 8-4〉, is journalized as follows.

(Numbers in billions of ₩)

(Dr.) Depreciation expense	10	(Cr.) Accumulated depreciation	10

As shown above, under the indirect method, the acquisition cost of a plant asset is maintained and the accumulated total depreciation expense from the acquisition date until today is recorded in a separate account.

IFRS[2] requires to disclose the acquisition cost of plant assets and accumulated depreciation. Therefore, plant assets should be accounted for in the indirect method, under which the acquisition cost is maintained and accumulated depreciation is recorded.

2.5 Reporting in the statement of financial position

Plant assets can be reported in the statement of financial position, either by the gross or the net method.

(1) Gross method

Under the gross method, we report plant assets in a style in which we deduct accumulated depreciation from acquisition cost. The following 〈Table 8-4〉 is machinery we report in the statement of financial position, using the gross method for the case of 〈Illustration 8-4〉, under the straight-line method of depreciation.

〈Table 8-4〉 Partial statement of financial position (gross method)

B Semi-conductor Ltd. As of December 31, 20×1 (Numbers in billions of ₩)

Account titles	Amount	
Non-current assets		
Tangible assets :		
Machinery	110	
Accumulated depreciation	(-)10	100

Under this method, the acquisition cost of machinery of ₩110 billion is reported as it is, the accumulated depreciation of ₩10 billion is deducted from the acquisition cost, and book value of ₩100 billion is reported.

(2) Net method

The net method is a method under which we report only the net amount, which is acquisition cost of the plant asset less accumulated depreciation. The following ⟨Table 8-5⟩ is machinery we report in the statement of financial position using the net method for the case of ⟨Illustration 8-4⟩, under the straight-line method of depreciation.

⟨Table 8-5⟩ Partial statement of financial position (net method)

B Semi-conductor Ltd. As of December 31, 20×1 (Numbers in billions of ₩)

Account titles	Amount	
Non-current assets		
Tangible assets :		
Machinery		100

As shown above, if the plant asset is reported in the statement of financial position using the net method, acquisition cost and accumulated depreciation are not reported.

IFRS allows both the gross method and the net method. The sample format of the statement of financial position that IFRS[3] provides is the one using the net method. And the statement of financial position that IFRS[4] provides to show the format and method of preparing the statement of cash flows is the one using the gross method. As reviewed above, IFRS requires to disclose the acquisition cost of the plant asset and accumulated depreciation. Therefore, if we report the plant asset in the statement of financial position using the net method, we should disclose the acquisition cost of the plant asset and accumulated depreciation in footnotes.

This book uses the gross method of reporting plant assets in the statement of financial position, which allows more information to be reported on the face of the statement of financial position. In the past, Korean accounting standards required the gross method, and US GAAP also requires the gross method.

2.6 A partial year depreciation expense

Companies usually purchase plant assets during the year, rather than on January 1 (or December 31). If a company purchases a plant asset during the year, it has to calculate a partial year depreciation. The most accurate method of computing the partial year depreciation is counting the number of days from the date of purchase till the year end. But if the task of counting the number of days is cumbersome, we can compute it on a monthly basis or a half year basis. In the case of a monthly basis, the number of months from the month of purchase till the end of year is the partial year. In the case of the half-year basis, which is allowed by corporate tax codes, one full year's depreciation expense is recorded for any plant asset purchased in the first half of the year, and one half-year's depreciation expense is recorded for any plant asset purchased in the second half of the year. To compute a partial year for a certain plant asset, one can select any one of these bases among the daily, monthly, or half-year base. Once selected, it should be used continuously.

In 〈Illustration 8-4〉, let's assume that B Semi-Conductor Ltd. purchased a semi-conductor testing equipment on April 10, 20×1 and computed a partial year on a monthly base. In that case, depreciation expenses under the fixed rate on diminishing balance method for 20×1 and 20×2 are computed as shown in 〈Table 8-6〉 below.

〈Table 8-6〉 Depreciation expense for 20×1 and 20×2

Depreciation method	20×1	20×2
Fixed rate on diminishing balance method	23.1 billion × 9/12 ≒ ₩17.3 billion	(110 billion − 17.3 billion) × 21% ≒ ₩19.5 billion

The monthly base partial year for 20×1, the acquisition year is 9 months, from April till December. Because the depreciation expense for one year from the acquisition date is ₩23.1 billion as shown in 〈Table 8-2〉, the depreciation expense for 9 months is ₩17.3 billion. For every year, during the 9 years from 20×2 to 20Y0, a depreciation expense is computed by multiplying 21% into the book value at the beginning of the year as the fixed rate on diminishing balance method itself dictates. Depreciation expense for 3 months, from January to March of the last year of the useful life, is ₩1.1 billion that converts the book value into the residual value.

(Note : Because the depreciation expense for every year under the straight-line method is the same, a partial year depreciation expense should be computed for only each of the first year and the last year of the useful life. Because the depreciation expense for each year is different under the sum-of-years'-digits method of 〈Box 8-3〉, a partial year depreciation expense should be computed every year.)

Depreciation expense and cash flows

Depreciation expense is a result of allocating the cost of a plant asset over the useful life of that asset. Cash is paid when the plant asset is acquired and, after that, no additional cash is paid. Therefore, depreciation expense affects net income but does not affect cash flows. Using the following 〈Illustration 8-5〉, we will examine the relationship between depreciation expense and cash flows more specifically.

〈Illustration 8-5〉 Depreciation expense and cash flows

A Co.'s sales for 20×1 was ₩10 billion and operating expenses including cost of goods was ₩9 billion so net income was of ₩1 billion. All sales were made in cash and all operating expenses but depreciation expense of ₩3 billion were paid in cash. A Co.'s cash flows from operating activities and net income for 20×1 are as shown in 〈Table 8-7〉 below.

〈Table 8-7〉 Cash flows from operating activities and net income

(Numbers in billions of ₩)

Description	Amount	Description	Amount
Operating cash inflows	10	Sales	10
Operating cash outflows (9 − 3)	(−)6	Operating expenses	(−)9
Operating cash flows	4	Net income	1

In 〈Illustration 8-5〉, cash inflows from operating activities are ₩10 billion. Cash outflows from operating activities are ₩6 billion because the depreciation expense of ₩3 billion does not require cash outflows. Thus, cash flows from operating activities are ₩4 billion. Net income (₩1 billion) and cash flows from operating activities (₩4 billion) differ by the depreciation expense (₩3 billion), which does not require cash outflows. More details on this issue will be examined in Chapter 11 'Statement of Cash flows.'

Capital expenditures and revenue expenditures

After acquiring a plant asset, one must have repair and maintenance service to keep that asset in good working condition. For example, if we acquire an automobile, then anything out of order should be repaired; engine oil, tires, and battery should be routinely changed; and sometimes the whole body should be painted. All expenditures made for these repair and maintenance services are classified into capital expenditures and revenue expenditures, depending on the size and nature of the expenditures.

Capital expenditures are expenditures that are material in amount and improve the operating efficiency significantly or extend the asset's useful life, leading to an increase in real value of the asset. These expenditures should be added to the acquisition cost of the plant asset, and should be depreciated over the remaining useful life of the asset.

In contrast, revenue expenditures are expenditures that are immaterial in amount and are necessary to maintain the current levels of operating efficiency and useful life of the asset. Revenue expenditures are expensed because their effects are not sustainable to future periods. (In practice, revenue expenditures are called expenditures to be expensed, or expenditures that are expenses in nature). Through the following 〈Illustration 8-6〉, we examine the concepts of capital expenditures and revenue expenditures.

〈Illustration 8-6〉 Capital expenditures and revenue expenditures

A Co. acquired a vehicle paying ₩35 billion on January 1, 20×1. Useful life of the vehicle was estimated to be 5 years and residual value was estimated to be ₩5 billion and depreciated by the straight-line method. Starting from 20×1, every year the company paid ₩0.2 billion to have engine oil and oil filter changed. At the beginning of January 20×4 ₩3 billion was paid to have whole body painted to cover a lot of scratches and rusty spots and to have major parts of the engine replaced. Because of this major repair, efficiency of the vehicle was improved and useful life was extended from 5 years to 8 years. Expenditure for the vehicle and depreciation expenses from January 1, 20×1 to December 31, 20×4 are journalized as shown in ⟨Table 8-8⟩ below.

⟨Table 8-8⟩ Journal entries

(Numbers in billions of ₩)

Year	Journal entry			
20×1	(Dr.) Vehicle	35	(Cr.) Cash	35
Every year from 20×1 to 20×3	(Dr.) Repair and maintenance expense	0.2	(Cr.) Cash	0.2
	(Dr.) Depreciation expense*	6	(Cr.) Accumulated depreciation	6
20×4	(Dr.) Vehicle**	3	(Cr.) Cash	3
	(Dr.) Repair and maintenance expense	0.2	(Cr.) Cash	0.2
	(Dr.) Depreciation expense***	3	(Cr.) Accumulated depreciation	3

* Depreciation expense for each of 20×1, 20×2, 20×3 : (35 billion − 5 billion) / 5 = ₩6 billion

** Instead of vehicle account, the company can use accumulated depreciation account.

*** Depreciation expense for 20×4 : [(35 billion − 6 billion × 3) + 3 billion − 5 billion]/5 = ₩3 billion

In ⟨Illustration 8-6⟩, because the ordinary repair and maintenance expense of ₩0.2 billion, paid every year from 20×1 to 20×4, are revenue expenditures, they were expensed in the year of occurrence. In contrast, because ₩3 billion, paid at the beginning of 20×4 for a major repair, was a capital expenditure, it is added to the book value of the vehicle and is depreciated over its remaining useful life (5 years). Depreciation expense for 20×4 is computed to be ₩3 billion by dividing the remaining useful life (5 years) into the amount (₩15 billion) obtained by adding capital expenditure (₩3 billion) and subtracting residual value (₩5 billion) from the book value of the vehicle at the beginning of 20×4 (remaining balance of ₩17 billion, after taking 3 years' depreciation expense of ₩18 billion from the acquisition cost of ₩35 billion).

Disposal of tangible assets

Tangible assets can be disposed of, either after using them up to the end of their useful life or by selling them during their useful life. Gain or loss on the disposal of a tangible asset is computed by comparing the book value of the tangible asset at the time of disposition and the proceeds received from the disposal. The following 〈Illustration 8-7〉 and 〈Illustration 8-8〉 show how to account for the disposal of a tangible asset in detail.

〈Illustration 8-7〉 Disposal of land

On January 1, 20×4 A Co. sold a piece of land for ₩21 billion, which was purchased at ₩20 billion on January 1, 20×1. The gain or loss on the disposal of land is computed as follows :

1. Computation of disposal gain or loss
   (1) Book value of land at the time of disposal : ₩20 billion
   (2) Proceeds from sales of land : ₩21 billion
   (3) Gain on disposal : (2) − (1) = 21 billion − 20 billion = ₩1 billion

2. Journal entry

(Numbers in billions of ₩)

(Dr.) Cash	21	(Cr.) Land	20
		Gain on disposal of tangible asset	1

We do not depreciate land, because it is assumed that the value of land does not decrease. Therefore, the book value of the land at the time of disposal is the acquisition cost of ₩20 billion. Gain on the disposal of land of ₩1 billion is computed by subtracting the book value of ₩20 billion from the sales proceeds of

₩21 billion.

〈Illustration 8-8-1〉 Disposal of a machinery

B Co. acquired a piece of machinery at ₩100 billion on January 1, 20×1. The company used it for 3 years and sold it at ₩63 billion in cash on January 1, 20×4. It was estimated that the useful life of the machinery was 10 years and the residual value was '0.' The company uses the straight-line method of depreciation for the machinery. Gain or loss on disposal of machinery is computed as follows.

1. Computation of gain or loss on disposal
   (1) Acquisition cost of machinery : ₩100 billion
   (2) Accumulated depreciation at the time of disposition :
   (100 billion/10) × 3 = ₩30 billion
   (3) Book value at the time of disposition :
   (1) − (2) = 100 billion − 30 billion = ₩70 billion
   (4) Proceed from sales of machinery : ₩63 billion
   (5) Loss on disposal :
   (4) − (3) = 63 billion − 70 billion = (−)₩7 billion

2. Journal entry

(Numbers in billions of ₩)

Debit		Credit	
(Dr.) Cash	63	(Cr.) Machinery	100
Accumulated depreciation	30		
Loss on disposal of tangible asset	7		

In 〈Illustration 8-8-1〉, the book value of the machinery at the time of disposal is ₩70 billion, reflecting the acquisition cost of ₩100 billion less the accumulated depreciation of ₩30 billion, and the sale proceeds are ₩63 billion. Therefore, loss on the disposal of machinery is ₩7 billion, which is the difference between the book value and the sale proceeds.

Machinery is generally disposed of during the year, rather than at the beginning of the year. 〈Illustration 8-8-2〉 shows how to compute a gain or loss on the disposal of tangible assets when a plant asset is disposed of during the year.

〈Illustration 8-8-2〉 Disposal of a machinery during the year

If everything is the same as 〈Illustration 8-8-1〉 but the company sold the machinery on July 1, 20×4, then the gain on disposal of machinery is computed as follows.

1. Computation of gain or loss on disposal
   (1) Depreciation expense from Jan. 1, 20×4 to Jul. 1, 20×4 :
   100 billion/10 × 6/12 = ₩5 billion
   (2) Book value of machinery at the time of disposition :
   100 billion − 30 billion − 5 billion = ₩65 billion
   (3) Proceed from sales of machinery : ₩63 billion
   (4) Loss on disposal :
   (3) − (2) = 63 billion − 65 billion = (−)₩2 billion

2. Journal entries

(Numbers in billions of ₩)

Debit		Credit	
(Dr.) Depreciation expense	5	(Cr.) Accumulated depreciation	5
(Dr.) Cash	63	(Cr.) Machinery	100
Accumulated depreciation	35		
Loss on disposal of tangible asset	2		

When a plant asset is disposed of during the year, as shown in 〈Illustration 8-8-2〉, first, the depreciation expense for the period from the beginning of the year to the date of disposition must be recorded. Then, the gain or loss on disposal is computed by comparing the book value with the sales proceeds. In 〈Illustration 8-8-2〉, the loss on disposal (₩2 billion) is the difference between the book value (₩65 billion) after recording depreciation expense (₩5 billion) for 6 months, from the beginning of 20×4 till the disposal date of July 1, and the proceeds from selling machinery (₩63 billion).

The disposal of tangible assets is also an investing activity, just as is their acquisition. The proceeds from the sale of tangible assets are reported as cash inflows from investing activities on the statement of cash flows. Because a gain or loss on disposal of tangible assets is not from operating activities, it must not be included as cash flow from operating activities. Therefore, a gain or loss on the disposal of a tangible asset is reversely adjusted back to net income when operating cash flows is computed by the indirect method. More detail on this issue will be reviewed in Chapter 11, 'Statement of Cash Flows.'

〈Box 8-4〉 Characteristics and types of intangible assets

Characteristics of intangible assets

Intangible assets are assets without physical substance that are used for a long time in a company's operating activities. Intangible assets include **industrial property rights, mining rights, goodwill, and development costs**. The cost of intangible assets, except for goodwill, should be allocated and reported as depreciation expenses over the useful life of the asset. The depreciation expense of an intangible asset is called the **amortization expense (무형자산상각비)**. As an amortization method, a company should choose amongst the straight-line method, the diminishing balance method, or the units of production method, which reflect the decrease in the real value of the asset. IFRS[5] requires that the straight-line method should be used if the pattern of decrease in real value of the asset cannot be observed objectively. Except for in situations where there is a commitment by a third party to purchase the asset at the end of its useful life and where there is an active market for the asset, it is assumed that intangible assets do not have residual value. The amortization method and useful life should be checked at least once every year to assure that they reflect reality. If they do not, they should be adjusted.

Goodwill is not amortized. Instead, we should check every year (or when there are indications of impairments) whether goodwill is impaired. If there is an impairment, then an impairment loss should be recorded. Intangible assets other than goodwill should be reviewed for impairments also, and if there is an impairment, then impairment loss and recovery of impairment loss should be recorded, applying the same accounting procedures applicable to the impairment loss of tangible assets.

IFRS[6] requires to disclose the acquisition cost of intangible assets and accumulated amortization (including accumulated impairment loss). We can report intangibles assets in the statement of financial position, using either 1) the **gross method** under which we report tangible assets in a style in which we deduct accumulated amortization from acquisition cost, or 2) the **net method** under which we report only the net amount, which is acquisition cost less accumulated amortization. (Refer to 3.5 methods of presenting plant assets.) If we report the intangible asset in the statement of financial position using the net method, we should disclose the acquisition cost and accumulated amortization in footnotes.

Types of intangible assets

1. Industrial property rights

Industrial property rights are intangible assets, including patents, copyrights, trademarks, trade names, franchises, and licenses. Industrial property rights are generally effective for a period fixed by law.

A patent is an exclusive right given by the Office for Patent Administration, to manufacture and sell inventions or newly developed products exclusively for a specific period fixed by law. Copyrights are exclusive rights, given by the government, to reproduce or sell an artistic work or a publication. A word, phrase, jingle, or symbol about a particular product is called a trademark and those about a particular enterprise is called a trade name. A franchise is a contractual arrangement under which the franchisor grants the franchisee the right to sell certain products, to render specific services, or to use certain trademarks or trade names within a designated location. A license is a right given by the government to an enterprise to use public facilities to provide a specific service. An example is the allotment of frequency bands by the government to a specific broadcasting company so the company can provide over-the-air broadcasting service.

2. Mining rights

Mining rights are rights to extract natural resources, such as minerals, oil, or gas, within a permitted specific mining zone. We depreciate mining rights by the units of production method. The depreciation expense of natural resources is called depletion expense (감모상각비).

3. Goodwill

Goodwill is a premium paid over the fair value of a company. It is recorded only when the company is purchased. This is because internally generated goodwill cannot be measured objectively. Key money paid when a store is transferred is the same as goodwill.

4. Development costs

Among development costs, one that is directly identified with the development of a specific product, and through which it is probable that future economic benefits can be generated, is reported as an intangible asset.

Impairment of tangible assets

A company should review, at the end of every year, whether the economic benefits from tangible assets have decreased significantly— that is, whether there is a sign of an impairment. If there is a sign of impairment, then the company should estimate the recoverable amount from the asset, and should report the amount below book value as an impairment loss. The recoverable amount from an asset is the higher of amount received by selling the tangible asset or amount of its value in use that is value will be obtained from continuous use of the asset.

The impairment loss of a tangible asset should be reported as an expense for the current year and should be accumulated in the accumulated impairment loss account, which is an account contra to the asset account (this is the same as done for a depreciation expense). Therefore, if there is an impairment, the book value of the tangible asset is the original cost of the tangible asset less the accumulated depreciation and the accumulated impairment loss.

If the recoverable amount of the asset increases in years subsequent to the recognition of impairment, then the increase is accounted for as a reversal of impairment loss. The increased book value, due to a reversal of an impairment loss, may not exceed the book value that would have existed if no impairment loss had been recognized for the asset in prior years per IFRS[7].

〈Illustration 8-9〉 Impairment of tangible asset

Daehan Ltd. purchased a piece of land at ₩10 billion on January 1, 20×1. At the end of 20×1, the recoverable amount from the land was ₩ 9 billon. In this case, impairment loss is journalized as follows.

(Numbers in billions of ₩)

(Dr.) Impairment loss on land 1	(Cr.) Accumulated impairment loss-land 1

If the recoverable amount from the land increases to ₩11 billion, then the reversal of impairment loss is journalized as follows.

(Numbers in billions of ₩)

(Dr.) Accumulated impairment loss-land 1	(Cr.) Reversal of impairment loss on land 1*

* Reversal is allowed only up to the point where the book value becomes the book value without impairment loss in prior years, which is ₩10 billion. Only ₩1 billion out of the ₩2 billion increase in the recoverable amount, then, is recognized as a reversal.

As shown in 〈Illustration 8-9〉, on December 31, 20×1, because the recoverable amount of land (₩9 billion) was less than the original cost (₩10 billion) by ₩1 billion, we recorded this amount as an impairment loss of land. On December 31, 20×2, the recoverable amount of land (₩11 billion) was ₩2 billion more than the book value (₩9 billion). But because the book value after a reversal cannot be more than ₩10 billion that in the book value would be without impairment in prior years, we recognize only the accumulated impairment loss of ₩1 billion as a reversal.

〈Box 8-5〉 Impairment of depreciable asset

Hankuk Ltd. purchased a building for ₩500 billion on January 1, 20×1. It was estimated that the useful life of the building was 20 years and residual value was '0.' The company uses the straight-line method to depreciate this building. The recoverable amount of the building was estimated at ₩456 billion at the end of 20×1. Impairment loss on the building is journalized as follows :

(Numbers in billions of ₩)

(Dr.) Impairment loss on building 19	(Cr.) Accumulated impairment loss—building 19

Book value [500 billion − 25 billion (500 billion/20)]	₩475 billion
Recoverable amount	₩456 billion
Impairment loss	₩19 billion

If recoverable amount of the building at the end of 20×2 was ₩455 billion, reversal of impairment loss was journalized as follows :

(Dr.) Accumulated impairment loss-building 18	(Cr.) Reversal of impairment loss on building 18

The reversal of impairment loss of ₩18 billion is finalized in the following 4 steps.

(Step 1) Compute the book value at end of 20×2.

Aquisition cost	₩500 billion
Accumulated depreciation (25 billion* + 24 billion**)	(−)₩49 billion
Accumulated impairment loss	(−)₩19 billion
Book value	₩432 billion

* Depreciation expense for 20×1 : Acquisition cost/(Useful life)
= 500 billion/20 = ₩25 billion

** Depreciation expense for 20×2 : Book value at beginning of 20×2/(Remaining useful life) = (500 billion − 25 billion − 19 billion)/19
= ₩24 billion

(Step 2) Compare the book value and recoverable amount at the end of 20×2 and compute a potential reversal of impairment loss. Because the book value at the end of 20×2 was ₩432 billion and recoverable amount was ₩455 billion, the potential reversal of impairment loss is ₩23 billion.

(Step 3) Compute the maximum limit of reversal of impairment loss. Book value after the reversal of impairment loss cannot exceed what the book value would be without impairment loss in prior years. If there was no impairment loss in prior years, the book value at end of 20×2 is computed as follows :

Acquisition cost	₩500 billion
Accumulated depreciation (25 billion + 25 billion)	(−)₩50 billion
Book value	₩450 billion

The maximum limit of reversal of impairment loss is ₩18 billion, which is the difference between ₩432 billion book value at the end of 20×2 and ₩450 billion book value that would have existed if there had been no impairment loss in prior years.

(Step 4) Determine the amount of reversal to be recognized by comparing the **potential amount** computed in (Step 2) and the **maximum limit** computed in (Step 3). The potential amount (₩23 billion) in (Step 2) exceeds the maximum limit (₩18 billion) in (Step 3). Thus, the maximum limit of ₩18 billion is recognized as a reversal of impairment loss, as done by the above journal entry.

The book value, after recording the maximum limit of ₩18 billion becomes the book value of ₩450 billon, which is what the balance would have been if there was no impairment loss in prior, as shown below.

Acquisition cost		₩500 billion
Accumulated depreciation	(25 billion + 24 billion)	(−)₩49 billion
Accumulated impairment loss	(19 billion* − 18 billion**)	(−)₩1 billion
Book value		₩450 billion

* Impairment loss at the end of 20×1

** Reversal of impairment loss at the end of 20×2

Related financial ratios

Financial ratios related to non-current assets include the average useful life of plant assets, the average age of plant assets, and the non-current asset turnover (as activity ratios) and the fixed assets to long-term capital ratio [as a (financial) safety ratio].

7.1 Financial ratios evaluating activity

(1) Average useful life of plant assets

The useful life of plant assets is estimated by management's subjective judgement. By estimating a longer useful life, a company spreads the cost of its plant assets over a longer period. Thus, the depreciation expense reported in each year is lower and net income is higher. If, on the other hand, a shorter useful life is estimated, depreciation expense for each year will be higher and net income will be lower. Thus, the average useful life of plant assets shows whether the company estimates the useful life of plant assets conservatively (shorter) or liberally (longer), so that it reports net income conservatively (less) or liberally (more). The average useful life of plant assets is computed as the following, based on the assumption that the company uses the straight-line depreciation method.

$$\text{Average useful life of plant assets} = \frac{\text{Average acquisition cost of plant assets}}{\text{Depreciation expense}}$$

(Daehan Department Store's ratio)

$$20\times2 : \frac{(160 \text{ billion} + 310 \text{ billion}) / 2}{10 \text{ billion}} = 23.5 \text{ years}$$

$$20\times1 : \frac{160 \text{ billion}}{6 \text{ billion}^{*}} = 26.7 \text{ years}$$

* In 20×1, plant assets were purchased at the end of June, so depreciation expense was reported only for six months. If converted for 1 year, it would be ₩6 billion.

Daehan Department Store is in its early stages of operation and does not own many plant assets. Thus, it is rather difficult to have a meaningful interpretation of the average useful life of plant assets. However, if a company has a lot of plant assets, then we can use this ratio to check whether net income is reported conservatively or not.

(2) Average age of plant assets

This ratio computes how many years plant assets have been used, based on the assumption that the company uses the straight line method of depreciation. This measure shows the degree of deterioration of plant assets. It can be computed by dividing accumulated depreciation by depreciation expense, as follows.

$$\textbf{Average age of plant assets} = \frac{\textbf{Accumulated depreciation of plant assets}}{\textbf{Depreciation expense}}$$

(Daehan Department Store's ratio)

$$20\times2 : \frac{13 \text{ billion}}{10 \text{ billion}} = 1.3 \text{ years}$$

$$20\times1 : \frac{3 \text{ billion}}{3 \text{ billion}} = 1 \text{ year}$$

Because Daehan Department Store 20×1 is in its early stages of operation and does not own many plant assets, the average age of plant assets, like the average useful life of plant assets above, may also lack significant meaning. However, if a company does have a lot of plant assets, this ratio would be a useful measure to assess the degree of deterioration of the firm's plant assets.

(3) Non-current assets turnover

As shown in Chapter 5, there are two ways to improve the return on an asset : one is to increase the profit margin on sales, the other is to increase the total assets turnover. To improve the total assets turnover, a company must increase the turnover of non-current assets, those that are used in operating activities. The non-current assets turnover is computed as follows.

$$\text{Non-current assets turnover} = \frac{\text{Sales}}{\text{Average non-current assets}} = \frac{\text{Sales}}{(\text{Beginning non-current assets} + \text{Ending non-current assets})/2}$$

(Daehan Department Store's ratio)

$$20\times2 : \frac{430\text{ billion}}{(257\text{ billion} + 439\text{ billion})/2} = 1.24\text{ times}$$

$$20\times1 : \frac{220\text{ billion}}{257\text{ billion}^{*}} = 0.86\text{ times}$$

* Because 20×1 was the year of foundation, the ending balance of non-current assets was used as the denominator.

The non-current assets turnover of Daehan Department Store increased from 0.86 times in 20×1, to 1.24 times in 20×2. This means that, compared with the prior year, in 20×2 the non-current assets were used efficiently in operating activities. As a result, profitability might have improved.

7.2 Financial ratios evaluating safety (financial)

(1) Non-current assets to long-term funds ratio

The non-current assets to long-term funds ratio is the ratio of non-current assets to long-term funds composed of non-current liabilities and equity, as shown below.

$$\text{Non-current assets to long-term funds ratio} = \frac{\text{Non-current assets}}{\text{Non-current liabilities + Equity}}$$

It is ideal to purchase non-current assets like plant assets, which are used for a long time, with long-term funds. If the acquisition of non-current assets is made via short-term borrowing, then the financial burden of paying back the borrowing is increased. The non-current assets to long-term funds ratio shows us how much of a firm's non-current assets are financed by long-term funds. (In Korean, this ratio is called the fixed long-term fit ratio because non-current assets used to be called fixed assets.) If this ratio is in excess of 100%, then an excess proportion of the purchase of non-current assets was made using short-term funds. If this ratio is below 100%, then a deficient proportion of long-term funds are available for the purchase of non-current assets.

(Daehan Department Store's ratio)

$$20\times2 : \frac{\text{439 billion}}{\text{126 billion + 323 billion}} = 97.77\%$$

$$20\times1 : \frac{\text{257 billion}}{\text{112 billion + 147 billion}} = 99.23\%$$

This ratio shows that, in 20×2 and 20×1, nearly all (97.77% in 20×2 and 99.23% in 20×1) non-current assets were acquired with long-term funds.

■ Note : Financial ratios reviewed in this chapter are summarized in Appendix 2 〈Table B-1〉 'Key financial ratios' at the end of this book.

IFRS references (http://www.kasb.or.kr)

[1] IAS 16 *Property, Plant and Equipment*, par. 60, 61.
[2] *Ibid*, par. 73(d).
[3] IAS 1 *Presentation of Financial Statements*, IG Part 1.
[4] IAS 7 *Statement of Cash Flows*, Appendix A.
[5] IAS 38 *Intangible Assets*, par. 97, 104.
[6] *Ibid*, par. 118(c).
[7] IAS 36 *Impairment of Assets*, par. 117.

Key terms

Accumulated depreciation (감가상각누계액) : The accumulated amount of depreciation from the acquisition date to the end of current year. (p.375)

Amortization expense (무형자산상각비) : Depreciation expense of an intangible asset. (p.385)

Capital expenditures (자본적 지출) : Large expenditures by which the efficiency of a plant asset is improved or the useful life of a plant asset is extended, which should be capitalized (recorded as an asset). (p.380)

Deletion (감모상각비) : Depreciation expense of a natural resource. (p.386)

Depreciation expense (감가상각비) : The expense of using a plant asset, which means a decrease in value of that asset because of usage and is computed by allocating the acquisition cost over the useful life of a plant asset. (p.371)

Diminishing balance method (체감잔액법) : A depreciation method such as the fixed rate on diminishing balance method or the double declining balance method under which a larger amount of depreciation is reported in earlier years in useful life of an asset than in the later years and the depreciation expense is computed by multiplying a constant rate to the book value at the beginning of the year, which is diminishing every year. (p.372)

Double declining balance method (이중체감법) : A depreciation method under which depreciation expense is computed by multiplying double the rate of the straight-line method to the book value at the beginning of the year, which is declining every year. (p.374)

Fixed rate on diminishing balance method (정률법) : A depreciation method under which the depreciation expense is computed by multiplying a constant rate obtained from a specific formula to the book value at the beginning of the year, which is diminishing every year. (p.372)

Goodwill (영업권) : A premium paid over the fair value of a company and is recorded and reported only when a company is purchased. (p.386)

Impairment loss (손상차손) : The deficient amount, when the recoverable amount from an asset is less than its book value. (p.387)

Residual value (잔존가치) : The expected value of a plant asset after its useful life is exhausted. (p.371)

Revenue expenditures (수익적 지출) : Small expenditures that are made to maintain the current operating efficiency and that are expenses in nature. (p.380)

Straight-line method (정액법) : A depreciation method under which the same amount is depreciated every year and depreciation expense is computed by dividing the amount subject to depreciation, which is acquisition cost less residual value, by the estimated useful life of the asset. (p.372)

Sum-of-the-years'-digits method (연수합계법) : A depreciation method under which depreciation expense is computed by multiplying the ratio composed of the remaining useful life at beginning of the year as a numerator and the sum of the years' digits in that useful life as a denominator into the amount subject to depreciation, which is the acquisition cost less residual value. (p.374)

Units of production method (생산량비례법) : A depreciation method under which depreciation expense is computed by multiplying the ratio of units of production during the period by the estimated total units of production into the amount subject to depreciation, which is the acquisition cost less residual value. (p.374)

Useful life (내용연수) : The time period during which a plant asset can be used. (p.371)

Exercises

1. Acquisition cost of tangible assets—a lump-sum purchase

J-Mart purchased a building and land in a lump-sum from H Co., which closed its business recently. Expenditures related to this lump-sum purchase are as follows :

Lump-sum price : ₩52 billion	Aquisition and registration tax : ₩2 billion

Fair values of the building and land at the time of the purchase are as follows.

Building : ₩40 billion	Land : ₩20 billion

《Question》 Determine the acquisition cost of each of building and land.

2. Acquisition cost of tangible assets—purchase on an installment plan

H-Mart purchased an automobile with cash purchase price of ₩50 million on an installment plan, paying ₩1 million every month for 60 months (paying in total ₩60 million). In addition, it paid acquisition and registration tax of ₩7 million.

《Question》 Compute the acquisition cost of the automobile? And explain reasons why.

3. Acquisition cost of tangible assets—capitalization of finance cost

Daejeon Corp. signed a contract to construct an office building on November 1, 20×1. The construction started on the date of the contract and was completed on December 31, 20×2. The contract's detailed contract price payment schedule is as follows.

Contract price : ₩140 billion

Payment schedule

(Numbers in billions of ₩)

Payment	Date	Amount
1st.	March 1, 20×2	60
2nd.	May 1, 20×2	50
3rd.	December 31, 20×2	30

* Daejeon Corp. paid the contract price by borrowing, with a maturity period of 1 year and an interest rate of 12%, from Chungcheong Bank on each payment date.

《Question》

Compute the interest that should be included in the acquisition cost of building.

4. Acquisition cost of plant assets and depreciation : straight-line method and fixed rate on diminishing balance method

The following is data concerning Shintan Logistics Co.'s acquisition of a vehicle.

The company purchased a vehicle with a cash purchase price of ₩55 million on January 1, 20×7. Cash of ₩28 million was paid on the date of purchase and the rest of the purchase price was to be paid in 24 monthly installments of ₩2 million. Acquisition tax of ₩3 million and registration tax of ₩2 million, which were incidental to the purchase, were paid in cash. It is estimated that useful life of this vehicle was 10 years and the residual value was '0.'

《Questions》

(1) Compute the acquisition cost of the vehicle

(2) Compute the depreciation expense for 20×7 under the straight-line method.

(3) Compute the depreciation expense for 20×8 under the fixed rate on diminishing balance method. (The fixed rate is assumed to be 20%.)

5. Lump-sum purchase and depreciation : straight-line method and fixed rate on diminishing balance method

On January 1, 20×1, Mirae Corp. purchased an office building and land together and paid ₩24 billion in cash. At the date of acquisition, the fair values of building and land were ₩25 billion and ₩5 billion, respectively. It was estimated that the useful life of building was 20 years and the residual value was '0.'

《Questions》

(1) Compute the cost of each (building and land), and prepare a journal entry for this purchase transaction.
(2) Under each of the straight-line method and the fixed rate on diminishing balance method, compute and journalize the depreciation expense for both 20×1 and 20×2. (The fixed rate is assumed to be 10%.)
(3) Explain the difference between the effects of each of the straight-line method and the fixed rate on diminishing balance method of depreciation, on the income statement and statement of financial position, as well as the differences between the effects of each method on income tax.

6. **Depreciation : sum-of-the-years'-digits method**

The following data concerns a machine owned by Daejeon Corp.

Acquisition date : January 1, 20×1 Purchase price : ₩26 million Cost of installation and a trial run : ₩5 million Residual value : ₩1 million Useful life : 5 years Depreciation method : Sum-of-the-years'-digits method

《Question》 Compute and journalize the depreciation expense for 20×1 and 20×3.

7. **Depreciation : units of production method**

Yuseong Co. purchased a tractor for ₩44 million on January 1 20x1. Residual value was estimated at ₩4 million and total usable milage was estimated at 200,000km. The milage used was 25,000 km and 15,000 km in 20×1 and 20×2, respectively.

《Question》

Compute and journalize the depreciation expense for 20×1 and 20×2, under the units of production method.

8. **Depreciation—comprehensive**

Sogang Corp. paid ₩100 billion in cash and purchased a new machine on January 1, 20×1. It was estimated that the useful life of the machine was 5 years and residual value was 10% of the acquisition cost. It was also estimated that the total usable machine hours is 20,000 hours. The machine was used 6,000 hours and 4,000 hours in 20×1 and 20×2, respectively. (The fixed rate, for the fixed rate on diminishing balance method, is assumed to be 40%.)

《Question》

Compute the depreciation expense for 20×1 and 20×2 under each of the four depreciation methods : the straight-line method, the fixed rate on diminishing balance method, the sum-of-the-years'-digit method, and the units of production method.

9. Depreciation expense and cash flows

Yuseong Co. purchased an office building for ₩80 billion on January 1, 20×1. It was estimated that useful life of this building was 40 years and the residual value was '0.' The straight-line method is used for depreciation. The following is a set of data gathered from the income statement for 20×3.

(Numbers in billions of ₩)

Account titles	Amount
Sales	70
Cost of goods sold	42
Operating expenses (except for depreciation expense)	25

* Sales, cost of goods sold, and operating expenses, excluding depreciation expense, were received or paid in cash.

《Questions》

(1) Compute depreciation expense and net income for 20×3.
(2) Compute cash flows from operating activities for 20×3.

10. Disposal of plant assets

Sogang Co. purchased a machine for ₩20 billion on January 1, 20×1 and sold it for ₩15 billion on June 30, 20×2. This machine was depreciated by the straight-line method. Its estimated useful life was 8 years and its estimated residual value was ₩4 billion.

《Questions》

(1) Compute gain or loss on disposal of machine
(2) Prepare journal entries for the disposal of machine

11. Disposal of tangible assets

K-Mart purchased land and a building on January 1, 20×1, at ₩12 billion and ₩22 billion, respectively. The useful life of the building was estimated to be 10 years and the residual value was estimated to be ₩2 billion. The straight-line method was used for depreciation. K-Mart sold land and building for ₩15 billion and ₩12 billion, respectively, on July 1, 20×5.

《Questions》

(1) Compute the book value of the building at the time of disposal.
(2) Compute the gain or loss on the disposal of the land and building.
(3) Journalize the disposal of the land and building.

12. Revenue expenditures and capital expenditures

The following data concerns a machine in a Daejeon Corp.'s warehouse.

Date of purchase : January 1, 20×1	Purchase price : ₩110 billion
Cost of installation and a trial run : ₩2 billion	Residual value : ₩12 billion
Useful life : 10 years	Depreciation method : straight-line method

The company conducts regular maintenance service, replacing parts and changing lubricant, every two months. Total annual expenditure for this repair and maintenance is ₩1 billion. Early in January of 20×6, the company carried out a major repair of the machine and had the core parts replaced for ₩30 billion. Thus, its useful life was estimated to be 15 years so its remaining useful life was 10 years.

《Questions》

(1) Compute the acquisition cost of machine.
(2) Journalize repair and maintenance and depreciation expense for every year from 20×1 to 20×5.
(3) Journalize the major repair in 20×6 and depreciation expense for 20×6.

13. Accounting for tangible assets—comprehensive

The following is information concerning the tangible assets of Sinchon Corp.

- The company purchased an office building and land for cash of ₩60 billion and ₩44 billion, respectively, on January 1, 20×1. It was estimated that the useful life of building was 20 years and the residual value was '0.'
- The company purchased a machine for cash of ₩95 billion with an additional expenditure of ₩5 billion in cash, which was made for installation. It was estimated that useful life of the machine was 5 years and its residual value was ₩10 billion.
- The company sold the machine for ₩40 billion in cash on July 1, 20×3.
- The company carried out roof waterproofing work on the building for ₩2 billion in cash in early January of 20×5. Thus, the useful life of the building was extended to 24 years.
- The company uses the straight-line method of depreciation for the building, and uses the fixed rate on diminishing balance method of depreciation for the machine. (The fixed rate is assumed to be 40%).

《Questions》

(1) Prepare a journal entry to record the aquisition of building and land on January 1, 20×5. Compute and journalize depreciation expense of the building for 20×1.

(2) Prepare a journal entry to record the aquisition of machine on July 1, 20×2. Compute and journalize depreciation expense of this machine for 20×2.

(3) Prepare journal entries to record the disposal of machine on July 1, 20×4.

(4) Prepare a journal entry to record the roof waterproofing work on the building in early January of 20×5. Compute and journalize depreciation expense of building for 20×5.

14. Amortization of intangible assets

The following is information on the intangible assets of Hanbat Software Co., as of December 31, 20×4.

(Numbers in billions of ₩)

Account titles	Amount	Date of aquisition	Useful life
Industrial property rights	40	January 1, 20×3	8 years*
Accumulated amortization—industrial property rights	(−)10		
Development costs	12	January 1, 20×4	6 years*
Accumulated amortization—development costs	(−)2		

* It was estimated that the residual value was '0.'

《Question》 Compute and journalize amortization expense for 20×5.

15. Impairment of tangible assets

The following is data concerning Daehan Corp.'s land used for business.

(Numbers in billions of ₩)

Date	Aquisition cost	Recoverable amount
January 1, 20×1	50	
December 31, 20×1		40
December 31, 20×2		55

《Question》

Prepare journal entries to record impairment of land as of December 31, 20×1 and December 31, 20×2.

16. Financial ratios related to non-current assets

The following is a set of data obtained from the financial statements of Hanbat Electronics Co., for 20×4.

(Numbers in billions of ₩)

Description	Amount	Description	Amount
Sales	20	Plant assets	15
Depreciation expense	1	Accumulated depreciation	10
Current assets	4	Current liabilities	1
Non-current liabilities	6	Equity	2

* There is no non-current asset, other than plant assets.

《Question》

Compute the average useful life of plant assets, the average age of plant assets, the non-current assets turnover, and the non-current assets to long-term funds ratio. (Use the ending balance instead of the average.)

Financing Activities—Liabilities

Chapter 9 Overview

In this chapter, we examine accounting methods for a company's borrowing from people other than stockholders. More specifically, we first study the reclassification of long-term borrowings into current liabilities. Next, we explain the nature of bonds and how bond prices are determined. After that, we introduce accounting methods for the issuance of bonds and interest payments, the amortization of a discount on bonds payable, and the retirement of bonds. We also examine how to account for provisions for product warranties and for refunds. Last, we explain methods for using accounting information that is related to liabilities.

Case of Daehan Department Store

Statement of financial position (Ft. 2.ⓐ)

As of December 31, 20×2
DDS As of December 31, 20×1 (Numbers in billions of ₩)

Account titles	December 31, 20×2		December 31, 20×1	
Assets				
Current assets				
Cash and cash equivalents(Ft. 4)		45		41
Trade receivables(Ft. 3ⓑ)	30		20	
Allowance for uncollectibe accounts (Ft. 3ⓑ, 5)	(−)4	26	(−)2	18
Inventory :				
Merchandise (Ft. 3ⓒ)		43		23
Total current assets		**114**		**82**
Non-current assets				
FVOCI financial asset (Ft. 3ⓓ, 6)		13		10
Investment in associate (Ft. 3ⓔ, 7)		24		−
Tangible assets (Ft. 8) :				
Land(Ft. 3ⓕ)		96		90
Plant assets (Ft. 3ⓕ, 16)	310		160	
Accumulated depreciation(Ft. 3ⓕ)	(−)13	297	(−)3	157
Intangible asset (Ft. 3ⓖ) :				
Industrial property right (Ft. 8)		9		−
Total non-current assets		**439**		**257**
Total assets		**553**		**339**
Liabilities				
Current liabilities				
Trade payables		42		18
Interest payable		5		4
Salaries payable		2		3
Income tax payable		14		5
Cost financial liabilities (Ft. 3ⓘ) :		38		48
Short-term borrowings (Ft. 9ⓐ)	10		30	
Current portion of long-term borrowings (Ft. 9ⓑ)	28		18	
Provision :				
Provision for refunds (Ft. 3ⓗ, 11)		3		2
Total current liabilities		**104**		**80**
Non-current liabilities				
Cost financial liability (Ft. 3ⓘ) :		126		112
Long-term borrowings (Ft. 9ⓑ)	84		72	
Amortized cost financial liability (Ft. 3ⓘ) :				
Bonds payable (Ft. 10)	42		40	
Total non-current liabilities		**126**		**112**
Total Liabilities		**230**		**192**

Equity				
Share capital				
Common stock(Ft. 13, 16)		150		100
Share premium				
Common stock(Ft. 16)		60		10
Accumulated other comprehensive income		20		11
Accumulated gain on valuation of FVOCI financial asset* (Ft. 3ⓓ, 6)	4		1	
Land revaluation surplus (Ft. 3ⓕ, 8)	16		10	
Retained earnings (Ft. 3ⓛ, 15)		93		26
Total equity		323		147
Total liabilities and equity		553		339

* FVOCI : Fair value through other comprehensive income

Comprehensive income statement (Ft. 2ⓑ)

From Jan. 1, 20×2 to Dec. 31, 20×2
DDS From Jan. 1, 20×1 to Dec. 31, 20×1 (Numbers in billions of ₩)

Account titles	20×2		20×1	
Sales (Ft. 3ⓐ)		430		220
Cost of goods sold		(−)230		(−)118
Gross profit		200		102
Operating expenses :		(−)85		(−)50
Salaries expense	(−)43		(−)26	
Bad debts expense (Ft. 3ⓑ)	(−)4		(−)2	
Depreciation expense (Ft. 3ⓕ)	(−)10		(−)3	
Rent expense	(−)24		(−)12	
Other operating expenses	(−)4		(−)7	
Income from operations		115		52
Other revenue		6		−
Equity income from associate (Ft. 7)	6		−	
Other expenses		(−)19		(−)14
Finance expense (Ft. 2ⓑ) :				
Interest expense	(−)19		(−)13	
Loss on disposal of tangible assets (Ft. 8)	−		(−)1	
Net income before income tax expense		102		38
Income tax expense		(−)30		(−)12
Net income		72		26
Other comprehensive income :		9		11
Item that will not be reclassified to profit or loss :				
Gain on revaluation of land (Ft. 3ⓕ, 8)	6		10	
Item that may be reclassified subsequently to profit or loss :				
Gain on valuation of FVOCI financial asset (Ft. 3ⓓ, 6)	3		1	
Total comprehensive income		81		37
Earnings per share (Ft. 12)		₩2,880		₩1,733

〈Footnotes〉

3. Important accounting policies

ⓗ Setting up provisions and contingent liabilities

Among liabilities for which the timing of payment and amount are not yet known, a liability for which 1) the possibility of its incurrence is more than 50%, and 2) its amount can be reliably estimated, is reported as a provision. Any liability that meets only one of the two above conditions is reported as a contingent liability. (The company reports provision for refunds and no contingent liability as of December 31, 20×1 and 20×2).

ⓘ Classification of financial liabilities

Financial liabilities are classified into cost financial liabilities, amortized cost financial liabilities, and fair value through profit or loss (FVPL) financial liabilities. Amortized cost means the cost after amortizing premium (discount) on issuance of financial liabilities by the effective interest method. (The company reports no FVPL financial liabilities as of December 31, 20×1 and 20×2).

9. Compositions of short-term and long-term borrowings

ⓐ Short-term borrowings

The company borrowed the following in short term to use as working capital.

(Numbers in billions of ₩)

Date of borrowing	Lender	Interest rate	Amount of borrowing	Terms
Apr.1 20×1	Seoul Bank	10% per annum	30	Matured in 1 year (Interest : after every 6 months)
Apr.1 20×2	Busan Bank	10% per annum	10	Matured in 1 year (Interest : after every 6 months)

ⓑ **Long-term borrowings**

(1) Composition of long-term borrowings : Long-term borrowings at the end of 20×2 and 20×1 are shown below :

(Numbers in billions of ₩)

Date of borrowing	Lender	Interest rate	Remaining balance		Terms
			At end of 20×2	At end of 20×1	
Mar. 1, 20×1	Daehan Capital	12% per annum	72	90	5 years installments (Interest : after every 6 months)
May 1, 20×2.	IBK	12% per annum	40	-	4 years installments (Interest : after every year)
Total			112	90	

(2) Retirement schedule : The long-term borrowing retirement schedule for each year is as below.

(Numbers in billions of ₩)

Year	Retirement amount
20×2	18
20×3	28
20×4	28
20×5	28
20×6	28

(3) Current portion of long-term borrowings : The company reclassified ₩28 billion and ₩18 billion of long-term borrowings into the current portion of long-term borrowings at the end of 20×2 and 20×1, respectively per the above retirement schedule.

(Numbers in billions of ₩)

Classification	Account titles	At end of 20×2	At end of 20×1
Current liability	Current portion of long-term borrowings	28	18
Non-current liability	Long-term borrowings	84	72
Total		112	90

10. Bonds payable

Bonds payable at the end of 20×2 and 20×1 are as follow.

(Numbers in billions of ₩)

Type	Issuance date	Maturity date	Face interest rate	Face value	Issuance price
Debenture bonds	July 1, 20×1	June 30, 20×6	6% per annum*	50	39

* Interest is paid after every 6 months. Effective interest rate is 12% per annum.

11. Provision for refunds

The following reconciliation schedule shows changes in provision for refunds.

Reconciliation of provision for refunds

(Numbers in billions of ₩)

Description		Provision for refunds
20×1	Beginning balance	–
	Actual refunds made	(–)1
	Estimated refunds	3*
	Ending balance	2
20×2	Actual refunds made	(–)2
	Estimated refunds	3*
	Ending balance	3

* Merchandise returned for a refund is scraped and the estimated amount of refunds is deducted from sales.

Explanation of case financial statements

■ Note: Numbers in superscripts are main text page numbers where the corresponding subjects are explained.

Accounts related to this chapter are short-term borrowings, the current portion of long-term borrowings,[415] and long-term borrowings (which are classified as cost financial liabilities[412] in the statement of financial position), bonds payable (which are classified as amortized cost financial liabilities[412]) and the provision for refunds[444] (which is reported as a provision) and interest expense in the comprehensive income statement. To avoid duplicate explanation, we explain mainly the case of 20×2 and omit explanation of 20×1. Daehan Department Store reports short-term borrowings of ₩30 billion and the current portion of long-term borrowings of ₩28 billion, as well as a provision for refunds of ₩3 billion as its current liabilities in the statement of financial position. It also reports long-term borrowings of ₩64 billion and bonds payable of ₩42 billion as long-term liabilities. On the other hand, the interest expense of ₩19 billion for short-term and long-term borrowings and bonds payable is reported as a financing expense in the comprehensive income statement.

In the footnotes, the amount and terms of borrowing and the repayment schedule are disclosed. Footnote 9 shows that short-term borrowings of ₩10 billion is made in 20×2 for 1 year, and the interest rate is 10% per annum. By examining Footnote 9, we find that long-term borrowings are ₩112 billion at the end of 20×2, of which ₩72 billion should be paid in installments of ₩18 billion every year for 4 years, and the interest rate is 12% per annum. Of this, ₩40 billion should be paid in installments of ₩10 billion every year for 4 years, and the interest rate is 12% per annum. The footnote also reveals that long-term borrowing of ₩28 billion, with a repayment date that falls within one year, is reclassified[414] as the current portion of long-term borrowing.

Footnote 3 ⓘ shows that amortized cost of amortized cost financial liabilities is the cost after amortizing discount (premium) on issuance of financial liabilities by the effective interest method[425]. By examining Footnote 10, we can find that the bonds payable of ₩42 billion, reported in the statement of financial position, were the amortized cost of bonds (amortization of discount on bonds payable of $ 1 billion and $ 2 billion in 20×1 and 20×2, respectively) with face value of ₩50 billion which was issued at a discount[420] at ₩39 billion on July 1, 20×1. The interest on these bonds is paid after every 6 months at the face interest rate of 6% per annum. (Effective interest rate is 12% per annum.) These bonds maturity date is June 30, 20×6.

Footnote 3 ⓘ shows that provisions were reported when the possibility of occurrence was more than 50% and the amount could be measured reliably.[443] Per Footnote 11, a provision of ₩3 billion, at the end of 20×2, is for refunds needed to cover possible sales returns.[444]

Financial liabilities and non-financial liabilities

Although liabilities are classified as current or non-current based on their maturity dates, liabilities can be also classified by financial or non-financial liabilities. Financial liabilities (금융부채) are created by contracts and should be paid off by financing assets such as cash, etc. For example, borrowings and bonds payable are financial liabilities because they occur by contracts between lenders and borrowers and should be paid off in cash on the maturity date.

Per IFRS[1], financial liabilities excluding amounts shown under trade payables and provisions are classified into amortized cost financial liabilities and fair value through profit or loss (FVPL) financial liabilities. Amortized cost refers to the cost after amortizing premium (discount) on issuance of financial liabilities by the effective interest method. (Refer to Section 3, 'Bonds payable,' in this chapter.) Amortized cost is the cost when there is no premium (discount). (This book has separated cost financial liabilities from amortized cost financial liabilities for educational purposes.) In general, borrowings of a company are cost financial liabilities and bonds payables are amortized cost financial liabilities.

FVPL financial liabilities include financial liabilities held for trading and designated FVPL financial liabilities. Held-for-trading financial liabilities are financial liabilities that are purchased and sold frequently for short-term profit-taking. For example, if a company make a short-sale of stock listed on the stock market (selling stock that the company dose not have), the stock is classified as held-for-trading financial liability. The company may designate amortized cost financial liabilities as FVPL financial liabilities in order to solve accounting mismatch (refer to 'FVPL financial assets' in the Appendix of this book) or to suit the purposes of management.

Information concerning the financial liabilities is very important for creditors, in evaluating liquidity risk (the possibility of being unable to pay interest and liabilities) of the subject company. Therefore, IFRS[2] requires financial liabilities to be presented as separate items in the statement of financial position, and the financial expense to be presented as a separate item in the comprehensive income statement. It also requires the disclosure of a maturity analysis of financial liabilities, and how the company manges the liquidity risk.

Non-financial liabilities (비금융부채), on the other hand, include liabilities created by contract but that are not to be paid off in cash, as well as liabilities that are to be paid off in cash but are not created by contract. For example, advances from customers and unearned revenues are non-financial liabilities because they are incurred by contracts but should be paid off by non-financial assets like goods and service. Income tax payable is also considered a non-financial liability because its payment is required by law, rather than by a contract, although it is to be paid off in cash. The provision, which is one kind of non-financial liability, is reviewed in Section 4.

Borrowings

We already reviewed the accounting method for the borrowings, the year-end adjusting entries for accrued interest and prepaid interest, the payment of interest, and the repayment of the borrowings in 〈Illustration 4-5〉 'Interest payable' and 〈Illustration 4-6〉 'Prepaid interest' in Chapter 4. Here we review the reclassification of long-term borrowings, a subject not covered in Chapter 4.

2.1 Reclassification of long-term borrowings

Long-term borrowing is to be paid off at any day before the date one year from the statement of financial position date, then long-term borrowing should be reclassified into the current liability. After that, if the principal is paid off as it matures, the long-borrowing, that was classified as a current liability, should be taken off from the accounting books.

Let's review accounting methods concerning reclassification of the long-term borrowing with 〈Illustration 9-1〉, below.

〈Illustration 9-1〉 Reclassification of long-term borrowing

On January 1, 20×1 Daehan Trading Inc. obtained a loan of ₩50 billion from a bank with an annual interest rate of 12% and terms requiring repayment of entire amount of the loan on December 31, 20×3. Interest is to be paid at the end of every year and Daehan Trading Inc.'s fiscal year ends at December 31. It is assumed that the borrowing and interest payments are recorded already. (Numbers in journal entries are in billions of ₩).

① Reclassification of long-term borrowing

As of December 31, 20×2, the maturity date of the loan falls within a year. Therefore, in the statement of financial position as of December 31, 20×2, this loan should be reported as a current portion of long-term borrowing, which is one kind of current liability. Journal entry for reclassification is as follows.

(Dr.) Long-term borrowings	50	(Cr.) Current portion of long-term borrowings	50

Because the reclassification of long-term borrowing is a change in the classification of a non-current liability which comes due within one year into a current liability, the total amount of liability is unchanged (the only change is that non-current liability is reduced and current liability is increased by the same amount).

② Repayment of long-term borrowing

If long-term borrowing, which was reclassified as the current portion of long-term borrowing, was paid off in cash on December 31, 20×3, then the following journal entry should be prepared.

(Dr.) Current portion of long-term borrowings	50	(Cr.) Cash	56

2.2 Long-term borrowings and cash flows

Let's review relationship between long-term borrowings and cash flows with 〈Illustration 9-2〉, below.

〈Illustration 9-2〉 Long-term borrowings and cash flows

The following 〈Table 9-1〉 is a partial statement of financial position of DH Trading as of December 31, 20×1 and December 31, 20×2.

〈Table 9-1〉 Partial statement of financial position

DH Trading (Numbers in billions of ₩)

Account titles	Amount		
	Dec. 31, 20×2	Dec. 31, 20×1	Increase or (decrease)
Current portion of long-term borrowings	50	15	35
Long-term borrowings	180	140	40

Based on the information given, we know that the company did the following during 20×2.

1) Reclassified ₩50 billion of long-term borrowings into the current portion of long term borrowings.
2) Paid off current portion of long-term borrowings of ₩15 billion.

(1) Amount of long-term borrowing in 20×2

The amount of long-term borrowing in 20×2 can be computed by T accounts analysis as shown in 〈Diagram 9-1〉 below.

〈Diagram 9-1〉 T account analysis

Current portion of long-term borrowings

(Numbers in billions of ₩)

		Beg. balance 15 (Cr.)
Retirement 15		–
	Reclassification 50	End. balance 50 (Cr.)

Long-term borrowings

(Numbers in billions of ₩)

				Beg. balance	140 (Cr.)
		Borrowing	(X)		230 (Cr.)
Reclassification	50			End. balance	180 (Cr.)

If the amount of long-term borrowing is X,

$140 + X - 50 = 180$

$X = 90$

(2) Presentation in statement of cash flows

The proceeds from long-term borrowings of ₩90 billion and the payment of current portion of long-term borrowings of ₩15 billion are reported as cash flows from financing activities in the statement of cash flows as shown in 〈Table 9-2〉 below.

〈Table 9-2〉 Statement of cash flows

From Jan. 1, 20×2 and Dec. 31, 20×2

DH Trading (Numbers in billions of ₩)

Description	Amount
Cash flows from financing activities :	
Proceeds from long-term borrowings	90
Retirement of current portion of long-term borrowings	(-)15

Bonds payable

3.1 Nature of bonds payable

A bond is a document issued by a company as a debt certificate to numerous people in the general public, from whom the company borrows money for a long period of time. On the face of a bond, the face value, interest rate, interest payment dates, and maturity date are shown. Face value is the principal amount of the loan that is to be paid off on the maturity date. Interest rate is the annual interest rate at which the company has to pay. The interest payment dates are the dates on which the company has to pay. The maturity date is the date on which the loan is matured. On that date, the company has to pay off the principal amount (that is, the face value).

There is an advantage, in using bonds, of being able to borrow money from the general public. Therefore, a lot of companies issue bonds to generate large amounts of funds, which are needed for a long period of time to invest in facilities, etc. Meanwhile, from the viewpoint of the people providing the funds, bonds are a financial instrument that offers a fixed interest income.

Bonds and stock are similar to each other, in that they provide a company with funds from the general public that can be used with stability for a long period of time. But there are differences between the two, as below :

First, funds generated from stockholders by issuing stock are owners' capital and do not have to be paid back later. Money borrowed by issuing bonds, on the other hand, is called 'capital from people other than owners' and must be paid back on the maturity date.

Second, dividends can be paid to stockholders as a return to their investment, though neither dividend payment nor the amount of dividend is pre-determined. For bondholders, on the other hand, a fixed amount of interest computed by a pre-determined interest rate must be paid.

Third, although stockholders and bondholders both provide funds to the company, stockholders are part-owners of the company and can participate in the company's management by casting votes in the stockholders' meeting. Bondholders, however, do not have voting rights so they can't participate in the management of the company.

Fourth, the interest paid to bondholders is an expense, for corporate income tax purposes, and thus provides tax savings. Dividends paid to stockholders, in contrast, are considered a distribution of income so they are not tax deductible.

Fifth, in the case of dividends, taxes are paid twice : once at a corporate level (corporate income tax), and once at an individual level (tax on dividend income).

The following 〈Table 9-3〉 is a summary of the differences between bonds and stock.

〈Table 9-3〉 Differences between bonds and stock

	Bonds	Stock
Obligation to repay principal	Yes	No
Return on fund invested	Interest (fixed)	Dividends (not pre-determined)
Participation in management	No	Yes
Tax savings	Yes	No
Double taxation	No	Yes
Classification	Liabilities (capital from other people)	Equity (owner's capital)

3.2 Issuance of bonds and determination of bond issuance price

3.2.1 Issuance of bonds

To generate funds through bonds, the company has to issue bonds to the ones lending money. Bond issuance price is the amount of money received by issuing the bond. It is determined by the interest rate stated on the face of bond and the market interest rate at the time of issuance. The face interest rate is the rate by which the issuing company computes the interest payment in cash. This is also called the 'surface interest rate' or 'stated interest rate' because it is stated on the surface of the bond. The cash amount of the interest payment is computed by multiplying the face value by the face interest rate. The market interest rate is a rate on which a company burdens in financial market. It is also called 'effective interest rate.' From the viewpoint of bondholders, because the market interest rate is the rate of interest income that is earned by investing in bonds, it is called the 'yield rate.'

① Issuance at face value

If the face interest rate on the bond is the same as the market interest rate, bonds are issued at face value, then we call this an 'issuance at face value'. If the face interest rate differs from the market interest rate, then the bond is issued at a value different from face value.

② Issuance at a discount

First, let's review a case in which the face interest rate is lower than the market interest rate. In this case, because investors can receive higher interest by investing in other financial instruments instead of in this bond, investors would not buy this bond. Therefore, the company has to issue bonds at a price lower than face value to attract investors. This is called 'issuance at a discount,' and the difference between face value and issuance price is noted as a 'discount on bonds payable'.

③ Issuance at a premium

On other hand, if the face interest rate is higher than the market interest rate, investors will prefer this bond because it is more beneficial to buy this bond than other financial instruments. In this case, investors may be willing to buy the bond at above face value, and the company can issue the bond at a price higher than face value. Issuing a bond at a price higher than face value, like this, is called 'issuance at a premium,' and the difference between face value and issuance price is called 'premium on bonds payable.'

The above can be summarized as shown in 〈Table 9-4〉 below.

〈Table 9-4〉 Bond issuance price and interest rate

①	Issuance at face value	Face interest rate	=	Market interest rate	⇒	Issuance price	=	Face value
②	Issuance at a discount	Face interest rate	<	Market interest rate	⇒	Issuance price	<	Face value
③	Issuance at a premium	Face interest rate	>	Market interest rate	⇒	Issuance price	>	Face value

3.2.2 Determination of bond issuance price

As reviewed above, the reason bonds are issued at a discount or at a premium is that the face interest rate is different from the market interest rate. If the face rate is lower than the market rate, the bond is issued at a discount. In the opposite case, if the face rate is higher than the market rate, the bond is issued at a premium. If that is the case, how exactly is the bond issuance price determined? Whether bonds are issued at face value, at a discount, or at a premium, in all cases the issuing company must bear financing expenses equal to the market interest rate. (It is because the financial market is efficient.) Hence, issuance price is the price by which the company bears the market interest rate. It is the present value that is computed by discounting all future cash flows associated with the bond payable with the market interest rate (the effective interest rate) at the time of issuance. (Refer to this chapter's appendix, for an explanation of the concept of present value).

Let's examine how the bond-issuing price is determined with the following 〈Illustration 9-3〉.

〈Illustration 9-3〉 Determination of bond issuance price

On January 1, 20×1 Daehan Trading Inc. issued bonds as shown in 〈Table 9-5〉 below.

〈Table 9-5〉 Bonds issued

Face value	₩100 billion
Face interest rate	10% per year
Interest payment date	December 31 every year
Maturity date	December 31, 20×3
Fiscal year ends	December 31

① Computing bond issuance price when market interest rate is 10%—issuance at face value

As can be seen in ⟨Diagram 9-2⟩ below, future cash flows of Daehan Trading Inc. from bond issuance include the interest payments of ₩10 billion at the end of every year (20×1, 20×2, and 20×3), and the face value of the bond of ₩100 billion, which is to be paid when the bond reaches its maturity date at the end of 20×3. The interest payment of ₩10 billion, shown here at the end of every year, is computed by multiplying the face interest rate by the face value.

Bond issuance price is the sum of present values, as is computed by discounting the interest payment of ₩10 billion at the end of each year and the repayment of the face value of ₩100 billion on the maturity date, with the market interest rate at the time of bond issuance.

⟨Diagram 9-2⟩ Bond issuance price

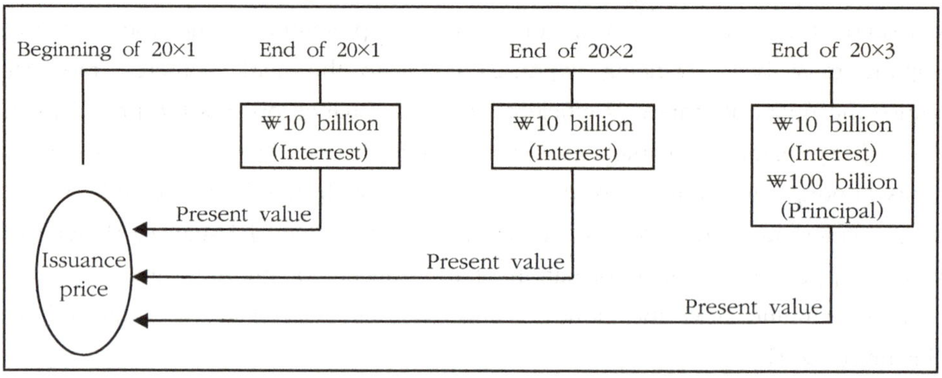

When the market interest rate is 10%, the bond issuance price is computed at ₩100 billion, as shown in ⟨Table 9-6⟩ below, which is a sum of ₩75.1 billion of present value of face value and ₩24.9 billion of present value of interest paid every year. In this case, because face interest rate and market interest rate are the same at 10%, the bond issuance price is the same as the face value. We call this an issuance at face value.

〈Table 9-6〉 Computation of bond issuance price—issuance at face value

① Present value of face value paid back on maturity date :		
100 billion × 0.7513 (10%, present value factor of 3 year)	≒	₩75.1 billion
② Present value of interest payment every year :		
10 billion × 2.4868 (10%, present value factor of 3 year annuity)	≒	₩24.9 billion
③ Bond issuance price :		
① 75.1 billion + ② 24.9 billion	=	₩100 billion

② Computing bond issuance price when market interest rate is 12%—issuance at a discount

Future cash flows associated with bond are the same, if face value and face interest rate are the same. Therefore, future cash flows, when market interest rate is 12%, are the same as those we had when the market interest rate was 10%, as reviewed above. When face interest rate is 10% and market interest rate is 12%, the bond issuance price is computed as shown in 〈Table 9-7〉 below.

〈Table 9-7〉 Computation of bond issuance price—issuance at discount

① Present value of face value paid back on maturity date :		
100 billion × 0.7118 (12%, 10%, present value factor of 3 year)	≒	₩71.2 billion
② Present value of interest payment every year :		
10 billion × 2.4018 (12%, present value factor of 3 year annuity)	≒	₩24 billion
③ Bond issuance price :		
① 71.2 billion + ② 24 billion	=	₩95.2 billion
④ Discount of band payable :		
Face value(100 billion) − ③ Issuance price (95.2 billion)	=	₩4.8 billion

If the bond is issued at a price of ₩95.2 billion, which is lower than the face value of ₩100 billion, as in the above case, it is called an issuance at a discount. The difference between the face value and issuance price of ₩4.8 billion is called a discount on bonds payable.

⟨Box 9-1⟩ A method of computing bond issuance price (a short cut approach) —issuance at a discount

(Introduced by L. Spurrell in *Issues in Accounting Education* 5 (1), 1990.)

In ⟨Illustration 9-3⟩ when market interest rate is 12%, the discount on bonds payable does not occur if the interest of ₩12 billion, based on the market interest rate of 12%, is paid every year. It occurs because only interest of ₩10 billion, based on face interest rate of 10%, is paid every year. Therefore, the discount on bonds payable is a present value of ₩2 billion (the difference between these two amounts) every year, and is computed to be ₩4.8 billion, as shown below. The bond issuance price can be computed by subtracting this discount on bonds payable from the face value of the bond as shown in ⟨Table 9-8⟩ below.

⟨Table 9-8⟩ Computation of bond issuance price (a short cut approach)—issuance at a discount

① Interest based on market interest rate of 12% to issue at face value :		
100 billion × 12%	=	₩12 billion
② Interest paid in cash based on face interest rate of 10% :		
100 billion × 10%	=	₩10 billion
③ Difference between ① and ② :		
12 billion − 10 billion	=	₩2 billion
④ Discount on bond payable = Present value of ③ every year :		
2 billion × 2.4018 (12%, present value factor of 3 year annuity)	≒	₩4.8 billion
⑤ Bond issuance price :		
Face value(100 billion) − ④ Discount on bond payable(4.8 billion)	=	₩95.2 billion

3.3 Amortization of discount on bonds payable

If a bond is issued at a discount, the difference between face value and issuance price is the discount on bonds payable, which is a compensation paid to bondholders in addition to the cash interest payments when the bond matures. Therefore, the total interest expense for the bond period, when a bond is issued at a discount, is the sum of cash interest payments and discount on bonds payable.

Here, let us take an example of 〈Illustration 9-3〉, in which Daehan Trading Inc. issued a bond at a discount. The market interest rate, which makes the issuance price possible, is computed to be 12%. In this illustration, the total interest expense for 3 years is ₩34.8 billion, which is a total addition of ₩30 billion (representing the sum of each year's cash interest payments) and ₩4.8 billion, which is a discount on bonds payable as shown in 〈Table 9-9〉 below.

〈Table 9-9〉 Total interest expense for 3 years when a bond is issued at a discount

① Cash interest payments : 100 billion × 10% × 3 times	=	₩30 billion
② Discount on bonds payable : 100 billion − 95.2 billion	=	₩4.8 billion
Total interest expense (① + ②)		₩34.8 billion

A discount on bonds payable is an additional interest expense for the bond period, as reviewed above. Hence, it should be recorded as an interest expense by a proper allocation method for every year. This process is called 'amortization of discount on bonds payable.' There are two amortization methods : the effective interest method and the straight-line method. We review the effective interest method here, in the main text, and we review the straight-line method in 〈Box 9-2〉.

3.3.1 Effective interest method

The effective interest method is a method for computing interest expense by multiplying effective interest rate (market interest rate) with the book value of the bonds at the beginning of the year. The amount of amortization of the discount on bonds payable is computed by subtracting the cash interest payment from the interest expense.

The interest expense for 20×1, the amortization amount of discount on bonds payable, and the book value at the end of 20×1 for 〈Illustration 9-3〉 can be computed using the effective interest method, as shown in 〈Table 9-10〉 below.

⟨Table 9-10⟩ Amortization of discount on bonds payable—effective interest method

① Interest expense for 20×1 :

Book value of bonds at beginning of 20×1 × Effective interest rate

= 95.2 billion × 12% ≒ ₩11.4 billion

② Amortization of discount on bonds payable for 20×1 :

① Interest expense for 20×1 − Cash interest payment on December 31, 20×1

= 11.4 billion − 10 billion = ₩1.4 billion

③ Book value of bonds at end of 20×1 :

Book value of bonds at beginning of 20×1 + ② Amortization of discount on bonds payable

= 95.2 billion + 1.4 billion = ₩96.6 billion

Interest expense for 20×1 is ₩11.4 billion, which is an outcome of the multiplication of the book value of bonds at the beginning of 20×1 with the effective interest rate of 12%. Interest paid in cash in 20×1 is ₩10 billion, which is computed by multiplying the face value of ₩100 billion with the face interest rate of 10%. Amortization of the discount on bonds payable for 20×1 is ₩1.4 billion, which is the interest expense of ₩11.4 billion less the cash interest payment of ₩10 billion. This amortization is the interest expense not paid in cash, so it is an additional liability. Therefore, the book value of bonds payable at the end of 20×1 becomes (amortized cost : ₩96.6 billion), which is the amount obtained by adding the amortization of discount on bonds payable (₩1.4 billion) to the book value of bonds payable at the beginning of 20×1 (cost : ₩95.2 billion).

The following ⟨Table 9-11⟩ is a schedule computing the interest expense and the amortization of discount on bonds payable for every year and the book value of bonds payable at the end of each year, by applying the above computing procedures for 20×2 and 20×3.

⟨Table 9-11⟩ Bond discount amortization schedule—effective interest method

(Numbers in billions of ₩)

Date	Interest expense	Interest payment	Amortization of discount on bonds payable	Book value of bonds payable (amortized cost)
January 1, 20×1				95.2
December 31, 20×1	11.4	10	1.4	96.6
December 31, 20×2	11.6	10	1.6	98.2
December 31, 20×3	11.8	10	1.8	100
Total	34.8	30	4.8	

As shown in the above amortization schedule, the book value of bonds payable increases by the amortization of discount on bonds payable every year. Eventually, it becomes the face value of ₩100 billion on the maturity date of December 31, 20×3.

3.3.2 Effective interest method vs. Straight-line method

Under the effective interest method, the interest expense is computed by multiplying the effective interest rate with the beginning book value of bonds payable. Thus, interest expense increases (decreases when issued at a premium) every year because the book value of bonds payable increases (decreases when issued at a premium) every year. The effective interest method—reporting interest expense proportional to the amounts of liability, which are the continuously changing book value of bonds payable—is more rational than the straight-line method (refer to ⟨Box 9-2⟩ below), which reports the same amount of interest expense regardless of the changing book value of the bonds payable. (A rational saying that if book value of liability increases, more interest expense should be reported.) IFRS[3] allows only the effective interest method.

⟨Box 9-2⟩ Straight-line method

Under the straight-line method, discounts on bonds payable are amortized by the same amount every year during the bond period. Amortization of the discount on bonds payable every year by the straight-line method is computed as below, for ⟨Illustration 9-3⟩.

$$\text{Every year amortization of discount on bonds payable} = \frac{\text{Discount on bonds payable}}{\text{Bonds period}} = \frac{4.8 \text{ billion}}{3 \text{ years}} = ₩\ 1.6\text{billion}$$

Under the straight-line method, the interest expense for every year and the book value of bonds payable at the end of every year are as shown in ⟨Table 9-12⟩ below.

⟨Table 9-12⟩ Bond discount amortization schedule—straight-line method

(Numbers in billions of ₩)

Date	Interest payment	Amortization of discount on bonds payable	Interest expense	Book value of bonds payable (amortized cost)
Jan. 1, 20×1				95.2
Dec. 31, 20×1	10	1.6	11.6	96.8
Dec. 31, 20×2	10	1.6	11.6	98.4
Dec. 31, 20×3	10	1.6	11.6	100
Total	30	4.8	34.8	

As shown in the above amortization schedule, every year's interest expense is ₩11.6 billion. This is an addition of the cash interest payment of ₩10 billion and the ₩1.6 billion amortization discount on bonds payable.

Because the straight-line method requires computation of amortization one time for the whole bond period, it has an advantage of simplicity of using over the effective method requiring a separate computation of amortization every year. But as can be seen in amortization schedule above, the straight-line method has a limitation of reporting interest expense same every year even though book value of bonds payable is changing. Therefore, US GAAP allows companies to use the straight-line method only when the differences between outcomes of those two methods are not materially significant.

3.4 Accounting for bond payable

3.4.1 Reporting in statement of financial position and comprehensive income statement

Per IFRS[4], the bonds payable should be reported at the amortized cost. The amortized cost means the amount after adding (or subtracting) the discount (premium) on bonds payable to the cost of bonds payable, which is the bond issuance price. (Numbers in all entries in 3.4.1 are in billions of ₩.)

(1) Issuance of bonds

① Issuance at face value

A journal entry for a bond issued at face value in 〈Illustration 9-3〉 is as follows.

(Dr.)	Cash	100	(Cr.)	Bonds payable	100

② Issuance at a discount

A journal entry for a bond issued at a discount in 〈Illustration 9-3〉 is as follows.

(Dr.)	Cash	95.2	(Cr.)	Bonds payable	95.2

(2) Interest expense and amortization of discount on bonds payable

① Issuance at face value

On the interest payment date, after the issuance of bonds, the interest computed by multiplying face interest rate with face value must be paid in cash. On each of the interest payment dates of December 31, 20×1, December 31, 20×2, and December 31, 20×3, the following journal entry should be prepared.

(Dr.)	Interest expense	10*	(Cr.)	Cash	10

* 100 billion × 10% = ₩10 billion

If bonds are issued at face value, because there is no amortization of discount or premium on bonds payable, the interest paid is the only interest expense. For the same reason, the amortized cost is just 'cost.' Therefore, the bonds payable reported in the statement of financial position at the end of 20×1 are simply the face value, that is the cost of the bonds as shown in 〈Table 9-13〉 below.

⟨Table 9-13⟩ Partial statement of financial position–issuance at face value

Daehan Trading Inc. As of December 31, 20×1 (Numbers in billions of ₩)

Account titles	Amount
Non-current liabilities	
Bonds payable	100

② **Issuance at a discount**

At the end of 20×1, the following journal entry of recording the amortization of discount on bonds payable should be prepared in addition to the journal entity to record interest payment.

(Dr.) Interest expense (20×1)	1.4	(Cr.) Bonds payable	1.4

As results of these journal entries, the interest expense of ₩11.4 billion is reported in the comprehensive income statement and the book value of bonds payable is increased by ₩1.4 billion. So bonds payable are reported at the amortized cost of ₩96.6 billion in the statement of financial position, as of December 31, 20×1, as shown in ⟨Table 9-14⟩ below.

⟨Table 9-14⟩ Partial statement of financial position–issuance at a discount

Daehan Trading Inc. As of December 31, 20×1 (Numbers in billions of ₩)

Account titles	Amount
Non-current liabilities	
Bonds payable	96.6

At the end of 20×2, the following journal entry should be prepared in addition to the journal entry to record interest payment.

(Dr.) Interest expense (20×2)	1.6	(Cr.) Bonds payable	1.6

(3) Reclassification of bonds payable

If the maturity date of the bonds falls within one year from the statement of financial position date, the bonds payable should be reclassified as a current portion of long-term borrowing.

① **Issuance at face value**

When bonds are issued at face value in ⟨Illustration 9-3⟩, the following journal entry should be prepared.

(Dr.)	Bonds payable	100	(Cr.)	Current portion of long-term borrowings	100

② **Issuance at a discount**

When bonds are issued at a discount in ⟨Illustration 9-3⟩, the book value of the bond payable on December 31, 20×2 is ₩98.2 billion. Therefore, the following journal entry should be prepared.

(Dr.)	Bonds payable	98.2	(Cr.)	Current portion of long-term borrowings	98.2

(4) Retirement of bonds

As bonds mature, the issuing company pays the face value of the bonds in cash to bondholders and retires the bonds.

① **When issued at face value**

In ⟨Illustration 9-3⟩ when bonds are issued at face value, the following journal entry should be prepared if the bonds are paid off on December 31, 20×3.

(Dr.)	Current portion of long-term borrowings	100	(Cr.)	Cash	100

② **When issued at a discount**

In ⟨Illustration 9-3⟩ when bonds are issued at a discount, the book value of bonds payable, reclassified as the current portion of long-term borrowing, is the amount before amortization of the discount on bonds payable for 20×3. Therefore, the following journal entry should be prepared to amortize the discount on bonds payable for 20×3.

(Dr.)	Interest expense (20×3)	1.8	(Cr.)	Current portion of long-term borrowings	1.8

By this journal entry, the book value of the current portion of long-term borrowing finally becomes the face value of the bonds—that is, the amount to be retired. The journal entry for bonds retirement is the same as the one prepared when bonds were issued at face value.

The following 〈Table 9-15〉 shows a comparison of the journal entries to be prepared when bonds were issued at face value and those to be prepared when bonds were issued at a discount, in 〈Illustration 9-3〉.

〈Table 9-15〉 Journal entries when bonds were issued at face value and at a discount

Date	① Issuance at face value		② Issuance at a discount	
Jan. 31, 20×1	Issuance of bonds			
	Dr.) Cash 100	Cr.) Bonds payable 100	Dr.) Cash 95.2	Cr.) Bonds payable 95.2
Dec. 31, 20×1	Interest expense and amortization of discount on bonds payable for 20×1			
	Dr.) Interest expense (20×1) 10	Cr.) Cash 10	Same as left when issued at face value.	
			Dr.) Interest expense (20×1) 1.4	Cr.) Bonds payable 1.4
Dec. 31, 20×2	Interest expense and amortization of discount on bonds payable for 20×2			
	Dr.) Interest expense (20×2) 10	Cr.) Cash 10	Same as left when issued at face value.	
			Dr.) Interest expense (20×2) 1.6	Cr.) Bonds payable 1.6
Dec. 31, 20×2	Reclassification of bonds payable			
	Dr.) Bonds payable 100	Cr.) Current portion of long-term borrowings 100	Dr.) Bonds payable 98.2	Cr.) Current portion of long-term borrowings 98.2
Dec. 31, 20×3	Interest expense and amortization of discount on bonds payable for 20×3			
	Dr.) Interest expense (20×3) 10	Cr.) Cash 10	Same as left when issued at face value.	
			Dr.) Interest expense (20×3) 1.8	Cr.) Current portion of long-term borrowings 1.8
Dec. 31, 20×3	Retirement of bonds			
	Dr.) Current portion of long-term borrowings 100	Cr.) Cash 100	Same as left when issued at face value.	

3.4.2 Reporting in statement of cash flows

Issuance of bonds, payment of interest, and retirement of bonds are all financing activities. Interest expense is reported as an 'other expense' in the comprehensive income statement, so it affects net income but does not affect net cash flows from operating activities. Here we compare and examine cash flows from operating activities and financing activities, when bonds are issued at face value in ⟨Illustration 9-3-1⟩ and at a discount in ⟨Illustration 9-3-2⟩.

⟨Illustration 9-3-1⟩ Bonds payable and cash flows – issuance at face value

Everything is the same as in ⟨Illustration 9-3⟩ and Daehan Trading Inc. issues bonds at face value. It is assumed that Daehan Trading Inc.'s sales and operating expenses for 20×1, 20×2, and 20×3 are the same as shown in ⟨Table 9-16⟩ below and all of them are made in cash.

⟨Table 9-16⟩ Income statement–issuance at face value

Daehan Trading Inc. (Numbers in billions of ₩)

Account titles	Amount		
	20×1	20×2	20×3
Sales	230	230	230
Operating expenses	(−)180	(−)180	(−)180
Income from operations	50	50	50
Interest expense	(−)10	(−)10	(−)10
Net income	40	40	40

〈Table 9-17〉 Operating cash flows and financing cash flows—issuance at face value

Daehan Trading Inc. (Numbers in billions of ₩)

Description	Amount		
	20×1	20×2	20×3
Cash flows from operating activities :			
Operating cash inflows	230	230	230
Operating cash outflows	(−)180	(−)180	(−)180
Net cash from operating activities	**50**	**50**	**50**
Or			
Net income	**40**	**40**	**40**
Interest expense	10	10	10
Net cash from operating activities	**50**	**50**	**50**
Cash flows from financing activities :			
Issuance of bonds	100		
Retirement of bonds			(−)100
Individually reporting item :			
Interest paid	(−)10	(−)10	(−)10
Net cash from financing activities	**90**	**(−)10**	**(−)110**

We can directly compute cash flows from operating activities by subtracting operating cash outflows from operating cash inflows. Alternatively, we can indirectly compute them by adding interest expense to net income, as shown in 〈Table 9-17〉 above. Net cash from operating activities for 20×1, 20×2, and 20×3 is the same at ₩50 billion. When bonds are issued at face value, as in 〈Illustration 9-3-1〉, interest expense (₩10 billion) to be added to net income to compute net cash from operating activities indirectly is the same as interest paid (₩10 billion), to be reported as a cash flow from financing activities. Interest paid is an individually reporting item. Issuance of bonds (₩100 billion) is also reported as a cash flow from financing activities in 20×1, which is same as the retirement of bonds (₩100 billion) reported as a cash flow from financing activities in 20×3. The method to compute net cash from operating activities indirectly, will be reviewed in detail in Chapter 11, 'Statement of Cash Flows.'

〈Illustration 9-3-2〉 Bonds payable and cash flows – issuance at a discount

Everything is the same as in 〈Illustration 9-3〉 and Daehan Trading Inc. issues bonds at a discount. It is assumed that Daehan Trading Inc.'s sales and operating expenses for 20×1, 20×2, and 20×3 are the same as shown in 〈Table 9-18〉 below and all of them are made in cash.

〈Table 9-18〉 Income statement–issuance at a discount

Daehan Trading Inc. (Numbers in billions of ₩)

Account titles	Amount		
	20×1	20×2	20×3
Sales	230	230	230
Operating expenses	(–)180	(–)180	(–)180
Income from operations	50	50	50
Interest expense	(–)11.4	(–)11.6	(–)11.8
Net income	38.6	38.4	38.2

〈Table 9-19〉 Operating cash flows and financing cash flows–issuance at a discount

Daehan Trading Inc. (Numbers in billions of ₩)

Description	Amount		
	20×1	20×2	20×3
Cash flows from operating activities :			
Operating cash inflows	230	230	230
Operating cash outflows	(–)180	(–)180	(–)180
Net cash from operating activities	50	50	50
Or			
Net income	38.6	38.4	38.2
Interest expense	11.4	11.6	11.8
Net cash from operating activities	50	50	50
Cash flows from financing activities :			
Issuance of bonds	95.2		
Retirement of bonds			(–)100
Individually reporting item :			
Interest paid	(–)10	(–)10	(–)10
Net cash from (or used in) financing activities	85.2	(–)10	(–)110

Because all items, excluding interest expense, are the same every year as in 〈Illustration 9-3-1〉 when issued at face value, net cash from operating activities is ₩50 billion each year. The issuance of bonds (₩95.2 billion) reported in 20×1 as a cash inflow from financing activities is the issuance price and retirement of bonds (₩100 billion) reported in 20×3 as a cash outflow from financing activities is face value.

When bonds are issued at a discount, as in 〈Illustration 9-3-2〉, the interest expense to be added to net income to compute net cash from operating activities is different from the interest paid, reported as a cash outflow from financing activities, as shown in 〈Table 9-19〉. The following 〈Table 9-20〉 shows the relationship between interest expense and interest paid.

〈Table 9-20〉 Interest expense and interest paid—issuance at a discount

(Numbers in billions of ₩)

Description	Amount		
	20×1	20×2	20×3
Interest expense	11.4	11.6	11.8
Amortization of discount on bonds payable	(-)1.4	(-)1.6	(-)1.8
Interest paid	10	10	10

〈Table 9-20〉 shows that the interest paid, reported in the statement of cash flows, can be computed by subtracting the amortization of discount on bonds payable (increase in book value of bonds payable) from the interest expense reported in the comprehensive income statement.

3.5 Issuance of bonds during the year

3.5.1 Interest expense and amortization of discount on bonds payable

Because bonds were issued at the beginning of the year in the cases we've reviewed so far, there was no need to prepare an adjusting journal entry for interest at year-end. But, if bonds are issued during the year, then we should prepare adjusting journal entries for interest expense at the end of the year.

① When issued at face value

Let's review the year-end adjusting journal entries and journal entries for interest payments, when bonds were issued at face value, with the following 〈Illustration 9-3-3〉.

〈Illustration 9-3-3〉 Issuance of bonds during the year—issuance at face value

Everything is the same as in 〈Illustration 9-3〉, but Daehan Trading Inc. issues bonds at face value on July 1, 20×1. Only the interest payment date and maturity date are different, as shown in table below.

Interest payment dates	June 30 every year
Maturity date	June 30, 20×4

In 〈Illustration 9-3-3〉, unlike in the previous cases, bonds were not issued at the beginning of the year (January 1) but instead were issued during the year (July 1), and the interest payment date is June 30 every year. Journal entries to be prepared at year-end and on the interest payment dates are as follow. (Numbers in all journal entries are in billions of ₩).

(1) Adjusting journal entry for interest expense on December 31, 20×1

Interest on bonds payable of ₩10 billion is paid in cash on June 30 each year (20×2, 20×3, and 20×4). There is no interest paid in 20×1. However, at the end of 20×1, 6 months' interest, for a period from July 1 to December 31, had been accrued as below.

Interest accrued for the period of 6 months = 100 billion × 10% × 6 months/12 months
= ₩5 billion

Therefore, we should prepare the following journal entry and record accrued interest as interest expense and as a liability of interest payable.

(Dr.)	Interest expense (20×1)	5	(Cr.)	Interest payable	5

(2) Journal entry for interest payment on June 30, 20×2

On the interest payment date of June 30, 20×2, interest of ₩10 billion is paid in cash. ₩5 billion out of ₩10 billion is a payment of the interest payable, reported as a liability at the end of 20×1. The remaining ₩ 5 billion is a payment of the interest expense for 20×2. A journal entry for this transaction is as follows.

(Dr.)	Interest payable	5	(Cr.)	Cash	10
	Interest expense (20×2)	5			

An adjusting journal entry as in (1), above, should be repeated at the end of 20×2 and at the end of 20×3. Journal entry (2) should be repeated on June 30, 20×3 and June 30, 20×4.

② When issued at a discount

Let's review the year-end adjusting journal entries when a bond is issued at a discount, with the following ⟨Illustration 9-3-4⟩.

> ⟨Illustration 9-3-4⟩ Issuance of bonds during the year—issuance at a discount
>
> Everything is the same as in ⟨Illustration 9-3-3⟩ but Daehan Trading Inc. issues bonds at ₩95.2 billion on July 1, 20×1.

If bonds are issued at a discount during the year then, first, we should compute yearly amortization of discount on bond payable from bond issuance date every year (bond year) until maturity. Then we should allocate the amount of amortization for a bond year among fiscal years based on the number of months in each fiscal year. For example, if bonds are issued on July 1, as in ⟨Illustration 9-3-4⟩, then amortization of the discount on bonds payable should be allocated by a rate of 6 to 6 between two fiscal years, as shown in the following ⟨Table 9-21⟩.

⟨Table 9-21⟩ Amortization of discount on bonds payable

(Numbers in billions of ₩)

Year	Amortization of discount on bonds payable				
	From Jan. 1 to Jun. 30		From Jul. 1 to Dec. 31		Total
20×1			1.4 × 6/12	0.7	0.7
20×2	1.4 × 6/12	0.7	1.6 × 6/12	0.8	1.5
20×3	1.6 × 6/12	0.8	1.8 × 6/12	0.9	1.7
20×4	1.8 × 6/12	0.9			0.9

If bonds are issued at a discount, then the journal entries of (1) below should be added to the ones prepared when bonds are issued at face value. The value of bonds payable [(2) below] to be reclassified at the end of 20×3 is different from that prepared when bonds are issued at face value. (Numbers in all journal entries are in billions of ₩).

(1) Additional adjusting journal entries to record amortization of discount on bonds payable

December 31, 20×1

(Dr.) Interest expense (20×1)	0.7	(Cr.) Bonds payable	0.7

December 31, 20×2

(Dr.) Interest expense (20×2)	1.5	(Cr.) Bonds payable	1.5

December 31, 20×3

(Dr.) Interest expense (20×3)	1.7	(Cr.) Bonds payable	1.7

December 31, 20×4

(Dr.) Interest expense (20×4)	0.9	(Cr.) Current portion of long-term borrowings	0.9

(2) Journal entry to reclassify bonds payable on December 31, 20×3

(Dr.) Bonds payable	99.1	(Cr.) Current portion of long-term borrowings	99.1

The following ⟨Table 9-22⟩ shows a comparison between the journal entries to be prepared when bonds were issued at face value in ⟨Illustration 9-3-3⟩ and when bonds were issued at a discount, in ⟨Illustration 9-3-4⟩.

⟨Table 9-22⟩ Journal entries when bonds were issued at face value and at a discount

<table>
<tr><th>Date</th><th colspan="2">① Issuance at face value</th><th colspan="2">② Issuance at a discount</th></tr>
<tr><td rowspan="2">Jul. 1, 20×1</td><td colspan="4">Issuance of bonds</td></tr>
<tr><td>Dr.) Cash 100</td><td>Cr.) Bonds payable 100</td><td>Dr.) Cash 95.2</td><td>Cr.) Bonds payable 95.2</td></tr>
<tr><td rowspan="3">Dec. 31, 20×1</td><td colspan="4">Interest expense and amortization of discount on bonds payable for 20×1</td></tr>
<tr><td>Dr.) Interest expense (20×1) 5</td><td>Cr.) Interest payable 5</td><td colspan="2">Same as left when issued at face value.</td></tr>
<tr><td colspan="2"></td><td>Dr.) Interest expense (20×1) 0.7</td><td>Cr.) Bonds payable 0.7</td></tr>
<tr><td rowspan="2">Jun. 30, 20×2</td><td colspan="4">Interest payment</td></tr>
<tr><td>Dr.) Interest expense (20×2) 5
Interest payable 5</td><td>Cr.) Cash 10</td><td colspan="2">Same as left when issued at face value.</td></tr>
<tr><td rowspan="3">Dec. 31, 20×2</td><td colspan="4">Interest expense and amortization of discount on bonds payable for 20×2</td></tr>
<tr><td>Dr.) Interest expense (20×2) 5</td><td>Cr.) Interest payable 5</td><td colspan="2">Same as left when issued at face value.</td></tr>
<tr><td colspan="2"></td><td>Dr.) Interest expense (20×2) 1.5</td><td>Cr.) Bonds payable 1.5</td></tr>
<tr><td rowspan="2">Jun. 30, 20×3</td><td colspan="4">Interest payment</td></tr>
<tr><td>Dr.) Interest expense (20×3) 5
Interest payable 5</td><td>Cr.) Cash 10</td><td colspan="2">Same as left when issued at face value.</td></tr>
<tr><td rowspan="3">Dec. 31, 20×3</td><td colspan="4">Interest expense and amortization of discount on bonds payable for 20×3</td></tr>
<tr><td>Dr.) Interest expense (20×3) 5</td><td>Cr.) Interest payable 5</td><td colspan="2">Same as left when issued at face value.</td></tr>
<tr><td colspan="2"></td><td>Dr.) Interest expense (20×3) 1.7</td><td>Cr.) Bonds payable 1.7</td></tr>
<tr><td rowspan="2">Dec 31. 20×3</td><td colspan="4">Reclassification of bonds payable</td></tr>
<tr><td>Dr.) Bonds payable 100</td><td>Cr.) Current portion of long-term borrowings 100</td><td>Dr.)Bonds payable 99.1</td><td>Cr.) Current portion of long-term borrowings 99.1</td></tr>
<tr><td rowspan="2">Jun. 30 20×4</td><td colspan="4">Interest payment</td></tr>
<tr><td>Dr.) Interest expense (20×4) 5
Interest payable 5</td><td>Cr.) Cash 10</td><td colspan="2">Same as left when issued at face value.</td></tr>
<tr><td rowspan="3">Jun. 30, 20×4</td><td colspan="4">Amortization of discount on bonds payable for 20×4 and retirement of bonds</td></tr>
<tr><td colspan="2"></td><td>Dr.) Interest expense (20×4) 0.9</td><td>Cr.) Current portion of long-term borrowings 0.9</td></tr>
<tr><td>Dr.) Bonds payable 100</td><td>Cr.) Current portion of long-term borrowings 100</td><td colspan="2">Same as left when issued at face value.</td></tr>
</table>

3.5.2 Interest expense and interest paid

① When issued at face value

When bonds were issued at face value, the interest expense reported in the comprehensive income statement and interest paid reported in the statement of cash flows of Daehan Trading Inc. for 20×1, 20×2, 20×3, and 20×4 are as shown in ⟨Table 9-23⟩ below.

⟨Table 9-23⟩ Interest expense and interest paid – issuance at face value

(Numbers in billions of ₩)

Description	Amount			
	20×1	20×2	20×3	20×4
Interest payable at year end	5	5	5	–
Interest expense	5	10	10	5
(Increase) or decrease in interest payable	(–)5	–	–	5
Interest paid	–	10	10	10

⟨Table 9-23⟩ shows that interest paid reported in the statement of cash flows can be computed by subtracting (or adding) increase (or decrease) in interest payable to interest expense reported in the comprehensive income statement, as reviewed in Chapter 5.

② When issued at a discount

When bonds were issued at a discount, interest expense reported in the comprehensive income statement and interest paid reported in the statement of cash flows of Daehan Trading Inc. for 20×1, 20×2, 20×3, and 20×4 are as shown in ⟨Table 9-24⟩ below.

〈Table 9-24〉 Interest expense and interest paid–issuance at a discount

(Numbers in billions of ₩)

Description	Amount			
	20×1	20×2	20×3	20×4
Interest payable at year end	5	5	5	–
Interest expense	5.7	11.5	11.7	5.9
(Increase) or decrease in interest payable	(–)5	–	–	5
Amortization of discount on bonds payable	(–)0.7	(–)1.5	(–)1.7	(–)0.9
Interest paid	–	10	10	10

〈Table 9-24〉 shows that interest paid reported in the statement of cash flows can be computed by subtracting (or adding) increase (or decrease) in interest payable and subtracting amortization of discount on bonds payable (increase in book value of bonds payable) from the interest expense reported in the comprehensive income statement.

Provisions

4.1 Nature of provision and contingent liabilities

Provisions (충당부채) are liabilities of uncertain timing of a payment or amount. For example, when a seller guarantees free repair of any defect found in a product they've sold, a warranty obligation occurs. In this case, although there exists a warranty obligation, the questions of when those free services will be provided and how much they will cost are uncertain at the time of sale. Per IFRS[5], if 1) the probability of providing free repair service is more than 50% and 2) the amount of free service can be estimated reliably, then we should recognize a provision (in this case, a provision for product warranties). We should also disclose a brief description of the obligation and of the increases and decreases in provisions, during the year.

Provisions can be either non-financial liabilities or financial liabilities. Although provisions for product warranties reviewed above are borne by a contract, they are called non-financial liabilities because they are redeemed by goods or services rather than by financial assets such as cash, etc.. Provisions for refunds reviewed below are financial liabilities because they are borne by a contract and redeemed by financial assets such as cash, etc.

Per IFRS[6], contingent liabilities (우발부채) are either possible obligations whose existence can be confirmed by future events, or present obligations that meet only one of two conditions set up for the recognition of provision as explained above. A good example of a contingent liability is the expected loss from a lawsuit where the probability of losing is less than 50%. Contingent liabilities should be disclosed in the footnotes.

4.2 Provision for product warranties

Let's review how to account for provision for product warranties with ⟨Illustration 9-4⟩ below.

〈Illustration 9-4〉 Provision for product warranties

Daejun Motors Inc. manufactures and sells automobiles and warranties 5 years' free repair service. In 20×1, the company sold 2 millions of Model X. Based on past experience the company estimates that 20% of sales require repair services of ₩100 thousand per unit and 5% of sales require repair services of ₩500 thousand per unit. In 20×1, the company paid ₩8 billion for warranty repair service. (All numbers in journal entries are in billions of ₩).

① Recording payment for warranty repair services

Payment made for warranty repair service of ₩8 billion in 20×1 is recorded as a redemption of provision for product warranties, which will be set up at the end of 20×1.

(Dr.)	Provision for product warranties	8	(Cr.)	Cash	8

② Setting up provision for product warranties

The estimated amount of warranty repair services to be provided for 2 millions of Model X sold in 20×1 is ₩90 billion. The company should set up a provision for product warranty for this amount at end of 20×1. This amount is the product warranty expense for the year.

(Dr.)	Product warranty expense	90*	(Cr.)	Provision for product warranties	90

* 2 million units × 20% × 100 thousand + 2 million units × 5% × 500 thousand = ₩90 billion

As a result of these two journal entries, the provision for product warranties reported in the statement of financial position, as of December 31, 20×1, is ₩82 billion. [Provision set up at end of year (₩90 billion)—warranty repair service actually provided during the year (₩8 billion)].

4.3 Provision for refunds

Companies may provide refunds for a certain period on a product sold, to promote sales. In these cases, if customers return goods with which they are unsatisfied and ask for a refund, companies must refund sales proceeds. The expected refunds in the future is a provision for refunds. In general, a provision for refunds is estimated by analyzing the refund period and the past refunding experience of the company.

〈Illustration 9-5〉 Provision of refunds

Daejun Internet Mall Inc. started its business at the beginning of 20×1. The company sells variety goods and has a sales policy by which customers can return unsatisfied merchandise for a refund within 3 months from sale. The company had sales of ₩100 billion in 20×1. Actual amount of refunds in 20×1 was ₩2 billion. Based on customers' pattern of returning merchandise, it is estimated that 3% of sales will be returned. The company scraps all returned merchandise. The acquisition cost of merchandise is 60% of the selling price. The merchandise purchases for 20×1 were ₩85 billion and ending merchandise inventory per the physical inventory taken was ₩25 billion. The company uses the periodic inventory system. (All numbers in journal entries are in billions of ₩).

① Recording refunds in cash

Actual cash refunds of ₩2 billion in 20×1 are recorded as a reduction of the provision for refunds, which will be set up at the end of 20×1.

(Dr.)	Provision for refunds	2	(Cr.)	Cash	2

② Setting up provision for refunds at the end of the year

At the end of 20×1, the estimated amount of expected refunds from sales of 20×1 is ₩3 billion. This amount should be recorded as a deduction from sales(or sales returns) and provision for refunds as shown below.

(Dr.)	Sales	3*	(Cr.)	Provision for refunds	3

* 100 billion × 3% = ₩3 billion

③ Recording cost of goods sold at the end of the year

The following adjusting journal entry should be prepared to record the cost of goods sold.

(Dr.)	Cost of goods sold	60*	(Cr.)	Purchases	85
	Merchandise	25**			

* 100 billion × 60% = ₩60 billion
** Purchases − Cost of goods sold = 85 billion − 60 billion = ₩25 billion (Verified by the physical inventory taken.)

The merchandise of ₩25 billion and the provision of refund of ₩1 billion [3 billion (provision set up at the end of the year) − 2 billion (refunds actually made in cash during the year)] are reported in the statement of financial position at the end of 20×1. The net sales of ₩97 billion [100 billion (gross sales) − 3 billion (sales returns)] and the cost of goods sold of ₩60 billion are reported in the comprehensive income statement.

〈Box 9-3〉 Provision for refunds : when a company resells returned merchandise

Everything is the same as in 〈Illustration 9-5〉. However, the company resells returned merchandise and has resold 70% of the returned merchandise in 20×1. The resale price is 80% of the regular sale price. When resale price is higher than cost (60% of the regular sale price), the returned merchandise should be recorded at the cost. Per the physical inventory taken, the ending returned merchandise inventory was ₩0.36 billion (All numbers in journal entries are in billions of ₩)

Journal entries to be prepared for ① Recording refunds in cash and ② Setting up provision for refunds at the end of the year are the same as ones prepared in 〈Illustration 9-5〉.

③ Recording cost of goods sold at the end of the year

(Dr.)	Cost of goods sold	59.04	(Cr.)	Purchases	85
	Merchandise	25*			
	Returned merchandise	0.36**			
	Merchandise expected to be returned	0.6***			

* From the physical inventory taken.
** Refunds paid × (Cost/Regular sale price) × (1 − Portion sold) = 2 billion × 60% × (1 − 70%) = ₩0.36 billion (Verified by the physical inventory taken.)
*** Provision for refunds at the end of the year × (Cost/Regular sale price) = 1 billion × 60% = ₩0.6 billion

The merchandise expected to be returned is merchandise to be returned when the provision for refunds at the end of the year is paid and should be included in the ending merchandise inventory together with the ending returned merchandise per IRFS[7]. If the returned merchandise is scrapped as in 〈Illustration 9-5〉, there is no need to report the merchandise expected to be returned because the merchandise to be returned, when the provision for refunds is paid, has no value. But if the merchandise to be returned has some value as in this case, the merchandise expected to be returned of that value should be recognized as a merchandise inventory. The merchandise of ₩25.96 billion [Merchandise (25 billion) + Returned merchandise(0.36 billion) + Merchandise expected to be returned (0.6 billion)] and the provision for refunds of ₩1 billion are reported in the statement of financial position at the end of 20×1.

The sales of returned merchandise are computed as follow.

Sale of returned merchandise : Refunds paid × (Resale price/Regular sale price) × Portion sold = 2 billion × 80% × 70% = ₩1.12 billion

The gross sales are ₩101.12 billion [Gross sales of merchandise (100 billion) + Sales of returned merchandise (1.12 billion)]. Therefore, the net sales of ₩98.12 [Gross sales (101.12 billion) - Sales returns (3 billion)] and the cost of goods sold of ₩59.04 billion are reported in the comprehensive income statement.

The resale price of returned merchandise can be lower than the cost. In that case the returned merchandise inventory and the inventory of merchandise expected to be returned should be valued at the resale price per LCNRV (lower of cost or net realizable value) reviewed in Chapter 7.

Related financial ratios

Financial ratios related with liabilities are ratios by which we evaluate the safety(financial) of a company. These include the times interest earned, the operating income to interest coverage ratio, and the borrowings to total assets ratio.

5.1 Financial ratios evaluating safety (financial)

(1) Times interest earned

'Times interest earned' is a ratio by which we evaluate a company's interest-paying capability. The more income a company earns, the more capable the company is of paying interest. Income by which a company pays interest is income before interest expense and income tax expense. Therefore, the times interest earned ratio is computed by dividing income before interest expense and income tax expense by interest expense, as shown below.

$$\text{Times interest earned} = \frac{\text{Net income} + \text{Interest expense} + \text{Income tax expense}}{\text{Interest expense}}$$

(Daehan Department Store's ratio)

$$20\times2 : \frac{72 \text{ billion} + 19 \text{ billion} + 30 \text{ billion}}{19 \text{ billion}} = 6.37 \text{ times}$$

$$20\times1 : \frac{26 \text{ billion} + 13 \text{ billion} + 12 \text{ billion}}{13 \text{ billion}} = 3.92 \text{ times}$$

We know that Daehan Department Store's interest paying capability has improved, because 6.37 times interest earned for 20×2 is a lot higher than 3.92 times for 20×1.

Generally, the time interest earned should be higher than '1' at the minimum, to pay interest expense. If this multiple is lower than '1', it means income is not high enough to pay even interest expense, so it is evaluated that a creditor's risk is quite high. It is because if income is not enough to pay even the interest expense, then there is a high possibility for creditors of having a problem with receiving interest and collecting the principal of a loan.

(2) Operating income interest coverage ratio

The operating income interest coverage ratio is an interest-paying capability evaluation index that is similar to the times interest earned ratio. Times interest earned is a multiple of income from all operating, investing, and financing activities, prior to interest expense and income tax expense on interest expense. In contrast, the operating income interest coverage ratio is a multiple of the income from a company's main operating activities on interest expense. Thus, it enables us to evaluate whether income from operations, specifically, is high enough to pay interest expense. Operating income interest coverage ratio is computed as follows.

$$\text{Operating income interest coverage ratio} = \frac{\text{Income from operations}}{\text{Interest expense}}$$

(Daehan Department Store's ratio)

$$20\times2: \frac{115\text{ billion}}{19\text{ billion}} = 6.05\text{ times*}$$

$$20\times1: \frac{52\text{ billion}}{13\text{ billion}} = 4\text{ times}$$

* Stated in times to be compatible with 'times interest earned' ratio.

Daehan Department Store's operating income interest coverage ratio for 20×2 is 6.05 times. This has increased from 4 times for 20×1, so it can be evaluated that the company's interest paying capability has improved quite a bit.

If there is no other revenue, and other expense in the comprehensive income statement is composed of only interest expense, income before interest expense and income tax expense equals operating income. In that case, the ratios for times interest earned and operating income interest coverage become the same. In the case of Daehan Department Store, since other expenses include not only interest expense but also loss on the disposal of tangible assets, the time interest earned ratio is different from the operating income interest coverage ratio.

(3) Borrowings to total assets ratio

Among liabilities, borrowings from non-owners of a company includes short-term and long-term borrowings and bonds payable. The borrowings to total assets ratio is a company's safety (financial) evaluation index, showing how much of a company's total assets is financed by borrowings. Borrowings to total assets ratio is computed as follows.

$$\textbf{Borrowings to total assets ratio} = \frac{\textbf{Borrowings}}{\textbf{Total assets}}$$

(Daehan Department Store's ratio)

$$20\times2:\ \frac{10\text{ billion} + 28\text{ billion} + 84\text{ billion} + 42\text{ billion}}{553\text{ billion}} = 29.66\%$$

$$20\times1:\ \frac{30\text{ billion} + 18\text{ billion} + 72\text{ billion} + 40\text{ billion}}{339\text{ billion}} = 47.2\%$$

Daehan Department Store's borrowings are composed of short-term borrowings, the current portion of long-term borrowings, long-term borrowings, and bonds payable. Because the borrowings to total assets ratio decreased from 47.2% in 20×1 to 29.66% in 20×2, we know that the firm's borrowings to total assets ratio was improved.

■ Note : Financial ratios reviewed in this chapter are summarized in Appendix 2 〈Table B-1〉 'Key financial ratios' at the end of this book.

⟨Appendix⟩ Present value and future value

An amount of cash right now can become a larger amount of cash in the future, this is because of interest. For example, if we make a deposit of ₩100 billion in a bank paying 10% interest, we can withdraw ₩110 billion a year from now because interest is added. We convert an amount at the present time into a value at a specific point in future time as shown above, and call that value 'future value.' On the other hand, the 'present value' is a value obtained by converting an amount to give or receive in future into value in the present time.

The following ⟨Diagram 9-3⟩ illustrates the relationship between future value and present value.

⟨Diagram 9-3⟩ Present value and future value

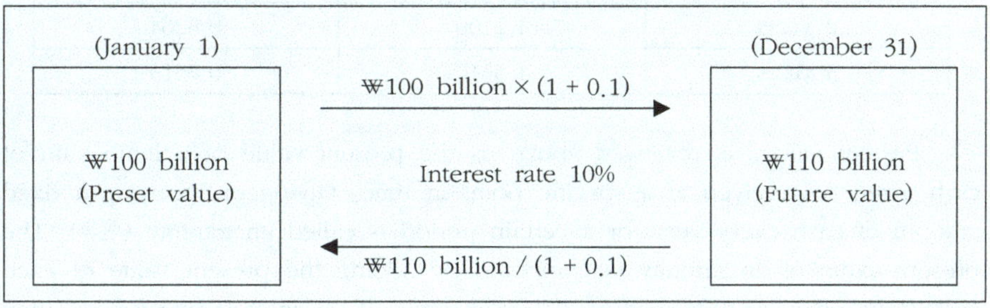

As shown in above diagram, if interest rate is 10% per year, the future value as of December 31 for ₩100 billion, as of January 1, is ₩110 billion [₩100 billion × (1 + 0.1)]. This means that ₩100 billion now has the same value of ₩110 billion 1 year from now, when the annual interest rate is 10%. On the other hand, present value as of January 1 for ₩110 billion on December 31 is ₩100 billion [₩100 billion / (1 + 0.1)]. This means that ₩110, a year from now, has the same value of ₩100 billion now if the annual interest rate is 10%.

Future value and present value are, like the face and tail of a coin. Given interest rate and time period, if the present amount is given, then future value can be computed. If the future amount is given, then the present value can likewise be computed. Designating future value (미래가치) as FV and present value (현재가치) as PV, interest rate as i, and time period as t, we can draw formulas computing future value and present value as follow.

$$FV = \text{Present amount} \times (1 + i)^t$$

$$PV = \text{Future amount} \times [1/(1 + i)^t]$$

As shown in the above formulas, the present amount is multiplied by $(1 + i)^t$ to get future value and future amount is multiplied by $[1/(1 + i)^t]$ to get present value. If the future value table and present value table are available, we can use the factors in tables without computing, $(1 + i)^t$ or $[1/(1 + i)^t]$ one by one. If interest rate and time period are given, then we can easily compute future value and present value by finding the proper factors from the tables and multiplying them by the cash amount.

For example, when the interest rate is 10% and time periods are 1 year, 2 years, and 3 years, the future value factors and present value factors of ₩1 are as shown in ⟨Table 9-25⟩ below.

⟨Table 9-25⟩ Future value factor and present value factor

Period	Future value factor	Present value factor
1 year	1.1000	0.9091
2 years	1.2100	0.8264
3 years	1.3310	0.7513

Present value, as reviewed above, is the present value of a lump sum of cash given or received at a specific point in time. Giving or receiving a fixed amount of cash every year for a certain period is called an annuity (연금). The present value of an annuity is computed by adding the present value of each cash to be given or to be received. For example, if the interest rate is 10%, then the present value of an annuity of receiving ₩100 billion at the end of every year for 3 years is computed as shown in ⟨Table 9-26⟩ below.

⟨Table 9-26⟩ Computation of present value of an annuity

① Present value of ₩100 billion 1 year after = ₩100 billion × $\frac{1}{(1 + 0.1)^1}$ =	₩90.91 billion
② Present value of ₩100 billion 2 years after = ₩100 billion × $\frac{1}{(1 + 0.1)^2}$ =	₩82.64 billion
③ Present value of ₩100 billion 3 years after = ₩100 billion × $\frac{1}{(1 + 0.1)^3}$ =	₩75.13 billion
Present value of the annuity (① + ② + ③)	₩248.68 billion

But if we use the present value factor, we can easily compute the present value of an annuity without going through the above process. If the interest rate and time period are given, then we can compute the present value of an annuity by finding the proper factor in the present value of annuity table and multiplying it only once by the amount of the annuity.

For example, if interest rate is 10% and time periods are each of 1 year, 2 years, and 3 years, then the annuity present value factors are as shown in ⟨Table 9-27⟩ below.

⟨Table 9-27⟩ Annuity present value factors

Periods	Annuity present value factors
1 year	0.9091
2 years	1.7355
3 years	2.4868

We can compute the present value of an annuity in the previous example, above, by multiplying the annuity amount of ₩100 billion with the annuity present value factor (10%, 3 years) of 2.4868.

Present value of annuity
= Amount of annuity × Annuity present value factor
= ₩100 billion × 2.4868
= ₩248.68 billion

IFRS references (http://www.kasb.or.kr)

[1] IFRS 9 *Financial Instruments*, par. 4.2.1, 4.2.2, BA.6, BA.7, Appendix A, Defined terms, FVPL financial liabilities.

[2] IAS 1 *Presentation of Financial Statements*, par. 54(m), 82(b).
IFRS 7 *Financial Instruments : Disclosures*, par. 39(a), (c).

[3] IFRS 9 *op. cit.*, par. 4.2.1, 5.3.1.

[4] IFRS 9 *op. cit.*, Appendix A, Defined terms, Amortized cost of a financial asset or financial liability.

[5] IAS 37 *Provisions, Contingent Liabilities and Contingent Assets*, par. 13(a), 14, 15, 84.

[6] *Ibid.*, par. 13(b), 27.

[7] IFRS 15 *Revenue from Contracts with Customers*, IE115C.

Key terms

Amortized cost (상각후원가) The amount after adding (or subtracting) discount (premium) on bonds payable to (from) the cost of bonds payable. (p.428)

Bond (사채) : A document issued by a company, as evidence of borrowing money from the general public for a long period of time. (p.418)

Contingent liabilities (우발부채) : Possible obligations that their existences can be confirmed by future events or present obligations that meet only one of two conditions set up for the recognition of provision. (p.443)

Current portion of long-term borrowings (유동성장기차입금) : Long-term borrowings that are reclassified from non-current liabilities to current liabilities, because their maturity dates now fall within 1 year. (p.415)

Discount on bonds payable (사채할인발행차금) : The difference between face value and issuance price when bonds were issued at a price lower than face value because the face interest rate was lower than the market interest rate. (p.420)

Effective interest method (유효이자율법) : A method by which a discount (or premium) on bonds payable is amortized by the difference between the interest expense (which is computed by multiplying the balance of bonds at the beginning of the year with the effective interest rate [the market interest rate]) and the interest payment (which is computed multiplying the face value of bonds with the face interest rate). (p.425)

Financial liabilities (금융부채) : Liabilities that occur because of a contract and that will be redeemed by financial assets such as cash, etc. (p.412)

Future value (미래가치) : Value at a specific point in the future for a certain amount of money at the present time. (p.451)

Non-financial liabilities (비금융부채) : Liabilities that are either not paid off by financial assets such as cash, etc., or are not based on contractual obligations. (p.413)

Present value (현재가치) : The value, at the present time, of an amount of money to be given or to be received at a specific point in the future. (p.451)

Provisions (충당부채) : Obligations whose amount and timing of redemption are not determined but recognized as liabilities because 1) the probability of settling down the obligations is more than 50% and 2) the amount of obligations can be estimated reliably. (p.443)

Straight-line method (정액법) : A method of amortizing discount (or premium) on bonds payable by the same amount every year, for the bonds period. (p.427)

Exercises

1. Reclassification of long-term borrowings

Jungsan Inc. borrowed ₩300 billion from a bank on May 1, 20×1. The terms are annual interest rate of 12% and a lump sum repayment on April 30, 20×3. Interest is paid on April 30 every year and Jungsan Inc.'s fiscal year ends on December 31.

《Question》

Prepare necessary journal entries needed on the following dates.

(1) May 1, 20×1
(2) December 31, 20×1
(3) April 30, 20×2
(4) December 31, 20×2
(5) April 30, 20×3

2. Current liabilities and non-current liabilities

The following are details of borrowings Hanbat Electronics Inc. had as of December 31, 20×2.

(Numbers in billions of ₩)

Classification as of borrowing dates	Amount	Borrowing dates	Due dates
Short-term borrowing	50	Jul. 1. 20×2	Jun. 30, 20×3
Short-term borrowing	30	Oct. 1, 20×2	Mar. 31, 20×3
Long-term borrowing	150	Dec. 1, 20×0	Nov. 30, 20×3
Long-term borrowing	120	May 1, 20×1	Apr. 30, 20×4
Long-term borrowing	230	Nov. 1, 20×2	Oct. 31, 20×4

《Questions》

(1) How much of borrowings should be reported as current liabilities in the statement of financial position as of December 31, 20×2.
(2) How much of borrowings should be reported as non-current liabilities in the statement of financial position as of December 31, 20×2.

3. **Determination of bond issuance price**

Daesan Inc. plans to issue bonds with face value of ₩100 billion (maturity period of 3 years, face interest rate of 10%) on January 1, 20×1.

Present value table

Interest rate	Present value of a lump sum of ₩1			Present value of annuity of ₩1		
	1 year	2 years	3 years	1 year	2 years	3 years
8%	0.9259	0.8573	0.7938	0.9259	1.7833	2.5771
10%	0.9091	0.8264	0.7513	0.9091	1.7355	2.4868
12%	0.8929	0.7972	0.7118	0.8929	1.6901	2.4018

《Question》

Compute the issuance price of the bonds when the market interest rate is following, using the present value table above.

(1) When the market interest rate is 10%
(2) When the market interest rate is 12%
(3) When the market interest rate is 8%

4. **Bonds issuance at face value**

On January 1, 20×1 Far East Trading Inc. issued bonds with face value of ₩100 billion, face interest rate of 8%, and a maturity period of 3 years. The market interest rate, as of issuance date, was the same as the face interest rate of 8%. Interest payment dates are December 31 every year, and Far East Trading Inc.'s fiscal year ends on December 31.

《Questions》

(1) What is the bond issuance price?
(2) Prepare a journal entry for bond issuance on January 1, 20×1.
(3) Prepare a journal entry for a payment of interest on December 31, 20×1.
(4) Prepare journal entries for a payment of interest and reclassification of the bonds payable on December 31, 20×2.
(5) Prepare journal entrics for a payment of interest and the retirement of bonds on December 31, 20×3.

5. **Preparation of a bond discount (or premium) amortization schedule**

On January 1, 20×1 Jusung Industries Inc. issued bonds with face value of ₩100 billion, face interest rate of 6%, and a maturity period of 3 years. The market interest rate, as of issuance date, was 8%. Interest is paid on December 31 every year, and Jusung Industries Inc.'s fiscal year ends December 31.

《Questions》

(1) Compute bond issuance price. (Use the present value table in Excercise 3.)
(2) Prepare a bond discount (or premium) amortization schedule, assuming the straight-line method is used to amortize discount (or premium) on bonds payable.
(3) Prepare a bond discount (or premium) amortization schedule, assuming the effective interest method is used to amortize discount (or premium) on bonds payable.
(4) Explain the reasons why the effective interest method is more rational than the straight-line method of amortizing discount (or premium) on bonds payable.

6. Issuance of bonds at a discount ①

On December 31, 20×1 Gusan Inc. issued bonds with face value of ₩200 billion, face interest rate of 8%, and a maturity period of 3 years at ₩190 billion. The market interest rate, as of issuance date, was 10%. Interest is paid on December 31 every year, and Gusan Inc.'s fiscal year ends on December 31. The company uses the effective interest method to amortize discount on bonds payable.

《Questions》

(1) Prepare a journal entry for issuance of bonds on January 1, 20×1.
(2) Prepare a bond discount amortization schedule.
(3) Prepare a journal entry for interest payment and amortization of discount on bonds payable on December 31, 20×1.
(4) Show where and how these bonds are reported in the statement of financial position, as of December 31, 20×1.
(5) Prepare a journal entry for interest payment and amortization of discount on bonds payable on December 31, 20×2.
(6) Prepare a journal entry to reclassify these bonds as current liabilities on December 31, 20×2.
(7) Prepare a journal entry for interest payment and amortization of discount on bonds payable on December 31, 20×3.
(8) Prepare a journal entry for the retirement of bonds on December 31, 20×3.

7. Issuance of bonds at a discount ②

On January 1, 20×1 Sangdang Electronics Inc. issued bonds with face value of ₩100 billion that matures in 3 years. Interest is paid on December 31 every year, and Sangdang Electronics Inc.'s fiscal year ends on December 31. Sangdang Electronics Inc. reported interest expense for 20×1, 20×2, and 20×3 as below.

(Numbers in billions of ₩)

Account title	20×1	20×2	20×3
Interest expense	6.6	6.8	6.9

Sangdang Electronics Inc. reported bonds in the statement of financial position at the end of 20×1, 20×2, and 20×3 as follows.

(Numbers in billions of ₩)

Account titles	Dec. 31, 20×1	Dec. 31, 20×2	Dec. 31, 20×3
Bonds payable	96.3	–	–
Current portion of long-term borrowings	–	98.1	–

《Questions》

(1) How much are cash payments for interest, on interest payment dates for each of 20×1, 20×2, and 20×3?

(2) What is the amount of amortization of discount on bonds payable for each of 20×1, 20×2, and 20×3?

(3) At what price these bonds were issued?

(4) What journal entries should be prepared to record interest expense at the end of 20×1 and at the end of 20×2?

(5) What journal entry should be prepared to reclassify bonds payable as current liabilities at the end of 20×2?

(6) What journal entries should be prepared to record interest expense for 20×3 and the retirement of the bonds at the end of 20×3?

8. **Issuance of bonds at a discount ③**

On January 1, 20×1 Yousung Development Inc. issued bonds and prepared the following bond discount amortization schedule.

Bond discount amortization schedule

(Numbers in billions of ₩)

Dates	Interest expense	Interest payment	Amortization of discount on bonds payable	Book value of bonds payable (amortized cost)
Jan. 1. 20×1				185
Dec. 31, 20×1.	18.5	14	4.5	189.5
Dec. 31, 20×2	19	14	5	194.5
Dec. 31, 20×3	19.5	14	5.5	200
Total	57	42	15	

8-1. Computing interest rates

《Questions》

(1) How much is the face value of the bond?
(2) How much is the face interest rate?
(3) How much is the bond issuance price?
(4) How much is the market interest rate at time of bond issuance?

8-2. Bonds payable and cash flows

The net income of Yousung Development Inc. for each of 20×1, 20×2, and 20×3 is as per the following table. All items in the income statement except interest expense were transacted in cash, and there was no transaction other than the issuance of bonds in financing activities. It is assumed that no exception is allowed in classifying interest payment.

Net income

(Numbers in billions of ₩)

Description	20×1	20×2	20×3
Net income	21.5	31	40.5

《Questions》

(1) Compute net cash from operating activities for each of 20×1, 20×2, and 20×3.
(2) Compute net cash from financing activities for each of 20×1, 20×2, and 20×3.

9. Issuance of bonds during accounting period ①

On April 1, 20×1 Misan Inc. issued bonds with face value of ₩500 billion, face interest rate of 10%, a maturity period of 3 years, and interest payment dates of March 31 every year, at ₩476 billion. The market interest rate, at the time of issuance, was 12%. Misan Inc.'s fiscal year ends on December 31.

9-1. Straight-line method of amortizing discount on bonds payable

Misan Inc. amortizes the discount on bonds payable using the straight-line method.

《Questions》

(1) Prepare a year-end adjusting journal entry needed on December 31, 20×1.
(2) Show where and how these bonds are reported in the statement of financial position as of December 31, 20×1.
(3) Prepare a journal entry for interest payment on March 31, 20×2.
(4) Prepare a year-end adjusting journal entry needed on December 31, 20×2.

9-2. Effective interest method of amortizing discount on bonds payable

Misan Inc. amortizes the discount on bonds payable using the effective interest method.

《Questions》

(1) Prepare a year-end adjusting journal entry needed on December 31, 20×1.
(2) Show where and how these bonds are reported in the statement of financial position as of December 31, 20×1.
(3) Prepare a journal entry for interest payment on March 31, 20×2.
(4) Prepare a year-end adjusting journal entry needed on December 31, 20×2.

10. Provision for refunds

Suwon Internet Mart carries out a refund policy as a sales promotion. If customers return back merchandise within 3 months from purchase, the company refunds the total amount of sales proceeds. Suwon Internet Mart's sales for 20×1 was ₩200 billion, and based on customers' pattern of returning merchandise, it was estimated that 2% of all merchandise sold would be returned for refunds. Suwon Internet Mart actually paid ₩3 billion for merchandise returned in 20×1. The company uses the periodic inventory system.

10-1. When returned merchandise is scraped

The company scraps all returned merchandise.

《Questions》

(1) Prepare a journal entry for refunds actually made in 20×1.
(2) Prepare a journal entry to record the provision for refunds at the end of 20×1.

10-2.* When returned merchandise is resold

The returned merchandise is resold at 80% of the regular sale price. 70% of the merchandise returned in 20×1 was sold. The cost of merchandise is 60% of the regular sale price. The physical inventory taken at the end of 20×1 reveals that there was no inventory shortage loss.

《Questions》

(1) Compute the returned merchandise inventory at the end of 20×1.
(2) Compute the inventory of merchandise expected to be returned at the end of 20×1.
(3) Compute the sales of returned merchandise in 20×1.
(4) Compute the net sales in 20×1.
(5) Compute the cost of goods sold in 20×1.

* The level of difficulty is high.

Financing Activities—Equity

Section 1 Issuance of stock

Section 2 Dividends

Section 3 Treasury stock

Section 4 Statement of changes in equity

Section 5 Related financial ratios

Chapter 10 Overview

In this chapter, we explain the accounting procedures for the issuance of stock and dividend payments, and treasury stock transactions which affect the components of equity. We also review a statement reporting changes in components of the equity called 'the statement of changes in equity'. Last, we explain method for using accounting information that is related with equity.

Case of Daehan Department Store

Statement of financial position (Ft. 2.ⓐ)

As of December 31, 20×2

DDS As of December 31, 20×1 (Numbers in billions of ₩)

Account titles	December 31, 20×2		December 31, 20×1	
Assets				
Current assets				
Cash and cash equivalents(Ft. 4)		45		41
Trade receivables(Ft. 3ⓑ)	30		20	
Allowance for uncollectibe accounts (Ft. 3ⓑ, 5)	(−)4	26	(−)2	18
Inventory :				
Merchandise (Ft. 3ⓒ)		43		23
Total current assets		**114**		**82**
Non-current assets				
FVOCI financial asset (Ft. 3ⓓ, 6)		13		10
Investment in associate (Ft. 3ⓔ, 7)		24		-
Tangible assets (Ft. 8) :				
Land(Ft. 3ⓕ)		96		90
Plant assets (Ft. 3ⓕ, 16)	310		160	
Accumulated depreciation(Ft. 3ⓕ)	(−)13	297	(−)3	157
Intangible asset (Ft. 3ⓖ) :				
Industrial property right (Ft. 8)		9		-
Total non-current assets		**439**		**257**
Total assets		**553**		**339**
Liabilities				
Current liabilities				
Trade payables		42		18
Interest payable		5		4
Salaries payable		2		3
Income tax payable		14		5
Cost financial liabilities (Ft. 3ⓘ) :		38		48
Short-term borrowings (Ft. 9ⓐ)	10		30	
Current portion of long-term borrowings (Ft. 9ⓑ)	28		18	
Provision :				
Provision for refunds (Ft. 3ⓗ, 11)		3		2
Total current liabilities		**104**		**80**
Non-current liabilities				
Cost financial liability (Ft. 3ⓘ) :		126		112
Long-term borrowings (Ft. 9ⓑ)	84		72	
Amortized cost financial liability (Ft. 3ⓘ) :				
Bonds payable (Ft. 10)	42		40	
Total non-current liabilities		**126**		**112**
Total Liabilities		**230**		**192**

Equity				
Share capital				
Common stock(Ft. 13, 16)		150		100
Share premium				
Common stock(Ft. 16)		60		10
Accumulated other comprehensive income		20		11
Accumulated gain on valuation of FVOCI financial asset* (Ft. 3ⓓ, 6)	4		1	
Land revaluation surplus (Ft. 3ⓕ, 8)	16		10	
Retained earnings (Ft. 3ⓙ, 15)		93		26
Total equity		323		147
Total liabilities and equity		553		339

* FVOCI : Fair value through other comprehensive income

Statement of changes in equity (Ft. 2ⓓ)

From Jan. 1, 20×2 to Dec. 31, 20×2

DDS From Jan. 1, 20×1 to Dec. 31, 20×1 (Numbers in billions of ₩)

Description	Share capital	Share premium	Retained earnings	Accumulated other comprehensive income		Total
	Common stock	Common stock		Accumulated gain on valuation of FVOCI financial asset	Land revaluation surplus	
Balance as of January 1, 20×1	–	–	–	–	–	–
Changes in 20×1 :						
Issuance of common stock (Ft. 13)	100	10				110
Total comprehensive income (Ft. 3ⓓ, 3ⓕ, 6, 8)			26	1	10	37
Balance as of December 31, 20×1	100	10	26	1	10	147
Changes in 20×2 :						
Issuance of common stock (Ft. 13)	50	50				100
Cash dividends (Ft. 14)			(−)5			(−)5
Total comprehensive income (Ft. 3ⓓ, 3ⓕ, 6, 8)			72	3	6	81
Balance as of December 31, 20×2	150	60	93	4	16	323

⟨Footnotes⟩

2. Formats of financial statements

ⓓ Format of statement of changes in equity

In the statement of changes in equity, the company reports its total comprehensive income by reconciling each item of 'other comprehensive income' with the corresponding 'accumulated other comprehensive income.'

3. Important accounting policies

ⓙ Reporting appropriated retained earnings and unappropriated retained earnings

In the statement of financial position, the company reports the total amount of appropriated retained earnings and unappropriated retained earnings as retained earnings. It reports them separately only in the statement of retained earnings (a proposal), which is disclosed in the footnotes.

13. Share capital

The composition of share capital at the end of each year is as follow.

Year end	Type of stock	Par value	Number of share issued
20×2	Common stock	₩5,000	30 million shares
20×1	Common stock	₩5,000	20 million shares

14. Dividends

Computations of dividends and payout ratio for each year are as follow.

(Numbers in billions of ₩)

Year	Type of stock	Number shares subject to dividends	Par value dividend rate	Amount of dividends
20×2	Common stock	30 million shares	10%	15
20×1	Common stock	20 million shares	5%	5

* The same diviend rate is applied to all stock outstanding at the end of the regardless of the issuance date of stock per the company's charter.

(Numbers in billions of ₩)

Year	Amount of dividends (1)	Net income (2)	Payout ratio [(1)/(2)]
20×2	15*	72	20.83%
20×1	5**	26	19.23%

* This represents the dividend payment plan of the management. If the plan is finalized by ballot at the stockholders meeting to be held on March 15, 20×3, they will be paid on March 22, 20×3.

** This was finalized by ballot at the stockholders meeting on March 14, 20×2 and paid on March 21, 20×2.

15. Appropriation of retained earnings

The appropriation of retained earnings (a proposal) for each year is as below.

Statement of retained earnings (a proposal)

From Jan. 1, 20×2 to Dec. 31, 20×2

DDS From Jan. 1, 20×1 to Dec. 31, 20×1 (Numbers in billions of ₩)

Description	Retained earnings			
	Legally appropriated	Discretionary appropriated	Unappropriated	Total
	Income	For business expansion		
Balance at beginning of 20×1	–	–	–	–
Changes in retained earnings in 20×1 :				
Net income			26	26
Appropriation per commercial codes[**]	1		(–)1	
Appropriation for business expansion[**]		2	(–)2	
Cash dividends[**]			(–)5	(–)5
Balance at end of 20×1	1	2	18	21
Changes in retained earnings in 20×2 :				
Net income			72	72
Appropriation per commercial codes[***]	2		(–)2	
Appropriation for business expansion[***]		4	(–)4	
Cash dividends[***]			(–)15	(–)15
Balance at end of 20×2	3	6	69	78

* Appropriate more than 10% of each year's dividends until it reaches 1/2 of share capital.
** Finalized by ballot at the stockholders meeting on March 14, 20×2.
*** This is the management's plan and will be finalized by ballot at the stockholders meeting, which will be held on March 16, 20×3.

Explanation of case financial statements

■ Note : Numbers in superscripts are main text page numbers where the corresponding subjects are explained.

Accounts related with this chapter are share capital—common stock (classified as share capital); share premium—common stock (classified as share premium); and retained earnings. To avoid duplicate explanation, we do the case explanation for 20×2 and omit the explanation of 20×1. As of December 31, 20×2, Daehan Department Store's share capital—common stock[472] is at ₩150 billion. Its share premium—common stock[472] is at ₩60 billion, retained earnings are ₩93 billion. Footnote 3 ⓙ shows that the retained earnings, in the statement of financial position, are total amount of the unappropriated retained earnings (not restricted in paying dividends) and the appropriated retained earnings (restricted in paying dividends).[475]

Daehan Department Store's changes in components of equity in 20×2 are reported in the statement of changes in equity.[481] Because of the issuance of common stock in 20×2, share capital—common stock is increased by ₩50 billion and share premium—common stock is increased by ₩50 billion. As a result, the number of common stock (par value of ₩5,000) issued is increased by 10 million shares to 30 million shares (Footnote 13). As explained in Footnote 2 ⓓ, comprehensive income is presented in detail, item by item,[481] and is reconciled with the components of equity in the statement of changes in equity. The net income of ₩72 billion increased retained earnings. The gain on valuation of FVOCI financial asset[583] of ₩3 billion and the land revaluation gain[588] of ₩6 billion increased the accumulated gain on valuation of FVOCI financial asset and land revaluation surplus, respectively. On the other hand, cash dividends[473] of ₩5 billion for 20×1 but paid in 20×2 (Footnote 14 and 15) reduced retained earnings.

In the footnotes, more detailed information about the components of equity is reported. Footnote 14 reports that the cash dividend plan of ₩15 billion in 20×2 is 10%[474] of par value and the dividend payout ratio[486] is 20.83%. Footnote 15 shows the retained earnings appropriation plan[475] to be reported at next year's meeting of stockholders. According to this plan, retained earnings will be appropriated by ₩2 billion for the legally appropriated income, ₩4 billion for the discretionary appropriated for business expansion, and ₩15 billion for dividends. If this plan is approved in next year's stockholder meeting, the unappropriated retained earnings available for dividends at the end of 20×1 will be ₩69 billion.

Issuance of stock

1.1 Classes of stock

If a company issues stock, the company receives its issuance price in cash. Those who receive stock by contributing money become stockholders. The amount stated on face of stock is par value. Par value should be more than ₩100 and issuing companies can decide the par value by themselves. No matter what par value is set, the par value per share of all stock issued must be the same. If no par value stock is issued, more than 1/2 of the amount issued should be set up as share capital.

In general, stock issued by companies is either common stock or preferred stock. A common stock is an ordinary stock so it is also called an ordinary share. Common stock holders can participate in the management of the company by casting votes at stockholders' meetings; they may also receive dividends. A preferred stock is a stock that give its holder a preferential right, over common stock, in a specific area. In general, a preferential right to receive certain dividends over common stock is given. Yet the right to vote in stockholder meetings is not given.

〈Box 10-1〉 Preferred stock

A **preferred stock (우선주)** is a stock to which a specific preference right is attached. In general, the right to receive a certain percentage of dividends over **common stock (보통주)** is attached to preferred stock. But it is common that voting right in stockholders' meeting given to common stock is not attached to preferred stock.

Depending on rights on the dividends attached to it, a preferred stock is classified as either a cumulative preferred stock or a participative preferred stock. A **cumulative preferred stock** is a stock that includes a right to retroactively receive dividends in following year, if dividends are not paid in a certain year.

A preferred stock without this kind of retroactive right is called a **non-cumulative preferred stock.**

A **participative preferred stock** is a stock that provides a right to participate in additional dividends with common stock after receiving a certain percentage of dividends. A preferred stock that the right to participate in additional dividends is not given is called a non-participative preferred stock.

A **convertible preferred stock** is the one gives stockholder a right to covert into common stock if certain preset conditions are met. Some times, a right to call and retire preferred stock if certain preset conditions are met is given to issuing company. A preferred stock with this kind of right is called as a **callable preferred stock.**

There are two kinds of preferred stock in Korea, old style and new style. **Old style preferred stock** is a participative preferred stock receiving dividends 1% more of par value than common stock. **New style preferred stock** is a preferred stock receiving more dividends than minimum percentage of par value specified in the corporate charter. Some of new style preferred stock is cumulative one receiving dividends in following year if dividends are not paid in current year, and some of them are convertible preferred stock having a converting feature enabling holders convert into common stock if they wish after a certain period of time, 3~10 years.

1.2 Accounting for issuance of stock

From the viewpoint of a company, issuing stock is the act of selling stock to stockholders who invest money in the company. The selling price of the stock is the stock issuance price. If the issuance price is same as par value, it is called issuance at par. Stock is not always issued at par value ; it can instead be issued at price above or below par value. Issuing stock at a price higher than par value is called 'issuance at a premium,' and issuing stock at a price lower than face value is called 'issuance at a discount.' Issuance at a discount is extremely restricted in Korea by the commercial codes, so there is almost no real issuance at a discount.

Let's review how to account for the issuance of stock with 〈Illustration 10-1〉.

〈Illustration 10-1〉 Issuance of stock

Daehan Trading Inc. needed an additional fund after its foundation and issued 20 million shares of common stock (par value of ₩5,000 per share) at ₩7,000 per share and generated cash of ₩140 billion from stockholders.

This transaction should be journalized as follows.

(Numbers in billions of ₩)

(Dr.) Cash	140	(Cr.) Share capital—common stock	100
		Share premium—common stock	40

If preferred stock is issued, the par value should be recorded in 'share capital—preferred stock' and the premium should be recorded in 'share premium—preferred stock.'

IFRS[1] requires to disclose, for each class of stock issued, 1) number of shares authorized, 2) number of shares issued, 3) par value, and 4) reconciliation schedule of the number of shares outstanding. The number of shares authorized is the maximum number that a company can issue, based on its corporate charter. The reconciliation schedule is the one that shows changes in number of outstanding shares from the beginning of the period to the end of the period.

The number of shares outstanding is number of shares being held by external stockholders thus outstanding. Hence, difference between the number of shares issued and the number of shares outstanding is number of treasury shares as shown in the formula below.

Number of shares issued	−	Number of shares outstanding	=	Number of treasury shares

The treasury stock will be reviewed in Section 3.

Dividends

Dividends are a distribution of income to stockholders. The source of dividends is retained earnings, and dividends cannot be paid from any other equity items apart from retained earnings. Dividends are usually paid in cash, but in some cases are paid in stock. Per IFRS[2], dividends and dividends per share should be disclosed either in the financial statements or the footnotes.

2.1 Cash dividends

Cash dividends are dividends paid to stockholders in cash. If cash dividends are paid, then the dividend amount of cash is paid out of the company. Therefore, we must evaluate a company's cash position thoroughly, when deciding whether to make a cash dividend payment and, if so, of what amount. This is because, if a company with a poor cash position pays out too much cash dividends, it may experience difficulties due to a cash shortage.

Let's review the accounting procedures for cash dividends with 〈Illustration 10-2〉 below.

〈Illustration 10-2〉 Cash dividends

Daehan Trading Inc., has issued 20 million shares of common stock (par value of ₩5,000 per share) as of December 31, 20×1. The company paid cash dividends of ₩500 per share on March, 31 20×2.

A journal entry that should be prepared on the dividend payment date is as follows.

(Numbers in billions of ₩)

(Dr.)	Retained earnings*	10	(Cr.)	Cash	10**

* It can be recorded on the dividends account and closed to the retained earnings account through a closing journal entry.

** (20 million × 500) = ₩10 billion

As can be seen in the above journal entry, if cash dividends are paid, then retained earnings and cash are decreased by the dividend amount. Because retained earnings is an equity account, total equity is reduced by the dividend amount in the case that cash dividends are paid.

⟨Box 10-2⟩ Par value dividend rate vs. Market value dividend rate

The **par value dividend rate** is the rate of the dividends over the par value of a stock. The **market value dividend rate** is the rate of the dividends over the market value of a stock on the dividend date of record, which is the last day of a fiscal year. If the market value of a stock is significantly different from its par value, the par value dividend rate poses the problem of not showing dividend yield, which is a return on investment from the perspective of an investor.

Let's take an example of Co. A. The par value of Co. A's common stock is ₩5,000 and it is traded on the stock market at ₩1,000,000 on the dividend date of record. Co. A plans to pay cash dividends of ₩20,000 for the current year. In this case, the par value dividend rate is 400% (20,000/5,000), yet the market value dividend rate is 2% (20,000/1,000,000). If we buy a share of this stock and receive dividends, our return on investment will actually be 2%, not 400%.

This is why the Securities and Exchange Act in Korea, requires companies listed on the stock markets to disclose the **market value dividend rate** when they disclose their dividends starting from 2003. However, a number of companies still disclose the **par value dividend rate** for their common stock because preferred stock dividends are determined by the par value dividend rate (that rate of common stock in case of old style and that rate of preferred stock in case of new style).

2.2 Stock dividends

Stock dividends are company stock distributed as dividends instead of cash. If stock dividends are distributed, then retained earnings are decreased by the par value of the stock distributed and share capital is increased by the same amount. The total number of stock owned by a stockholder is increased by stock dividends. But because such dividends are distributed in proportion to each stockholder's equity, there will be no change in the percentage of equity held by each stockholder after stock dividends are distributed.

Let's review the accounting procedures for stock dividends with 〈Illustration 10-3〉 below.

> **〈Illustration 10-3〉 Stock dividends**
>
> Daehan Trading Inc.'s number of common stock issued is 20 million shares (par value of ₩5,000 per share) as of December 31, 20×1. The company distributed stock dividends of 10% on March 15, 20×2.

A journal entry that should be prepared on the stock dividend distribution date is as follows.

(Numbers in billions of ₩)

(Dr.) Retained earnings*	10	(Cr.) Share capital—common stock 10**

* It can be recorded on the dividends account and closed to the retained earnings account through a closing journal entry.
** (20 million × 10%) × 5,000 = ₩10 billion

Both retained earnings and share capital-common stock are equity accounts. Therefore, in the case of stock dividends, there is no change in the total equity because a decrease in equity (retained earnings) and an increase in equity (share capital-common stock) are happening simultaneously.

If stock dividends are of more than 20~25%, it is considered as a stock split. If there is a stock split, only par value is reduced by the proportion of the split, while the number of stock are increased, so there is nothing to be journalized. We should only note these facts in a memorandum.

〈Box 10-3〉 Composition of statement of retained earnings

Appropriation of retained earnings is a process of deciding how much of income should be paid as dividends and how much income should be restricted on dividend payment. The restrictions on dividend payment may be made because the commercial codes legally require companies to protect creditors, or because the companies themselves want to meet a specific need. Earnings appropriated by law, as in the former example above, are called '**legally appropriated retained earnings**.' Earnings voluntarily appropriated by a company, as in the latter example, are called '**discretionary appropriated retained earnings**.'

The legally appropriated retained earnings refers to **legally appropriated income** per the commercial codes (which requires the appropriation of over 10% of cash dividends for the current year, until the accumulated amount reaches 50% of share capital). Examples of discretionary appropriated retained earnings include appropriated retained earnings for **stable dividend payments** and appropriated retained earnings for **business expansion**. Unappropriated retained earnings are retained earnings that are neither appropriated legally nor discretionarily; they represent retained earnings that are not restricted on dividend payment. These are carried forward to the next year and become retained earnings that are available for dividends in the following year.

Statement of retained earnings is a report showing management's plan to appropriate retained earnings. This plan is finalized only if it is approved in stockholders meeting. In the past, the statement of retained earnings used to be one of the basic financial statements. Yet the K-IFRS[3] no longer includes this statement amongst the basic financial statements, and does not require the classification of retained earnings into detailed appropriations and unappropriated retained earnings in the statement of financial position. It does, however, require that the statement of retained earnings be reported in the **footnotes**, because such appropriation constitutes a restriction on the dividends that can be paid to stockholders.

Current year dividend plan in the statement of retained earnings is actually carried out after it is approved in the stockholders meeting that will be held in next year. Therefore, there is one year time lag between the dividend plan in the statement of retained earnings and the actual dividend payment.

Treasury stock

3.1 Nature of treasury stock

Treasury stock (자기주식) is a stock repurchased by the issuing company, mainly to manage stock price. If the issuing company purchases a certain quantity of treasury stock, then the number of stock that can be bought and sold by general investors (the number of outstanding stock) is decreased by that same quantity. No dividends and no voting right in stockholders' meetings are given to treasury stock.

IFRS[4] requires to report treasury stock at the acquisition cost in the statement of financial position as a reduction to total equity. And it also requires to disclose the number of treasury stock.

Companies can resell treasury stock. The selling price in excess of the book value of treasury stock is called share premium—treasury stock, because it is paid-in capital from treasury stock without any changes in share capital. If the selling price is below the book value of treasury stock, the deficiency should be charged first against the share premium—treasury stock account. If there is no balance in the share premium—treasury stock account, the deficiency is considered to be dividends to stockholders and is charged to retained earnings.

3.2 Accounting for treasury stock

Let's review the accounting procedures for the purchase and disposal of treasury stock with ⟨Illustration 10-4⟩, below.

⟨Illustration 10-4⟩ Acquisition and sales of treasury stock

Yousung Trading Inc. issued 50 million shares of par value ₩5,000 common stock at ₩6,000 per share on its foundation date of March 1, 20×1. The following ⟨Table 10-1⟩ are treasury stock transactions.

⟨Table 10-1⟩ Treasury stock transactions

No.	Date	Transactions
①	March 15, 20×4	Bought 4 million shares of common stock at ₩8,000 per share in cash.
②	August 27, 20×4	Sold 2 million shares of treasury stock at ₩9,000 per share in cash.
③	June 26, 20×5	Sold 1 million shares of treasury stock at ₩7,000 per share in cash.
④	November 11, 20×6	Sold 1 million shares of treasury stock at ₩6,000 per share.

The following are journal entries for the transactions in ⟨Illustration 10-4⟩. (Numbers in all journal entries are in billions of ₩).

① March 15, 20×4 : Acquisition of treasury stock

(Dr.) Treasury stock	32*	(Cr.) Cash	32

* 4 million × 8,000 = ₩32 billion

② August 27, 20×4 : Sale of treasury stock

(Dr.) Cash	18*	(Cr.) Treasury stock	16**
		Share premium—treasury stock	2

* 2 million × 9,000 = ₩18 billion
** 2 million × 8,000 = ₩16 billion

If the statement of financial position is prepared as of December 31, 20×4, then share capital—common stock and treasury stock, as well as the share premium related with these items, are reported as shown in 〈Table 10-2〉 bellow.

〈Table 10-2〉 Partial statement of financial position

Yousung Trading Inc. As of December 31, 20×4 (Numbers in billions of ₩)

Account titles	Amount	
Equity		
Share capital		250
Common stock	250	
Share premium		52
Common stock	50	
Treasury stock	2	
Retained earnings		×××
Accumulated other comprehensive income		×××
Accumulated gain on valuation of FVOCI financial assets*	×××	
Other components of equity		(-)16
Treasury stock	(-)16	
Total equity		×××

* FVOCI : Fair value through other comprehensive income

Share premium—treasury stock of ₩2 billion are reported under the caption of share premium, in the statement of financial position. Treasury stock of ₩16 billion, which are an item in 'other components of equity,' are reported as a reduction to equity.

③ June 26, 20×5 : Sale of treasury stock

(Dr.)		(Cr.)	
Cash	7*	Treasury stock	8**
Share premium—treasury stock	1		

* 1 million × 7,000 = ₩7 billion
** 1 million × 8,000 = ₩8 billion

The deficiency in selling price (₩7 billion) against the acquisition cost (₩8 billion) is ₩ 1 billion. Because this deficiency is smaller than the share premium—treasury stock of ₩2 billion carried forward from the previous year, all of ₩1 billion is debited to the share premium—treasury stock account. The share premium—treasury stock reported in the statement of financial position as of December 31, 20×5 became ₩1 billion.

④ November 11, 20×6 : Sale of treasury stock

(Dr.)			(Cr.)		
	Cash	6*		Treasury stock	8**
	Share premium—treasury stock	1			
	Retained earnings	1			

* 1 million × 6,000 = ₩6 billion
** 1 million × 8,000 = ₩8 billion

The deficiency in selling price (₩6 billion) against acquisition cost (₩8 billion) is ₩2 billion. The share premium—treasury stock account balance carried forward from last year was ₩1 billion. Therefore, ₩1 billion out of the deficiency of ₩2 billion should be debited to the share premium—treasury stock account and the remaining ₩1 billion is debited to the retained earnings account, treating it as dividends to stockholders (in a fashion that buying 1 share from a stockholder at ₩8,000 and resell it at ₩6,000).

Statement of changes in equity

4.1 Nature of statement of changes in equity

The statement of changes in equity is a financial statement that reports both the changes and the reasons for said changes in each component of equity : share capital, share premium, retained earnings, accumulated other comprehensive income, and other components of equity for an accounting period. IFRS[5] requires that accumulated other comprehensive income should be separately reported by each component in the statement of changes in equity or in the footnotes, so that they are reconciled with other comprehensive income reported in the statement of comprehensive income.

4.2 An illustration of preparing a statement of changes in equity

〈Illustration 10-5〉 Preparing a statement of changes in equity

The following 〈Table 10-3〉 and 〈Table 10-4〉 are Yousung Trading Inc.'s partial statement of financial position that shows the equity section, as of December 31, 20×1 and December 31, 20×2, and the partial comprehensive income statement that displays net income and other comprehensive income for the period from January 1, 20×2 to December 31, 20×2, respectively.

〈Table 10-3〉 Partial statement of financial position

Yousung Trading Inc. (Numbers in billions of ₩)

Account titles	Amount			
	Dec. 31, 20×2		Dec. 31, 20×1	
Equity				
Share capital		**140**		**100**
Common stock	140		100	
Share premium		**90**		**60**
Common stock	80		60	
Treasury stock	10		-	
Retained earnings		**104**		**80**
Accumulated other comprehensive income		**20**		**14**
Accumulated gain on valuation of FVOCI financial assets*	20		14	
Other components of equity		-		**(−)30**
Treasury stock	-		(−)30	
Total equity		**354**		**224**

* FVOCI : Fair value through other comprehensive income

〈Table 10-4〉 Partial comprehensive income statement

From Jan. 1, 20×2
Yousung Trading Inc. to Dec. 31, 20×2 (Numbers in billions of ₩)

Account titles	Amount	
Net income		**42**
Other comprehensive income		**6**
Gain on valuation of FVOCI financial assets*	6	
Total comprehensive income		**48**

* FVOCI : Fair value through other comprehensive income

(1) T account analyses of component of equity

To prepare the statement of changes in equity, we must find out how much each component of equity has changed and what caused those changes by conducting T account analyses. The following 〈Diagram 10-1〉 are the results of T account analyses of each component of equity. The analyses are performed by tracking debit and credit entries of each a0ccount during the year.

〈Diagram 10-1〉 T account analyses

Share capital—common stock

(Numbers in billions of ₩)

			Beginning	100(Cr.)
	① Issuance of common stock	40	Ending	140(Cr.)

Share premium—common stock

			Beginning	60(Cr.)
	① Issuance of common stock	20	Ending	80(Cr.)

Share premium—treasury stock

			Beginning	–
	② Sale of treasury stock	10	Ending	10(Cr.)

Treasury stock

			Beginning	30(Cr.)
	② Sale of treasury stock	30	Ending	–

Retained earnings

			Beginning	80(Cr.)
③ Cash dividends 18				62(Cr.)
	Net income	42*	Ending	104(Cr.)

* Obtained from the comprehensive income statement.

Accumulated gain on valuation of FVOCI financial assets

		Beginning	14(Cr.)
Gain on valuation	6*	Ending	20(Cr.)

* Obtained from the comprehensive income statement. This is reviewed in the Appendix.

Additional information obtained from T account analyses is as shown in ⟨Table 10-5⟩ below.

⟨Table 10-5⟩ Additional information

	Transactions
①	Issued common stock with par value of ₩40 billion at ₩60 billion.
②	Sold treasury stock with acquisition cost of ₩30 billion at ₩40 billion.
③	Paid cash dividends of ₩18 billion.

(2) Preparation of the statement of changes in equity

The following ⟨Table 10-6⟩ is the statement of changes in equity of Yousung Trading Inc. for 20×2, reflecting the findings from the above T account analyses,

⟨Table 10-6⟩ Statement of changes in equity

Yousung Trading Inc. From Jan. 1, 20×2 to Dec. 31, 20×2 (Numbers in billions of ₩)

Description	Share capital	Share premium		Retained earnings	Accumulated other comprehensive income	Other components of equity	Total
	Common stock	Common stock	Treasury stock		Accumulated gain on valuation of FVOCI financial assets	Treasury stock	
Balance as of January 1, 20×2	100	60	–	80	14	(–)30	224
Changes in equity during 20×2 :							
Cash dividends				(–)18			(–)18
Issuance of common stock	40	20					60
Sale of treasury stock			10			30	40
Total comprehensive income				42	6		48
Balance as of December 31, 20×2	140	80	10	104	20	–	354

* FVOCI : Fair value through other comprehensive income

As we examine the above statement, we find that the statement of changes in equity reports detailed changes in each component of equity. Yet it also reports the total amount of changes in equity, by each type of change, during the year. The total amount of changes in equity, reported by each type in this statement, include : cash dividends of ₩18 billion, the price of common stock additionally issued of ₩60 billion, the sale of treasury stock at ₩40 billion, and the total comprehensive income of ₩48 billion.

Related financial ratios

Financial ratios that are related with equity include : the payout ratio, by which the profitability of a company can be evaluated ; the book-value per share, by which the safety (financial) of a company can be evaluated ; and the price book-value ratio, which is one of the price multiples.

5.1 Financial ratio evaluating profitability

(1) Payout ratio

The payout ratio (배당성향) shows what proportion of the net income is paid as common stock dividends. We compute the payout ratio by dividing the common stock cash dividends into the net income applicable to common stockholders, as shown below. The numerator should be the one matching with the denominator, net income for current year. Therefore, the management's dividend plan for the current period in the statement of retained earnings, which is disclosed in the footnotes, is a proper numerator. In most cases, the original dividend plan is approved in the stockholders' meeting. If the dividend plan is instead modified, the payout ratio should be recomputed. The net income applicable to common stockholders is the net income after deducting preferred stock dividends.

$$\text{Payout ratio} = \frac{\text{Common stock cash dividends}}{\text{Net income} - \text{Preferred stock dividends}}$$

(Daehan Department Store's ratio)

$$20\times2 : \frac{15 \text{ billion}}{72 \text{ billion}} = 20.83\%$$

$$20\times1 : \frac{5 \text{ billion}}{26 \text{ billion}} = 19.23\%$$

In the case of Daehan Department Store, there is no preferred stock dividend because no preferred stock was issued. The common stock cash dividends in 20×1 are the management's dividend plan of ₩5 billion in the statement of retained earnings. These dividends were actually paid in the following year and were reported in the statement of changes in equity and statement of cash flows for 20×2. The dividend plan of ₩15 billion for 20×2 will be voted in the stockholders meeting and paid in the following year, 20×3. It will likewise be reported in the financial statements for 20×3. The payout ratio of Daehan Department Store for 20×2 was 20.83%, which was a bit higher than that for 20×1 (19.23%).

If the payout ratio is high, it means that a large proportion of the income earned by the company is returned to its stockholders. But the higher the payout ratio, the lower the ratio of earning that is retained for reinvestment. Therefore, the payout ratio should be determined at the proper levels considering the company's relationship with its stockholders, its future investment plan, etc.

5.2 Financial ratio evaluating safety (financial)

(1) Book-value per share

Book-value per share (BPS) means the book value of net assets applicable to one share of common stock. Therefore, it is called net assets per share (주당순자산) in Korean. Net assets are the total assets less the total liabilities ; that is, equity. Net assets per share are computed by dividing the book value of the equity, less the preferred stock, by the number of common shares outstanding at the end of the year. The reason for subtracting the preferred stock is that the net assets applicable to common stock should be used as the numerator. The number of shares outstanding is the number of shares issued, less the number of treasury shares.

$$\text{Book-value per share (BPS)} = \frac{\text{Book-value of equity} - \text{Preferred stock}}{\text{Number of common shares outstanding at the end of the year}}$$

(Daehan Department Store's ratio)

$$20\times2: \frac{\text{323 billion}}{\text{30 million shares}} = ₩10,767$$

$$20\times1: \frac{\text{147 billion}}{\text{20 million shares}} = ₩7,350$$

In the case of Daehan Department Store, because no preferred stock was issued, the book value of net assets (that is, the book value of equity) is used as the numerator without any adjustment. The numbers of common shares outstanding for 20×2 and 20×1 is 30 million shares and 20 million shares, respectively. Because Daehan Department Store did not have treasury stock, the number of common shares outstanding are the same as the number of common shares issued in Footnote 14. Daehan Department Store's BPS at the end of 20×2 was ₩10,767. This amount shows an increase by ₩3,417 from the BPS at the end of 20×1, which was ₩7,350.

5.3 Price multiple

(1) Price book-value ratio

The price book-value ratio (PBR : 주가순자산비율) is an index that shows how high stock price is in comparison with book-value per share. As noted, book-value per share is called net assets per share in Korean. Because of this, the PBR is called the price net assets ratio in Korean. The ratio is computed as follows.

$$\text{Price book-value ratio (PBR)} = \frac{\text{Common stock price}}{\text{Book-value per share (BPS)}}$$

(Daehan Department Store's ratio)

It is assumed that the common stock prices of Daehan Department Store at the end of 20×2 and at the end of 20×1 were ₩15,000 and ₩10,000, respectively.

$$20\times2 : \frac{15,000}{10,767} = 1.39 \text{ times}$$

$$20\times1 : \frac{10,000}{7,350} = 1.36 \text{ times}$$

The PBR of Daehan Department Store at the end of 20×2 was 1.39 times, and it is a bit higher than 1.36 times at the end of 20×1. A high PBR usually means that the stock price is formed at a high level, in relation to BPS, because the expected future growth potential of the company is high.

■ Note : Financial ratios reviewed in this chapter are summarized in Appendix 2 〈Table B-1〉 'Key financial ratios' at the end of this book.

IFRS references (http://www.kasb.or.kr)

[1] IAS 1 *Presentation of Financial Statements*, par. 79(a)(i), (ii), (iii), (iv), 82(b).
[2] IAS 1 *Ibid*. par. 107.
[3] IAS 1 *Ibid*. par. 79(a)(v), 137(a), Korean 138.1.
[4] IAS 32 *Financial Instruments : Presentation*, par. 33, 34.
IAS 1 *op. cit.*, par. 79(a)(vi).
[5] IAS 1 *op. cit.*, par. 106(d)(ii), 106A.

Key terms

Common stock (보통주) : Ordinary stock representing ownership of the company. (p.470)

Dividends (배당금) : Distribution of income to stockholders in cash or company's own stock. (p.473)

Preferred stock (우선주) : Stock that allows holders to receive preferred treatment, in terms of certain rights, over common stock holders. (p.470)

Statement of retained earnings (이익잉여금처분계산서) : A statement reporting a plan to appropriate retained earnings. (p.475)

Treasury stock (자기주식) : A company's own stock that is repurchased and kept by the issuing company. (p.477)

Exercises

1. Relationship of income and dividends with equity

The following is data gathered from the financial statements of Dongsan Inc. for 20×1.

(Numbers in billions of ₩)

Description	Amount	Description	Amount
Assets (beginning)	400	Liabilities (beginning)	230
Total revenue	300	Total expense	200
Dividends	20		

《Question》 Compute the equity at the end of 20×1.

2. Issuance of stock and presenting in statement of financial position

Sersan Inc. was founded with funds of ₩160 billion, generated by issuing 20 million shares of common stock, with par value of ₩5,000, at ₩8,000 per share on January 1, 20×1. The company generated additional funds of ₩50 billion by issuing 10 million shares of preferred stock, with par value of ₩5,000, at ₩5,000 on July 1, 20×1.

《Questions》

(1) Prepare journal entries for the issuance of stocks on the following dates.
  1) January 1, 20×1 2) July 1, 20×1

(2) Show where and how these issued stocks are presented in the statement of financial position, as of December 31, 20×1.

3. Cash dividends and stock dividends

Dongyang Electronics reported share capital-common stock of ₩500 billion (number of shares issued : 100 million shares ; par value per share : ₩5,000) and retained earnings of ₩370 billion on December 31, 20×1. The company paid cash dividends of ₩400 per share on March 10, 20×2 and distributed 10% stock dividends on September 10, 20×2.

《Questions》

(1) Prepare journal entries for the cash dividends on March 10, 20×2 and the stock dividends on September 10, 20×2.

(2) How much are 1) share capital-common stock and 2) retained earnings after stock dividends of September 10, 20×2.

4. Statement of retained earnings

The following are the details of appropriated retained earnings of Daesan Inc., as of December 31, 20×1.

Details of appropriated retained earnings

Daesan Inc. As of December 31, 20×1 (Numbers in billions of ₩)

Description	Amount	
Retained earnings		
Legally appropriated		100
Appropriated income by commercial codes	100	
Discretionary appropriated		300
Appropriated for business expansion	180	
Appropriated for stable dividend payments	120	
Unappropriated retained earnings		200
Total		600

The management of Daesan Inc. decided that the net income of ₩330 billion for 20×2 should be appropriated as follows, and that they would propose their plan to the stockholders' meeting to be held on March 9, 20×3.

① Appropriation of income by commercial codes : ₩10 billion
② Appropriation for business expansion : ₩30 billion
③ Appropriation for stable dividend payments : ₩10 billion
④ Cash dividends : ₩100 billion

《Question》

Prepare a statement of retained earnings (a proposal) of Daesam Inc. for 20×2.

5. **Classification of equity**

The following items comprise equity in the statement of financial position of Suwon Inc., as of December 31, 20×1.

(Numbers in billions of ₩)

Account titles	Amount	Account titles	Amount
Share premium—treasury stock	5	Share premium—common stock	113
Retained earnings	120	Share capital—common stock	350
Treasury stock	7	Share capital—preferred stock	150

《Question》

How much of each of the following items should be reported in the statement of financial position of Suwon Inc., as of December 31, 20×1?

(1) Share capital (2) Share premium (3) Retained earnings
(4) Other components of equity (5) Total equity

6. **Acquisition and sales of treasury stock**

SB Co. issued 80 million shares of common stock (par value ₩5,000) at ₩6,000 per share, and received cash of ₩480 billion, on its foundation date of March 1, 20×1. The following are treasury stock transactions :

① Mar. 15, 20×4 : Bought 4 million shares of common stock in cash at ₩10,000 per share and paid ₩40 billion.
② Aug. 27, 20×4 : Sold 2 million shares of treasury stock in cash at ₩11,000 per share and received ₩22 billion.
③ Jun. 26, 20×5 : Sold 1 million shares of treasury stock in cash at ₩9,000 per share and received ₩9 billion.
④ Nov. 11, 20×6 : Sold 1 million shares of treasury stock in cash at ₩7,000 per share and received ₩7 billion.

《Questions》

(1) Prepare journal entries for treasury stack transactions.
(2) Prepare a partial statement of financial position as of December 31, 20×4, showing share capital-common stock and treasury stock and share premium related with those stocks.

7. Equity transactions and presentation in the statement of financial position

The following is Buksan Inc.'s partial statement of financial position as of December 31, 20×1 showing equity part.

Partial statement of financial position

Buksan Inc. As of December 31, 20×1 (Numbers in billions of ₩)

Account titles	Amount	
Equity		
Share capital		**100**
Common stock	100	
Share premium		**40**
Common stock	40	
Retained earnings		**10**
Total equity		**150**

The following equity transactions occurred in 20×2.

① Feb. 15 : Issued 40 million shares of common stock with par value of ₩5,000 at ₩7,000, and received ₩28 billion in cash.
② Mar. 11 : Paid dividends of ₩5 billion in cash.
③ Net income for 20×2 : ₩12 billion

《Question》

How much each of the following items is reported in the statement of financial position of Buksan Inc. as of December 31, 20×2?

(1) Share capital—common stock (2) Share premium—common stock
(3) Retained earnings

8. Changes in equity

Dukmyoung Inc. issued 10 million shares of common stock (par value per share of ₩5,000) at ₩7,000 per share, and received ₩70 billion in cash, on its founding date of January 1, 20×1. The following are the details of equity transactions of the company from 20×1 to 20×3.

① Net income for 20×1 : ₩14 billion
② Mar. 14, 20×2 : Paid cash dividends of ₩400 per share, total ₩4 billion.
③ Net income for 20×2 : ₩16 billion
④ Mar. 15, 20×3 : Distributed stock dividends of 0.1 share per share.
⑤ Net income for 20×3 : ₩19 billion

《Question》

The following is Dukmyoung Inc.'s partial statement of financial position as of December 31, 20×3 and December 31, 20×2, showing the equity section. Fill in the blanks with the correct amounts.

Partial statement of financial position

Dunmyoung Inc. (Numbers in billions of ₩)

Account titles	Amount	
	Dec. 31, 20×3.	Dec. 31, 20×2
Equity		
Share capital		
Common stock	( )	( )
Share premium		
Common stock	( )	( )
Retained earnings	( )	( )
Total equity	( )	( )

9. **Statement of changes in equity**

The following are Chungju Inc.'s partial statement of financial position as of December 31, 20×2 and December 31, 20×1, showing the equity section and partial comprehensive income statement for 20×2.

Partial statement of financial position

Chungju Inc. (Numbers in billions of ₩)

Account titles	Amount			
	Dec. 31, 20×2		Dec. 31, 20×1	
Equity				
Share capital		**75**		**50**
Common stock	75		50	
Share premium		**54**		**30**
Common stock	45		30	
Treasury stock	9		–	
Retained earnings		**59**		**46**
Accumulated other comprehensive income		**7**		**4**
Accumulated gain on valuation of FVOCI financial assets*	7		4	
Other components of equity		–		**(–)8**
Treasury stock	–		(–)8	
Total equity		**195**		**122**

* FVOCI : Fair value through other comprehensive income.

Partial comprehensive income statement

Chungju Inc. From Jan. 1, 20×2 to Dec. 31, 20×2 (Numbers in billions of ₩)

Account titles	Amount	
Net income		21
Other comprehensive income		3
Gain on valuation of FVOCI financial assets	3	
Total comprehensive income		24

The following are equity transactions for 20×2 identified by conducting T account analyses for the equity accounts of Chungju Inc.

① Issued 5 million shares of common stock with par value of ₩5,000, at ₩8,000 per share in cash.
② Paid cash dividends of ₩8 billion.
③ Purchased 1 million shares of its own common stock at ₩8,000 per share.
④ Sold 2 million shares of all treasury stock owned at ₩10,000 per share.

《Question》
Prepare a statement of changes in equity of Chungju Inc. for 20×2.

10. Price book-value ratio

The following is data obtained from Inkae Inc.'s financial statements for 20×1.

(Numbers in billions of ₩)

Description	Amount	Description	Amount
Assets (ending)	550	Liabilities (ending)	310
Net income	67	Cash dividends*	23

* Per the cash dividend plan for 20×1 which is disclosed in the statement of retained earnings, in the footnotes to the financial statement for 20×1.

The number of common stock outstanding at year-end was 20 million shares and the price of common stock per share at year-end was ₩14,000.

《Questions》
Compute the following financial ratios of Inkae Inc.

(1) Book-value per share (BPS) (2) Price book-value ratio (PBR) (3) Payout ratio

Statement of Cash Flows

Chapter 11 Overview

In this chapter, we closely examine key issues such as items that multiple classifications are allowed and explain the methods for reporting cash flows from each of operating activities, investing activities, and financing activities. We review, in particular detail, the indirect method of reporting cash generated from operations by adding and subtracting adjustments to and from net income before income tax expense. In the last part of this chapter we introduce a comprehensive illustration for preparing a statement of cash flows using an income statement and a statement of financial position. We also explain financial ratios, using information from the statement of cash flows.

Case of Daehan Department Store

Statement of cash-flows (Ft. 2ⓒ)

From Jan. 1, 20×2 to Dec. 31, 20×2

DDS From Jan. 1, 20×1 to Dec. 31, 20×1 (Numbers in billions of ₩)

Description	20×2		20×1	
Cash flows from operating activities				
Net income before income tax expense (NIBITE)		102		38
Adjustments (Ft. 2ⓒ) :				
NIBITE expense related with individually reporting item				
Interest expense		19		13
Gain and loss from non-operating activities		(−)6		1
Loss on disposal of tangible assets (Ft. 8)	−		1	
Equity income from associate (Ft. 7)	(−)6		−	
Operating expense without cash outflows				
Depreciation expense		10		3
Changes in assets and liabilities due to operating activities :		(−)4		(−)18
Increase in trade receivables	(−)8		(−)18	
Increase in merchandise	(−)20		(−)23	
Increase in trade payables	24		18	
Increase (decrease) in salaries payables	(−)1		3	
Increase in provision for refunds (Ft. 11)	1		2	
Cash generated from operations		121		37
Individually reporting item :				
Income tax paid (Ft. 2ⓒ)		(−)21		(−)7
Net cash from operating activities		100		30
Cash flows from investing activities				
Proceeds from sales of land (Ft. 8)	−		39	
Individually reporting item :				
Dividends received (Ft. 7)	2			
Purchase of FVOCI financial asset (Ft. 6)	−		(−)9	
Purchase of stock of associate (Ft. 7)	(−)20		−	
Purchase of land (Ft. 8)	−		(−)120	
Purchase of plant assets (Ft. 8)	(−)150		(−)100	
Purchase of intangible assets (Ft. 8)	(−)9		−	
Net cash used in investing activities		(−)177		(−)190
Cash flows from financing activities				
Proceeds from short-term borrowings (Ft. 9ⓐ)	10		30	
Proceeds from long-term borrowings (Ft. 9ⓑ)	40		90	
Proceeds from Issuing bonds (Ft. 10)	−		39	
Proceeds from issuing common stock (Ft. 13)	100		50	

Retirement of short-term borrowings (Ft. 9ⓐ)	(-)30		-	
Retirement of current portion of long-term borrowings (Ft. 9ⓑ)	(-)18		-	
Individually reporting items :				
Interest paid (Ft. 2ⓒ)	(-)16		(-)8	
Dividends paid (Ft. 2ⓒ, 14)	(-)5		-	
Net cash from financing activities		81		201
Net increase in cash and cash equivalents		4		41
Cash and cash equivalents at beginning of period (Ft. 4)		41		-
Cash and cash equivalents at end of period		45		41

〈Footnotes〉

2. Formats of financial statements

© Format of statement of cash flows

The company prepares its statement of cash flows using the indirect method. It classifies adjustments made to income before income tax expense (NIBITE), to compute cash generated from operations into : NIBITE revenue and expense related with individually reporting items ; gain and loss from non-operating activities ; operating expense without cash outflows ; and changes in assets and liabilities due to operating activities. The company also classifies income tax paid as an operating activity dividends received as an investing activity, and interest paid and dividends paid as financing activities, and reports these items individually.

4. Cash and cash equivalents

Cash and cash equivalents include cash on hand and bank deposits, as well as financial instruments that can be readily convertible to a known amount of cash and that are subject to an insignificant risk of change in value because they are matured less than 3 months from their acquisition date. Cash equivalents are valued at the quoted price on the active market. 'Cash and cash equivalents' in the statement of financial position is the same as 'cash and cash equivalent' in the statement of cash flows.

6. Fair value through other comprehensive income (FVOCI) financial asset

The company purchased the following stock for long-term investment purpose and decided to classify this investment in stock as a FVOCI financial asset on the acquisition day. They are valued at the quoted price (market price).

(Numbers in billions of ₩)

Investment in stock	Acquisition date	Number of shares	Base price per share		Year-end market price per share	Valuation gain
KM-Mart	Nov. 1, 20×1	1 million share	20×1	₩9,000 (Acquisition cost)	₩10,000	₩1,000 × 1 million share = 1
			20×2	₩10,000 (Market price at beginning of the year)	₩13,000	₩3,000 × 1 million share = 3

7. Investment in associate

Shown below is the content of investment in associate and the reconciliation of the investment in associate account, revealing changes in that account.

Composition of investment in associate

Associate	Aquisition date	Number of shares	Equity
Sohan Inc.	January 2, 20×2	20,000 shares	20%

Reconciliation of investment in associate

(Numbers in billions of ₩)

Balance at the beginning of 20×2	Changes in 20×2			Balance at the end of 20×2
	Investment	Add : Equity income	Less : Dividends received	
–	20	6	2	24

8. Aquisition and disposal of tangible and intangible assets

The acquisition and disposal of tangible and intangible assets for each year are as follow.

(Numbers in billions of ₩)

Description		Land	Plant assets	Intangible assets
20×1	Beginning balance	–	–	–
	Acquisition in cash	120	100	–
	Acquisition by issuing stock	–	60	–
	Disposal	(–)40*	–	–
	Gain on revaluation	10		
	Ending balance	90	160	–
20×2	Acquisition in cash	–	150	9**
	Gain on revaluation	6		
	Ending balance	96	310	9

* Proceeds from sales were ₩39 billion.
** An industrial property right (patent) acquired at the end of 20×2.

9. Compositions of short-term and long-term borrowings

ⓐ Short-term borrowings

The company borrowed the following in short term to use as working capital.

(Numbers in billions of ₩)

Date of borrowing	Lender	Interest rate	Amount of borrowing	Terms
Apr. 1 20×1	Seoul Bank	10% per annum	30	Matured in 1 year (Interest : after every 6 months)
Apr. 1 20×2	Busan Bank	10% per annum	10	Matured in 1 year (Interest : after every 6 months)

ⓑ Long-term borrowings

(1) Composition of long-term borrowings : Long-term borrowings at the end of 20×2 and 20×1 are shown below :

(Numbers in billions of ₩)

Date of borrowing	Lender	Interest rate	Remaining balance		Terms
			At end of 20×2	At end of 20×1	
Mar. 1, 20×1	Daehan Capital	12% per annum	72	90	5 years installments (Interest : after every 6 months)
May 1, 20×2.	IBK	12% per annum	40	-	4 years installments (Interest : after every year)
Total			112	90	

(2) Retirement schedule : The long-term borrowing retirement schedule for each year is as below.

(Numbers in billions of ₩)

Year	Retirement amount
20×2	18
20×3	28
20×4	28
20×5	28
20×6	28

(3) Current portion of long-term borrowings : The company reclassified ₩28 billion and ₩18 billion of long-term borrowings into the current portion of long-term borrowings at the end of 20×2 and 20×1, respectively per the above retirement schedule.

(Numbers in billions of ₩)

Classification	Account titles	At end of 20×2	At end of 20×1
Current liability	Current portion of long-term borrowings	28	18
Non-current liability	Long-term borrowings	84	72
Total		112	90

10. Bonds payable

Bonds payable at the end of 20×2 and 20×1 are as follow.

(Numbers in billions of ₩)

Type	Issuance date	Maturity date	Face interest rate	Face value	Issuance price
Debenture bonds	July 1, 20×1	June 30, 20×6	6% per annum*	50	39

* Interest is paid after every 6 months. Effective interest rate is 12% per annum.

11. Provision for refunds

The following reconciliation schedule shows changes in provision for refunds.

Reconciliation of provision for refunds

(Numbers in billions of ₩)

Description		Provision for refunds
20×1	Beginning balance	-
	Actual refunds made	(-)1
	Estimated refunds	3*
	Ending balance	2
20×2	Actual refunds made	(-)2
	Estimated refunds	3*
	Ending balance	3

* Merchandise returned for a refund is scraped and the estimated amount of refunds is deducted from sales.

13. Share capital

The composition of share capital at the end of each year is as follow.

Year end	Type of stock	Par value	Number of share issued
20×2	Common stock	₩5,000	30 million shares
20×1	Common stock	₩5,000	20 million shares

14. Dividends

Computations of dividends and payout ratio for each year are as follow.

(Numbers in billions of ₩)

Year	Type of stock	Number shares subject to dividends	Per value dividend rate	Amount of dividends
20×2	Common stock	30 million shares	10%	15
20×1	Common stock	20 million shares	5%	5

* The same dividend rate is applied to all stock outstanding at the end of the year regardless of the issuance date of stock per the company's charter.

(Numbers in billions of ₩)

Year	Amount of dividends (1)	Net income (2)	Payout ratio [(1)/(2)]
20×2	15*	72	20.83%
20×1	5**	26	19.23%

* This represents the dividend payment plan of the management. If the plan is finalized by ballot at the stockholders meeting to be held on March 15, 20×3, they will be paid on March 22, 20×3.

** This was finalized by ballot at the stockholders meeting on March 14, 20×2 and paid on March 21, 20×2.

16. Statement of cash flows : non-cash transactions

Significant non-cash financing and investing transactions for each year are as follow.

(Numbers in billions of ₩)

Description	Amount	
	20×2	20×1
Acquisition of plant assets by issuing stock	–	60*

* It was the cash selling price of plant assets acquired. The company issued and distributed 10 million shares of common stock with par value of ₩5,000 on July 1, 20×1 to the seller.

An explanation of the case financial statements

▪ Note : Numbers in superscripts are main text page numbers where the corresponding subjects are explained.

The financial statements for 20×1 of Daehan Department Store that are related with this chapter are the statement of cash flows and the footnotes thereto. First, per Footnote 2 ©, we can find that Daehan Department Store computes the cash generated from operations using the indirect method[518], by adjusting net income before income tax expense (NIBITE) in the comprehensive income statement. Daehan Department Store also classifies the individually reporting items of income tax paid as an operating activity, of dividends received as inventing activities, and of interest paid and dividend paid as financing activities.[511] Footnote 4 instructs us that cash and cash equivalents[511] in the statement of cash flows are the same as cash and cash equivalents in the statement of financial position.

To avoid redundant explanation, here we explain in detail only the case of 20×2 ; we omit explanation of the case of 20×1. Daehan Department Store had net cash of ₩121 billion from operating activities, net cash of ₩177 billion used in investing activities, and net cash of ₩81 billion from financing activities, so there was a ₩4 billion increase in cash. Therefore, by adding the cash increase of ₩4 billion to the beginning cash balance of ₩41 billion, the ending cash balance of ₩45 was reported.

Items adjusted to NIBITE to compute the cash generated from operations are mainly 1) NIBITE expense related with individually reporting item,[519] 2) gain and loss from non-operating activities,[520] 3) operating expense without cash outflows and[522] 4) changes in assets and liabilities due to operating activities.[522] NIBITE for 20×2 was ₩102 billion. As NIBITE expense related with individually reporting item, the interest expense of ₩19 billion was added as an adjustment.[519] As gain and loss from non-operating activities, the equity income[522] of ₩6 billion (Footnote 7) was deducted as an adjustment. [In addition, the loss on the disposal of plant assets[520] in 20×1 (Footnote 8) was added back as an adjustment]. As an operating expense without cash outflows, the depreciation expense[522] of ₩10 billion was added as an adjustment. As changes in assets and liabilities due to operating activities,[522] the increase in trade receivables of ₩8 billion and the increase in merchandise of ₩20 billion were deducted as adjustments ; meanwhile, the increase in trade payables of ₩24 billion and the increase in provision for refunds of ₩1 billion (Footnote 11) were added back as adjustments. The decrease in salaries payable of ₩1 billion was subtracted as an adjustment. (In 20×1, on the contrary, the increase in salaries payable was added back as an adjustment). Because of these adjustments, the cash generated from operations was ₩121 billion. Then, an item to be reported individually was the income tax paid[524] of ₩21 billion (Income tax expense 30 billion - Increase in income tax payable 9 billion). It was deducted from cash generated from operations, and the 'net cash from operating activities' of ₩100 billion was computed.

In investing activities, cash of ₩2 billion dividends received (Footnote 7), an individually reporting item, flowed in.[525] And cash of ₩20 billion for the acquisition of stock of an associate (Footnote 7) ; ₩150 billion for acquisitions of plant assets (Footnote 8) ; and ₩9 billion for the acquisition of intangible assets (Footnote 8) flowed out.[525] As a result, net cash of ₩177 billion was reported as 'net cash used in investing activities.' In financing activities, cash of ₩10 billion from short-term borrowings (Footnote 9 ⓐ) ; ₩40 billion from long-term borrowings (Footnote 9 ⓑ) ; and ₩100 billion from the issuance of common stock (Footnote 13) flowed in.[527] And cash of ₩30 billion for the payment of short-term borrowings (Footnote 9 ⓐ) and ₩18 billion for the payment of the current portion of long-term borrowings (Footnote 9 ⓑ), as well as individually reporting items of ₩16 billion (Interest expense 19 billion - Increase in interest payable 1 billion - Amortization of discount on bonds payable 2 billion) for interest payment and ₩5 billion (dividends of 20×1) for dividend payment (Footnote 14) flowed out.[527] As a result, net cash of ₩81 billion was reported as 'net cash from financing activities.'

Footnote 16 reveals that the acquisition of plant assets by issuing stock on July 1, 20×1 was a noncash transaction.[528] Therefore, it was not reported in the statement of cash flows but was disclosed in the footnotes because it was an important investing and financing activity.

Key issues

The statement of cash flows reports how much cash inflows and outflows have occurred due to the firm's various activities over a one-year period. Therefore, if we examine this statement, we can find out how cash balance has changed over the year.

To aid in understanding the statement of cash flows, this book has reviewed issues related with the statement of cash flows in each chapter, as listed in the following 〈Table 11-1〉. In this chapter, we review subjects that we have not yet covered, particularly the indirect method of preparation.

〈Table 11-1〉 Subjects reviewed

Text	Subjects reviewed
Chapter 1	Three activities of a company and the statement of cash flows
Chapter 2	Nature and compositions of the statement of cash flows (direct method)
Chapter 3	Preparation of a statement of cash flows (direct method)
Chapter 4	Cash basis vs. Accrual basis (when there is no beginning balance)
Chapter 5	Cash basis vs. Accrual basis (when there are beginning balances)
Chapter 6	Sales, trade receivables and cash flows
Chapter 7	Purchases, inventory, cost of goods sold, trade payables, and cash flows
Chapter 8	Depreciation expense and cash flows
Chapter 9	Long-term borrowings and paying off current portion of long-term borrowings Bond interest expense, interest payable, amortization of discount on bonds payable, and cash flows
Chapter 10	Acquisitions and sales of treasury stock and dividends paid

1.1 Cash and cash equivalents

What should be considered cash in the statement of cash flows? Cash and cash equivalents are both considered 'cash' in this statement. Cash includes currency (paper money), coins, checks, and deposits in the bank. When a company temporarily has excess cash, rather than keeping that cash in a safe, it invests in financial instruments that give stable income and are marketable so they can be resold easily. When the company needs cash again, it sells those instruments and uses the cash proceeds. Reflecting the common use of these practices, 'cash,' in the statement of cash flows, includes financial instruments that are used as payment tools like cash. These financial instruments are called cash equivalents (현금성자산). To qualify as cash equivalents per IFRS[1], financial instruments must be readily convertible to a known amount of cash and must be subject to an insignificant risk of changing value because their maturity dates are within three months. Examples are MMFs (Money Market Funds), CDs (Certificates of Deposit), and government bonds and corporate bonds with maturity dates within 3 months. Cash equivalents are valued at the market value at active market. Cash and cash equivalents in the statement of financial position are the same as those in the statement of cash flows. In the statement of cash flows in this book, we simply use 'cash' to refer to 'cash and cash equivalents.'

1.2 Items for which multiple classification methods are allowed

Companies classify cash flows, such as interest received, dividends received, interest paid, dividends paid, and income tax paid, in various ways. IFRS[2] allows all different methods rather than unifying them. But it does require that these items should each be reported individually, so that a comparison between companies can be possible by making simple additions and deductions. (In this book, we present a caption of 'individually reporting items' in the statement of cash flows to highlight that these items should be reported individually. The caption can be omitted, as long as these items are reported individually).

1) Interest received and dividends received, and interest paid and dividends paid

In theory, interest received and dividends received should be classified as investing activities, because they are returns on investments. Interest paid, on the other hand, should be classified as a financing activity because it is paid for money-generating financing activities. If we classify these items according to the theory, then the operating activities applied to compute income from operations in the comprehensive income statement and those applied to compute operating cash flows in the statement of cash flows are the same.

Companies either classify interest received, dividends received, and interest paid per the theory, as explained above, or they classify all those items as operating activities, applying the old Korean accounting standards (This is presently still required by the US GAAP.). This kind of exception to the theory is allowed so that firms can compute their cash flows from operating activities by the same method they use to compute net income in the comprehensive income statement. In other words, because interest received, dividends received, and interest paid are related, respectively, to interest income, dividend income, and interest expense—which are included in computing net income—firms classify them as operating activities. This classification method has an advantage: Users of accounting information can compare net income with cash flows from operating activities easily, without additional reconciliations. But it has the disadvantage of confusion, because operating activities considered in the comprehensive income statement are different from operating activities considered in the statement of cash flows.

Per the theory, dividends paid should be classified as a financing activity because they are related to fund-generating financing activities, as is interest paid. Some companies classify dividends paid as a financing activity, following this theory. However, other companies exceptionally classify dividends paid as an operating activity, because they consider the fact that companies pay dividends with cash generated from operations.

IFRS[3] accepts all the above-mentioned: the theory, the old Korean standards, and the exception in practice for dividend payment. Therefore, it allows companies to classify each instance of interest received and dividends received as investing activities or operating activities, and to classify each instance of interest paid and dividends paid as financing activities or operating activities, as seen in 〈Table 11-2〉 below. This standard, of allowing 2 classification methods for each of 4 items, creates a total of 16 ($2 \times 2 \times 2 \times 2$) different ways to report these four items.

〈Table 11-2〉 IFRS classification–interest and dividends

Description	Investing activities	Financing activities	Operating activities
Interest received	O		O
Dividends received	O		O
Interest paid		O	O
Dividends paid		O	O

2) Income tax paid

Companies pay income tax for income not only from operating activities, but also from investing and financing activities. It is, however, rather difficult to identify income tax by activity. Even when income tax is identified by activity, it is almost impossible to report income tax paid on these different activities because the timing of payment and timing of transaction that cause the income tax are different. For this reason, income tax expense is not divided between operating income and other income, but is reported in an aggregate amount in the comprehensive income statement. Therefore, IFRS[4] allows companies to report income tax by different activities in the statement of cash flows if it is possible to identify income tax by different activities and to report the total amount of tax as an operating activity if it is not possible as shown in 〈Table 11-3〉 below. If a company reports income tax paid by each activity in the statement of cash flows, it should disclose a total amount in a footnote.

〈Table 11-3〉 IFRS classification–income tax paid

Description	Possible to identify by each activities			Impossible to identify by each activities		
	Operating activities	Investing activities	Financing activities	Operating activities	Investing activities	Financing activities
Income tax paid	Applicable amount	Applicable amount	Applicable amount	Total amount		

Following most companies' practice, this book classifies income tax paid as an operating activity, under the assumption that it is impossible to identify income tax by each activity.

3) Individually reporting of interest received, dividends received, interest paid, dividends paid, income tax paid

Multiple classification methods reviewed above allow companies to report different factors in each activity and jeopardize the comparability of accounting information among companies. IFRS[5] requires companies to report all these items individually in the statement of cash flows, no matter what activities these items are classified under, and to separately report 'cash generated from operations,' exclusive of these items in the statement of cash flows. This is so that users of accounting information can easily compare one company's cash flows with another company's cash flows.

4) Four examples of multiple classification methods

Items that the multiple classifications are allowed are interest received, dividends received, interest paid, and dividends paid. We will review four examples of different classification methods of these items with 〈Illustration 11-1〉 below.

〈Illustration 11-1〉 Multiple classification methods

The following 〈Table 11-4〉 are data gathered for preparation of a statement of cash flows for Songho Trading Co. for 20×2.

〈Table 11-4〉 Data to prepare a statement of cash flows

(Numbers in billions of ₩)

Description	Amount
Cash generated from operations	47
Investing cash flows other than interest and dividends received	(−)62
Financing cash flows other than interest and dividends paid	29
Individually reporting items :	
Income tax paid	(−)6
Interest received	2
Dividends received	8
Interest paid	(−)7
Dividends paid	(−)9

〈Table 11-5〉 Statements of cash flows by four different classification methods

From January 1, 20×2 to December 31, 20×2

Songho Trading Co. (Numbers in billions of ₩)

Description	Theory	Past standards	Most net cash from operating activities	Least net cash from operating activities
Cash flows from operating activities				
Cash generated from operations	**47**	**47**	**47**	**47**
Individually reporting items :				
Income tax paid	(−)6	(−)6	(−)6	(−)6
Interest received		2	2	
Dividends received		8	8	
Interest paid		(−)7		(−)7
Dividends paid				(−)9
Net cash from operating activities	**41**	**44**	**51**	**25**
Cash flows from investing activities				
Cash flows other than interest received and dividends received	(−)62	(−)62	(−)62	(−)62
Individually reporting items :				
Interest received	2			2
Dividends received	8			8
Net cash used in investing activities	**(−)52**	**(−)62**	**(−)62**	**(−)52**
Cash flows from financing activities				
Cash flows other than interest paid and dividends paid	29	29	29	29
Individually reporting items :				
Interest paid	(−)7		(−)7	
Dividends paid	(−)9	(−)9	(−)9	
Net cash from financing activities	**13**	**20**	**13**	**29**
Net increase in cash	**2**	**2**	**2**	**2**

〈Table 11-5〉 shows 4 different classification methods, from among the 16 possible methods allowed by IFRS. As seen in this table, 'cash generated from operations' is the operating cash flows before the individually reporting items. The individually reporting items, as noted, can be classified by theory (as shown in 'Theory' column) or by the old accounting standards (as shown in 'Past standards' column). Depending on the incentives of reporting companies, these items can be classified as shown in 'Most net cash from operating activities' column or in 'Least net cash from operating activities' column. 'Most net cash from operating activities' is a classification method by which a company can report the maximum amount of net cash from operating activities, when compared with the other methods. In this method, items generating cash inflows (such as interest received and dividends received) are classified as 'operating activities,' while items requiring cash outflows (such as interest paid and dividends paid) are classified as 'financing activities.' 'Least net cash from operating activities,' in contrast, is a classification method by which a company can report the minimum amount of net cash from operating activities, as compared to other methods. In this method, items requiring cash outflows (such as interest paid and dividends paid) are classified as 'operating activities,' while items generating cash inflows (such as interest received and dividends received) are classified as 'investing activities.'

This book is based on 'Theory,' i.e., the theory noted in the preceding pages. It classifies interest received and dividends received as investing activities, and interest paid and dividends paid as financing activities.

Cash flows from operating activities

Net cash from operating activities is computed by adding or subtracting individually reporting items from the cash generated from operations. As previously noted, there are two methods—direct and indirect—to compute cash generated from operations. The same amount of cash generated from operations is obtained, using either of two methods. In practice, most companies use the indirect method because it is easy to prepare the statement.

2.1 Direct method

In Chapters 3 through 5, the direct method of preparing a statement of cash flows was reviewed. ⟨Table 11-6⟩ shows a format for directly reporting cash generated from operations, in the statement of cash flows.

⟨Table 11-6⟩ Format of statement cash flows using direct method

Description	Amount	
Cash flows from operating activities :		
Cash receipts from customers	×××	
Cash paid to suppliers and employees	(−)×××	
Cash generated from operations	×××	
Individually reporting item :		
Income taxes paid	(−)×××	
Net cash from operating activities		×××

If cash flows from operating activities are computed by the direct method, then, first, the cash generated from operations is computed by subtracting cash paid to suppliers and employees from the cash receipts from customers. Next, individually reporting items are added or subtracted. The composition of individually reporting items (as reviewed above) depends upon how interest received, dividends received, interest paid, dividends paid, and income tax paid are classified. This book adopts the classification method by theory, as explained above. So we report only income tax paid as an individually reporting item in operating activities.

Because the statement of cash flows, when prepared in the direct method, reports cash inflows and outflows from operating activities by their causes, it is easy even for those with a limited accounting background to understand how much cash was received from what source and how much cash was paid for what purpose in operating activities. The direct method also makes it easy to forecast future cash flows, because it reports cash flows by their generating sources. Because of this, IFRS[6] recommends the direct method. Yet it takes a lot of effort to report cash flows from operating activities in the direct method. Transactions with customers and suppliers are made so frequently, and are sometimes done in cash and sometimes on credit. To compute cash receipts from customers and cash paid to suppliers and employees, one must classify and compute cash flows separately. That process is very complex and cumbersome. Therefore, even though the statement of cash flows is prepared in the direct method, the cash flow from each item is computed in the indirect method (See 5.6 'Preparing a direct method statement of cash flows by the indirect method'). In practice, most companies (all listed companies in Korea, when the old accounting standards were applied) are using the indirect method because it is easy to use.

2.2 Indirect method

The indirect method is a method that indirectly computes cash generated from operations, by adding or subtracting adjusting items to a certain income in the comprehensive income statement, using information in the statement of financial position and comprehensive income statement. Although any income in the comprehensive income statement can be adjusted, net income or net income before income tax expense are the ones that are adjusted because other comprehensive income does not generate cash flows. Following an illustration given by IFRS[7], this book adjusts net income before income tax expense to compute cash generated from operations.

Items that should be adjusted to net income before income tax expense (NIBITE), to compute cash generated from operations, are called adjusting items. IFRS shows adjusting items under the caption of 'adjustments,' in the illustrations. ⟨Table 11-7⟩ is a classification of these adjusting items, to aid in understanding them better. Adjusting items can be classified as: 1) NIBITE revenue and expense related with individually reporting items, 2) gain and loss from non-operating activities, 3) operating expense without cash outflows, and 4) changes in assets and liabilities due to operating activities.

〈Table 11-7〉 Format of statement of cash flows using indirect method

Description	Amount	
Cash flows from operating activities		
Net income before income tax expense (NIBITE)		×××
Adjustments :		
NIBITE revenues and expense related with individually reporting items		×××
Interest revenue	(−)×××	
Dividends revenue	(−)×××	
Interest expense	×××	
Gain and loss from non-operating activities		(−)×××
Gain on disposal of tangible assets	(−)×××	
Equity income	(−)×××	
Loss on retirement of debts	×××	
Operating expense without cash outflows		×××
Depreciation expense	×××	
Changes in assets and liabilities due to operating activities		
Increase in assets due to operating activities	(−)×××	
Decrease in assets due to operating activities	×××	
Increase in liabilities due to operating activities	×××	
Increase in liabilities due to operating activities	(−)×××	
Cash generated from operations		×××
Individually reporting item :		
Income tax paid		(−)×××
Net cash from operating activities		×××

(1) NIBITE revenues and expense related with individually reporting items

The first items to be adjusted back to net income before income tax expense (NIBITE), to compute cash generated from operations, are NIBITE revenues and expense related to individually reporting items. The reason for making these adjustments is to avoid reporting these items twice.

Individually reporting items should be presented after cash generated from operations is presented. As can be seen in 〈Table 11-8〉, interest revenue, dividends revenue and interest expense are all reflected already in 'NIBITE.' If these items are individually reported without reverse-adjustments, then they are reported once when NIBITE is reported and then again as individually reporting items, thus creating a problem of double-reporting. Therefore, interest revenue and dividends revenue should be deducted and interest expense should be added back to NIBITE. Because income tax expense and dividends paid are not reflected in NIBITE, there is no need to adjust them.

⟨Table 11-8⟩ Adjustments of NIBITE revenues and expense related with individually reporting items

Description	Individually reporting items				
Net income before income tax expense (NIBITE)	Interest revenue	Dividends revenue	Interest expense	Income tax expense	Dividends paid
	'After'	'After'	'After'	'Before'	'Before'
Adjustments in statement of cash flows :	Subtract back	Subtract back	Add back	-	-

Instead of adjusting NIBITE, one can adjust net income to compute cash generated from operations. Net income is 'after' income tax expense. Therefore, income tax expense should be additionally added back to net income after adjusting the three items noted above (interest revenue, dividends revenue, and interest expense), so not to report this item twice.

(2) Gain and loss from non-operating activities

Non-operating activities are investing activities and financing activities. Because gain and loss from investing activities and financing activities—regardless of cash flows—do not come from operating activities, they should not be included in 'cash flows from operating activities.' Yet these gain and loss are reflected in NIBITE. Therefore, gain and loss from non-operating activities should be subtracted and added, respectively, to NIBITE.

A typical example of a gain from non-operating activities is a gain on the disposal of tangible assets. This is a gain incurred by selling a tangible asset, such as land or a plant asset, at a price higher than the book value of that asset. Selling tangible assets is not an operating activity but an investing activity. Therefore, it should not be included in cash flows from operating activities. Because a gain on disposal of tangible assets is included in NIBITE, a gain on the disposal of tangible assets should be deducted from NIBITE, to compute cash generated from operations.

⟨Illustration 11-2⟩ shows an adjustment of gain on the disposal of tangible assets to NIBITE.

〈Illustration 11-2〉 Adjustment of gain on disposal of tangible asset

The following 〈Table 11-9〉 is Daehan Trading Ltd.'s condensed income statement for 20×1. Gain on disposal of tangible assets was made by selling land with book value of ₩120 billion at ₩130 billion. There was no depreciation expense and all revenues and expenses were made in cash. Income tax paid was the same as income tax expense.

〈Table 11-9〉 Condensed income statement

From Jan. 1, 20×1
Daehan Trading Ltd. to Dec. 31, 20×1 (Numbers in billions of ₩)

Account titles	Amount
Sales	300
Cost of goods sold	(−)230
Salaries expense	(−)20
Gain on disposal of tangible asset	10
Net income before income tax expense (NIBITE)	60
Income tax expense	(−)12
Net income	48

The following 〈Table 11-10〉 are Daehan Trading Ltd.'s cash flows from operating activities computed by indirect method and direct method.

〈Table 11-10〉 Cash flows from operating activities (direct method and indirect method)

From Jan. 1, 20×1
Daehan Trading Ltd. to Dec. 31, 20×1 (Numbers in billions of ₩)

Description	Indirect method	Direct method
Sales	300	300
Cost of goods sold	(−)230	(−)230
Salaries expense	(−)20	(−)20
Gain on disposal of tangible asset	10	
Net income before income tax expense (NIBITE)	60	
Adjustment : Gain on disposal of tangible asset	(−)10	
Cash generated from operations	50	50
Income tax paid	(−)12	(−)12
Net cash from operating activities	38	38

NIBITE of Daehan Trading Ltd. for 20×1 is ₩60 billion, and cash generated from operations using the direct method is ₩50 billion. The difference between these items is the gain on disposal of tangible assets of ₩10 billion. Hence, we should deduct the gain on disposal of tangible assets of ₩10 billion from NIBITE, to compute cash generated from operations. On the other hand, net cash from operating activities is ₩38 billion, which is obtained by subtracting income tax paid of ₩12 billion from cash generated from operations of ₩50 billion.

A gain or loss on the retirement of debts is from non-operating activities. The details concerning this item will be reviewed in the Intermediate Accounting course. Equity income which will be reviewed in Appendix is also from non-operating activities.

(3) Operating expense without cash outflows

Although operating expense without cash outflows was reflected in NIBITE, that should not be included in cash generated from operations because that was not accompanied by any cash flows. Therefore, we should add operating expense without cash flows to NIBITE.

A typical example of an operating expense without cash outflows is a depreciation expense. The relationship between depreciation expense and cash flows was already reviewed in Chapter 8. Other examples of operating expenses without cash outflows are impairment loss of tangible assets, amortization of intangible assets. Impairment loss of tangible assets and amortization expense of intangible assets are the same kind of operating expense as a depreciation expense, as reviewed in Chapter 8. Amortization of discount on bonds payable is interest expense without cash outflows as reviewed in Chapter 9. Because interest expense is not an operating expense, amortization of discount on bonds payable should be considered when interest paid is computed in '3.2 (2)' below.

(4) Changes in assets and liabilities due to operating activities

In the supplementary material in Chapter 5, Section 1, we closely examined the differences between the information shown in the statement of cash flows and in the income statement. These differences involve changes in assets and liabilities due to operating activities, to be adjusted to NIBITE in order to compute cash generated from operations. To avoid redundant explanations, here we will exclusively review how to adjust changes in assets and liabilities due to operating activities, to NIBITE.

Changes in assets and liabilities due to operating activities involve the increase or decrease of the ending balance, in comparison with the beginning balance, of each of those assets and liabilities. To compute cash generated from operations, we should subtract an increase in those assets and a decrease in those liabilities from NIBITE as shown in ⟨Table 11-11⟩ below. (Logic : In a cash transaction, if there is an increase in an asset or a decrease in a liability, cash will be decreased.) We should likewise add a decrease in those assets and an increase in those liabilities to NIBITE (Logic : In a cash transaction, if there is an decrease in an asset or an increase in a liability, cash will be increased.).

⟨Table 11-11⟩ Adjustments of changes in assets and liabilities due to operating activities

Description	Adjustment to net income before income tax expense (NIBITE)	
	Increase	Decrease
Assets related with operating activities (Trade receivables, Accrued revenue, Inventory, Prepaid expense)	(-)	(+)
Liabilities related with operating activities (Unearned revenue, Trade payables, Accrued expense)	(+)	(-)

Changes in assets and liabilities that are related with individually reporting items are not included in 'changes in assets and liabilities due to operating activities.' This is because changes in these assets and liabilities should be considered when individually reporting items are computed. For example, prepaid income tax and income tax payable are assets and liabilities related to operating activities. Yet changes in them are not reported as changes in assets and liabilities due to operating activities. This is because the changes in prepaid income tax and income tax payable should be considered when income tax paid—an individually reporting item—is computed. (Refer to (5) 'Individually reporting item : income tax paid' below).

(5) Individually reporting item : income tax paid

Net cash from operating activities is computed by deducting individually reporting items from the cash generated from operations. As this book applies theoretical classification and assumes income tax paid cannot be classified amongst operating, investing and financing activities, only the total amount of income tax paid is reported as an individually reporting item in operating activities. Income tax paid is computed by adjusting changes in prepaid income tax and in income tax payable to the income tax expense, as shown in 〈Table 11-12〉 below.

〈Table 11-12〉 Computation of income tax paid

<table>
<tr><th>Description</th><th colspan="3">Computation</th></tr>
<tr><td rowspan="2">Income tax paid
(−)XXX</td><td rowspan="2">Income tax expense
(−)XXX</td><td>Prepaid income tax</td><td>Increase (−)×××
Decrease (+)×××</td></tr>
<tr><td>Income tax payable</td><td>Increase (+)×××
Decrease (−)×××</td></tr>
</table>

Cash flows from investing and financing activities

3.1 Cash flows from investing activities

Investing activities include activities of acquiring and disposing of a piece of land or a plant asset, as well as providing and collecting loans. Cash flows from investing activities are reported by segregating each transaction by cash inflows and cash outflows, as shown in the following 〈Table 11-13〉. As this book applies theoretical classification, interest received by making loans and dividends received by investing in stock are reported as individually reporting items in investing activities.

〈Table 11-13〉 Cash inflows and outflows from inventing activities

Cash inflows from investing activities	Collecting short-term loans, Collecting long-term loans, Disposing a piece of land, Disposing a plant asset
	Individually reporting items : Interest received, Dividends received
Cash outflows for investing activities	Making short-term loans, Making long-term loans, Purchasing a piece of land, Purchasing a plant asset, Investing in stock

(1) Acquisition and disposition of an asset, making and collecting loans

If a piece of land or a plant asset is acquired, then corresponding assets are increased. If these assets are disposed of, corresponding assets are decreased. Likewise, if loans are made, then the loans are increased and if the loans are collected, the loans are decreased. If an asset is only increased or only decreased by investing activities, then we can find the monetary impact of the investing activities by examining the increase or decrease in the corresponding asset in the statement of financial position. However, if increases and decreases in the corresponding asset occur together, we cannot find the monetary impact of investing activities by examining the net increase or net decrease in the corresponding asset in the statement of financial position, because they have offset each other. Therefore, to make it possible to find cash inflows and outflows from investing activities, we should conduct T account analyses and identify the increase and decrease in the corresponding accounts in the statement of financial position. Detailed procedures of identifying increase and decrease through T account analyses are reviewed in the following Section 5, 'A comprehensive illustration of preparing a statement of cash flows.'

(2) Individually reporting items

Interest received and dividends received, which are reported as individually reporting items in investing activities, are computed as shown in 〈Table 11-14〉 below. Interest received is computed by adjusting changes in interest receivable and in unearned interest to interest revenue. Dividends received are computed by adjusting changes in dividends receivable to dividend revenue.

〈Table 11-14〉 Computations of interest received and dividends received

<table>
<tr><th>Description</th><th colspan="3">Computation</th></tr>
<tr><td rowspan="2">Interest received
(+)×××</td><td rowspan="2">Interest revenue
(+)×××</td><td>Interest receivable</td><td>Increase (−)×××
Decrease (+)×××</td></tr>
<tr><td>Unearned interest</td><td>Increase (+)×××
Decrease (−)×××</td></tr>
<tr><td>Dividends received
(+)×××</td><td>Dividends revenue
(+)×××</td><td>Dividends receivable</td><td>Increase (−)×××
Decrease (+)×××</td></tr>
</table>

3.2 Cash flows from financing activities

Financing activities are activities associated with generating funds, such as issuing stock; issuing bonds and retiring bonds; and borrowing money and paying back the money borrowed. Cash flows from financing activities are reported by segregating each transaction by cash inflows and cash outflows as shown in the following 〈Table 11-15〉. As this book applies theoretical classification, interest paid on borrowing and dividends paid to stockholders are reported as individually reporting items in financing activities.

⟨Table 11-15⟩ Cash inflows and outflows from financing activities

Cash inflows from financing activities	Short-term borrowings, Long-term borrowings, Issuing bonds, Issuing stock
Cash outflows for financing activities	Paying off short-term borrowings, Paying off current portion of long-term borrowings
	Individually reporting items : Interest paid, Dividends paid

(1) Borrowings and paying off borrowings

As with investing activities, by comparing the statement of financial position at the end of last year with the same statement at the end of the current year, financing cash inflows and outflows cannot be found. Therefore, to find cash inflows and outflows from financing activities we should identify the increase and decrease in the corresponding accounts in the statement of financial position through T account analyses of these accounts.

(2) Individually reporting items

Interest paid and dividends paid, which are reported as individually reporting items in financing activities, are computed as shown in ⟨Table 11-16⟩ below. Interest paid is computed by adjusting changes in interest payable and in prepaid interest, and amortization of discount or premium on bonds payable (reviewed in Chapter 9) to interest expense. Dividends paid are computed by adjusting changes in dividends payable to dividends.

⟨Table 11-16⟩ Computations of interest paid and dividends paid

Description	Computation		
Interest paid (−)×××	Interest expense (−)×××	Prepaid interest	Increase (−)××× Decrease (+)×××
		Interest payable	Increase (+)××× Decrease (−)×××
		Amortization of (*) on bonds payable	(*) Premium (−)××× (*) Discount (+)×××
Dividends paid (−)×××	Dividends (−)×××	Dividends payable	Increase (+)××× Decrease (−)×××

Non-cash transactions

The statement of cash flows reports cash inflows and outflows of a company for a given period. Therefore, in this statement only transactions accompanying cash flows are reported ; transactions not accompanying cash flows (non-cash transactions) are not reported. Yet there could be a non-cash transaction amongst a firm's important investing and financing activities. For example, a company could acquire an asset by issuing stock instead of paying cash. In that case, since there was no cash flow, the transaction is not reported in the statement of cash flows. But it is in fact a very important investing and financing transaction, changing an asset and equity ; therefore, we should report it to users of the company's financial statements. Hence, IFRS[8] requires a footnote disclosure of non-cash investing and financing transactions.

A comprehensive illustration of preparing a statement of cash flows

In the previous section, we have reviewed the direct and indirect methods for computing cash flows from operating activities, as well as how to report cash flows from investing and financing activities. Here we introduce an illustration of the indirect method of preparing a statement of cash flows, using a two-year comparative statement of financial position and an income statement. In addition, we show the direct method of preparing a statement of cash flows, using the outcomes of the indirect method.

Because the indirect method introduced here in this book uses reference tables, we may call this method as the 'reference table method.' If there is a cash inflow or a cash outflow, the financial position of the company is changed. Applying this notion reverse, the reference table method is a method explaining the changes in financial position with cash inflows and outflows using reference tables.

5.1 Statement of financial position and income statement

The following ⟨Table 11-17⟩ and ⟨Table 11-18⟩ are Heemang Department Store's statement of financial position at the end of 20×2 and 20×1, and its income statement for 20×2, respectively. The company classifies income tax paid as an operating activity; interest received as an investing activity; and interest paid and dividends paid as financing activities.

〈Table 11-17〉 Statement of financial position

Heemang Department Store (Numbers in billions of ₩)

Account titles	Dec. 31, 20×2		Dec. 31, 20×1	
Assets				
Current assets				
Cash		17		13
Trade receivables		18		43
Short-term loans		25		20
Interest receivable		2		3
Prepaid insurance		3		2
Merchandise		29		17
Non-current assets				
Land		80		56
Building	109		67	
Accumulated depreciation	(-)34	75	(-)28	39
Total assets		249		193
Liabilities				
Current liabilities				
Trade payables		26		18
Short-term borrowings		15		22
Current portion of long-term borrowings		11		5
Unearned rent		1		4
Interest payable		4		2
Income tax payable		3		2
Non-current liability				
Long-term borrowings		36		17
Bonds payable		19		18
Total liabilities		115		88
Equity				
Share capital-common stock		120		100
Share premium-common stock		2		2
Retained earnings		12		3
Total equity		134		105
Total liabilities and equity		249		193

〈Table 11-18〉 Income statement

From January 1, 20×2 to December 31, 20×2

Heemang Department Store (Numbers in billions of ₩)

Account titles	Amount	
Sales		211
Cost of goods sold		(−)124
Gross profit		87
Operating expenses		(−)69
Salaries expense	(−)47	
Depreciation expense	(−)6	
Insurance expense	(−)16	
Other operating revenue:		5
Rent revenue	5	
Income from operations		23
Other revenues		10
Interest revenue	1	
Gain on disposal of tangible assets	9	
Other expense		(−)9
Interest expense	(−)9	
Net income before income tax expense (NIBITE)		24
Income tax expense		(−)6
Net income		18

5.2 T account analysis

Statement of financial position accounts for which we do and do not need to conduct the T account analysis are listed in the following 〈Table 11-19〉. The accounts not requiring the analysis are the ones we need to directly show the difference between the balances at the beginning of the year and at the end of the year in the statement of cash flows. The accounts requiring the analysis are the ones we need to show increasing factors and decreasing factors causing the difference between the balances at the beginning of the year and at the end of the year in the statement of cash flows. The increasing factors and decreasing factors of each account are computed by analysing debit and credit entries of the corresponding account over the year.

〈Table 11-19〉 Accounts subject to T account analysis

No need	Need
Cash, Trade receivables, Interest receivable, Prepaid insurance, Merchandise, Trade payables, Unearned rent. Interest payable, Income tax payable	Short-term loans, Land, Building, Accumulated depreciation, Short-term borrowings, Current portion of long-term borrowings, Long-term borrowings, Bonds payable, Share capital-common stock, Retained earnings

The following 〈Diagram 11-1〉 are results of the T accounts analyses of Heemang Department Store's applicable statement of financial position accounts.

〈Diagram 11-1〉 T account analyses

(Numbers in billions of ₩)

Short-term loans

		Beginning 20(Dr.)
① Loans made 30		50(Dr.)
	② Collection 25	Ending 25(Dr.)

Land

		Beginning 56(Dr.)
③ Purchase 40		96(Dr.)
	④ Disposal 16	Ending 80(Dr.)

Building

		Beginning 67(Dr.)
⑤ Purchase 42		Ending 109(Dr.)

Accumulated depreciation

		Beginning 28(Cr.)
	ⓚ Depreciation expense 6	Ending 34(Cr.)

ⓚ : Obtained from the income statement

Short-term borrowings

				Beginning	22(Cr.)
		⑥ Borrowing	30		52(Cr.)
⑦ Retirement	37			Ending	15(Cr.)

Current portion of long-term borrowings

				Beginning	5(Cr.)
⑧ Retirement	5				–
		⑨ Reclassification	11	Ending	11(Cr.)

Long-term borrowings

				Beginning	17(Cr.)
		⑩ Borrowing	30		47(Cr.)
⑨ Reclassification	11			Ending	36(Cr.)

Bonds payable

				Beginning	18(Cr.)
		⑪ Amortization of discount	1	Ending	19(Cr.)

Share capital—common stock

				Beginning	100(Cr.)
		⑫ Issuance of common stock	20	Ending	120(Cr.)

Retained earnings

				Beginning	3(Cr.)
		① NIBITE	24		
					27(Cr.)
ⓜ Income tax expense	6				21(Cr.)
⑬ Dividends	9			Ending	12(Cr.)

①ⓜ : Obtained from the income statement

The following ⟨Table 11-20⟩ is a summary of income statement items used in

T account analyses.

〈Table 11-20〉 Income statement items used in T account analyses

	Income statement items
ⓚ	Depreciation expense was ₩6 billion.
ⓛ	NIBITE was ₩24 billion.
ⓜ	Income tax expense was ₩6 billion.

The following 〈Table 11-21〉 is a summary of information obtained from T account analyses.

〈Table 11-21〉 Additional information obtained from T account analyses

	Additional information
①	Made short-term loans of ₩30 billion.
②	Collected short-term loans of ₩25 billion.
③	Purchased land and paid ₩40 billion in cash.
④	Sold a piece of land with acquisition cost of ₩16 billion.
⑤	Purchased a building and paid ₩42 billion in cash.
⑥	Borrowed ₩30 billion for short term.
⑦	Paid off ₩37 billion of short-term borrowings.
⑧	Paid off ₩5 billion of current portion of long-term borrowings.
⑨	Reclassified long-term borrowings of ₩11 into current portion of long-term borrowings
⑩	Borrowed ₩30 billion for long term.
⑪	Amortization of discount on bonds payable was ₩1 billion.
⑫	Issued 4 million shares of common stock (par value of ₩5,000 per share) at par value, and received cash of ₩20 billion.
⑬	Paid dividends of ₩9 billion in cash.

5.3 Preparation of reference tables

To effectively prepare a statement of cash flows using the indirect method, we should, as shown 〈Table 11-22〉, 〈Table 11-23〉 and 〈Table 11-24〉 below: 1) compute changes in financial position during the current year [indicate (−) for increase in asset and decrease in liability, and (+) for decrease in asset and increase in liability] and create a reference column in the statement of financial position, 2) make a reference column in the income statement, 3) prepare a statement of cash flows format that includes a reference column.

〈Table 11-22〉 Statement of financial position reference table

Heemang Department Store (Numbers in billions of ₩)

Account titles	Dec. 31, 20×2	Dec. 31, 20×1	Change	Reference
Assets				
Current assets				
Cash	17	13	(−)4	
Trade receivables	18	43	25	
Short-term loans	25	20	(−)5	
Interest receivable	2	3	1	
Prepaid insurance	3	2	(−)1	
Merchandise	29	17	(−)12	
Non-current assets				
Land	80	56	(−)24	
Building	109	67	(−)42	
Accumulated depreciation	(−)34	(−)28	6	
	75	39	(−)36	
Total assets	249	193	(−)56	
Liabilities				
Current liabilities				
Trade payables	26	18	8	
Short-term borrowings	15	22	(−)7	
Current portion of long-term borrowings	11	5	6	
Unearned rent	1	4	(−)3	
Interest payable	4	2	2	
Income tax payable	3	2	1	
Non-current liability				
Long-term borrowings	36	17	19	
Bonds payable	19	18	1	
Total liabilities	115	88	27	
Equity				
Share capital-common stock	120	100	20	
Share premium-common stock	2	2	-	
Retained earnings	12	3	9	
Total equity	134	105	29	
Total liabilities and equity	249	193	56	

〈Table 11-23〉 Income statement reference table

From January 1, 20×2 to December 31, 20×2

Heemang Department Store (Numbers in billions of ₩)

Account titles	Amount		Reference
Sales		211	
Cost of goods sold		(−)124	
Gross profit		87	
Operating expenses		(−)69	
Salaries expense	(−)47		
Depreciation expense	(−)6		
Insurance expense	(−)16		
Other operating revenue		5	
Rent revenue	5		
Income from operations		23	
Other revenues		10	
Interest revenue	1		
Gain on disposal of tangible assets	9		
Other expense		(−)9	
Interest expense	(−)9		
Net income before income tax expense (NIBITE)		24	
Income tax expense		(−)6	
Net income		18	

⟨Table 11-24⟩ Statement of cash flows reference table

From January 1, 20×2 to December 31, 20×2

Heemang Department Store (Numbers in billions of ₩)

Description	Amount	Reference
Cash flows from operating activities		
Net income before income tax expense (NIBITE)		
Adjustments :		
NIBITE revenue and expense related with individually reporting items		
Interest revenue		
Interest expense		
Gain from non-operating activities		
Gain on disposal of tangible assets		
Operating expense without cash outflows		
Depreciation expense		
Changes in assets and liabilities due to operating activities		
Decrease in trade receivables		
Increase in prepaid insurance		
Increase in merchandise		
Increase in trade payables		
Decrease in unearned rent		
Cash generated from operations		
Individually reporting item :		
Income tax paid		
Net cash from operating activities		
Cash flows from investing activities		
Disposal of land		
Collection of short-term loans		
Individually reporting item :		
Interest received		
Short-term loans (made)		
Purchase of land		
Purchase of building		
Net cash used in investing activities		
Cash flows from financing activities		
Proceeds from short-term borrowings		
Proceeds from long-term borrowings		
Proceeds from issuing common stock		
Retirement of short-term borrowings		
Retirement of current portion of long-term borrowings		
Individually reporting items :		
Interest paid		
Dividends paid		
Net cash from financing activities		
Net increase in cash		
Cash at beginning of period		
Cash at end of period		

5.4 Cross referencing

The reference table method prepares a statement of cash flows by making cross reference among reference tables. Items in the statement of cash flows can be classified items that can be explained by changes in financial position and items that can not be explained by changes in financial position. The later items are the income statement items.

5.4.1 Items that can not be explained by changes in financial position

Income statement ⇨ Statement of cash flows

Items in the statement of cash flows that can not be explained by changes in financial position are some of items reflected in NIBITE that need to reclassify activities. They can be classified into (1) items related with individually reporting items and (2) items related with non-operating activities.

(1) NIBITE revenue and expense related with individually reporting items

Look for NIBITE revenue and expense related with individually reporting items in the income statement. In case of Heemang Department store, its interest revenue and interest expense are NIBITE revenue and expense related with individually reporting items. Identify interest revenue of ₩1 billion and interest expense of ₩9 billion and mark ⓤ and ⓥ, respectively, in the income statement reference table as shown in 〈Table 11-25〉 below. You should also mark ⓤ and ⓥ and record the amounts twice as additions and deductions in the statement of cash flows reference table, as shown in 〈Table 11-26〉 below.

〈Table 11-25〉 Income statement reference table–Interest revenue and Interest expense

From January 1, 20×2 to December 31, 20×2

Heemang Department Store (Numbers in billions of ₩)

Account titles	Amount		Reference
Other revenues			
Interest revenue	1		Ⓤ
Other expense			
Interest expense	(−)9		Ⓥ

〈Table 11-26〉 Statement of cash flows reference table–Interest received and Interest paid

From January 1, 20×2 to December 31, 20×2

Heemang Department Store (Numbers in billions of ₩)

Description	Amount		Reference*
Cash flows from operating activities			
NIBITE revenue and expense related with individually reporting items		8	
Interest revenue	(−)1		Ⓤ
Interest expense	9		Ⓥ
Cash flows from investing activities			
Individually reporting item :			
Interest received			Ⓤ 1**
Cash flows from financing activities			
Individually reporting item :			
Interest paid			Ⓥ (−)9***

* If there is only one item, we record the amount in the 'amount' column.

** There will be one more item from [5.1.2 (2) 2)] below, so we record the amount in the 'reference' column.

*** There will be two more items from [5.1.2 (2) 2) and 5.1.2 (3) 2)] below, so we record the amount in the 'reference' column.

(2) Gain and loss from non-operating activities

Look for gain and loss from non-operating activities in the income statement. In case of Heemang Department store, the gain on disposal of tangible assets is a gain from non-operating activities. Identify the gain on disposal of tangible assets of ₩9 billion in the income statement reference table as shown in 〈Table 11-27〉 below, and mark Ⓧ. Likewise, mark Ⓧ and record the amount twice as an addition and deduction in the statement of cash flows reference table as shown in 〈Table 11-28〉 below.

⟨Table 11-27⟩ Income statement reference table—Gain on disposal of tangible assets

From January 1, 20×2 to December 31, 20×2

Heemang Department Store (Numbers in billions of ₩)

Account titles	Amount		Reference
Other revenues			
Gain on disposal of tangible assets	9		ⓧ

⟨Table 11-28⟩ Statement of cash flows reference table—Disposal of land

From January 1, 20×2 to December 31, 20×2

Heemang Department Store (Numbers in billions of ₩)

Description	Amount		Reference*
Cash flows from operating activities			
Gain from non-operating activities		(−)9	
Gain on disposal of tangible assets	(−)9		ⓧ
Cash flows from investing activities			
Disposal of land			ⓧ 9**

* If there is only one item, we record the amount in the 'amount' column.

** There will be one more item from [5.1.2 (3) 2)] below, so we record the amount in the 'reference' column.

5.4.2 Items that can be explained by changes in financial position

The most items in the statement of cash flows are the ones that can be explained by changes in financial position. They can be classified into (1) items that are explained directly by changes in financial position, (2) income statement items that are explained by T account analysis, and (3) items that are explained by T account analysis.

(1) Statement of financial position ⇨ Statement of cash flows

1) Changes in assets and liabilities due to operating activities

Look for changes in assets and liabilities due to operating activities, in the statement of financial position. In case of Heemang Department store, the decrease in trade receivables, the increase in prepaid insurance, the increase in merchandise, the increase in trade payables, and the decrease in unearned rent are changes in assets and liabilities due to operating activities. In the statement of financial position reference table, as shown in ⟨Table 11-29⟩ below, identify and mark ⓐ for the decrease in trade receivables of ₩25 billion, ⓑ for the increase in prepaid insurance of (−)₩1 billion, ⓒ for the increase in merchandise of (−)₩12 billion, ⓓ for the increase in trade payables of ₩8 billion, and ⓔ for the decrease in unearned rent of (−)₩3 billion. Also mark ⓐ, ⓑ, ⓒ, ⓓ, ⓔ and record the amounts in the statement of cash flows reference table, as shown in ⟨Table 11-30⟩ below.

⟨Table 11-29⟩ Statement of financial position reference table–Changes in assets and liabilities due to operating activities

Heemang Department Store (Numbers in billions of ₩)

Account titles	Dec. 31, 20×2	Dec. 31, 20×1	Change	Reference*
Trade receivables	18	43	25	ⓐ
Prepaid insurance	3	2	(−)1	ⓑ
Merchandise	29	17	(−)12	ⓒ
Trade payables	26	18	8	ⓓ
Unearned rent	1	4	(−)3	ⓔ

* If there is only one item, we do not record the amount.

⟨Table 11-30⟩ Statement of cash flows reference table–Changes in assets and liabilities due to operating activities

From January 1, 20×2 to December 31, 20×2

Heemang Department Store (Numbers in billions of ₩)

Description	Amount		Reference*
Cash flows from operating activities			
Changes in assets and liabilities due to operating activities		17	
Decrease in trade receivables	25		ⓐ
Increase in prepaid insurance	(−)1		ⓑ
Increase in merchandise	(−)12		ⓒ
Increase in trade payables	8		ⓓ
Decrease in unearned rent	(−)3		ⓔ

* If there is only one item, we record the amount in the 'amount' column.

2) Changes in assets and liabilities related with individually reporting items.

Look for changes in assets and liabilities related with individually reporting items, in the statement of financial position. In case of Heemang Department store, the decrease in interest receivable, the increase in interest payable, and the increase in income tax payable are changes in assets and liabilities related with individually reporting items. Identify the decrease in interest receivable of ₩1 billion, the increase in interest payable of ₩2 billion, and the increase in income tax payable of ₩1 billion, and mark ⓟ, ⓠ and ⓡ, respectively, in the statement of financial position reference table, as shown In ⟨Table 11-31⟩ below. Also mark ⓟ, ⓠ and ⓡ and record the amounts in the statement of cash flows reference table, as shown in ⟨Table 11-32⟩ below. In addition, add ⓤ ₩1 billion and ⓟ ₩1 billion and record total of ₩2 billion as interest received in the statement of cash flows reference table.

⟨Table 11-31⟩ Statement of financial position reference table—Changes in assets and liabilities related with individually reporting items

Heemang Department Store (Numbers in billions of ₩)

Account titles	Dec. 31, 20×2	Dec. 31, 20×1	Change	Reference*
Interest receivable	2	3	1	ⓟ
Interest payable	4	2	2	ⓠ
Income tax payable	3	2	1	ⓡ

* If there is only one item, we do not record the amount.

⟨Table 11-32⟩ Statement of cash flows reference table—Changes in assets and liabilities related with individually reporting items

From January 1, 20×2 to December 31, 20×2

Heemang Department Store (Numbers in billions of ₩)

Description	Amount		Reference
Cash flows from operating activities			
Individually reporting item :			
Income tax paid			ⓡ1*
Cash flows from investing activities			
Individually reporting item :			
Interest received	2		Ⓤ1 ⓟ1**
Cash flows from financing activities			
Individually reporting item :			
Interest paid			Ⓥ(−)9 ⓠ2***

* There will be one more item from [5.1.2 (3) 1) below], so we record the amount in the 'reference' column.

** Record ⓟ 1 in the 'reference' column and add Ⓤ ₩1 billion and ⓟ ₩1 billion and record ₩2 billion as interest received.

*** There will be one more item from [5.1.2 (3) 2) below], so we record ⓠ 2 in the 'reference' column and do not compute the amount of interest paid yet.

(2) Income statement ⇨ T account analysis ⇨ Statement of cash flows

Mark Ⓚ, Ⓛ and Ⓜ (capital letters) for income statement items used in T account analysis of ⟨Table 11-20⟩ in the income statement reference table, as shown in ⟨Table 11-33⟩ below. Also mark ⓚ, ⓛ and ⓜ (smaller letters) and record the amount in the statement of financial position reference table and the statement of cash flows reference table, as shown in ⟨Table 11-34⟩ and ⟨Table 11-35⟩ below. In addition, add ⓡ ₩1 billion and Ⓜ (-)₩6 billion and record (-)₩5 billion as income tax paid in the statement of cash flows reference table.

⟨Table 11-33⟩ Comprehensive income statement reference table–T account analysis

From January 1, 20×2 to December 31, 20×2

Heemang Department Store (Numbers in billions of ₩)

Account titles	Amount		Reference
Operating expenses			
Depreciation expense	(-)6		Ⓚ
Net income before income tax expense (NIBITE)		24	Ⓛ
Income tax expense		(-)6	Ⓜ

⟨Table 11-34⟩ Statement of financial position reference table–(Income statement → T account analysis)

Heemang Department Store (Numbers in billions of ₩)

Account titles	Dec. 31, 20×2	Dec. 31, 20×1	Change	Reference*
Accumulated depreciation	(-)34	(-)28	6	ⓚ
Retained earnings	12	3	9	ⓛ24 ⓜ(-)6

* If there is only one item, we do not record the amount.

⟨Table 11-35⟩ Statement of cash flows reference table–(Income statement → T account analysis)

From January 1, 20×2 to December 31, 20×2

Heemang Department Store (Numbers in billions of ₩)

Description	Amount		Reference*
Cash flows from operating activities			
Net income before income tax expense (NIBITE)		24	ⓛ
Operating expense without cash outflows			
Depreciation expense	6		ⓚ
Individually reporting item :			
Income tax paid		(-)5	ⓡ1 ⓜ(-)6**

* If there is only one item, we record the amount in the 'amount' column.

** Record ⓜ(-)6 in the 'reference' column and add ⓡ ₩1 billion and ⓜ (-)₩6 billion and record (-)₩5 billion as income tax paid.

(3) T Account analysis ⇨ Statement of cash flows

Mark ① ~ ⑬ for the additional information obtained from T account analyses of 〈Table 11-21〉 in the statement of financial position reference table, as shown in 〈Table 11-36〉 below. Also mark ① ~ ⑬ and record the amounts in the statement of cash flows reference table, as shown in 〈Table 11-37〉 below. In addition, add Ⓧ ₩9 billion and ④ ₩16 billion and record ₩25 billion as a disposal of land in the statement of cash flows reference table. Add Ⓥ (-)₩9 billion, ⓠ ₩2 billion, and ⑪ ₩1 billion, and record (-)₩6 billion as interest paid.

〈Table 11-36〉 Statement of financial position reference table—T account analyses

Heemang Department Store (Numbers in billions of ₩)

Account titles	Dec. 31, 20×2	Dec. 31, 20×1	Change	Reference*
Short-term loans	25	20	(-)5	①(-)30 ②25
Land	80	56	(-)24	③(-)40 ④ 16
Building	109	67	(-)42	⑤
Short-term borrowings	15	22	(-)7	⑥30 ⑦(-)37
Current portion of long-term borrowings	11	5	6	⑧(-)5 ⑨11
Long-term borrowings	36	17	19	⑨(-)11 ⑩30
Bonds payable	19	18	1	⑪
Share capital-common stock	120	100	20	⑫
Retained earning	12	3	9	ⓘ24 ⓜ(-)6 ⑬(-)9

* If there is only one item, we do not record the amount.

〈Table 11-37〉 Statement of cash flows reference table—T account analyses

From January 1, 20×2 to December 31, 20×2

Heemang Department Store (Numbers in billions of ₩)

Description	Amount		Reference*
Cash flows from investing activities			
Disposal of land	25		Ⓧ9 ④16**
Collection of short-term loans	25		②
Short-term loans made	(-)30		①
Purchase of land	(-)40		③
Purchase of building	(-)42		⑤
Cash flows from financing activities			
Proceeds from short-term borrowings	30		⑥
Proceeds from long-term borrowings	30		⑩
Proceeds from issuing common stock	20		⑫
Retirement of short-term borrowings	(-)37		⑦
Retirement of current portion of long-term borrowings	(-)5		⑧
Individually reporting item :			
Interest paid	(-)6		Ⓥ(-)9 ⓠ2 ⑪1***
Dividends paid	(-)9		⑬

* If there is only one item, we record the amount in the 'amount' column.

** Record ④ 16 in the 'reference' column and add Ⓧ ₩9 billion and ④ ₩16 billion and record ₩25 billion as a disposal of land.

*** Record ⑪ 1 in the 'reference' column and add ⓥ (-)₩9 billion, ⓠ ₩2 billion and ⑪ ₩1 billion and record (-)₩6 billion as interest paid.

5.4.3 Cash account

Mark the beginning and ending balances, and change in cash as ⓕ, ⓖ and ⓗ, respectively, in the statement of financial position reference table and the statement of cash flows reference table, as shown in 〈Table 11-38〉 and 〈Table 11-39〉 below.

〈Table 11-38〉 Statement of financial position reference table—Cash

Heemang Department Store (Numbers in billions of ₩)

Account titles	Dec. 31, 20×2	Dec. 31, 20×1	Change	Reference
Cash	17ⓖ	13ⓕ	(-)4	ⓗ

〈Table 11-39〉 Statement of cash flows reference table—Cash

From January 1, 20×2 to December 31, 20×2

Heemang Department Store (Numbers in billions of ₩)

Description	Amount		Reference
Net increase in cash		4	ⓗ*
Cash at beginning of period		13	ⓕ
Cash at end of period		17	ⓖ

* Because an increase in asset is marked (−) in the statement of financial position, the increase in cash is reported as (+)₩4 billion in the statement of cash flows.

5.5 Finished reference tables

The statement of financial position reference table ; the income statement reference table ; and the statement of cash flows reference table , after making all cross reference, are 〈Table 11-40〉, 〈Table 11-41〉 and 〈Table 11-42〉, respectively as follow. We know that all items in the statement of cash flows were explained by changes in financial position except Ⓤ, Ⓥ and Ⓧ which were the income statement items.

⟨Table 11-40⟩ Statement of financial position reference table—Finished

Heemang Department Store (Numbers in billions of ₩)

Account titles	Dec. 31, 20×2	Dec. 31, 20×1	Change	Reference*
Assets				
Current assets				
Cash	17ⓖ	13ⓕ	(−)4	ⓗ
Trade receivables	18	43	25	ⓐ
Short-term loans	25	20	(−)5	①(−)30 ②25
Interest receivable	2	3	1	ⓟ
Prepaid insurance	3	2	(−)1	ⓑ
Merchandise	29	17	(−)12	ⓒ
Non-current assets				
Land	80	56	(−)24	③(−)40 ④16
Building	109	67	(−)42	⑤
Accumulated depreciation	(−)34	(−)28	6	ⓚ
	75	39	(−)36	
Total assets	249	193	(−)56	
Liabilities				
Current liabilities				
Trade payables	26	18	8	ⓓ
Short-term borrowings	15	22	(−)7	⑥30 ⑦(−)37
Current portion of long-term borrowings	11	5	6	⑧(−)5 ⑨11
Unearned rent	1	4	(−)3	ⓔ
Interest payable	4	2	2	ⓠ
Income tax payable	3	2	1	ⓡ
Non-current liability				
Long-term borrowings	36	17	19	⑨(−)11 ⑪30
Bonds payable	19	18	1	⑪
Total liabilities	115	88	27	
Equity				
Share capital-common stock	120	100	20	⑫
Share premium-common stock	2	2	–	
Retained earnings	12	3	9	ⓛ24 ⓜ(−)6 ⑬(−)9
Total equity	134	105	29	
Total liabilities and equity	249	193	56	

* If there is only one item, we do not record the amount.

⟨Table 11-41⟩ Income statement reference table–Finished

From January 1, 20×2 to December 31, 20×2

Heemang Department Store (Numbers in billions of ₩)

Account titles	Amount		Ref.*
Sales		211	
Cost of goods sold		(–)124	
Gross profit		87	
Operating expenses		(–)69	
Salaries expense	(–)47		
Depreciation expense	(–)6		Ⓚ
Insurance expense	(–)16		
Other operating revenue:		5	
Rent revenue	5		
Income from operations		23	
Other revenues		10	
Interest revenue	1		Ⓤ
Gain on disposal of tangible assets	9		Ⓧ
Other expense		(–)9	
Interest expense	(–)9		Ⓥ
Net income before income tax expense (NIBITE)		24	Ⓛ
Income tax expense		(–)6	Ⓜ
Net income		18	

* If there is only one item, we do not record the amount.

⟨Table 11-42⟩ Statement of cash flows reference table—Finished

From January 1, 20×2 to December 31, 20×2

Heemang Department Store (Numbers in billions of ₩)

Description	Amount		Ref.*
Cash flows from operating activities			
Net income before income tax expense (NIBITE)		24	Ⓘ
Adjustments :			
NIBITE revenue and expense related with individually reporting items		8	
Interest revenue	(−)1		Ⓤ
Interest expense	9		Ⓥ
Gain from non-operating activities		(−)9	
Gain on disposal of tangible assets	(−)9		Ⓧ
Operating expense without cash outflows		6	
Depreciation expense	6		ⓚ
Changes in assets and liabilities due to operating activities		17	
Decrease in trade receivables	25		ⓐ
Increase in prepaid insurance	(−)1		ⓑ
Increase in merchandise	(−)12		ⓒ
Increase in trade payables	8		ⓓ
Decrease in unearned rent	(−)3		ⓔ
Cash generated from operations		46	
Individually reporting item :			
Income tax paid		(−)5	ⓡ1 ⓜ(−)6
Net cash from operating activities		41	
Cash flows from investing activities			
Disposal of land	25		Ⓧ9 ④16
Collection of short-term loans	25		②
Individually reporting item :			
Interest received	2		Ⓤ1 ⓟ1
Short-term loans (made)	(−)30		①
Purchase of land	(−)40		③
Purchase of building	(−)42		⑤
Net cash used in investing activities		(−)60	
Cash flows from financing activities			
Proceeds from short-term borrowings	30		⑥
Proceeds from long-term borrowings	30		⑩
Proceeds from issuing common stock	20		⑫
Retirement of short-term borrowings	(−)37		⑦
Retirement of current portion of long-term borrowings	(−)5		⑧
Individually reporting items :			
Interest paid	(−)6		Ⓥ(−)9 ⓠ2 ⑪1
Dividends paid	(−)9		⑬
Net cash from financing activities		23	
Net increase in cash		4	ⓗ
Cash at beginning of period		13	ⓕ
Cash at end of period		17	ⓖ

* If there is only one item, we record the amount in the amount column.

5.6 Preparing a direct method statement of cash flows by the indirect method

5.6.1 Computation of cash generated from operations

The cash generated from operations, under the direct method, is computed by deducting cash paid to suppliers and employees from cash receipts from customers. It can be computed by using information in the statement of cash flows prepared in the indirect method as the following ⟨Table 11-43⟩.

⟨Table 11-43⟩ Computing direct method cash generated from operation using information from the indirect method

(Numbers in billions of ₩)

Description	Computation			Amount
	Description	Amount	Ref.	
Cash receipts from customers	Sales	211	*	238
	Rent revenue	5	*	
	Decrease in trade receivables	25	ⓐ	
	Decrease in unearned rent	(-)3	ⓔ	
Cash paid to suppliers and employees	Cost of goods sold	(-)124	*	(-)192
	Operating expenses	(-)69	*	
	Depreciation expense	6	ⓚ	
	Increase in prepaid insurance	(-)1	ⓑ	
	Increase in merchandise	(-)12	ⓒ	
	Increase in trade payables	8	ⓓ	
Cash generated from operations				46

* Obtained from the income statement.

5.6.2 Preparation of direct method statement of cash flows

The direct method statement of cash flows prepared using information from ⟨Table 11-43⟩ is as the following ⟨Table 11-44⟩.

⟨Table 11-44⟩ Statement of cash flows (direct method)

From January 1, 20×2 to December 31, 20×2

Heemang Department Store (Numbers in billions of ₩)

Description	Amount		Reference
Cash flows from operating activities			
Cash receipts from customers		238	⟨Table 11-43⟩
Cash paid to suppliers and employees		(-)192	⟨Table 11-43⟩
Cash generated from operations		46	

The remaining part of the statement are the same as under the indirect method.

Related financial ratios

Financial ratios related with cash flows are cash-flow per share ; cash flow to total assets ratio evaluating profitability, operating cash flows to current liabilities ratio ; operating cash flows to total liabilities ratio ; and operating cash flows interest coverage ratio evaluating safety (financial), and price cash-flows ratio as a price multiple.

6.1 Financial ratios evaluating profitability

(1) Cash-flows per share

Cash-flows per share (CPS : 주당현금흐름) shows how much cash has been made from operating activities per share of common stock. It is computed by dividing operating cash flows less preferred stock dividends, by weighted average common shares outstanding (as shown below).

$$\text{Cash-flows per share (CPS)} = \frac{\text{Operating cash flows} - \text{Preferred stock dividends}}{\text{Weighted average common shares outstanding}}$$

Daehan Department Store's weighted average common shares outstanding for 20×2 and 20×1 were 25 million shares and 15 million shares, respectively, and there was no preferred stock dividend.

(Daehan Department Store's CPS)

$$20\times2 : \frac{\text{100 billion}}{\text{25 million shares}} = ₩4{,}000$$

$$20\times1 : \frac{\text{30 billion}}{\text{15 million shares}} = ₩2{,}000$$

It is understood that Daehan Department Store's CPS has increased significantly, from ₩2,000 for 20×1 to ₩4,000 for 20×2.

Cash-flows per share is an index that is contrasted with earnings per share. Earnings per share are used extensively as an operating performance index ; the greater the earnings per share, the better the evaluation of operating performance. But because income is computed based on an accrual basis, it can be different from cash flows from operating activities, which are computed on a cash basis. If cash flows are lower than income, cash-flows per share are reported lower than are earnings per share. If earnings per share remain the same, then the higher the cash-flows per share, the sounder the net income. Therefore, to evaluate the operating performance of a firm properly, we should examine cash-flows per share as a supplemental index to earnings per share.

(2) Operating cash flows to total assets ratio

Net income is accrual basis income and operating cash flow is cash basis income. Therefore, the operating cash flows to total assets ratio is a cash basis income to total assets ratio. It should be used as an index supplement to the return on assets (ROA), which was reviewed in Chapter 5. In general, persistent income is the income that shows an accompanying cash flow. Hence, the operating cash flows to total assets ratio can be considered as a return on investment (ROI), incorporating persistency of income.

The operating cash flows to total assets ratio is computed as follows.

$$\text{Operating cash flows to total assets ratio} = \frac{\text{Operating cash flows}}{\text{Average total assets}}$$

(Daehan Department Store's ratio)

$$20\times2 : \frac{100 \text{ billion}}{(553 \text{ billion} + 339 \text{ billion}) / 2} = 22.42\%$$

$$20\times1 : \frac{30 \text{ billion}}{339 \text{ billion}^{*}} = 8.85\%$$

* Because it is the first year of operation, the total assets at the end of 20×1 was used.

Daehan Department Store's operating cash flows to total assets ratio is significantly increased, from 8.85% for 20×1 to 22.42% for 20×2. The return on assets for 20×2 and 20×1 were 16.14% and 7.67%, respectively. It is understood that the operating cash flow to total assets ratios are higher than the return on assets for 20×2 and 20×1.

6.2 Financial ratios evaluating safety

(1) Operating cash flows current liabilities coverage ratio

The operating cash flows current liabilities coverage ratio is a ratio by which one can evaluate a firm's ability to pay short-term debts. This ratio shows whether operating cash flows are sufficient to pay off current liabilities, as shown in the following formula.

$$\text{Operating cash flows current liabilities coverage ratio} = \frac{\text{Operating cash flows}}{\text{Current liabilities}}$$

(Daehan Department Store's ratio)

$$20\times2 : \frac{100 \text{ billion}}{104 \text{ billion}} = 96.15\%$$

$$20\times1 : \frac{30 \text{ billion}}{80 \text{ billion}} = 37.5\%$$

Because Daehan Department Store's operating cash flows to current liabilities coverage ratio was increased significantly, to 96.15% for 20×2 from 37.5% for 20×1, it is understood that the company's ability to pay current liabilities with operating cash flows has improved substantially.

In general, the current ratio (current assets / current liabilities) is used to a great extent to evaluate a firm's ability to pay short-term debts. If the current ratio is high, firm's ability to pay short-term debts is evaluated to be high. But, if assets such as inventory and trade receivables, which cannot be used to pay debts right away, represent a significant portion of current assets, then the company may face difficulty in paying off current debts although the current ratio is high. Because the operating cash flows current liabilities coverage ratio is a current debt-paying-ability index that is based on cash flows rather than on current assets, it can mitigate the above-mentioned problems of the current ratio. Therefore, it is desirable to use the operating cash flows current liabilities coverage ratio, together with the current ratio, to evaluate a firm's short-term debt-paying ability correctly.

(2) Operating cash flows total liabilities coverage ratio

The operating cash flows total liabilities coverage ratio is computed as follows. It shows whether operating cash flows are sufficient to pay off total liabilities.

$$\text{Operating cash flows total liabilities coverage ratio} = \frac{\text{Operating cash flows}}{\text{Total liabilities}}$$

(Daehan Department Store's ratio)

$$20\times2 : \frac{100 \text{ billion}}{230 \text{ billion}} = 43.48\%$$

$$20\times1 : \frac{30 \text{ billion}}{192 \text{ billion}} = 15.63\%$$

The operating cash flows total liabilities coverage ratio of Daehan Department Store increased from 15.63% for 20×1 to 43.48% for 20×2, so it is understood that the firm's ability to pay its total liabilities with its operating cash flows was improved significantly.

(3) Operating cash flows interest coverage ratio

The operating cash flows interest coverage ratio is a financial ratio by which one can evaluate whether operating cash flows, before paying income tax and interest, are enough to pay interest. The operating cash flows before income tax and interest are the actual cash by which a company can pay interest. Therefore, this ratio can be considered a ratio that shows a company's real interest-paying capability.

The operating cash flows interest coverage ratio is computed as follows.

$$\text{Operating cash flows interest coverage} = \frac{\text{Operating cash flows} + \text{Interest} + \text{Income tax}}{\text{Interest}}$$

If interest paid and interest expense are very close in amount and income tax paid and income tax expense are also very close in amount, then interest expense may be substituted for interest paid and income tax expense may be substituted for income tax paid.

(Daehan Department Store's ratio)

$$20\times2: \frac{100 \text{ billion} + 16 \text{ billion} + 21 \text{ billion}}{16 \text{ billion}} = 8.56 \text{ times}^{*}$$

$$20\times1: \frac{30 \text{ billion} + 8 \text{ billion} + 7 \text{ billion}}{8 \text{ billion}} = 3.46 \text{ times}$$

* Stated in times to be compatible with the 'times interest earned' ratio.

The operating cash flows interest coverage ratio of Daehan Department Store increased from 3.46 times for 20×1 to 8.56 times for 20×2. Thus it is understood that the firm's ability to pay interest with its operating cash flow, before paying interest and income tax, improved significantly.

6.3 Price multiple

(1) Price cash-flows ratio

The price cash-flows ratio (PCR : 주가현금흐름비율) is a ratio showing how much cash-flows per share is reflected in the common stock price. It is computed as follows.

$$\text{Price cash-flows ratio (PCR)} = \frac{\text{Common stock price}}{\text{Cash-flows per share (CPS)}}$$

Daehan Department Store's common stock prices at end of 20×2 and at end of 20×1 were ₩15,000 and ₩10,000, respectively.

(Daehan Department Store's PCR)

$$20\times2 : \frac{15{,}000}{4{,}000} = 3.75 \text{ times}$$

$$20\times1 : \frac{10{,}000}{2{,}000} = 5 \text{ times}$$

It is understood that PCR of Daehan Department Store decreased to 3.75 times, at the end of 20×2, from 5 times, at the end of 20×1.

The price cash-flows ratio is affected by a company's expected future growth. The price cash-flows ratio, together with the price earnings ratio (common stock price/earnings per share), is used as a useful investment index in the stock market.

▪ Note : Financial ratios reviewed in this chapter are summarized in Appendix 2 〈Table B-1〉 'Key financial ratios' at the end of this book.

IFRS references (http://www.kasb.or.kr)

[1] IAS 7 *Statement of Cash Flows*, par. 7.
[2] *Ibid*. par. 31, 35.
[3] *Ibid*. par. 31.
[4] *Ibid*, par. 35, 36.
[5] *Ibid*, par. 31, 35.
[6] *Ibid*, par. 19.
[7] *Ibid*, Illustrative Example A.
[8] *Ibid*, par. 43.

Key terms

Cash equivalents (현금성자산): Financial instruments that are readily convertible to a known amount of cash and that are subject to an insignificant risk of changing value because their maturity dates fall within three months. (p.511)

Changes in assets and liabilities due to operating activities (영업활동으로 인한 자산과 부채의 변화): Increases and decreases in assets (such as trade receivables, accrued revenue, inventory, and prepaid expense) and in liabilities (such as trade payables, accrued expense, and unearned revenue) due to operating activities. (p.522)

Direct method (직접법): A method of directly computing and reporting cash flows from operating activities, by listing all revenues accompanying cash inflows and all expenses accompanying cash outflows. (p.517)

Gain and loss from non-operating activities (비영업활동에 의한 이익과 손실): Gain and loss incurred from investing and financing activities which are not operating activities. (p.520)

Indirect method (간접법): A method for indirectly computing and reporting operating cash flows by adjusting a certain income in the comprehensive income statement (e.g. net income before income tax expense). (p.518)

Non-cash investing and financing transactions (비현금흐름 투자와 재무거래): Important investing and financing transactions not accompanying cash flows, which are not reported in the statement of cash flows but disclosed in footnotes to the financial statements. (p.528)

Operating expense without cash outflows (현금유출이 없는 영업비용): Operating expense not accompanying cash outflows, such as depreciation expense. (p.522)

Exercises

▪ Note : In all exercises, the classification method based on theory is applied. Therefore, income tax paid should be classified as an operating activity ; interest received and dividends received should be classified as investing activities ; and interest paid and dividends paid should be classified as financing activities.

1. Computing cash flows by each activity

The following is data concerning the cash inflows and outflows of Hanbat Inc. in 20×1.

(Numbers in billions of ₩)

Description	Amount	Description	Amount
Payment of employees' salaries	8	Cash purchases of merchandise	22
Cash sales of merchandise	55	Payment of proceeds of merchandise purchases on credit	16
Acquisition of machines and equipment	36	Short-term borrowings	12
Collection of proceeds of merchandise sales on credit	17	Early retirement of long-term borrowings	6
Long-term borrowings	15	Payment of interest on borrowings	2
Paying off short-term borrowings	5	Disposition of a building	13
Dividends paid	4	Insurance premium paid	3
Income tax paid	7	Rent paid	1

《Questions》

(1) Compute the amount reported as cash flows for each of following activities in the statement of cash flows.

1) Operating activities 2) Investing activities 3) Financing activities

(2) What is the amount to be reported as increase (or decrease) in cash in the statement of cash flows?

2. Cash inflows from sales

Sales reported in the comprehensive income statement of Hanbat Inc. for 20×2 are ₩560 billion. Trade receivables reported in the statement of financial position, as of December 31, 20×2 and December 31, 20×1, are as below.

(Numbers in billions of ₩)

Account titles	December 31, 20×2	December 31, 20×1
Trade receivables	74	45

《Question》 Compute Hanbat Inc.'s cash inflows from sales in 20×2.

3. Cash outflows for merchandise purchases

The cost of goods sold, reported in the comprehensive income statement of Hanyang Inc. for 20×2, is ₩340 billion. Merchandise and trade payable, reported in the statement of financial position as of December 31, 20×2 and December 31, 20×1, are as below.

(Numbers in billions of ₩)

Account titles	December 31, 20×2	December 31, 20×1
Merchandise	33	52
Trade payables	47	24

《Question》 Compute Hanbat Inc.'s cash flows for merchandise purchases in 20×2.

4. Computing cash inflows form sales, cash outflows for merchandise purchases, depreciation expense, and dividends paid

The following are Daejeun Inc.'s statements of financial position as of December 31, 20×2 and December 31, 20×1.

Statement of financial position

Daeheon Inc. (Numbers in billions of ₩)

Account titles	December 31, 20×2	December 31, 20×1
Cash	36	22
Trade receivables	54	38
Merchandise	40	30
Land	20	20
Building	280	240
Accumulated depreciation	(−)80	(−)60
Total assets	350	290
Trade payables	38	32
Long-term borrowings	152	140
Share capital-common stock	60	40
Retained earnings	100	78
Total liabilities and equity	350	290

〈Additional data〉

① Sales, cost of goods sold, and net income of Daejeun Inc. for 20×2 were ₩480 billion, ₩200 billion, and ₩26 billion, respectively.

② During 20×2, the company sold a building with book value of ₩32 billion (acquisition cost of ₩60 billion, accumulated depreciation of ₩28 billion) and received cash of ₩36 billion.

《Question》 Compute Daejun Inc.'s following items for 20×2.

(1) Cash inflows from sales
(2) Cash outflows for merchandise purchases
(3) Depreciation expense
(4) Dividends paid

5. **Structure of statement of cash flows ①**

The following is the format of the statement of cash flows, reporting cash flows from operating activities indirectly.

Statement of cash flows

Description		Amount	
Cash flows from operating activities			
Net income before income tax expense (NIBITE)			xxx
Adjustments :			
NIBITE revenue and expense related with individually reporting items :			xxx
(1))		(−)xxx	
(2))		(−)xxx	
(3))		xxx	
Gain and loss from non-operating activities	Ⓐ		xxx
Operating expense without cash outflows	Ⓑ		xxx
Changes in assets and liabilities due to operating activities			xxx
Increase in assets due to operating activities	Ⓒ	(−)xxx	
Decrease in assets due to operating activities	Ⓓ	xxx	
(4))	Ⓔ	xxx	
Decrease in liabilities due to operating activities	Ⓕ	(−)xxx	
Cash generated from operations			xxx
Individually reporting item :			
(5))			(−)xxx
Net cash from operating activities			xxx

《Questions》

(1) Write down the correct items for each of 1), 2), 3), 4), and 5) in the statement of cash flows.

1) ______________________ 2) ______________________

3) ______________________ 4) ______________________

5) ______________________

(2) Find the correct items for each of Ⓐ, Ⓑ, Ⓒ, Ⓓ, Ⓔ, Ⓕ in the statement of cash flows from the table below and write down the numbers.

Ⓐ Gain and loss from non-operating activities : ______________

Ⓑ Operating expense without cash outflows : ______________

Ⓓ Decrease in assets due to operating activities : ______________

Ⓔ Increase in liabilities due to operating activities : ______________

Ⓕ Decrease in liabilities due to operating activities : ______________

① Depreciation expense	② Decrease in fees receivable
③ Gain on disposal of tangible assets	④ Decrease in trade payables
⑤ Increase in trade receivables	⑥ Decrease in merchandise
⑦ Decrease in salaries payable	⑧ Increase in unearned rent
⑨ Increase in prepaid rent	⑩ Loss on disposal of tangible assets

6. Structure of statement of cash flows ②

The following is the statement of cash flows of Yousung Inc. for 20×1.

Statement of cash flows

Yousong Inc. From Jan. 1, 20×1 to Dec. 31, 20×1 (Numbers in billions of ₩)

Description	Amount	
Cash flows from operating activities		
Net income before income tax expense (NIBITE)		(④)
Adjustments :		
NIBITE expense related with individually reporting item		20
Interest expense	20	
Gain and loss from non-operating activities		(−)1
Gain on disposal of tangible assets	(−)4	
Loss on disposal of tangible assets	(②)	
Operating expense without cash outflows		160
Depreciation expense	160	
Changes in assets and liabilities due to operating activities		(−)150
Increase in trade receivables	(−)70	
Decrease in merchandise	(③)	
Increase in trade payables	50	
Decrease in rent payable	(−)5	
Cash generated from operations		93
Individually reporting item		
Income tax paid		(−)14
Net cash from operating activities		(①)
Cash flows from investing activities		
Disposal of equipment	10	
Disposal of machinery	30	
Acquisition of building	(⑤)	
Net cash used in investing activities		(−)530
Cash flows from financing activities		
Proceeds from long-term borrowings	(⑥)	
Retirement of short-term borrowings	(−)160	
Individually reporting item :		
Interest paid	(−)22	
Net cash from financing activities		453
Net increase in cash		(⑦)
Cash at beginning of period		(⑧)
Cash at end of period		11

《Question》

Compute the amount for each of ①, ②, ③, ④, ⑤, ⑥, ⑦, and ⑧ in the statement of cash flows.

7. Computing cash flows from operating activities (indirect method) ①

The following are the income statement of Hangdo Inc for 20×2 and partial statements of the financial position of the company as of December 31, 20×2 and December 31, 20×1, showing accounts related with operating activities.

Income statement

Hangdo Inc. From Jan. 1, 20×2 to Dec. 31, 20×2 (Numbers in billions of ₩)

Account titles	Amount
Sales	135
Cost of goods sold	(−)71
Salaries expense	(−)6
Depreciation expense	(−)8
Gain on disposal of tangible assets	2
Net income before income tax expense (NIBITE)	52
Income tax expense	(−)9
Net income	43

Partial statement of financial position

Hangdo Inc. (Numbers in billions of ₩)

Account titles	December 31, 20×2	December 31, 20×1
Trade receivables	15	22
Merchandise	20	18
Trade payables	13	16

《Question》

Prepare a partial statement of cash flows of Hangdo Inc. for 20×2, showing cash flows from operating activities computed by the indirect method.

8. Computing cash flows from operating activities (indirect method) ②

Hanshin Inc. reported cash generated from operations of ₩19 billion in its statement of cash flows for 20×1. The following are items adjusted to net income before income tax expense, to compute the cash generated from operations.

(Numbers in billions of ₩)

Description	Amount	Description	Amount
Increase in trade receivables	20	Decrease in merchandise	16
Decrease in trade payables	15	Increase in salaries payable	7
Decrease in fees receivable	5	Decrease in prepaid rent	8
Decrease in unearned rent	3	Depreciation expense	10

《Question》

Compute net income before income tax expense of Hanshin Inc. for 20×1.

9. **Computing cash flows from operating activities (indirect method) ③**

Net income before income tax expense (NIBITE) of Bodong Inc. for 20×2 was ₩450 billion. The following is the data needed to compute cash flows from operating activities using the indirect method.

Income statement data

(Numbers in billions of ₩)

Account titles	Amount
Depreciation expense	80
Gain on disposal of tangible assets	15
Loss on disposal of tangible assets	20
Interest revenue	12
Interest expense	35
Income tax expense	125

Statement of financial position data

(Numbers in billions of ₩)

Account titles	Dec. 31, 20×2	Dec. 31, 20×1	Increase (Decrease)
Trade receivables	220	270	(−)50
Merchandise	110	150	(−)40
Prepaid insurance	50	30	20
Rent receivable	18	15	3
Trade payables	100	170	(−)70
Rent payable	40	20	20

《Question》

Prepare a partial statement of cash flows of Bodong Inc. for 20×2, showing cash flows from operating activities computed by the indirect method.

10. Computing cash flows from investing activities

The following is data obtained from the statement of financial position of Komil Inc., as of December 31, 20×2 and December 31, 20×1.

(Numbers in billions of ₩)

Account titles	December 31, 20×2	December 31, 20×1
Short-term loans	100	80
Land	450	320

The following are a part of the company's cash transactions in 20×2 concerning short-term loans and land.

① Made a loan of ₩50 billion to a supplier company for short term.
② A piece of land was acquired and ₩330 billion was paid.
③ Sold land and received ₩240 billion.

《Questions》

(1) Compute the following.
  1) Short-term loans collected 2) Gain or loss on disposal of land
(2) Prepare a partial statement of cash flows for 20×2, showing cash flows from investing activities.

11. Computing cash flows from financing activities

The following is data obtained from the statement of financial position of Danyang Inc., as of December 31, 20×2 and December 31, 20×1.

(Numbers in billions of ₩)

Account titles	December 31, 20×2	December 31, 20×1
Short-term borrowings	50	45
Bonds payable	450	400

The following are a part of the company's cash transactions in 20×2 concerning short-term borrowings and bonds payable.

① Borrowed ₩40 billion from a bank for short term.
② Issues bonds with face value of ₩200 billion at face value.

《Questions》

(1) Computer the following.

1) Retirement of short-term borrowings 2) Early retirement of bonds payable (There was no gain or loss on paying off short-term borrowings and no gain or loss on early retirement of bonds payable.)

(2) Prepare a partial statement of cash flows for 20×2, showing cash flows from financing activities.

12. Preparation of statement of cash flows

The following are Duckmyung Inc.'s statements of financial position at the end of 20×2 and at the end of 20×1, as well as the firm's income statement for 20×2.

Statement of financial position

Duckmyung Inc. (Numbers in billions of ₩)

Account titles	December 31, 20×2	December 31, 20×1
Cash	10	9
Trade receivables	104	88
Merchandise	83	56
Land	140	80
Building	290	293
Accumulated depreciation	(-)36	(-)40
Total assets	591	486
Trade payables	170	100
Salaries payable	40	60
Rent payable	28	44
Short-term borrowings	22	40
Long-term borrowings	40	32
Share capital—common stock	100	75
Share premium-common stock	91	76
Retained carnings	100	59
Total liabilities and equity	591	486

Income statement

Duckmyung Inc. From Jan. 1, 20×2 and Dec. 31, 20×2 (Numbers in billions of ₩)

Account titles	Amount	
Sales		366
Cost of goods sold		(−)178
Gross profit		188
Operating expenses		(−)120
Salaries expense	(−)77	
Depreciation expense	(−)8	
Rent expense	(−)35	
Income from operations		68
Interest expense		(−)7
Loss on disposal of tangible assets		(−)3
Net income before income tax expense (NIBITE)		58
Income tax expense		(−)8
Net income		50

〈Additional data concerning cash transactions〉

① Purchased a piece of land for operations at ₩60 billion.

② Sold a building with book value of ₩43 billion (acquisition cost of ₩55 billion, accumulated depreciation of ₩12 billion) at ₩40 billion.

③ Acquired a building at ₩52 billion.

④ Paid off short-term borrowings of ₩18 billion.

⑤ Early retired long-term borrowing of ₩22 billion.

⑥ Borrowed additional ₩30 billion for long term.

⑦ Issued 5 million shares of common stock with par value of ₩5,000 per share at ₩8,000 per share and received ₩40 billion.

⑧ Paid dividends of ₩9 billion.

12-1. Preparing direct method statement of cash flows by indirect method

《Question》

(1) Prepare an indirect method statement of cash flows.

(2) Compute the cash generated from operations by the direct method using the indirect method statement of cash flows.

12-2. Statement of cash flows by 3 different classification methods

The following table is a summary of Duckmyung Inc.'s statement of cash flows.

Statement of cash flows

Duckmyung Inc. From Jan. 1, 20×2 to Dec. 31, 20×2 (Numbers in billions of ₩)

Description	Amount
Cash flows from operating activities	
Cash generated from operations	67
Individually reporting item :	
Income tax paid	(−)8
Net cash from operating activities	59
Cash flows from investing activities	
Net cash used in investing activities	(−)62
Cash flows from financing activities	
Cash flows other than interest paid and dividends paid	20
Individually reporting items :	
Interest paid	(−)7
Dividends paid	(−)9
Net cash from financing activities	4
Net increase in cash	1

《Question》

Compute Duckmyung Inc.'s cash flows from operating activities, cash flows from investing activities, and cash flows from financing activities if interest paid and dividends paid are classified under each of 1) the past standards, 2) the method providing the most net cash from operating activities, and 3) the method providing the least net cash from operating activities.

Special Issues

Section 1 Other comprehensive income and net income

Section 2 Accounting for fair value through other comprehensive income financial assets

Section 3 Accounting for revaluation of tangible assets

Section 4 Equity method and consolidated financial statements

Case of Daehan Department Store

Statement of financial position (Ft. 2.ⓐ)

As of December 31, 20×2
DDS As of December 31, 20×1 (Numbers in billions of ₩)

Account titles	December 31, 20×2		December 31, 20×1	
Assets				
Current assets				
Cash and cash equivalents(Ft. 4)		45		41
Trade receivables(Ft. 3ⓑ)	30		20	
Allowance for uncollectibe accounts (Ft. 3ⓑ, 5)	(-)4	26	(-)2	18
Inventory :				
Merchandise (Ft. 3ⓒ)		43		23
Total current assets		**114**		**82**
Non-current assets				
FVOCI financial asset (Ft. 3ⓓ, 6)		13		10
Investment in associate (Ft. 3ⓔ, 7)		24		-
Tangible assets (Ft. 8) :				
Land(Ft. 3ⓕ)		96		90
Plant assets (Ft. 3ⓕ, 16)	310		160	
Accumulated depreciation(Ft. 3ⓕ)	(-)13	297	(-)3	157
Intangible asset (Ft. 3ⓖ) :				
Industrial property right (Ft. 8)		9		-
Total non-current assets		**439**		**257**
Total assets		**553**		**339**
Liabilities				
Current liabilities				
Trade payables		42		18
Interest payable		5		4
Salaries payable		2		3
Income tax payable		14		5
Cost financial liabilities (Ft. 3ⓘ) :		38		48
Short-term borrowings (Ft. 9ⓐ)	10		30	
Current portion of long-term borrowings (Ft. 9ⓑ)	28		18	
Provision :				
Provision for refunds (Ft. 3ⓗ, 11)		3		2
Total current liabilities		**104**		**80**
Non-current liabilities				
Cost financial liability (Ft. 3ⓘ) :		126		112
Long-term borrowings (Ft. 9ⓑ)	84		72	
Amortized cost financial liability (Ft. 3ⓘ) :				
Bonds payable (Ft. 10)	42		40	
Total non-current liabilities		**126**		**112**
Total Liabilities		**230**		**192**

Equity				
Share capital				
Common stock (Ft. 13, 16)		150		100
Share premium				
Common stock (Ft. 16)		60		10
Accumulated other comprehensive income		**20**		**11**
Accumulated gain on valuation of FVOCI financial asset (Ft. 3ⓓ, 6)	4		1	
Land revaluation surplus (Ft. 3ⓕ, 8)	16		10	
Retained earnings (Ft. 3ⓛ, 15)		93		26
Total equity		323		147
Total liabilities and equity		553		339

* FVOCI : Fair value through other comprehensive income

Comprehensive income statement (Ft. 2ⓑ)

From Jan. 1, 20×2 to Dec. 31, 20×2

DDS From Jan. 1, 20×1 to Dec. 31, 20×1 (Numbers in billions of ₩)

Account titles	20×2		20×1	
Sales (Ft. 3ⓐ)		430		220
Cost of goods sold		(−)230		(−)118
Gross profit		200		102
Operating expenses :		(−)85		(−)50
Salaries expense	(−)43		(−)26	
Bad debts expense (Ft. 3ⓑ)	(−)4		(−)2	
Depreciation expense (Ft. 3ⓕ)	(−)10		(−)3	
Rent expense	(−)24		(−)12	
Other operating expenses	(−)4		(−)7	
Income from operations		115		52
Other revenue		6		−
Equity income from associate (Ft. 7)	6		−	
Other expenses		(−)19		(−)14
Finance expense (Ft. 2ⓑ) :				
Interest expense	(−)19		(−)13	
Loss on disposal of tangible assets (Ft. 8)	−		(−)1	
Net income before income tax expense		102		38
Income tax expense		(−)30		(−)12
Net income		72		26
Other comprehensive income :		**9**		**11**
Item that will not be reclassified to profit or loss :				
Gain on revaluation of land (Ft. 3ⓕ, 8)	6		10	
Item that may be reclassified subsequently to profit or loss :				
Gain on valuation of FVOCI financial asset (Ft. 3ⓓ, 6)	3		1	
Total comprehensive income		81		37
Earnings per share (Ft. 12)		₩2,880		₩1,733

Statement of cash-flows (Ft. 2ⓒ)

From Jan. 1, 20×2 to Dec. 31, 20×2

DDS From Jan. 1, 20×1 to Dec. 31, 20×1 (Numbers in billions of ₩)

Description	20×2		20×1	
Cash flows from operating activities				
Net income before income tax expense (NIBITE)		**102**		**38**
Adjustments (Ft. 2ⓒ) :				
NIBITE expense related with individually reporting item				
Interest expense		**19**		**13**
Gain and loss from non-operating activities		**(−)6**		**1**
Loss on disposal of tangible assets (Ft. 8)	−		1	
Equity income from associate (Ft. 7)	(−)6		−	
Operating expense without cash outflows				
Depreciation expense		**10**		**3**
Changes in assets and liabilities due to operating activities :		**(−)4**		**(−)18**
Increase in trade receivables	(−)8		(−)18	
Increase in merchandise	(−)20		(−)23	
Increase in trade payable	24		18	
Increase (decrease) in salaries payable	(−)1		3	
Increase in provision for refunds (Ft. 11)	1		2	
Cash generated from operations		**121**		**37**
Individually reporting item :				
Income tax paid (Ft. 2ⓒ)		**(−)21**		**(−)7**
Net cash from operating activities		**100**		**30**
Cash flows from investing activities				
Proceeds from sales of land (Ft. 8)	−		39	
Individually reporting item :				
Dividends received (Ft. 7)	2			
Purchase of FVOCI financial asset (Ft. 6)	−		(−)9	
Purchase of stock of associate (Ft. 7)	(−)20		−	
Purchase of land (Ft. 8)	−		(−)120	
Purchase of plant assets (Ft. 8)	(−)150		(−)100	
Purchase of intangible assets (Ft. 8)	(−)9		−	
Net cash used in investing activities		**(−)177**		**(−)190**
Cash flows from financing activities				
Short-term borrowings (Ft. 9ⓐ)	10		30	
Long-term borrowings (Ft. 9ⓑ)	40		90	
Issuance of bonds (Ft. 10)	−		39	
Issuance of common stock (Ft. 13)	100		50	
Retirement of short-term borrowings (Ft. 9ⓐ)	(−)30		−	
Retirement of current portion of long-term borrowings (Ft. 9ⓑ)	(−)18		−	
Individually reporting items :				
Interest paid (Ft. 2ⓒ)	(−)16		(−)8	
Dividends paid (Ft. 2ⓒ, 14)	(−)5		−	

Net cash from financing activities		810		201
Net increase in cash and cash equivalents		4		41
Cash and cash equivalents at beginning of period(Ft. 4)		41		-
Cash and cash equivalents at end of period		45		41

Statement of changes in equity (Ft. 2ⓓ)

From Jan. 1, 20×2 to Dec. 31, 20×2

DDS From Jan. 1, 20×1 to Dec. 31, 20×1 (Numbers in billions of ₩)

Description	Share capital	Share premium	Retained earnings	Accumulated other comprehensive income		Total
	Common stock	Common stock		Accumulated gain on valuation of FVOCI financial asset	Land revaluation surplus	
Balance as of January 1, 20×1	-	-	-	-	-	-
Changes in 20×1 :						
Issuance of common stock (Ft. 13)	100	10				110
Total comprehensive income (Ft. 3ⓓ, 3ⓕ, 6, 8)			26	1	10	37
Balance as of December 31, 20×1	100	10	26	1	10	147
Changes in 20×2 :						
Issuance of common stock (Ft. 13)	50	50				100
Cash dividends (Ft. 14)			(-)5			(-)5
Total comprehensive income (Ft. 3ⓓ, 3ⓕ, 6, 8)			72	3	6	81
Balance as of December 31, 20×2	150	60	93	4	16	323

〈Footnotes〉

3. Important accounting policies

ⓓ Classification of financial assets

Financial assets are classified into cost financial assets, amortized cost financial assets, fair value through profit or loss (FVPL) financial assets, and fair value through other comprehensive income (FVOCI) financial assets. The amortized cost is cost after amortizing premium (discount) on financial assets by the effective interest method. (The company reports no amortized cost financial assets and FVPL financial assets as of December 31, 20×1 and 20×2). Because valuation gains on FVOCI financial assets may be reclassified to profit or loss when these assets are sold, it is reported as an 'item that may be reclassified subsequently to profit or loss.' And the accumulated sum of these gains are reported as 'accumulated gain on valuation of FVOCI financial assets,' in the equity section of the statement of financial position.

ⓔ Valuation of investment in associate

When the company invests in more than 20% of another company's stock, with voting right, and can thus influence the investee company significantly, those investments are reported as 'investments in associates.' Investments in associates are valued by the equity method, and equity income is reported as 'other income' in the comprehensive income statement.

ⓕ Aquisition cost, depreciation methods, and revaluation of tangible assets

(3) Land is revaluated at an appraisal value, which is determined by an external and independent appraiser, every 3 years or whenever there is a large change in fair value. The gain on revaluation, that is, the amount of increase in the book value of the asset due to the revaluation, is an item in other comprehensive income in the comprehensive income statement. This gain on revaluation is reported as an 'item that will not be reclassified to profit or loss' Accumulated gain on revaluation is reported as revaluation surplus, in the equity section of the statement of financial position.

6. Fair value through other comprehensive income (FVOCI) financial asset

The company purchased the following stock for long-term investment purpose and decided to classify this investment in stock as a FVOCI financial asset on the acquisition day. They are valued at the quoted price (market price).

(Numbers in billions of ₩)

<table>
<tr><th>Investment in stock</th><th>Acquisition date</th><th>Number of shares</th><th colspan="2">Base price per share</th><th>Year-end market price per share</th><th>Valuation gain</th></tr>
<tr><td rowspan="2">KM-Mart</td><td rowspan="2">Nov. 1, 20×1</td><td rowspan="2">1 million share</td><td>20×1</td><td>₩9,000 (Acquisition cost)</td><td>₩10,000</td><td>₩1,000 × 1 million share = 1</td></tr>
<tr><td>20×2</td><td>₩10,000 (Market price at beginning of the year)</td><td>₩13,000</td><td>₩3,000 × 1 million share = 3</td></tr>
</table>

7. Investment in associate

Shown below is the content of investment in associate and the reconciliation of the investment in associate account, revealing changes in that account.

Composition of investments in associate

Associate	Aquisition date	Number of shares	Equity
Sohan Inc.	January 2, 20×2	20,000 shares	20%

Reconciliation of investment in associate

(Numbers in billions of ₩)

<table>
<tr><th rowspan="2">Balance at the beginning of 20×2</th><th colspan="3">Changes in 20×2</th><th rowspan="2">Balance at the end of 20×2</th></tr>
<tr><th>Investment</th><th>Add : Equity income</th><th>Less : Dividends received</th></tr>
<tr><td>-</td><td>20</td><td>6</td><td>2</td><td>24</td></tr>
</table>

An explanation of case financial statements

▪ Note : Numbers in superscripts are main text page numbers where the corresponding subjects are explained.

Accounts related to this appendix include fair value through other comprehensive income (FVOCI) financial asset, investment in associate, land, accumulated gain on valuation of FVOCI financial asset and land revaluation surplus in the statement of financial position, and equity income from associate, gain on revaluation of land and gain on valuation of FVOCI financial asset in the comprehensive income statement. In the statement of cash flows, equity income from associate was reported as an adjustment to compute the cash generated from operations indirectly[599], and the purchase of FVOCI financial asset[587] and the purchase of stock of associate and dividends received are reported as investing activities[599]. In the statement of changes in equity, other comprehensive income was reported as a part of the total comprehensive income, and was reflected in each component of accumulated other comprehensive income. So as not to repeat explanations, here we explain items of 20×2 in detail while we omit an explanation of 20×1.

FVOCI financial asset[582] of ₩13 billion and land of ₩96 billion are reported in the statement of financial position of Daehan Department Store, as of December 31, 20×2. According to Footnote 3 ⓓ and Footnote 6, the company evaluates its FVOCI financial asset at the quoted price (market price). Daehan Department Store recognized ₩3 billion and ₩1 billion as gains on the valuation of FVOCI financial asset in 20×2 and 20×1, respectively. Each of those gains was reported as other comprehensive income classified as an 'item that may be reclassified subsequently to profit or loss'[583] in the comprehensive income statement. As shown in the statement of changes in equity, gain on valuation of FVOCI financial asset for each year was accumulated in accumulated gain on valuation of FVOCI financial asset to be ₩4 billion at the end of 20×2. According to Footnote 3 ⓕ (3) and 8, ₩6 billion and ₩10 billion gains on revaluation of land[588] were recognized for 20×2 and 20×1, respectively. Each of these was reported as other comprehensive income classified as an 'item that will not be reclassified to profit or loss.'[588] The statement of changes in equity shows that the gain in revaluation of land for each year was accumulated in the revaluation surplus to be ₩16 billion at the end of 20×2.

Investment in associate[596] of the company is ₩24 billion, as of December 31, 20×2. As described in Footnote 7, this is a result of the purchase of 20% interest in common stock of Sohan Inc. for ₩20 billion on January 20, 20×2. The purchase of stock of this associated company is reported as an investing activity in the statement of cash flows. Daehan Department Store can exercise significant influence on Sohan Inc. because of this investment, so this investment is accounted for as an investment in associate, which is evaluated by the equity method[596]. Sohan Inc. reported a net income of ₩30 billion in 20×2. Daehan Department Store reported ₩6 billion of equity income from associate on the comprehensive income statement, which is 20% of Sohan Inc.'s reported net income. Because this equity income is an income from a non-operating activity (investing activity), it was deducted from the net income before income tax expense (NIBITE), to indirectly compute the cash generated from operations in the statement of cash flows[600]. Dividends of ₩2 billion received[600] from Sohan Inc. decrease the investment of associate and they were reported as cash inflows from investing activities, under the caption of 'individually reporting item,' in the statement of cash flows.

Other comprehensive income and net income

1.1 Other comprehensive income

In general, revenue less expense is called net income. However, some types of income are not permitted to be included in net income. This is because, if they were included, they could distort net income and increase the volatility of net income over time. Income (or loss) that is not included in net income for this reason is called 'other comprehensive income (or loss).' Other comprehensive income is usually comprised of gain or loss from valuing assets at fair value. Examples are gain or loss on the valuation of fair value through other comprehensive income (FVOCI) financial assets, and gain or loss on the revaluation of tangible assets.

Per IFRS[1], other comprehensive income is classified into two types : (1) 'items that may be reclassified subsequently to profit or loss', and (2) 'items that will not be reclassified to profit or loss.' Gain on valuation of FVOCI financial assets is an example of the former, while gain on revaluation of tangible assets is an example of the later.

The purpose of acquiring FVOCI financial assets is to obtain gains from the price difference. Therefore, a gain on the disposal of FVOCI financial assets is computed by taking difference between the disposal amount and the acquisition cost. Because the base of disposal gain is acquisition cost, valuation gains recognized up to the disposal are included in the gain on disposal, which is an item in profit or loss. Therefore, gain on valuation of FVOCI financial assets is classified as one of 'items that may be reclassified subsequently to profit or loss.'

The purpose of purchasing tangible assets is to use them for operation, not to gain a price difference as in the case of FVOCI financial assets. Therefore, the gain on disposal of a revalued tangible asset is computed by taking the difference between the disposal amount and the book value of the asset disposed of. Because the base of disposal gain is the book value, revaluation gains recognized up to the disposal are not included in the gain on disposal, which is an item in profit or loss. Therefore, gain on revaluation of tangible assets is classified as one of 'items that will not be reclassified to profit or loss.'

This book assumes that there is no income tax on other comprehensive income. Income tax effects on other comprehensive income will be reviewed in Intermediate Accounting.

Total comprehensive income is the sum of net income and other comprehensive income. The following 〈Diagram A-1〉 shows this relationship.

〈Diagram A-1〉 Other comprehensive income and net income

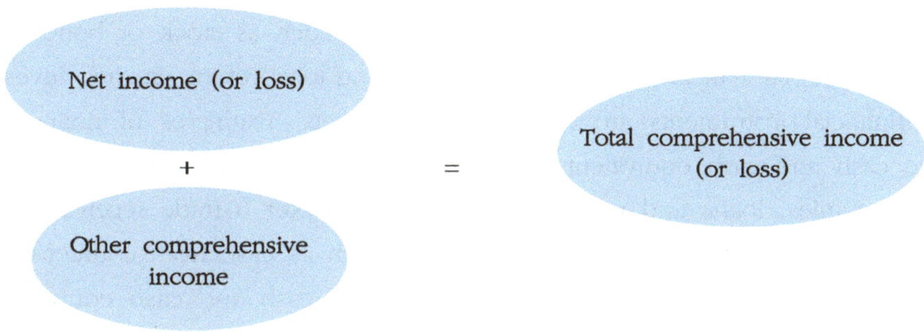

1.2 Retained earnings and accumulated other comprehensive income

Net income in the comprehensive income statement is closed to retained earnings. But other comprehensive incomes are closed to accumulated other comprehensive income. The following 〈Diagram A-2〉 shows this relationship.

〈Diagram A-2〉 Net income and retained earnings, other comprehensive income and accumulated other comprehensive income

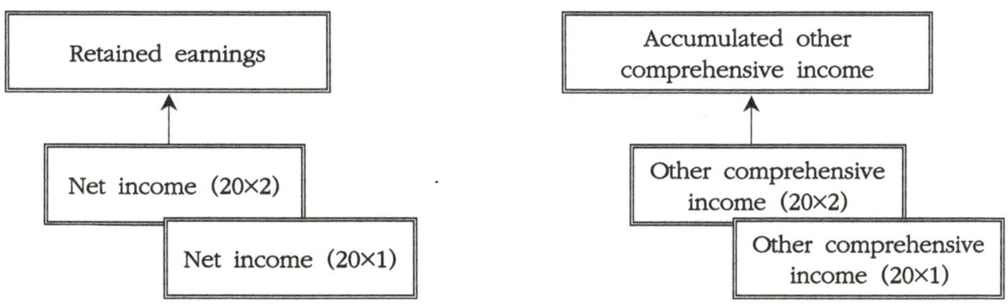

Accounting for fair value through other comprehensive income financial assets

2.1 Nature and classification of financial assets

Companies may purchase financial instruments such as stock or bonds of other companies, etc. as a means of earning short or long term return on their investments. These financial instruments are called financial assets. Examples of financial assets include cash and cash equivalents (refer to Chapter 11, 11.2), stock and bonds of other companies, loans and receivables (refer to Chapter 6 trade receivables) which are contractual rights to receive financial assets such as cash from counter parties of a transaction. Per IFRS[2], financial assets excluding cash and cash equivalents and investment in associates (refer to Section 4 of this Appendix) are classified into amortized cost financial assets, fair value through profit or loss (FVPL) financial assets, and fair value through other comprehensive income (FVOCI) financial assets.

Amortized cost is cost after amortizing premium (discount) on financial assets by the effective interest method (Refer to Chapter 9, Section 3). If there is no premium (discount), the amortized cost is a cost. (This book has distinguished cost financial assets from amortized cost financial assets for educational purposes.) If a company acquires bonds at a premium (or at a discount) and holds them until maturity (purpose of 'holding to maturity'), the investment in those bonds is classified as an amortized cost financial asset. In general, loans made by a company are classified as cost financial assets.

FVOCI financial assets include stock that a company purchases and decides to value at the fair value and recognize valuation gain or loss as other comprehensive income at the time of acquisition. Bonds that a company purchases with the intent of not only 'holding to maturity' and but also 'selling' are also included in FVOCI financial assets. Financial assets that are not included as either amortized cost financial assets or FVOCI financial assets are classified as FVPL financial assets. A company may designate amortized cost financial assets or FVOCI financial assets as

FVPL financial assets to resolve an accounting mismatch. An accounting mismatch is an inconsistency that may arise from measuring assets and liabilities and recognizing the gains or losses on them on different bases.

2.2 Valuation and disposal of fair value through other comprehensive income (FVOCI) financial assets

An FVOCI financial asset is recorded at cost when it is purchased. After the purchase, it is measured at fair value. Fair value (공정가치) is the market price, if there is an active market. If there is no active market, valuation methods are used to compute the value. If the fair value of an FVOCI financial asset is different from its book value, it should be valued at the fair value and the difference between these two amounts should be reported as a gain or loss on valuation. This gain or loss on valuation is reported as other comprehensive income, and is classified as an 'item that may be reclassified subsequently to profit or loss.' As mentioned above, a gain or loss on valuation of FVOCI financial assets is accumulated in 'accumulated gain or loss on valuation of FVOCI financial assets.'

When FVOCI financial assets are disposed of, the gain on disposal is the difference between the disposal amount and the acquisition cost of the asset disposed of, as reviewed above. Therefore, to avoid double-reporting accumulated gain on the valuation of financial assets disposed of, IFRS[3] requires that the accumulated gain should be reclassified as another comprehensive loss. (Accumulated loss, on the contrary, should be reclassified into other comprehensive income.)

〈Illustration A-1〉 Valuation and disposal of FVOCI financial assets

Daehan Inc. purchased 1 million shares of common stock of Sohan Inc. at ₩10,000 per share to obtain investment income on July 1, 20×1 and decided to classify as FVOCI financial assets. On December 31, 20×1 and 20×2 the share price of Sohan Inc. were ₩12,000 and ₩11,000 respectively. On January 2, 20×3 Daehan Inc. sold all shares of stock of Sohan Inc. at ₩13,000 per share.

(1) Journal entries

Journal entries to be prepared, from the acquisition date of the stock of Sohan

Inc. on July 1, 20×1 to their disposal date of January 2, 20×3, are the following. (Numbers in all journal entries are in billions of ₩.)

July 1, 20×1 :

(Dr.) FVOCI financial assets	10	(Cr.) Cash	10*

* 1 million shares × 10,000 = ₩10 billion

December 31, 20×1 :

(Dr.) FVOCI financial assets	2	(Cr.) Gain on valuation of FVOCI financial assets	2*

* 1 million shares × (12,000 − 10,000) = ₩2 billion

December 31, 20×1 (Closing journal entry) :

(Dr.) Gain on valuation of FVOCI financial assets	2	(Cr.) Accumulated gains on valuation of FVOCI financial assets	2

December 31, 20×2 :

(Dr.) Loss on valuation of FVOCI financial assets	1*	(Cr.) FVOCI financial assets	1

* 1 million shares × (12,000 − 11,000) = ₩1 billion

December 31, 20×2 (Closing journal entry) :

(Dr.) Accumulated gains on valuation of FVOCI financial assets	1	(Cr.) Loss on valuation of FVOCI financial assets	1

January 2, 20×3 :

(Dr.) Reclassification adjustment	1*	(Cr.) FVOCI financial assets	1

(Dr.) Cash	13	(Cr.) FVOCI financial assets	10
		Gain on disposal of FVOCI financial assets	3**

* To change the FVOCI financial assets account balance to acquisition cost, we reclassify the valuation gain of ₩1 billion [= 1 million share × (11,000 − 10,000)], reflected in the FVOCI financial assets account balance. The reclassification adjustment should be reported as other comprehensive loss under the title of 'reclassification adjustment for gain included in profit or loss,' in the comprehensive income statement.

** 1 million shares × (13,000 − 10,000) = ₩3 billion

December 31, 20×3 (Closing journal entry) :

(Dr.)			(Cr.)		
	Gain on disposal of FVOCI financial assets	3		Retained earnings	3
	Accumulated gain on valuation of FVOCI financial assets	1		Reclassification adjustment	1*

* Reclassification adjustment, reported as other comprehensive loss, is closed to accumulated gain on valuation of FVOCI financial assets. As a result of this closing journal entry, the account balance for accumulated gain on valuation of FVOCI financial assets becomes '0.'

(2) The comprehensive income statement and the statement of financial position

The following 〈Table A-1〉 and 〈Table A-2〉 are the partial comprehensive income statement and the partial statement of financial position, respectively prepared after posing journal entries in (1).

〈Table A-1〉 Partial comprehensive income statement

Sohan Inc. (Numbers in billions of ₩)

Account titles	Amount		
	20×3	20×2	20×1
Other revenue			
Gain on disposal of FVOCI financial assets	Ⓧ 3	–	–
Net income before income tax expense (NIBITE)	Ⓜ 3		
Other comprehensive income			
Items that may be reclassified subsequently to profit or loss :			
Gain (loss) on valuation of FVOCI financial assets	–	Ⓑ (–)1	Ⓐ 2
Reclassification adjustment for gain included in profit or loss	Ⓒ (–)1	–	–
Total comprehensive income	2	(–)1	2

〈Table A-2〉 Partial statement of financial position

Sohan Inc. (Numbers in billions of ₩)

Account titles	Amount		
	End of 20×3	End of 20×2	End of 20×1
Assets			
Non-current assets			
FVOCI financial assets	–	11	12
Equity			
Accumulated other comprehensive income			
Accumulated gain on valuation of FVOCI assets	–	1	2

(3) The statement of cash flows

1) T account analyses

The following 〈Diagram A-3〉 are T account analyses to prepare the statement of cash flows.

〈Diagram A-3〉 T account analyses

FVOCI financial assets

① Purchase	10				10(Dr.)
ⓐ Gain on valuation	2			End of 20×1	12(Dr.)
		ⓑ Loss on valuation	1	End of 20×2	11(Dr.)
		ⓒ Reclassification	1		10(Dr.)
		② Sales	10	End of 20×3	-

Note : ⓐ, ⓑ, ⓒ are Ⓐ, Ⓑ, Ⓒ in the comprehensive income statement.

Retained earnings

		ⓜ NIBITE	2	End of 20×3	2(Cr.)

Note : ⓜ is Ⓜ in the comprehensive income statement.

Accumulated gain on valuation of FVOCI assets

		ⓐ Gain on valuation	2	End of 20×1	2(Cr.)
ⓑ Loss on valuation	1			End of 20×2	1(Cr.)
ⓒ Reclassification	1			End of 20×3	-

Note : ⓐ, ⓑ, ⓒ are Ⓐ, Ⓑ, Ⓒ in the comprehensive income statement.

2) Preparing the statement of cash flows

ⓐ, ⓑ, ⓒ are non-cash transactions so they are not reported in the statement of cash flows. The following ⟨Table A-3⟩ is the statement of cash flows prepared using the comprehensive income statement information and information obtained from T account analyses.

⟨Table A-3⟩ Partial statement of cash flows

Sohan Inc. (Numbers in billions of ₩)

Description	Amount		
	20×3	20×2	20×1
Cash flows from operating activities			
Net income before income tax expense (NIBITE)	ⓜ 3	–	–
Gain from non-operating activities			
Gain on disposal of FVOCI financial assets	Ⓧ (-)3	–	–
Net cash from operating activities	–	–	–
Cash flows from investing activities			
Proceeds from sales of FVOCI financial assets	Ⓧ 3 + ② 10 = 13	–	–
Purchase of FVOCI financial assets	–	–	① (-)10
Net cash used in investing activities	13	–	(-)10

Accounting for revaluation of tangible assets

3.1 Nature of revaluation of tangible assets

IFRS[4] allows us to revalue a tangible asset at fair value, if we can measure the fair value of that asset reliably after its acquisition. If a tangible asset is to be revalued, all of the family of assets to which that asset belongs should be revalued together. Examples of families of assets include land, buildings, machinery, ships, aircraft, motor vehicles, furniture and fixtures, office equipment, etc. If an asset is revalued, the book value of the asset should be fair value at the revaluation date, less subsequent accumulated depreciation and accumulated impairment losses. Fair value is the exchange price that would be received or paid between independent, knowledgeable, and willing parties in an arm's length transaction. Appraised value, determined by a certified appraisal institute, can be a proxy of fair value.

IFRS[5] requires us to conduct revaluation every year, if the changes in fair value of assets already revalued are significant. If changes in fair value are not significant; however, we may do revaluation every three or five years.

3.2 Revaluation and disposal of tangible assets

If the book value of an asset is increased as a result of a revaluation, the increase shall be reported as a gain on revaluation. Gain on revaluation is another type of comprehensive income that is classified as an 'item that will not be reclassified to profit or loss.' Gain on revaluation is closed to revaluation surplus, which is an equity, at the end of the year. IFRS[6] requires that if the book value of an asset is decreased as the result of a revaluation, we should report the decrease as a loss on revaluation, to the extent of the balance in the revaluation surplus associated with that asset. However, if book value is decreased below the original acquisition cost, then the decrease should be reported as a part of net loss for the current period. If book value is increased after a loss on revaluation was recognized as a net loss for the current period, the increase should be recognized as net income for the current period, to the extent of the amount reported as net loss in the past.

There is no duplicate reporting problem, because the gain or loss on disposal of revalued tangible assets is computed based on the net book value, not based on the acquisition cost. There is merely a question as to whether we should reclassify revaluation surplus into retained earnings or not. This reclassification, if made, does not affect the total amount of equity, because this reclassification is an adjustment within the equity. IFRS[7] allows companies to decide whether or not the reclassification within equity should be made.

〈Illustration A-2〉 Revaluation and disposal of tangible assets

Daehan Inc. purchased land at ₩10 billion on January 1, 20×1. The company made a decision to revaluate this land at end of every year. The following 〈Table A-4〉 is fair value of this land for 4 years.

〈Table A-4〉 Fair value of land

(Numbers in billions of ₩)

Date	Fair value
December 31, 20×1	13
December 31, 20×2	11
December 31, 20×3	8
December 31, 20×4	11

Daehan Inc. sold the revalued land on April 3, 20×5 and received ₩13 billion in cash.

(1) Journal entries

The following are journal entries Daehan Inc. should prepare from January 1, 20×1 to December 31, 20×5. (Numbers in all entries are in billions of ₩).

January 1, 20×1

(Dr.) Land	10	(Cr.) Cash	10

December 31, 20×1

(Dr.) Land	3	(Cr.) Gain on revaluation of land (OCI*)	3

* OCI: Other comprehensive income

December 31, 20×1 (Closing journal entry)

(Dr.) Gain on revaluation of land (OCI)	3	(Cr.) Land revaluation surplus	3

December 31, 20×2

(Dr.) Loss on revaluation of land (OCI)	2	(Cr.) Land	2

December 31, 20×2 (Closing journal entry)

(Dr.) Land revaluation surplus	2	(Cr.) Loss on revaluation of land (OCI)	2

After this closing entry, the land revaluation surplus shall be ₩1 billion.

December 31, 20×3

(Dr.) Loss on revaluation of land (OCI)	1	(Cr.) Land	3
Land revaluation loss (Profit or loss)	2		

To the extent of the balance of land revaluation surplus of ₩1 billion from total decrease of book value due to revaluation of ₩3 billion should be recognised as a loss on revaluation of land that is classified as an other comprehensive income, and remaining ₩2 billion should be recognized as land revaluation loss that is reflected in profit or loss.

December 31, 20×3 (Closing journal entry)

(Dr.) Retained earnings	2	(Cr.) Land revaluation loss (Profit or loss)	2

(Dr.) Land revaluation surplus	1	(Cr.) Loss on revaluation of land (OCI)	1

After this closing journal entry, land revaluation surplus shall be '0.'

December 31, 20×4

(Dr.) Land	3	(Dr.) Land revaluation gain (Profit or loss)	2
		Gain on revaluation of land (OCI)	1

In this case, there was a land revaluation loss of ₩2 billion, which was reflected in net income in the past. Therefore, ₩2 billion out of the total increase in book value of ₩3 billion, due to revaluation, should be reported as a land revaluation gain and be reflected in profit or loss. The remaining ₩1 billion should be reported as a gain on the revaluation of land, which is classified as other comprehensive income.

December 31, 20×4 (Closing journal entry)

(Dr.) Land revaluation gain (Profit or loss)	2	(Cr.) Retained earnings	2

(Dr.) Gain on revaluation of land (OCI)	1	(Cr.) Land revaluation surplus	1

After this closing journal entry, land revaluation surplus shall be ₩1 billion.

April 3, 20×5

(Dr.) Cash	13	(Cr.) Land Gain on disposal of land (Profit or loss)	11 2

Gain on disposal of land, of ₩2 billion, is included in profit or loss.

December 31, 20×5 (Closing journal entry)

(Dr.) Gain on disposal of land (Profit or loss)	2	(Cr.) Retained earnings	2

Concerning the land disposed of, there is a revaluation surplus of ₩1 billion. Companies can select either one of the following two accounting methods :

① Land revaluation surplus is reclassified

(Dr.) Land revaluation surplus	1	(Cr.) Retained earnings	1

Land revaluation surplus of ₩1 billion is reclassified to retained earnings, because it was realized by the disposal. Total equity after this reclassification is ₩3 billion, because the retained earning is ₩3 billion after this reclassification (Gain on disposal ₩2 billion + Reclassification of ₩1 billion) and land revaluation surplus is '0.'

② Land revaluation surplus is not reclassified

No journal entry.

In this case, total equity is ₩3 billion because retained earnings are ₩2 billion (Gain on disposal) and revaluation surplus is ₩1 billion. Likewise, total equity is the same as in (1), above, in which reclassification was made.

(2) The comprehensive income statement and the statement of financial position

The following 〈Table A-5〉 and 〈Table A-6〉 are the partial comprehensive income statement and the partial statement of financial position, respectively after posing journal entries in (1).

〈Table A-5〉 Partial comprehensive income statement

Daehan Inc. (Numbers in billions of ₩)

Account titles	Amount				
	20×5	20×4	20×3	20×2	20×1
Other revenues					
Gain on disposal of land	Ⓧ 2				
Land revaluation gain		Ⓛ 2			
Other expense					
Land revaluation loss			Ⓚ (−)2		
Net income before income tax expense (NIBITE)	Ⓖ 2	Ⓕ 2	Ⓔ (−)2		
Other comprehensive income					
Items that will not be reclassified to profit or loss					
Gain on revaluation of land		Ⓓ 1			Ⓐ 3
Loss on revaluation of land			Ⓒ (−)1	Ⓑ (−)2	
Total comprehensive income	2	3	(−)3	(−)2	3

〈Table A-6〉 Partial statement of financial position

Daehan Inc. (Numbers in billions of ₩)

Account titles	Amount					
	End of 20×5		End of 20×4	End of 20×3	End of 20×2	End of 20×1
	Reclass.					
	Yes	No				
Assets						
Non-current assets						
Land	−		11	8	11	13
Equity						
Retained earnings	3	2		(−)2		
Accumulated other comprehensive income						
Land revaluation surplus	−	1	1		1	3

(3) The statement of cash flows

1) T account analysis

The following ⟨Diagram A-4⟩ are T account analyses to prepare the statement of cash flows.

⟨Diagram A-4⟩ T account analyses

Land

Debit		Credit			
① Purchase	10				10(Dr.)
ⓐ Gain on revaluation	3			End of 20×1	13(Dr.)
		ⓑ Loss on revaluation	2	End of 20×2	11(Dr.)
		ⓒ Loss on revaluation	1		10(Dr.)
		ⓚ Revaluation loss	2	End of 20×3	8(Dr.)
ⓛ Revaluation gain	2				10(Dr.)
ⓓ Gain on revaluation	1			End of 20×1	11(Dr.)
		② Sales	11	End of 20×5	-

Note : ⓐ, ⓑ, ⓒ, ⓓ, ⓚ, ⓛ are Ⓐ, Ⓑ, Ⓒ, Ⓓ, Ⓚ, Ⓛ in the comprehensive income statement.

Retained earnings

Debit		Credit			
ⓔ NIBITE	2			End of 20×3	2(Dr.)
		ⓕ NIBITE	2	End of 20×4	-
		ⓖ NIBITE	2	End of 20×5	2(Cr.)
If reclassified :					
		ⓡ Reclassification	1	End of 20×5	3(Cr.)

Note : ⓔ, ⓕ, ⓖ are Ⓔ, Ⓕ, Ⓖ in the comprehensive income statement.

Land revaluation surplus

Debit		Credit			
		ⓐ Gain on revaluation	3	End of 20×1	3(Cr.)
ⓑ Loss on revaluation	2			End of 20×2	1(Cr.)
ⓒ Loss on revaluation	1			End of 20×3	-
		ⓓ Gain on revaluation	1	End of 20×2	1(Cr.)
If reclassified :					
ⓡ Reclassification	1			End of 20×5	-

Note : ⓐ, ⓑ, ⓒ, ⓓ are Ⓐ, Ⓑ, Ⓒ, Ⓓ in the comprehensive income statement.

2) Preparing the statement of cash flows

ⓐ, ⓑ, ⓒ, ⓓ, (if reclassified ⓡ) are other comprehensive income and non-cash transactions so they are not reported in the statement of cash flows. The following ⟨Table A-7⟩ is the statement of cash flows prepared using comprehensive income statement information and information obtained from T account analyses.

⟨Table A-7⟩ Partial statement of cash flows

Daehan Inc. (Numbers in billions of ₩)

Description	Amount				
	20×5	20×4	20×3	20×2	20×1
Cash flows from operating activities					
Net income before income tax expense (NIBITE)	ⓖ 2	ⓕ2	ⓔ (−)2	−	−
Gains and loss from non-operating activities					
Land revaluation gain		Ⓛ(−)2			
Land revaluation loss			Ⓚ 2		
Gain on disposal of land	Ⓧ (−)2			−	−
Net cash from operating activities	−	−	−	−	−
Cash flows from investing activities					
Land revaluation gain	−	Ⓛ2	−	−	−
Increase in land by revaluation gain	−	ⓛ (−)2	−	−	−
Land revaluation loss	−	−	Ⓚ (−)2	−	−
Decrease in land by revaluation loss	−	−	ⓚ 2	−	−
Proceeds from sales of land	Ⓧ 2 + ② 11 = 13	−	−	−	−
Purchase of land	−	−	−	−	① (−)10
Net cash used in investing activities	13	−	−	−	(−)10

Equity method and consolidated financial statements

4.1 Investments in associates

Companies may hold stock of other companies to make use of idle cash or to pursue a long-term return on investment. In some instances, the investment company (investor) may invest in the investee company's (investee's) stock with voting rights, to exercise significant influence on the investee. We call investments in stock that are made for this purpose as 'investments in associates.' The associates are the investees, on whom the investor can have significant influence.

In general, the more shares of an investee's stock with voting right an investor holds, the more influence the investor has over the investee. Per IFRS[8], if an investor holds, directly or indirectly, 20% or more shares of an investee's stock with voting right, it is presumed that the investor can exercise a significant influence unless there is a contradictory real evidence.

4.2 Equity method and cost method

If an investor has a significant influence on an associate's appropriation of earnings as dividends, the investor can make the associate pay dividends at the investor's will. Therefore, the investor can recognize the associate's share of the associate's profit as the investor's income, when the associate reports profit. In this context, the equity method is an accounting method by which the investor recognizes its share of the associate's profit as income and adjusts 'investment in associates' upward by the same amount when the associate reports profit.

Under the equity method, the investment in associate account is adjusted upward every time the associate reports profit. But if the associate pays dividends, the balance of investment in associate should be reduced by the amount of dividends received. This is because dividends are considered to be a conversion of recognized the associate's income into cash.

If an investor does not have a significant influence on the company invested, the cost method should be used. Per IFRS[9], as required in Korea, investment in associate can be reported by the cost method in separate financial statements when additional consolidated financial statements (reflecting equity income in consolidated net income) should be prepared. (Refer to 4.3 'Consolidated financial statements.') Under the cost method, investments in stock are recorded at the cost and dividends received are recorded as revenues.

〈Illustration A-3〉 Equity method and cost method

On January 1, 20×1, Daehan Inc. purchased 30% of Seoul Inc.'s stock with voting right at ₩10 billion and could exercise significant influence on Seoul Inc. Seoul Inc. reported net income of ₩20 billion on December 31, 20×1. The company reported net income of ₩30 billion on December 31, 20×2 and paid dividends of ₩10 billion on April 15, 20×2.

(1) Journal entries

1) Equity method

The following are journal entries Daehan Inc. should prepare when the equity method is applied. (Numbers in all journal entries are in billions of ₩).

January 1, 20×1 : Purchase of associate stock

(Dr.) Investment in associate	10	(Cr.) Cash	10

December 31, 20×1 : Reporting net income by associate

(Dr.) Investment in associate	6	(Cr.) Equity income from associate	6*

* 20 billion × 30% = ₩6 billion

April 15, 20×2 : Receipt of associate dividends

(Dr.) Cash	3	(Cr.) Investment in associate	3*

* 10 billion × 30% = ₩3 billion

December 31, 20×2 : Reporting net income by associate

(Dr.) Investment in associate	9	(Cr.) Equity income from associate	9*

* 30 billion × 30% = ₩9 billion7

2) Cost method

The following are journal entries Daehan Inc. should prepare when the cost method is applied. (Numbers in all journal entries are in billions of ₩).

January 1, 20×1 : Purchase of associate stock

(Dr.) Investment in associate	10	(Cr.) Cash	10

April 15, 20×2 : Receipt of associate dividends

(Dr.) Cash	3	(Cr.) Dividends revenue	3*

* 10 billion × 30% = ₩3 billion

3) Comparison of journal entries under equity method and cost method

The following 〈Table A-8〉 is a comparison of journal entries under the equity method with those under the cost method.

〈Table A-8〉 Journal entries under equity method and cost method

(Numbers in billions of ₩)

<table>
<tr><th>Date</th><th colspan="2">Equity method</th><th colspan="2">Cost method</th></tr>
<tr><td rowspan="2">Jan. 1, 20×1</td><td colspan="4">Purchase of associate stock</td></tr>
<tr><td>(Dr.) Investment in associate 10</td><td>(Cr.) Cash 10</td><td colspan="2">Same as equity method.</td></tr>
<tr><td rowspan="2">Dec. 31, 20×1</td><td colspan="4">Reporting of net income from associate by associate</td></tr>
<tr><td>(Dr.) Investment in associate 6</td><td>(Cr.) Equity income from associate 6</td><td colspan="2">No journal entry.</td></tr>
<tr><td rowspan="2">Apr. 15, 20×2</td><td colspan="4">Receipt of associate dividends</td></tr>
<tr><td>(Dr.) Cash 3</td><td>(Cr.) Investment in associate 3</td><td>(Dr.) Cash 3</td><td>(Cr.) Dividends revenue 3</td></tr>
<tr><td rowspan="2">Dec. 31, 20×2</td><td colspan="4">Reporting of net income from associate by associate</td></tr>
<tr><td>(Dr.) Investment in associate 9</td><td>(Cr.) Equity income from associate 9</td><td colspan="2">No journal entry.</td></tr>
</table>

(2) Income statement, statement of financial position, and statement of cash flows

1) Equity method

The following 〈Table A-9〉 and 〈Table A-10〉 are the partial income statement and the partial statement of financial position to be reported when the equity method is used.

〈Table A-9〉 Partial income statement—equity method

Daehan Inc. (Numbers in billions of ₩)

Account titles	Amount	
	20×2	20×1
Other revenue		
Equity income from associate	Ⓛ 9	Ⓚ 6
Net income before income tax expense (NIBITE)	Ⓝ 9	Ⓜ 6

〈Table A-10〉 Partial statement of financial position—equity method

Daehan Inc. (Numbers in billions of ₩)

Account titles	Amount	
	End of 20×2	End of 20×1
Assets		
Non-current assets		
Investment in associate	22	16

The following 〈Diagram A-5〉 are T account analyses to prepare the statement of cash flows under the equity method.

〈Diagram A-5〉 T account analyses—equity method

Investment in associate

① Purchase	10			10(Dr.)
ⓚ Equity income	6			End of 20×1 16(Dr.)
		② Dividends	3	End of 20×2 13(Dr.)
ⓛ Equity income	9			22(Dr.)

Note : ⓚ, ⓛ are Ⓚ, Ⓛ in the income statement.

Retained earnings

	ⓜ NIBITE	6	End of 20×1 6(Cr.)
	ⓝ NIBITE	9	End of 20×2 15(Cr.)

Note : ⓜ, ⓝ are Ⓜ, Ⓝ in the income statement.

The following ⟨Table A-11⟩ is the statement of cash flows—equity method prepared using the income statement information and information obtained from T account analyses.

⟨Table A-11⟩ Partial statement of cash flows—equity method

Daehan Inc. (Numbers in billions of ₩)

Description	Amount	
	20×2	20×1
Cash flows from operating activities		
Net income before income tax expense (NIBITE)	ⓝ 9	ⓜ 6
Income from non-operating activities		
Equity income from associate	ⓛ (-)9	ⓚ (-)6
Net cash from operating activities	-	-
Cash flows from investing activities		
Individually reporting item :		
Dividends received	② 3	-
Purchase of stock of associate	-	① (-)10
Net cash used for investing activities	3	(-)10

2) Cost method

The following ⟨Table A-12⟩ and ⟨Table A-13⟩ are the partial income statement and the partial statement of financial position to be reported when the cost method is used.

⟨Table A-12⟩ Partial income statement

Daehan Inc. (Numbers in billions of ₩)

Account titles	Amount	
	20×2	20×1
Other revenue		
Dividends revenue	Ⓚ 3	-
Net income before income tax expense (NIBITE)	Ⓛ 3	-

〈Table A-13〉 Partial statement of financial position

Daehan Inc. (Numbers in billions of ₩)

Account titles	Amount	
	End of 20×2	End of 20×1
Assets		
Non-current assets		
Investment in associate	10	10

The following 〈Diagram A-6〉 are T account analyses to prepare the statement of cash flows under the cost method.

〈Diagram A-6〉 T account analyses

Investment in associate

① Purchase 10		10(Dr.)

Retained earnings

	① NIBITE 3	End of 20×2 3(Cr.)

Note : ① is Ⓛ in the income statement.

The following 〈Table A-14〉 is the statement of cash flows—cost method prepared using the income statement information and information obtained from T account analyses.

〈Table A-14〉 Partial statement of cash flows—cost method

Daehan Inc. (Numbers in billions of ₩)

Description	Amount	
	20×2	20×1
Cash flows from operating activities		
Net income before income tax expense (NIBITE)	① 3	-
NIBITE revenue related with individually reporting items		
Dividends revenue	Ⓚ (-)3	-
Net cash from operating activities	-	-
Cash flows from investing activities		
Individually reporting item :		
Dividends received	Ⓚ 3	-
Purchase of stock of associate	-	① (-)10
Net cash used for investing activities	3	(-)10

4.3 Consolidated financial statements

(1) Nature of consolidated financial statements

When an investor holds the stock of another company to exercise control, we call said stock an investment in associate, as noted above. Per IFRS[10], if an investor has rights to returns from an investee and ability to affect those returns through its power over the investee, it is presumed that the investor has control over the investee. When an investor has such control, the investor is considered a parent. The subsidiary is an entity that is controlled by the parent. In this case, both parent and subsidiary can be treated as a single accounting entity, since the management of the parent can directly control the entire management of the subsidiary. For this reason, the parent needs to prepare consolidated financial statements that show the two companies as one company. [In Korea, consolidate financial statements should be prepared in addition to separate financial statements for parents per 'Law on External Audit of Corporations,' and K-IFRS (KAI issued)[11] requires, to apply international accounting standards when these financial statements are prepared.]

(2) Preparation of consolidated financial statements

Consolidated financial statements are prepared when two or more companies can be treated as a single company under the control of the parent, even though they are legally separated. Consolidated financial statements include the consolidated statement of financial position, the consolidated comprehensive income statement, the consolidated statement of cash flows, and the consolidated statement of changes in equity—just as with individual financial statements. Basically, consolidated financial statements are prepared by adding the financial statements of the parent to those of its subsidiaries. Let's prepare a consolidated statement of financial position, a consolidated income statement, a consolidated statement of cash flows, and a consolidated statement of changes in equity, using the following simple illustration.

〈Illustration A-4〉 Preparing consolidated financial statements

P Co. was founded on January 1, 20×1. P Co. invested ₩8 billion and set up an 80% owned subsidiary, S Co. on January 1, 20×1. The following 〈Table A-15〉 and 〈Table A-16〉 are P Co. and S Co.'s income statement for 20×1 and statement of financial position at the end of 20×1, respectively.

〈Table A-15〉 Income statement

From January 1, 20×1 to December 31, 20×1

(Numbers in billions of ₩)

Description	Amount	
	P Co.	S Co.
Sales	100	50
Expenses	70	30
Net income	30	20

〈Table A-16〉 Statement of financial position

As of December 31, 20×1

(Numbers in billions of ₩)

Description	Amount		Description	Amount	
	P Co.	S Co.		P Co.	S Co.
General assets	120	50	Liabilities	50	20
Investment in associate	8	-	Equity : Share capital-common stock Retained earnings	 48 30	 10 20
Total assets	128	50	Liabilities and equity	128	50

First, the consolidated income statement is prepared as the following 〈Table A-17〉. Consolidated sales is ₩150 billion (₩100 billion + ₩50 billion), consolidated expenses is ₩100 billion (₩70 billion + ₩30 billion), and consolidated net income is ₩50 billion (₩30 billion + ₩20 billion). The consolidated net income is classified into ₩46 billion for owners of the parent and ₩4 billion for non-controlling interest. Per IFRS[12], the non-controlling interest is defined as "equity in a subsidiary not attributable, directly or indirectly, to a parent."

⟨Table A-17⟩ Consolidated income statement

From January 1, 20×2 to December 31, 20×2

(Numbers in billions of ₩)

Description	Amount		
	P Co.	S Co.	Consolidated
Sales	100	50	150
Expense	70	30	100
Net income	30	20	50
Owners of parent	30	20 × 80%	46
Non-controlling interest		20 × 20%	4

Next, the consolidated statement of financial position should be prepared as following ⟨Table A-18⟩. P Co.'s investment in associate of ₩8 billion is not included in consolidated assets and S Co.'s share capital-common stock of ₩8 billion is not included in consolidated equity. The reason is that investment of ₩8 billion by P Co. to S Co. is a transaction within the consolidated companies, which does not affect consolidated financial position. Therefore, the consolidated assets are ₩170 billion (₩120 billion + ₩50 billion) and consolidated liabilities are ₩70 billion (₩50 billion + ₩20 billion). The consolidated equity is ₩100 billion is classified into owners of parent of ₩94 billion (share capital-common stock of 48 billion + retained earnings of 46 billion) and non-controlling interest of ₩6 billion (increase in non-controlling interest of 2 billion + retained earnings of 4 billion).

⟨Table A-18⟩ Consolidated statement of financial position

As of December 31, 20×2

(Numbers in billions of ₩)

Description	Amount			Description	Amount				
	P Co.	S Co.	Con.		P Co.	S Co.	Consoldated		
General assets	120	50	170	Liabilities	50	20			70
Investment in associate	8			Equity					100
Off-set	(−)8			Owners of parent				94	
				Share capital-common stock	48		48		
				Retained earnings	30	16(20×80%)	46		
				Non-controlling interest				6	
				Share capital-common stock		10			
				Off-set		(−)8	2		
				Retained earning		4(20×20%)	4		
Total assets			170	Total liabilities and equity					170

The consolidated statement of cash flows (indirect method) is prepared using the consolidated income statement and consolidated statement of financial position as shown in ⟨Table A-19⟩ below.

⟨Table A-19⟩ Consolidated statement of cash flows (indirect method)

P Co. From Jan. 1, 20×1 to Dec. 31, 20×1 (Numbers in billions of ₩)

Description	Amount	
Cash flows from operating activities*		
Net income	50	
Net cash from operating activities		**50**
Cash flows from investing activities		
Purchase of 80% owned subsidiary S Co.**	(−)8	
Purchase of general assets (170 − 30 × 80%)	(−)146	
Net cash used in investing activities		**(−)154**
Cash flows from financing activities		
Borrowings (70 − 20 × 80%)	54	
Issuance of common stock	48	
Increase in non-controlling interest	2	
Net cash from financing activities		**104**
Net increase in cash		−
Cash at beginning of period		−
Cash at end of period		−

* If the direct method is used, cash receipts from customers of ₩150 billion less cash paid to suppliers and employees of ₩100 billion, net of ₩50 billion is reported as cash flows from operating activities.

** Disclosure of detailed purchase of 80% owned subsidiary S. Co. − IFRS[13]

Assets (30 billion × 80%)	₩ 24 billion
Liabilities (20 billion × 80%)	(−)16 billion
Cash paid	₩ 8 billion

The statement of changes in equity is prepared analysing equity accounts in the consolidated statement of financial position as shown in ⟨Table A-20⟩ below.

⟨Table A-20⟩ Consolidated statement of changes in equity

From Jan. 1, 20×1 to Dec. 31, 20×1 (Numbers in billions of ₩)

Description	Owners of parent		Non-controlling interest	Total
	Share capital-common stock	Retained earning		
Balance at January 1, 20×1	-	-	-	-
Changes in equity for 20×1 :				
Issuance of common stock	48			48
Net income		46	4	50
Increase in non-controlling interest			2	2
Balance at December 31, 20×1	48	46	6	100

IFRS references (http://www.kasb.or.kr)

[1] IAS 1 *Presentation of Financial Statements*, par. 82A.
[2] IFRS 9 *Financial Instruments*, par. 4.1.2, 4.1.2A, 4.1.4.
[3] *Ibid.* par. 5.7.10.
IAS 1 *op. cit.* par. 93, 94.
[4] IAS 16 *Property, Plant and Equipment*, par. 31, 36.
[5] *Ibid.* par. 34.
[6] *Ibid*, par. 40.
[7] *Ibid*, par. 41.
[8] IAS 28 *Investments in Associates and Joint Ventures*, par. 5.
[9] IAS 27 *Separate Financial statements*, par. 10.
[10] IFRS 10 *Consolidated Financial Statements*, par. 5, 6, 7, 19.
[11] *Ibid*, par. Korean 3.1.
IAS 27 *op. cit.* par. Korean 1.1.
[12] IFRS 10 *op. cit.* Appendix A Defined terms.
[13] IAS 7 *Statement of Cash Flows,* par. 39, 40.

Key terms

Cost method (원가법) : An accounting method under which investments in stock are recorded at cost and dividends received are recorded as revenues. (p.597)

Consolidated financial statements (연결재무제표) : Financial statements that a parent prepares for an accounting entity that is composed of the parent and its subsidiaries together. (p.602)

Equity method (지분법) : An accounting method by which the investor recognize its share of the associates' profit reported as income and adjusts investments in associates upward by the same amount. (p.596)

Fair value through other comprehensive income (FVOCI) financial assets [공정가치 측정 기타포괄이익인식 (공가기포익) 금융자산] : Financial assets that a company decides to value at the fair value and recognize valuation gain or loss as other comprehensive income at the time of acquisition. (p.580)

Fair value through profit or loss (FVPL) financial assets [공정가치 측정 당기손익인식 (공가당손익) 금융자산] : Financial assets that are not include as either amortized cost financial assets or FVOCI financial assets. (p.582)

Financial assets (금융자산) : Stock or bonds of other companies purchased to earn short or long term return. (p.582)

Gain on revaluation (재평가차익) : Increase amount of book value due to revaluation of assets. (p.580)

Investments in associates (관계기업투자) : Investee company's stock with voting right that is purchased by an investor company to exercise significant influence on the investee company. (p.596)

Non-controlling interest (비지배지분) : Equity in a subsidiary not attributable, directly or indirectly, to a parent. (p.603)

Parent (지배기업) : An investor that has control over an investee company. (p.602)

Revaluation surplus (재평가잉여금) : Accumulated amount of gain on revaluation. (p.588)

Separate financial statements (별도재무제표) : Financial statements that a parent prepares for an accounting entity that excludes its subsidiaries but includes only the parent. (p.602)

Subsidiary (종속기업) : A company that is controlled by a parent company. (p.602)

Key Financial Ratios

Ⅰ. Evaluating profitability

Ⅱ. Evaluating growth

Ⅲ. Evaluating activity

Ⅳ. Evaluating safety (financial)

Ⅴ. Price multiples

〈Table B-1〉 Key financial ratios

C	Financial ratio	Formula	Use	Text*
I. P	Profit margin on sales	$\frac{\text{Net income}}{\text{Sales}}$	Evaluate how much net income is generated on every ₩1 of sales.	p.224
	Operating income to sales ratio	$\frac{\text{Income from operations}}{\text{Sales}}$	Evaluate how much income from operations is generated on every ₩1 of sales.	p.225
	Return on assets (ROA : 총자산이익률)	$\frac{\text{Net income}}{\text{Average total assets}}$	Evaluate how much net income is generated in relation to total assets.	p.226
	Return on equity (ROE : 자기자본이익률)	$\frac{\text{Net income}}{\text{Average equity}}$	Evaluate how much net income is generated in relation to equity.	p.227
	Earnings per share (EPS : 주당이익)	$\frac{\text{Net income} - \text{Preferred stock dividends}}{\text{Weighted average common shares outstanding}}$	Evaluate how much net income per share of common stock is generated.	p.229
	Payout ratio	$\frac{\text{Common stock cash dividends}}{\text{Net income} - \text{Preferred stock dividends}}$	Evaluate how much cash dividends are paid from net income applicable to common stock holders.	p.486
	Cash-flows per share (CPS : 주당현금흐름)	$\frac{\text{Operating cash flows} - \text{Preferred stock dividends}}{\text{Weighted average common shares outstanding}}$	Evaluate how much operating cash flows per share of common stock are generated.	p.552
	Operating cash flows to total assets ratio	$\frac{\text{Operating cash flows}}{\text{Average total assets}}$	Evaluate how much operating cash flows are generated in relation to total assets.	p.553
II. G	Sales growth rate	$\frac{\text{Sales for current period} - \text{Sales for prior period}}{\text{Sales for prior period}}$	Evaluate how much sales have grown from prior year.	p.230
	Total asset growth rate	$\frac{\text{Total assets at the end of current period} - \text{Total assets at the end of prior period}}{\text{Total assets at the end of prior period}}$	Evaluate how much total assets have grown from prior year.	p.231
	Operating income growth rate	$\frac{\text{Income from operations for current period} - \text{Income from operations for prior period}}{\text{Income from operations for prior period}}$	Evaluate how much income from operations has grown from prior year.	p.231
	Net income growth rate	$\frac{\text{Net income for current period} - \text{Net income for prior period}}{\text{Net income for prior period}}$	Evaluate how much net income has grown from prior year.	p.232

* Shaded ones : Basic financial ratios.

C	Financial ratio	Formula	Use	Text
III. A	Total assets turnover	$\frac{\text{Sales}}{\text{Average total assets}}$	Evaluate how efficiently assets are utilized to generate sales.	p.233
	Trade receivables turnover	$\frac{\text{Sales}}{\text{Average trade receivables}}$	Evaluate how many times trade receivables are collected in a year.	p.290
	Days' sales in trade receivables	$\frac{\text{365 days}}{\text{Trade receivable turnover}}$	Evaluate average time period of collecting trade receivables.	p.291
	Inventory turnover	$\frac{\text{Cost of goods sold}}{\text{Average inventory}}$	Evaluate how many times inventory is sold in a year.	p.346
	Days' sales in inventory	$\frac{\text{365 days}}{\text{Inventory turnover}}$	Evaluate average time period of selling inventory.	p.347
	Trade payables turnover	$\frac{\text{Purchases}}{\text{Average trade payables}}$	Evaluate how many times trade payables are paid off in a year.	p.348
	Days' sales in trade payables	$\frac{\text{365 days}}{\text{Trade payables turnover}}$	Evaluate average time period of paying off trade payables.	p.348
	Operating cycle	Days' sales in trade receivables + Days' sales in inventory	Evaluate time period required to sell merchandise on credit and collect trade receivables.	p.349
	Cash operating cycle	Days' sales in trade receivables + Days' sales in inventory − Days' sales in trade payables	Evaluate time period in which additional funds other than funds generated by trade payables are tried up with trade receivables and inventory.	p.350
	Average useful life of plant assets	$\frac{\text{Average acquisition cost of plant assets}}{\text{Depreciation expense}}$	Evaluate a company's conservativeness in estimating useful lives of plant assets.	p.391
	Average ages of plant assets	$\frac{\text{Accumulated depreciation for plant assets}}{\text{Depreciation expense}}$	Evaluate degree of deterioration of plant assets.	p.392
	Non-current assets turnover	$\frac{\text{Sales}}{\text{Average non-current assets}}$	Evaluate how efficiently non-current assets are utilized to generate sales.	p.393
IV. S	Debt ratio	$\frac{\text{Liabilities}}{\text{Equity}}$	Evaluate reliance on liabilities in relation to equity.	p.393
	Equity ratio	$\frac{\text{Equity}}{\text{Total assets}}$	Evaluate what portion of total assets is contributed by stockholders.	p.234
	Quick ratio	$\frac{\text{Quick assets}}{\text{Current liabilities}}$	Evaluate whether quick assets are enough in comparison with current liabilities.	p.235
	Current ratio	$\frac{\text{Current assets}}{\text{Current liabilities}}$	Evaluate whether current assets are enough in comparison with current liabilities.	p.235

C	Financial ratio	Formula	Use	Text
IV. S	Net working capital	Current assets − Current liabilities	Evaluate how much additional funds are spent after investing in production facilities.	p.236
	Trade receivables uncollectibility risk	$\frac{\text{Allowance for uncollectible accounts}}{\text{Trade receivables}}$	Evaluate degree of risk that trade receivables will be uncollected.	p.292
	Non-current assets to long-term funds ratio	$\frac{\text{Non-current assets}}{\text{Non-current liabilities + Equity}}$	Evaluate how much of non-current assets are acquired with long-term funds.	p.393
	Time interest earned	$\frac{\text{Net income + Interest expense + Income taxes expense}}{\text{Interest expense}}$	Evaluate whether net income before interest and income taxes expense is enough to pay interest.	p.448
	Operating income interest coverage ratio	$\frac{\text{Income from operations}}{\text{Interest expense}}$	Evaluate whether income from operations is enough to pay interest.	p.449
	Borrowings to total assets ratio	$\frac{\text{Borrowings}}{\text{Total assets}}$	Evaluate how much of total assets are financed by outside borrowings.	p.450
	Book-value per share (BPS : 주당순자산)	$\frac{\text{Book value of equity-Preferred stock}}{\text{Number of common shares outstanding at the end of the year}}$	Evaluate how much is book-value of equity per share of common stock.	p.487
	Operating cash flows current liabilities coverage ratio	$\frac{\text{Operating cash flows}}{\text{Current liabilities}}$	Evaluate whether operating cash flows are generated enough to pay off current liabilities.	p.554
	Operating cash flows total liabilities coverage ratio	$\frac{\text{Operating cash flows}}{\text{Total liabilities}}$	Evaluate whether operating cash flows are generated enough to pay off total liabilities.	p.555
	Operating cash flows interest coverage ratio	$\frac{\text{Operating cash flows + Interest + Income taxes}}{\text{Interest}}$	Evaluate whether operating cash flows before interest and income taxes are generated enough to pay interest.	p.555
V. PM	Price earnings ratio (PER : 주가이익비율)	$\frac{\text{Price of common stock}}{\text{Earnings per share (EPS)}}$	Evaluate how many times of EPS are reflected in the common stock price.	p.236
	Price book-value ratio (PBR : 주가순자산비율)	$\frac{\text{Price of common stock}}{\text{Book-value per share (BPS)}}$	Evaluate how many times of BPS are reflected in the common stock price.	p.488
	Price cash-flows ratio (PCR : 주가현금흐름비율)	$\frac{\text{Price of common stock}}{\text{Cash-flows per share (CPS)}}$	Evaluate how many times of CPS are reflected in the common stock price.	p.556

C : Characteristics, P : Profitability, G : Growth, A : Activity, S : Safety (financial), PM : Price multiples

Translation of terms and index (English-Korean)

A

B

D

G

J

K

S

V

W

About the authors

Dai-Sun Lee

B.S. in Accounting, University of Ozarks
M.S. and Ph. D. in Accounting University of Nebraska-Lincoln
Present, Professor Emeritus, Business School, Sogang University
American CPA

Kyung-Man Jung

B.A. in Business Administration, Sogang University
M.A. and Ph. D. in Accounting, Sogang University
Present, Professor, Department of Business Administration, Busan Digital University

Sung-Whan Park

B.A. in Business Administration, Sogang University
M.A. and Ph. D. in Accounting, Sogang University
Present, Professor, Department of Business Administration and Accounting, Hanbat National University
Korean CPA

Kee-Shin Song

B.A. in Business Administration, Sogang University
M.A. in Accounting, Sogang University
Ph. D. in Accounting, Korea University
Present, Professor, School of Business and Commerce, Baekseok University

Ho-Gap Lee

B.A. in Business Administration, Cheongju University
M.A. in Business Administration, Korea University
Ph. D. in Accounting, Sogang University
Present, Professor, Department of Business Administration and Accounting, Hanbat National University

Principles of Accounting
based on International Standards, 3e
(English Version)

First edition, First print	Aug. 30, 2010
Second edition, First print	Sep. 5, 2011
Third edition, First print	Mar. 6, 2019

Authors	Dai-Sun Lee, Kee-Shin Song, Kyung-Man Jung, Ho-Gap Lee, Sung-Whan Park

Publisher	Ki-Nam Park
Publishing Company	Yulgok Publishing Company
	84, 803 Ho, Ga-san Digital 1 Ro, Kum-chun-ku, Seoul 08590 Tel 82-2-718-9872~3 Fax 718-9874 http://www.yulgokbooks.co.kr e-mail : yulgokbook@naver.com Registered : Nov. 10, 1989. Registration number : 2014-00031

Price ₩ 34,000 ISBN 979-11-87897-58-3 94320